The Spirit Filled Journey

Experiencing God's Love

Daily Devotional Readings

Apostolic Church of God

www.xulonpress.com

Foreword

When I became pastor of the Apostolic Church of God June 1, 2008, we embarked upon a marvelous journey together. We have been blessed to inherit a phenomenal foundation from my father, Bishop Arthur Brazier, who was the pastor for the previous forty-eight years. His strong Bible teaching and sharp theological mind instilled within our congregation a deep love for the Word of God. Bishop was the quintessential pastor, a pastor's pastor. His love for the people of God was unparalleled, and he committed his entire life and ministry to serving God by serving God's people.

When I assumed the pastorate, I committed to be a pastor after the same kind as my father. I was blessed to serve for two years while my father yet lived. Bishop went home to be with the Lord October 22, 2010, and we miss him still.

A hallmark of Bishop's ministry, and a core theological principle intertwined into the very fabric of the church, was—and still is—salvation by grace and grace alone. When it was yet unpopular among Apostolic Pentecostals to embrace eternal security, Bishop advanced the theology of grace with missionary zeal, and it transformed our church. People who had been bound by legalism were transformed, not to live a life of license but of liberty in Christ by the Holy Spirit.

During the first year of my pastorate, the Lord laid on my heart to focus on living out the grace we had been given. Through this, the teaching of grace extends to future generations in our church. To bring this message to life, the Lord impressed upon me to institute what we now have come to call a series of spiritual growth ministry initiatives. In the fall of 2009, we held our first revival bringing all our spiritual growth auxiliaries together for a series of services aimed at igniting our spiritual walk. In January 2010, we launched our first pastor-led congregational prayer service. We started with a teaching series that culminated with a Friday-night prayer service. We continue to hold these special prayer services quarterly.

The Lord continued to deal with me about the spiritual life

of our members. We have always had a strong Bible foundation, engaging Bible study, well-attended Sunday Morning Bible Study classes, and other programs for the men, women, and youth of our church. But as we continued to grow as a congregation, we had to grow even deeper in our Word and in our relationship with the Lord.

Yet most members of our congregation had demanding schedules and needed a means to integrate consistent Bible reading into their daily lives. Hence the Scripture texting program of our church was birthed. Members began to sign up to receive from us daily Scripture texts on their cell phones during their workday, when they were often the most challenged and tested.

Still, I felt the Lord saying there was more. I began to discuss with the ministry staff the use of daily devotional books. Most of them already subscribed to and used devotional books on a regular basis. I began to review various devotionals that might be right for our congregation to use collectively. Not finding just the right one, I believe the Lord led us to write our own Pentecostal devotional. The first person with whom I conferred about this book was my father. And hence, *The Spirit-Filled Journey* devotional project began.

It is my prayer that this devotional will bless you and encourage you in your relationship with the Lord as you read it daily. There are some distinctive characteristics to this body of work.

The Spirit-filled life is the core theme of this devotional, honoring our Pentecostal roots. We believe in, and embrace, the active role of the Holy Spirit in our lives and in the church. As Christians, by God's grace we are born of the Spirit, we are led by the Spirit, we are enlightened by the Spirit, and we are comforted by the Spirit. The Holy Spirit assists us in praying and reveals God's will to us. Truly, the Holy Spirit is the agent of transformation for the believer.

The Spirit-Filled Journey: Experiencing God's Love is written by ministers and members of our church, twenty-five writers in all. Often writing from their own experiences, they have a heart for encouraging others in their daily walk in Christ. They write with different voices and styles, yet with the same purpose—to edify the body of Christ.

The Spirit-Filled Journey: Experiencing God's Love is dedicated to my father, Bishop Brazier, and it commemorates the great influence he had on this church and our spiritual life. One of our team members was able to sit down with Bishop before he died to hear his insights on the significance of such an endeavor. His insights are shared in the special commemorative article dedicated to him.

This first volume of the *The Spirit-Filled Journey* devotional series focuses on our *Experiencing God's Love* as He has saved us and filled us with the precious gift of the Holy Spirit. It consists of five sections: "We are Saved by Grace and Grace Alone," "We are Born of the Spirit," "We are Children of God," "We are Connected," and "We are Secured by Love." Each section speaks to the enduring presence of God in our lives as He has saved us, filled and sealed us with His Spirit.

Each entry opens with a guiding Scripture, followed by an inspirational message that helps you to connect to the Scripture. Each devotional entry closes with a prayer. Just as we engaged a multiplicity of writers, so we have a multiplicity of prayers. After you have read the devotional entry for a given day, I encourage you to spend some time reflecting on what you have read and considering what the Lord may be saying to you through that day's entry. Truly, that is the power of devotional books. They are tools used to help you draw closer to God through the disciplines of the Word of God and prayer.

I invite you to take this walk with us as we dive into *The Spirit-Filled Journey: Experiencing God's Love*. May you be blessed by the Word of God and encouraged to hold on as you stand on God' promises, as revealed through His Word.

Dr. Byron T. Brazier,
Pastor, Apostolic Church of God

Bishop Arthur Brazier: Our Tribute

Pastor of the Apostolic Church of God for forty-eight years, Bishop Arthur Monroe Brazier shaped the spirituality of our church and influenced the spiritual maturity of multiple generations of our congregation. Bishop, as we affectionately and reverently called him, was a man of vision, with a passion for ministry and a heart for the people of God. He was a true shepherd. His preaching of the gospel of Jesus Christ literally brought thousands to the Lord, and his clear and practical Bible teaching helped thousands grow and mature spiritually.

In early 2010, when Dr. Byron Brazier approached Bishop about writing a devotional book for the congregation, Bishop enthusiastically endorsed the project. Indeed, he so firmly supported the devotional project that he stopped a devotional book team member in the hall one day and began to share the importance of encouraging the saints in their walk. He thought it was crucial that the writing be inspirational—that it encourage and uplift the people of God. He noted that the *Apply the Word* section of our weekly Sunday morning bulletin was the type of inspiration that would be important to this project. He commended our church's newsletter editor, who writes that weekly segment, for her keen spiritual insight, and said it was that type of writing we needed in this devotional project. The devotional book had to touch people where they were and speak to them about the situations in their lives, as well as help give them hope that comes only from trusting in the Lord.

Up until a week before he was hospitalized, Bishop stayed strong at the helm of the two community groups he founded after his retirement. We would see him come to the church daily for meetings, even as he became visibly weaker. Yet he emphatically stated that he would make time to discuss the devotional project. He believed this endeavor was as important as those projects—because the devotional book dealt with the spiritual life of the believer. Perhaps Bishop was letting us know that we could not adequately work for transformation in our communities until we were on our own personal journey of transformation. Though transformation will not occur merely by reading a devotional book, transformation is a work of the Holy Spirit, and as one engages in the disciplines of prayer, listening to the Holy Spirit, and Scripture reading, one grows and matures in his or her Christian walk and service to the community.

Actually, Bishop's mark on this devotional book began long before the book was conceived. It goes without saying that, as pastor, he was devoted to the spiritual development of the people of our congregation. But Bishop had a way of personally touching the lives of parishioners, even as the congregation grew to mega-church status. There were countless times, for instance, after counseling a parishioner that Bishop would not only recommend resources for the person's spiritual growth, but he would also walk with the person to the church's bookstore to find just the right resource to help. He didn't just recommend the book and send the person on his or her way; he actually escorted the person to the bookstore and picked out the resources himself. Isn't that such a powerful model for, and symbol of, the walk of the believer on this Spirit-filled journey? Bishop showed us we can't always just point a person in the right direction; sometimes we must walk with one another.

Throughout this project, Bishop's influence on the devotional project was evident. We formed two core teams. The first was the theological framework team to guide our doctrinal framing of the devotional. Though it was to be inspirational, it had to be solidly anchored theologically. A few years prior, Bishop had formed a similar team to draft *The Articles of Faith* for our church. One of the clearest legacies he has left us is a clear doctrinal perspective. This devotional book is both informed and influenced heavily by that theological perspective.

We also formed a leadership team that was to guide the entire project. This team handled the details of every aspect of the project—selecting writers, editors, and proofreaders; leading the writer's workshop; conducting the theological review of every entry; leading the team of editors and proofreaders; designing and laying out the book; working with the publisher and the printer; and marketing. Bishop's teaching down through the years influenced us heavily in a number of ways.

During our writer's workshop, the editorial team leader made a provocative statement that in some ways may have intimidated some, but it reinforced the core values by which we were operating to produce this devotional to God's glory. We desired and aimed to produce a book of excellent quality. This team leader took it up a notch and recounted the days when she sang in the sanctuary choir. She declared during the writer's workshop, "Bishop would come in at the beginning of Tuesday rehearsals and have us repeat the following affirmation: *'We are striving for perfection, and we will settle for nothing less!'* And that's what we must accomplish in this project in honor of Bishop!" A lofty goal, clearly, but one that this team fastidiously worked toward, because of the legacy of excellence we have inherited from Bishop Brazier.

On another occasion, a devotional writer had written an entry dealing with an issue that had become politicized in the news. At first we reviewed it and passed it on to editing, as it was very well written. But the Holy Spirit did not let one of our team members rest. She revisited the entry with an editor, recounting Bishop's admonishments. "Stay away from as much controversy as you can," he had said. "Increase the faith of the believer without developing controversial thoughts or putting down another theology." So we did not use that entry. For Bishop, an inspirational devotional book was not the place to confront controversial issues but a vehicle to encourage and inspire the saints in their walk with the Lord.

Not that Bishop was afraid of controversy. An extremely well-read and enlightened man, Bishop could hold his own in any debate. In controversy, he would study both sides of an issue; and after much study, prayer, and reflection, he landed upon a position and held firm.

So it was with his position on eternal security. Bishop recounted that in his early years of ministry, as a traditional Pentecostal, he was wedded to the Arminian doctrine that a person could be saved and then lost. The Arminian doctrine was formulated by the sixteenth-century theologian Jacob Arminius, who taught that one could be saved and lost several times during one life period. However, John Calvin, another sixteenth-century theologian, developed another system of theology that stressed the sovereignty of God and the eternal security of the believer. Arminianism and Calvinism differed on a number of points as they related to the salvation of the believer, and the Pentecostal doctrine of Bishop's day was firmly entrenched in the Arminian position as opposed to the Calvinistic position. The then Elder Brazier accepted the Arminian position without question.

Bishop often recounted that even when he attended Moody Bible Institute, which he considered to be heavily Calvinistic, he never changed his traditional views. He often shared that students would talk to him after class about the merits of eternal security, but he never budged from his Arminian position. That was until he began to read passages that he felt many Pentecostals tended to avoid, such as Ephesians 1:4, which declares, "According as he hath chosen us in him before the foundation of the world, that we should be holy and without blame before him in love."

Bishop had grappled with the issue but eventually came to realize, "If we were chosen in Christ for salvation before the foundation of the world, then how could we, by our conduct negate what God had done?" He continued, "If, as is stated in Romans, we are predestinated to be conformed to the image of His Son, how can puny man change what God has already predetermined?" The strongest of the strong-willed humans were no match for the sovereign God, and it is inconceivable that humans could undo anything God set in motion. On that Bishop stood firm.

To get to this point, Bishop apparently had begun to weigh both sides. A deeply reflective man who relied heavily on the Bible, Bishop read John Calvin and expositors who believed in Calvinism, along with the Scriptures Calvinists used to support their view. He also read the writers of Arminianism. He compared the various references made by both sides and it became clear to him that salvation was eternal.

Bishop recounted, "Jesus said in St. John, 'My sheep hear my voice, and I know them, and they follow me: And I give unto them eternal life; and they shall never perish' (John 14:27). I concentrated on the word 'never' as to what never meant, and obviously never means without ending. Then, as I read and listened to other expositors on the Arminian side who quoted that same Scripture, they had an interpretation that differed. That interpretation placed in a sub-position, 'if they follow me I give unto them eternal life.' That's a word that is added to the statement of Jesus because it gives justification to the concept that you can lose what Jesus said you would never lose."[1]

What grew out of Bishop's arduous study, and embracing of eternal security, was a theology of grace that, when combined with our Pentecostal emphasis on the active role of the Holy Spirit in the life of the believer, created the Apostolic Church of God distinctive that we know today. That distinctive can be clearly seen in our *Spirit-Filled Journey: Experiencing God's Love* devotional: because of God's great love for us, we are saved by the grace of God through the atoning death of Jesus on the cross of Calvary, and we're empowered through His resurrection and sealed eternally by the indwelling Holy Spirit, who guides us into all truth.

In a spontaneous moment when Bishop was resting in his office on a Friday afternoon, after a day of meetings, some eleven weeks prior to his passing, he sat down with one of our devotional team members to reflect on what would become key elements of this devotional book.

Bishop believed emphatically that the people of God grew through the Word of God. He often stressed to members who came to him for guidance the necessity of attending Bible study. He knew the child of God grows strong through the very Word of God that nourishes our soul and transforms our mind. So it was. Bishop believed any tool that helped enhance or encourage believers to read Scripture would be a blessing to the people of God. Bishop was keenly aware that the life of faith is often a battle between belief and doubt, struggles and victories, and temptations and perseverance; and we as believers will only make it through by relying upon God's Word.

Bishop emphasized the devotional book must include, or incorporate, a series of thoughts on faith. For the Spirit-filled journey was a walk of faith. Faith, Bishop stressed, was about depending upon, and trusting wholeheartedly, in God.

First and foremost, he shared, faith in Jesus brings peace with God. In Romans 5, Paul lets us know that being justified by faith, we have peace with God through our Lord Jesus Christ. Bishop stressed that there is a difference between the peace of God and peace with God. The peace of God speaks of us finding solace in God, but peace with God says that we are no longer enemies, based upon Jesus going to the cross of Calvary for us. The war is over with God.

Having been a pastor for almost a half century, Bishop seemed particularly sensitive to the difficult times the people of God faced. He stressed, we've got to have faith through hard times. Like the prophet Habakkuk, he began to recall if our stalls are emptied, we still have to rejoice. During a particularly dire time in the life of ancient Israel, a time Habakkuk first deemed as unjust, but later determined to stand firm in his faith, the prophet declared:

> *Although the fig tree shall not blossom, neither shall fruit be in the vines; the labour of the olive shall fail, and the fields shall yield no meat; the flock shall be cut off from the fold, and there shall be no herd in the stalls: Yet I will rejoice in the LORD, I will joy in the God of my salvation. The LORD God is my strength, and he will make my feet like hinds' feet, and he will make me to walk upon mine high places.*
>
> Habakkuk 3:17-19

So it was that Bishop encouraged us to help readers of our devotional stand firm in faith—through economic recession, mortgage foreclosure, prolonged unemployment. In so doing, he admonished us to remind the saints that our strength is in the Lord God, and regardless of the outward circumstances, God will steady our feet as we walk through trials and troubles.

Bishop also stressed that the life of faith—the Spirit-filled journey—is a life of sacrifice. He quoted Romans 12:1-2:

> *I beseech you therefore, brethren, by the mercies of God, that ye present your bodies a living sacrifice, holy, acceptable*

unto God, which is your reasonable service. And be not conformed to this world: but be ye transformed by the renewing of your mind, that ye may prove what is that good, and acceptable, and perfect, will of God.

The old covenant of the law required that Israel come at set times to offer various types of sacrifices, but under the new covenant of grace, God requires our entire being as a living sacrifice to Him. Bishop was encouraging us to remind our readers that the walk of faith is a wholehearted endeavor. And the more we walk with God and grow in our relationship, the more we walk in the will of God

Along that same vein, Bishop stressed that the life of faith is about obedience. Jesus has said, if you love me keep my commandments. Bishop punctuated that lesson with a story he shared many times across the pulpit on the obedience of Abraham in offering up his son Isaac. In obedience to God, Abraham took his son up to Mt. Moriah to sacrifice him up. But just in the nick of time, the Angel of the Lord stopped him and told him, "now I know you fear God, since you have not withheld your son, your only son from me" (Genesis 22:12). And sure enough, Abraham lifted up his eyes and behind him there was a ram caught in the bush. Bishop was reminding us that first and foremost, God will provide for Himself the sacrifice as He did in Jesus, the Lamb slain for us from the foundation of the world. And if God provided the sacrificial lamb for us, would He not also provide everything else for us—even in hard times? Yes, Bishop was reminding us to trust in Jehovah-Jireh—God our provider!

Bishop proceeded to speak on the Holy Spirit in the believer's life. He stressed, the Spirit comes by faith not works—salvation is a gift from God. This gracious gift is the Holy Spirit in Acts 2:38; 8:30; and 11:17. It is the "gift" Jesus offers to the Samaritan woman at the well (John 4:10). It is the "free gift" (charisma) in Romans 5:15. It is the "unspeakable gift" in 2 Corinthians 9:15. A person cannot work for the Holy Spirit; He is truly a gracious gift from God. He quoted, "That the blessing of Abraham might come on the Gentiles through Jesus Christ; that we might receive the promise of the Spirit through faith" (Galatians 3:14). Just as Abraham, the "father of faith," was accounted righteous by faith, we inherit the same promises by faith, so that the righteousness of Jesus Christ is imputed to us by our faith in Jesus and we receive the promises of the Spirit likewise by faith.

Bishop reflected on this life of faith and spoke of missionaries the world over who may not have shared our denominational stands but were so fervent in their faith, they were willing to give up their lives for the cause of Christ. He reflected on Jim Elliot, the evangelical missionary who was killed in Ecuador, along with four others, while attempting to evangelize the Waodani people. He paraphrased Jim Elliott: "I do not have any trouble giving up what I cannot keep in order to gain what I cannot lose." The life of faith is one of sacrifice and one of eternal reward. And Bishop encouraged us to make the life of faith our priority.

What was striking about this interview was that, at eighty-nine years old, and somewhat weary from a long day, the passages of Scripture Bishop shared on that day came readily to mind. It was as the psalmist had declared centuries earlier, "Thy word have I hid in mine heart" (Psalm 119:11). And it was a living testimony to all that Bishop shared, not just on that day but through his entire ministry. The Word of God is essential to the life and spiritual health of the believer. So this devotional book, *The Spirit-filled Journey: Experiencing God's Love*, is dedicated to our beloved Bishop, Pastor, and friend—Arthur M. Brazier.

We miss Bishop still, and we are forever grateful for the influence and impact he had on us. His inspired teaching can be found in each section of this book. And we will be forever grateful to this great shepherd.

Humbly Submitted,
The *Spirit-Filled Life* Devotional Book Leadership Team

We are Saved by Grace and Grace Alone

For by grace are ye saved through faith;
and that not of yourselves: it is the gift of God.
Ephesians 2:8, KJV

A corpse can do nothing. It can't breathe. It can't move. It can't think. It's dead, rotting away in a grave. That's not unlike the spiritually dead, whose souls are decayed by sin. We were once dead in trespasses and sin, but God resurrected us (Ephesians 2:1-10). And only God could do that. He alone raised us from our graves, cleansed us from the unrighteousness of our sinful pasts, covered us with His mercy, and made us one with His Son. God redeemed us not because we did something to earn salvation, but He redeemed us because He loves us. Period. He loved us even before He established the world; and because of His abounding grace toward us, we are already victorious on our Spirit-filled journey.

As you begin a new year on your Spirit-filled journey, take sweet repose in God's love for you. Be inspired to walk out each day with a clearer understanding of what it means to be saved by grace, to be chosen from the foundation of the world by a holy and perfect God, and to be justified not by your works but by your faith.

THANK GOD FOR GRACE

For by grace you have been saved through faith, and that not of yourselves;
it is the gift of God, not of works lest anyone should boast.

EPHESIANS 2:8-9, NKJV

Salvation is a marvelous gift from God. Being "in Christ," "saved," granted "eternal life" are all terms used to define the position or state secured for us who believe in Jesus by means of the gratuitous actions of our loving God. God granted us this new life in Christ as a result of His own volition and will, and not as a reward for anything we had done or could do.

Remember, Adam and Eve were brought into this world spiritually and physically alive. Yet when they disobeyed God, they died spiritually and their intimate union with God was severed. In fact they were positioned outside of the idyllic Eden and blocked from freely communing with God. And every one of us born into this world from that point on has been born physically alive, but spiritually dead, unable to reach God on our own terms. And because we were spiritually dead, we walked according to the ways of the world, obeying the devil and succumbing to the desires of sinful flesh (Ephesians 2:1-4).

Yet God, rich in mercy and His great love for us, graciously made us alive together with Christ. He re-positioned us into a realm of safety, called the kingdom, where we are eternally secure in Christ. We did nothing to earn this new position. We did nothing to qualify for this new walk.

God offered us this new life purely out of His favor and kindness, unmerited and unwarranted on our part. We did not deserve it. We could not afford it. And that's the essence of this divine grace. Grace is the means by which God swoops us up out of our sinful, perilous conditions and extends His salvation to us—without charge, without fee.

❧

Dear God, I am grateful for Your grace, which swooped me up and lavished me with love. I am grateful for You saving me and placing me on this marvelous journey of drawing closer to You and becoming more like Christ. With a grateful heart I say, "Thank You for Your grace!" Amen.

LIFE GIFT

For the wages of sin is death; but the gift of God is eternal life through Jesus Christ our Lord.

ROMANS 6:23, KJV

Sin is a hard taskmaster—demanding lifelong commitment, only to be rewarded with death. The compensation for working under sin is not a minimum wage, nor a living wage, but a dying wage.

The Greek word translated as "wages" referred to the pay or allowance given to soldiers of the first century. A soldier was paid in exchange for his work and loyalty in the army. He was required to obey and follow orders that had to be scrupulously carried out. He was given assignments that were his duty to fulfill.

The life of sin, the life lived independently of God, is therefore likened unto enlistment in an army in which the soldier is to follow and obey orders in exchange for wages. In this case, the payment for the sinful life is ultimately death.

By contrast, the Greek word translated as "gift" means favor bestowed without merit on the part of the one who receives it. A gift, then, would have been given by a benefactor who gave to one who often could not afford the gift but definitely did not earn it. The gift was given purely as favor bestowed from the benefactor. The gift was not payment for anything done or any work performed.

So it is the apostle Paul used two contrasting metaphors to compare two walks of life: the life of sin under Satan's rule and life in the Spirit under God's rule. When viewed from the world's perspective, the sinful life can look glamorous, even enticing, especially to the flesh, or carnal nature. Yet when viewed from eternity, anyone following the sinful life pays a great toll—eternal death.

Without thought of payment or exchange for goods, God offers eternal life as a gift not to be earned but received. Instead of exacting a toll upon us, God gives us an eternal endowment—everlasting life!

Dear Heavenly Father, I thank You for the gift of life. No longer am I employed by the enemy in the life of sin. Thank You for sending the Holy Spirit to accompany me on this journey into eternity with You. I am grateful for Your gift of life. Amen.

THE MOSAIC MISSION

When the Gentiles heard this, they were glad and praised the word of the Lord; and as many as had been destined for eternal life became believers.

ACTS 13:48, NRSV

What started out as a message of hope to Jews of the first century has expanded to include people of every nation. It was not by happenstance that the gospel message spread throughout the various cultures of the world. To save people from every nation was always God's plan.

Ethnic and national divisions are not modern inventions. People of ancient days were also categorized by their national or ethnic groupings. The first followers of Jesus were Palestinian Jews, and Gentile described people from other nations.

Although the gospel was first sent to Jewish people, many rejected Jesus as the promised Messiah. So, on one missionary journey, the apostle Paul and his partner, Barnabas, declared their intentions to preach to the Gentiles. It would be to the "nations" that they would now announce the good news of salvation through Jesus Christ. According to Luke, the Gentiles rejoiced and glorified God! They were grateful that they, too, could receive God's grace.

Those who believed and rejoiced over God's grace had already been appointed or chosen by God to do so; they were responding to an act of God accomplished for them ages prior. This passage reminds us that God chooses whom He will and does not limit Himself to a specific ethnic group or nationality. The theme is consistent throughout Scripture: "in the last days I will pour out my spirit upon all flesh" (Joel 2:28). In the Revelation, John saw people from every tongue, tribe, and nation bowing before the throne of God (Revelation 7:14). These passages remind us that God is no respecter of persons (Acts 10:34) and selects people from every ethnic and national group for His Kingdom. Whether Jew, Gentile, black, white, red, brown, African, European, Asian, or Latino, God's appointment signifies entrance into a new nation— the kingdom of God.

❧

Lord, I thank You for including me in this mosaic assembly called the kingdom of God. Thank You for including me before others could reject me because of my ethnicity, race, or culture. Together we all make up Your kaleidoscope of believers. Amen.

GOD'S PEACE TREATY

Therefore being justified by faith, we have peace with God through our Lord Jesus Christ.

ROMANS 5:1, KJV

Nations sign peace treaties to end war and commit to work together in the future. For instance, the Treaty of Ghent ended the American Civil War. The Northern and Southern states fought over the issue of slavery. At the end of the war, the peace treaty was signed reconciling the two sides and committing them to work together to uphold the laws of the land.

The devil has been the archenemy of God since his rebellion (Isaiah 14:12-14). In many ways, he declared war against God. Furthermore, with Adam and Eve's disobedience, the human race entered into this conflict with God, aligned with Satan. Our separation from God was like trying to fight a war that could not be won. In fact, every one of us deserved to die in this war against righteousness.

For us to have peace with God, the terms of God's righteousness had to be satisfied. We needed to be justified, that is acquitted or declared righteous. We needed a means of getting out of this eternal war—an exit strategy, if you will. We needed a strategy that would satisfy the conditions of God's righteousness and eliminate the barrier between us and God. So God sent His only Son into the world to satisfy the terms and conditions of righteousness. In other words, Jesus died in our place. And in so doing He ended the war against righteousness, ratifying the treaty of peace with His own blood.

So now we have peace with God. Now we live under the terms of a treaty that has declared us righteous, has reconciled us back to God, and has given us access to God through the Spirit (Ephesians 2:18).

Having peace with God also gives us access to the peace *of* God. Through the power of the Spirit, we can walk in freedom, love, and power as we glorify God for what He has already done on our behalf through Jesus Christ our Lord.

❧

Heavenly Father, I am so thankful for the peace treaty signed at Calvary. I thank You for initiating the terms of this agreement when I had no strength or means of my own to end this war. I am forever grateful. Amen.

ABOUNDING GRACE

Moreover the law entered, that the offence might abound. But where sin abounded, grace did much more abound.

ROMANS 5:20, KJV

How many of us have ever driven through a red light, even though we knew that stoplight meant just that—to stop? In many cities, officials have installed cameras to monitor everything from traffic violations to violence. Yet, in spite of the laws and devices to enforce the law, people still violate these laws.

Violating the law seems to be part of human nature. God's law was a written code reflecting all His righteous commands. His law included commands around worship of God, ordinances related to how people ought to treat their neighbors, and statutes covering every realm of the human experience. In spite of those laws, God's people continued to sin. We now know that the law could not keep people from sinning. It could only show people "how sinful they were" (Romans 5:20, NLT).

The righteous requirements of the law still needed to be fulfilled. Yet there was no inherent power in the law to enable humans to fulfill its requirements. Throughout the history of God's relationship with His people, God would graciously intervene on their behalf, in spite of their shortcomings. When Adam and Eve sinned, God graciously covered them with skins of animals. Consider the Israelites, who strayed from God after entering the Promised Land; yet "God raised up judges" to save them from the nations that had taken them captive (Judges 2:16-19). Or when God's people continued to sin and act unjustly, God spoke to the prophets to let them know, though they would be overtaken by oppressive nations, He would ultimately bring them out.

So it is throughout the history of God's relationship with humanity: the more humans sinned, the more God was gracious. So much so, that in the fullness of time, God sent Jesus as a sacrifice for the sins of the world. Even now, while we are free from sin, we are not sinless. God's grace continues to abound. God's grace overflows and will always abound more than sin.

Lord, You are amazing! I thank You that I will never be able to deplete Your grace. You will never run out of grace. Your grace is greater than my sin. Your grace abounds over transgression. Amen.

No Campaign Promises

Knowing, brethren beloved, your election of God.

1 Thessalonians 1:4, KJV

Think back to the election of one of your favorite candidates. Perhaps you campaigned for him. Perhaps you donated to her campaign fund. And on the night of the election, you stayed up way past your bedtime to learn of her election results.

Now contrast the democratic process of election to the theological concept of election. We did not and could not campaign for our position in Christ! We had no platform upon which to stand. If called upon to vote for us to enter heaven, there may have been more than a few people to cast a vote against us. Instead, God in His sovereignty, His full and supreme power and authority, chose us for salvation, without input from us or anyone else.

In fact, the Greek word from which we get the term election in this passage is *ekloge*, a compound word stemming from two root words meaning out (*ek*) and to speak (*logos*). In essence, *ekloge* means to speak out, as in God's calling us out, hence choosing us. In theological terms, *ekloge* refers to God's decisive decree to choose us and to call us into salvation and kingdom blessing. In choosing us for life, God saved us from eternal damnation.

So it is that the apostle Paul in the beginning of his epistle to the church in Thessalonica reminded them that the Lord used the gospel and the power of the Holy Spirit to bring them to salvation. And now he calls them to know, to really understand or grasp, the significance of their election.

The implication of Paul's admonition is this: when one really comes to understand the significance of being chosen or elected by God, a deep and abiding joy is generated. Knowing through experience that we had neither platform nor purse—we could not purchase nor earn this salvation—the inward response to grasping and truly understanding the Lord's choosing of us is that of joy, thankfulness, humility, and confidence. We know that because no one voted us *in* to this office of salvation, no one can vote us *out!*

❧

Lord, thank You for choosing me and, through Your Spirit, helping me to really grasp the wonder of divine election. I am forever grateful. Amen.

THE PROOF OF THE PUDDING

Therefore … be all the more diligent to make your calling and election sure,
for if you practice these qualities you will never fall.

2 PETER 1:10, ESV

In the 1600s pudding was a staple dessert at British tables and different recipes for puddings abounded. No right–minded cook, however, would boast of having *the* recipe for pudding. Instead, the saying went, "the proof of the pudding is in the eating." In other words, how good the pudding was could be determined only after the pudding was tested or eaten. This phrase eventually came to mean "the true value of something can only be judged when it's put to use" or tested.[2]

So it was that the apostle Peter wrote two epistles to first-century Christians who were being tested because of their profession of faith in Jesus Christ (1 Peter 4:1-4, 12-16). Peter reminded these Christians that they were the elect of God and because of that very calling, they would experience resistance and opposition (1 Peter 1:2).

Peter proceeded to remind them that because they were divinely elected, God, by His divine power, had given believers all they needed to endure the tests and trials of life. Peter knew from experience that what they needed to endure tests was already in them!

Peter admonished these believers to accept that God had done His part by imparting His divine nature into them, even bringing their faith alive. He let them know that through testing, they will grow in God, and proof of their growth will be virtuous character (2 Peter 1:5-8).

Like those first century believers, our faith may be put to the test, but the real proof of our relationship with God (our calling and election) will be in the character that is evidenced through us. Our real value comes forth in testing. The life we lead, and the character that comes forth even in times of testing and difficulty, demonstrates to others who and Whose we are!

❧

Lord, thank You for giving me eternal life. Help me to live out the grace You have given, showing people around me who You are in me. Amen.

OUR EMANCIPATION PROCLAMATION

So Christ has truly set us free.

GALATIANS 5:1A, NLT

Legalized slavery in nineteenth-century America required that the slave live under the absolute rule of the slave master. The slave had to obey the dictates of the master and to endure often cruel and harsh conditions. The master owned the slave and controlled every aspect of the slave's life.

Yet on January 1, 1863, President Abraham Lincoln issued the Emancipation Proclamation, freeing all slaves in the rebel southern states. It would take the ending of the Civil War for all slaves to eventually be freed. After 250 years of institutionalized slavery, four million people of African descent were finally set free.[3]

As difficult as it is to imagine, there is another type of slavery that has held far more people than American chattel slavery ever did. This slavery is called sin—the state of rebellion and living contrary to God's righteousness. Yet the good news for born-again believers is that sin is no longer our master. We are no longer controlled by sin or the desire to rebel against and be independent from God and His righteousness.

According to the apostle Paul, the law revealed its righteous requirements but gave us no power to follow those requirements (Romans 6:14). Under the law, we know what is right but have no ability to do what is right; that condition is likened unto a state of slavery. In fact we continue to choose what is wrong because of the sin principle—the principle that governs all relationships not secured by God's grace.

Yet when the grace of God appears in our lives, it sets us free! Grace breaks the bondage of sin—it proclaims us emancipated from the bondage of sin and the law. To live under the freedom of God's grace is to freely live in the place or state of God's love and favor, knowing beyond a shadow of a doubt that Jesus secured our salvation at Calvary. We are free!

❧

Dear Lord, thank You for freeing me. You freed me from the chains of slavery. You freed me from the bondage of sin. You freed me from the yoke of the law. You freed me to walk freely in Your grace. And I am grateful. Amen.

Changed From the Inside Out

But we are bound to give thanks to God always for you, brethren beloved by the Lord, because God from the beginning chose you for salvation through sanctification by the Spirit and belief in the truth.

2 Thessalonians 2:13, NKJV

It is easier to change our clothes than our minds. Unfortunately, too many people have thought that living the Christian life was merely about changing their outward appearances and not their hearts.

In Paul's day, believers suffered persecutions and hardships, and were confronted with various forms of false teaching. Some people, affected by that false teaching, fell away from the church. They did so because they did not believe the truth about Jesus, and they had become easily "shaken in mind" (2 Thessalonians 2:2). You see, their hearts and minds had never truly been changed.

Yet there were those who persisted and did not walk away. So Paul gives thanks that these believers were the ones chosen by God to salvation. They were called, chosen, and saved from eternity past. And the very fact that they remained grounded in the truth was evidence that they were being sanctified by the Holy Spirit.

God has likewise called, chosen, and saved us from eternity past. Yet God desires that we remain steadfast in Him and be sanctified by the Holy Spirit. Unfortunately, some people define sanctification as looking holy on the outside. But the sanctification to which Paul refers is a process of change with the result of becoming more and more like Christ. It is the process of being transformed, or changed internally (Romans 12:2), that will be manifested outwardly.

The type of change to which Paul refers can only be wrought by the work of the Holy Spirit in our lives. The Holy Spirit strengthens us to withstand hardship, giving us that inner resolve to persevere. The Holy Spirit changes our hearts to trust God even through hardships and difficulty. The Holy Spirit changes us from the inside out so that we become more Christ-like.

❧

Dear God, I thank You for the sanctifying work of the Holy Spirit in my life! You are changing my heart, my mind, and my attitude, so that I more and more reflect You. Amen.

THE MYSTERY OF GRACE

Who hath saved us, and called us with an holy calling, not according to our works, but according to his own purpose and grace, which was given us in Christ Jesus before the world began.

2 TIMOTHY 1:9, KJV

Through unrestricted and irresistible grace we were set apart by God. There is no "rhyme or reason" as to why God chose us, no evidence as to why we deserve it. We were chosen before the earth was framed, before God divided light from darkness, and before He separated the waters from the spread of heaven and earth. Before God breathed into Adam the breath of life, He had a plan to choose those He would redeem. Before the serpent beguiled Eve, and Adam disobeyed through her invitation, we were chosen. God's decision, based purely in His love, is the essence of grace. His grace is unfathomable!

The belief in Jesus Christ, His death, burial, and resurrection, is pivotal. It is by saving grace that we are regenerated to be sons and daughters of God, reconciled to Him for eternity. We have been emancipated from the penalty of sin. The blood of Christ's atonement was the fulfillment of payment needed to spare us from the deserving wrath of God's judgment. Jesus' resurrection is the assurance that we will never be lost in darkness again, and our lives are hidden in Him with resurrection power.

But we must never forget that God's grace is indeed a mystery (Romans 11:25). It defies human logic, which says we should work for God's favor. Instead, God called us according to His own purpose. We can search the world from hemisphere to hemisphere and will not find any reason why God should love us and give us His grace. The best detective in the world would not be able to find clues as to why God chose us. With the world's advanced technology, there are no fingerprints to be lifted. The crime scene of sin is totally eliminated, and the Judge's heart has been turned in our favor. Who can discover the answers to such a mystery?

❧

Eternal Sovereign God, I do not understand the mysteries of Your ways, but I am grateful for Your choosing me and for the revelation of the election of grace. Amen.

ENLISTED TO SERVE

Soldiers don't get tied up in the affairs of civilian life, for then they cannot please the officer who enlisted them.

2 TIMOTHY 2:4, NLT

Joe enlisted in the military when he was but 19 years old. He served in a region of the world that was hot, dry, and rife with enemy combatants. There were none of the comforts of home. With a young wife and baby at home, his aim was to serve his tour of duty and return safely to his young family. Outside of keeping in touch with his family, Joe determined not to get enmeshed in the current events back home. It was not that Joe didn't care about others, but he could not afford to lose his focus, which was to serve his country and return to his loving family.

So it is that the apostle Paul admonishes his protégé Timothy to stay focused on the ministry God had entrusted to him. Paul and Timothy served in an age of the church when there was much opposition to the gospel of Jesus Christ. Yet both were called to Christian ministry by God. Their charge was to fight the opposition and take a stand against heretics and enemies of the cross. Paul tells Timothy from experience that, because of the call upon his life, Timothy would face hard times. Just as a soldier has to endure hardship, Paul admonished Timothy to do likewise.

God enlisted us into His "army" when He chose, called, and saved us. We did not go to a recruiter's office to enlist for this tour of duty. Instead, God—by His grace—enlisted us to serve. Just as a soldier stays focused on following the commands of his or her enlisting officer, so must we stay focused on pleasing our Enlisting Officer. We cannot get entangled or enmeshed in the world system and lose sight of our purpose and the true cause to which we have been called by God—to declare His name to others and bring glory to Him.

Yes, we have been chosen to serve. We have been enlisted to fight. The Holy Spirit will strengthen us, and we must stay focused.

Dear Lord, help me to stay focused to fight. My desire is to please You, my Enlisting Officer. My desire is to serve You with wholehearted devotion. Amen.

CAN YOU HEAR ME NOW?

And he said, The God of our fathers hath chosen thee, that thou shouldest know his will, and see that Just One, and shouldest hear the voice of his mouth.

ACTS 22:14, KJV

Remember that television commercial in which a cell phone provider sent a representative to different places with his cell phone? In each new place the representative would ask, "Can you hear me now?" The company's message was to assure us that, by using its network, we would be able to receive our calls and hear the voice on the other end of our calls. Are we as sure that we can hear the Lord's voice as clearly?

On this occasion, Paul was recounting his Damascus Road encounter with the Lord to an angry mob. He recounted his conversion, when he fell to his knees, blinded, and heard the voice of the Lord. The Lord Jesus was calling him into relationship so that Paul would know God's will and see Jesus as God's planned Redeemer for Jew and Gentile.

Like Paul, we were called first into relationship with God. Perhaps our conversion to Jesus was not as dramatic as Paul's, but it was no less significant. The Lord called our names in eternity past, and that call reverberated through the ages until it reached our hearts. And like Paul, we had to respond.

The Lord is still calling, still speaking. Can we hear the voice of the Lord?

Today, so many voices vie for our attention. Advertisers call out to us to buy this product or that one. Our electronic devices ping and ring notifying us of new messages. News people call out to us to pay attention to one event after another. But God is calling for us to "hear the voice of His mouth." For it is through His voice that we know His will and pay attention to what the Lord is doing in and around us.

Today we must decide, like Paul, to hearken to the voice of the Lord.

Dear Lord, it's to Your voice that called me in salvation and continues to call me daily that I desire to respond. Today, I quiet my soul that I may hear You above the noise. Your voice, whispered by Your Spirit within me, guides me in the path of Your will. I want to hear You now. Amen.

GOD'S CHOSEN VESSELS

*But the Lord said unto him, Go thy way: for he is a chosen vessel unto me,
to bear my name before the Gentiles, and kings, and the children of Israel.*

ACTS 9:15, KJV

Prior to his conversion, the apostle Paul was known by his Hebrew name, Saul. He was well-known in the Christian world for his persecution of the followers of Jesus. So much so that Ananias, when asked by the Lord to disciple the newly converted Saul, resisted. Ananias reminded God of Saul's evil ways.

Yet God had a plan for Saul. He assured Ananias that Saul was indeed chosen by God and had a distinct purpose to declare the name of Jesus to the nations. Ananias eventually embraced this former persecutor as a brother in the Lord (Acts 9:17).

The Lord called Saul a "chosen vessel." In ancient days, vessels were hollow household containers used to hold or carry goods. For instance, a waterpot was a vessel. Some vessels were made of costly material and were used to store treasures; while other vessels were made of more mundane materials such as wood and held more everyday goods.

The term came, metaphorically, to stand for humans—either people chosen for good works, or in a bad sense, those who assisted in the accomplishment of evil deeds.[4] God was saying to Ananias, "Saul is a person I have set apart to carry the good news of Jesus Christ." Saul was a human receptacle to be filled with the Holy Spirit (Acts 9:17) and used by God.

Some of us had pretty shady pasts also. We may not have attacked the church the way Saul did, but each of us did other things that opposed or resisted God. It could have been our lifestyles, our tendency to lie, or our mean attitudes. Yet when God chose us for salvation, He did it out of His great love for us. God chose us as His vessels, filled us with the Holy Spirit, and then commissioned us to bear witness to Jesus our Savior.

What an awesome privilege!

Dear Lord, thank You for selecting me for salvation and giving me the honor of sharing Your love and carrying the good news of Jesus to a dying world. I am Your chosen vessel. Use me to Your glory! In Jesus' Name. Amen.

WE ARE HEIRS

In whom also we have obtained an inheritance, being predestinated according to the purpose of him who worketh all things after the counsel of his own will.

EPHESIANS 1:11, KJV

Everything the Lord did, He did with us in mind, so we could receive the greatest inheritance on earth and in heaven—the gift of eternal life. That was His plan for us from the beginning of time. He chose to love us despite our shortcomings and disobedient behavior. God's love for us is unconditional, and His plan for our lives cannot be changed. Unlike the earthly inheritances that we receive, this inheritance does not come with a set of rules, just acceptance of our Lord. He gives us so many opportunities, even when we mess up, to get it right. His love reaches far beyond our human understanding; He forgives, redeems, and sets us free from all pain and bondage. His gift of the Holy Spirit allows us to be closely guided by Him. Our spiritual walk is more profound because we are open to hear and receive His instruction.

The Holy Spirit is our guide, who helps us along life's journey. As we read God's Word, we grow closer and understand His plan. As we pray, our relationship grows stronger and we discover in which direction we should go; and as we are still, we can hear His still, small voice.

No matter what, we have an inheritance that is for a lifetime. This inheritance will never run out, never be taken away, and never depreciate in value. We don't have to fight with siblings over it because we each receive our own according to our confession of faith in Jesus as Lord and Christ. This inheritance comes from a God who is alive and living inside of us! The dividends from this inheritance grow continually and are passed from generation to generation. What a plan and what a gift!

Lord, thank You for my inheritance of eternal life and the gift of the Holy Spirit, which guides me. Help me to be a better listener and follower of Your Word and to grow richer every day by applying the things You are teaching. I thank You that I am leaving a rich heritage by living my life according to Your will as an example to those around me. Amen.

DRAFTED INTO THE FAMILY

*According as he hath chosen us in him before the foundation of the world,
that we should be holy and without blame before him in love.*

EPHESIANS 1:4, KJV

Throughout our lives we experience different opportunities to
be chosen, but most of the time, we have to demonstrate some
type of great accomplishment that allows us to stand out above
everyone else so we are noticed. In the various sports arenas there
are drafts for new players, and scouts are sent out to the various
games to look for the best players. Players must apply to be in the
draft; sports teams review their records, and watch them in action.
Basically, the teams have some idea of the types of players that
would best fit their requirements

For instance, in football, each team selects new players and
awards them contracts according to their potential. Players must
then produce or face the possibility of being cut from the team or
traded. The whole idea is that teams want the best players so they
have a chance to win championship games.

With Christ, we didn't have to demonstrate anything. He paid
the price for us to be on His team! He already knew our track
record and decided that He wanted us anyway. He loved us so
much and He wanted us to experience the greatest love of all, His!
His love covers us; His love presents us before the Father blameless;
and His love keeps us. Even when we mess up, Christ has given us
the ability to confess our sins, and He willingly forgives us and
cleanses us from all unrighteousness (1 John 1:9). So being drafted
into, chosen for, and elected into the family of God is for life. This
is a great sign-on bonus and benefits package. We will never be cut
or traded because we are now part of His family!

*Lord, thank You for choosing me before the foundation of the world and
allowing me to be Your child. I ask You to continue to teach me how to love,
forgive, and be a light in the world that others will be drawn to You. Amen.*

A DESIGN FOR CHANGE

For we are his workmanship, created in Christ Jesus unto good works, which God hath before ordained that we should walk in them.

EPHESIANS 2:10, KJV

We are designer originals created in Christ unto good works. Before Christ entered our hearts, we were dead in trespasses and sin. The path we were on fulfilled our fleshly desires but destroyed us spiritually. When we accepted the free gift of salvation our lives were changed, and now we are walking in the Spirit and not fulfilling the lust of the flesh.

The fact that God chose us to be His workmanship is an act of love and grace. His love toward us caused us to move from darkness to light. His grace allows us to live with Him in eternity. He knew what we were capable of and how we would behave, but He still chose us to represent Him in the earth. He has given us the gift of the Holy Spirit, which leads us in making decisions.

Our lives have been reconstructed to fulfill His purpose in the earth. Our assignment can be on our job, at our school, or in our community. But we should never forget that we were created to bring Him glory.

Because we are new creatures in Christ, we now have a new way of handling life's situations. When people are talking about us and putting us down, we can pray in the Holy Ghost and build ourselves up. When we are being mistreated and abused, we can trust and believe that the Lord is fighting our battles so we do not have to take matters into our own hands. When we have been rejected, we can be comforted knowing that the Lord is our Shepherd and we shall not want. How can we do this? By choosing God's ways and principles above the world's and knowing that His grace and mercy shall follow us all the days of our lives. So living for Him is not an option—it is a necessity!

❧

Lord, thank You for each lesson that I learn from each trial that I have endured. Please continue to teach me how to press, even when it appears to be tough. Teach me to walk in the Spirit so that I will not fulfill the lust of the flesh. In Jesus' Name. Amen.

JUSTICE WITHOUT VIOLENCE

Behold my servant, whom I uphold; mine elect, (in whom) my soul delighteth; I have put my spirit upon him: he shall bring forth judgment to the Gentiles.

ISAIAH 42:1, KJV

In our world we have experienced many injustices. African Americans were not able to vote, to live where they wanted, to attend school in certain neighborhoods, or simply to ride at the front of the bus. Many marches were organized to bring awareness to those injustices. Rosa Parks' bus ride in Montgomery, Alabama, on December 1, 1955, stands out the most. She refused to give up her seat to a white passenger and was arrested and fined. That was one of the catalysts of the civil rights movement to bring freedom to those who were bound. She did not announce what she was going to do; her actions were not violent, but their impact began a movement that changed the course of our nation's history. People across the nation were blessed to sit in any seat on the bus because of one woman's brave stand.

Christ knew his assignment from the Father was to bring both reconciliation and judgment. Only He could judge the nations and bring about the justice of God and blessing the people. Jesus would complete His assignment without boasting and without arrogance, but rather by being meek, humble, and peaceful. He completed His task of teaching the masses and healing the sick. He did it even though He would encounter great persecution and suffer the ultimate betrayal. Because of His obedience, we can receive Him, live with Him eternally, and not be consumed by this world. Because of Christ we have a place in heaven for eternity.

Though Christ was lied on, beaten, and spat upon, He was not deterred. Nor did He respond violently. In fact, He prayed to the Father, "Lord, not my will but Your will be done." He did it all for us!

※

Lord, thank You for loving me so much that You were willing to die so that I can live. Amen.

Do You Know Who's on Your Team?

I speak not of you all: I know whom I have chosen: but that the scripture may be fulfilled, He that eateth bread with me hath lifted up his heel against me.

JOHN 13:18, KJV

Can you imagine the one you chose betraying you at your own table? Consider this scenario: You were given the opportunity to choose twelve people to be on your team. Of course you are looking for those who will help your team excel, as well as those with whom you can have a good working relationship. Your assignment is to teach them and to build trusting relationships. You eat and laugh together, and you know intricate details about each other. The team members have begun to gel and suddenly it's revealed that one of them is a spy, sent in to set you up for a monetary reward. Now, how are you going to handle this? What will be your response?

Jesus' response was *I chose him. Judas was the one who was set up, not Me.* Judas unwittingly was used to betray Jesus so that the people of God would receive the ultimate gift of salvation. God used Judas to fulfill His grand plan (Psalm 41:9). God used what was in Judas' heart to accomplish His purpose. Jesus loved him, taught him, and spent time with him despite the knowledge that Judas would betray Him. Judas' example teaches us to first pray to find out why certain people are in our lives, and then to trust God that whatever the plan, He will take care of us and give us the strength to walk alongside our enemies.

The fact that Judas was allowed to be one of the twelve disciples, shows us that we can face our enemies without fear because God chose us and He will deliver us.

🕊

Lord, thank You for protecting me and keeping me even when the enemy is on my track. Thank You for teaching me how to continue in Your ways and to not be distracted by the schemes of the enemy but to trust that You will deliver me when trouble is in my way. Amen.

CHOSEN AND ORDAINED

Ye have not chosen me, but I have chosen you, and ordained you, that ye should go and bring forth fruit, and that your fruit should remain: that whatsoever ye shall ask of the Father in my name, he may give it you.

JOHN 15:16, KJV

Jesus was giving comforting words to the disciples He had chosen to do a work for Him. He instilled in them everything that He had learned from the Father. Their assignment was clear—to spread the good news of the gospel to all that will hear. Jesus built a relationship with them that formed a friendship and a bond that would last forever. He initiated relationships that would change the world.

It is clear that the relationship we have with the Lord began with Christ. He placed a desire in us to follow Him. When we were busy with our own plans, He interrupted our lives with a public announcement that *we need Him.* He established us to a place, time, and a group of people to impact His Kingdom.

When we walk according to God's plan, it takes precedence over everything else. The cost doesn't matter because the reward outweighs the price. We have an assurance that because God chose us, He has equipped us with everything we need to fulfill the purpose He has set for us. So when life seems to turn upside down and depression tries to take over, remember that the joy of the Lord is our strength. When we are waiting for an important decision to be made and the answers are not coming as quickly as we would like, remember that we have peace that passes all understanding. When we are faced with people who negatively challenge us and cause us to really want to "go there," we should remember to walk in kindness. No matter what comes our way, our stance is the same, and whatever we need, God will provide. His fruit will continually grow in us as we trust in Him for the decisions in our lives—because He chose us.

❧

Lord, thank You for choosing me and allowing me to experience the fruit of the Spirit and for hearing my prayers and loving me so that I can know how to love others. In Jesus' Name. Amen.

"Father, Give Them What They Need"

I have manifested Your name to the men whom You have given Me out of the world. They were Yours, You gave them to Me, and they have kept Your word.

John 17:6, NJKV

News flash—Jesus never loses! Jesus was focused and knew His assignment. Jesus chose twelve disciples to walk alongside Him in His earthly ministry. He taught them, chastised them, and loved them. His earthly assignment was coming to a close, and He began to pray to the Father. His prayer was a three-part prayer. He prayed that He would be glorified, the disciples sanctified, and the believers of God unified.

Jesus prayed that whomever the Father gave Him would know Him and receive eternal life. He prayed that they would know the only true and living God and that He would be glorified.

Jesus prayed that the disciples would be sanctified. He taught them the Word, and they believed it. He kept them and never lost one. His prayer was that even though they would be in the world, that they would not be consumed by it. Jesus desired that they would experience the same oneness that He and the Father had. He was taking care of those that were given to Him, and He wanted them to be able to have immediate access to Him.

That is the same level of love Jesus has for us—that we would have joy, relationship with Him, and not be consumed by this world. So when we are faced with trials and tribulations, we can draw strength from His prayer because we are now the ones God has chosen. Jesus' prayer reminds us that the Lord already knew what we were going to have to endure, but He prayed for us and we can be assured that we have been given everything we need in order to walk according to His will. So don't get overwhelmed by the drama of life; draw from the fountain of life and know that if Jesus has already prayed, we already have what we need.

Lord, thank You for revealing Yourself to me and allowing me to develop a close and loving relationship with You. Your love overshadows all of the disappointments and challenges I have encountered. Thank You for Your Word and for never leaving me alone. In Jesus' Name. Amen.

HE HAS MY BACK

And shall not God avenge his own elect, which cry day and night unto him,
though he bear long with them?

LUKE 18:7, KJV

A ccording to *Encarta Dictionary*, persistence is the quality of continuing steadily despite problems or difficulties. There is a parable in Luke 18:1-8 that describes how a widow persistently pursued a judge to receive justice. The woman pursued the judge continuously until she received the justice she sought. The judge, who had no fear of God, nor regard for man (Luke 18:2), granted the woman's request because of her continued persistence. She basically wore him out!

There are times in our lives when we ask God to rescue us from a distressing situation. The situation might be self-inflicted or brought about by circumstances beyond our control. We may try to fix it ourselves, then we realize we can't do it alone. Thus we end up feeling helpless. Fortunately, the Lord has provided us access to Him, and He promises to help us through every situation. We learn from reading the book of Psalms that the Lord loves us and hears our cries. We don't have to worry; He hears our cries and will deliver us from our fears.

The key is prayer—persistent prayer. Scripture reminds us to pray without ceasing (1 Thessalonians 5:17), continue steadfastly in prayer (Romans 12:12), and that the Lord hears the prayers of the righteous (Proverbs 15:29). We can go to God with the assurance that He never tires of hearing our prayers and He will deliver us. He never gets tired and, no matter how long we are in, or how perilous our situation, He will be right there with us.

So when it seems as though God has not heard our prayers, we can be assured that He has, and more importantly, that He has an answer for us. We are to be patient, prayerful, and confident that our answer is on the way.

❧

Lord, thank You for being patient with me as I look to You for direction. I thank You for hearing my cries and for delivering me from the things that would have me bound. Amen.

PRAY BEFORE YOU CHOOSE

And when it was day, he called unto him his disciples: and of them he chose twelve, whom also he named apostles.

LUKE 6:13, KJV

Prayer is key, because Jesus did it. Jesus did not make a decision without spending time with the Father. Jesus' example to us is to first spend time with the Father before making decisions. The decisions don't always make sense or even appear rational. Jesus' choice of His twelve disciples might not have been ours. He chose fishermen, treasurers, tax collectors, and a betrayer. Who of us would pick someone to be in our camp who we know would betray us? Yet all of Jesus' choices were according to God's will.

Our obedience to God might not always lead to the most popular choice, but it is always the right one. As we seek God's direction, it is so much better to follow Him and His plans than our own. If we follow God, He will provide for us. He gives us strength to bear the rough times, peace to deal with the uneasy times, and love to deal with the difficult times. Our obedience aligns us with God's plan for us, which is good and not evil and gives us a hope and an expected end (Jeremiah 29:11).

Before the foundation of the world God chose us! He chose us to be a light in the midst of darkness, followers of Christ, a royal priesthood, and more importantly, His children. His plan has always had us in mind. He knows how much we can bear and whose lives we will impact. We might not have been someone else's choice, but that really doesn't matter; we were God's choice, and He doesn't make mistakes.

Today, we can glorify Him in all that we do and share His Word across the world—a living example of His grace. And we can encourage those who are struggling to have hope.

❧

Lord, thank You for choosing me for this season in life. I want to glorify You in all that I do and draw others to You. Thank You for saving me out of a life of darkness into a life that is full of hope and love. Amen.

INTERVENTION

And except that the Lord had shortened those days, no flesh should be saved:
but for the elect's sake, whom he hath chosen, he hath shortened the days.

MARK 13:20, KJV

As children, we experienced some growing pains. We were disobedient and did not want to listen. We thought we knew what was best for us, and even though destruction was ahead, we took the chance any way, not thinking about the consequences. Some of us had people who tried to warn us of the trouble that lay ahead; they could see that if we followed the path we were on, it would lead to our detriment. Our choice was to listen or continue and suffer the consequences. Of course, we minimized what we had done and tried to rationalize it in our heads, saying the punishment did not fit the action that we took.

Can you remember crying, wishing you could get another chance? You would say, "I won't do it again; I promise." Of course, as life continued, we made other mistakes. During those times, it was nice to have someone to intervene to help get us out of situations we got ourselves into. When a grandparent, aunt, uncle, or someone who cares for us came to our defense and caused our punishment to be lessened, or done away with altogether, it was a sigh of relief.

The Lord's love for us is just like that. Even though we deserve the punishment, His grace and mercy cover us and allow us to experience less suffering than we should have. His care has always been for those He came for. The Lord gave signs of the destruction that lay ahead and also instructed one of the disciples not to be fooled by the ones who were coming claiming to be the Messiah.

As we see prophecies being fulfilled—nation against nation, earthquakes, and famines—we can be assured that He is taking care of us in the midst. Jesus protects those that are His and gives us the strength to endure the hardships we will go through.

❧

Lord, thank You for intervening on my behalf, giving me warning signs of
the destruction that lay ahead and the strength to endure life circumstances
that I must face along my journey. Amen.

Equal Faithfulness, Equal Reward

So the last shall be first, and the first last: for many be called, but few chosen.

MATTHEW 20:16, KJV

Jesus spoke to His disciples in a parable in which workers in a vineyard began working at different times of the day. The first set of workers was given a contract and agreed to its terms. During the day, the vineyard owner noticed people watching on the sidelines, called them over, and offered them a position to work. They jumped right in and began working.

At the end of the day, the vineyard owner began paying the workers. He began with the workers who were last hired. They received the standard wage for the day. He then called the next crew and paid them the same day's wage. Last, he called the crew that had worked the longest and gave each the same wage. The crew that had worked the longest believed they should have received a higher wage because they had worked more hours. The landowner shared with them that they had agreed to the wage they were given, and that it was his choice to bless the new workers the way he pleased.

The Lord chooses whom He wants to bless and how He wants to do it. We shouldn't get discouraged when someone else is called to the front of the line. One day it might be our turn. Whatever we do for the Lord, we should do out of love and not for monetary reward. If we can just remember to be steadfast, unmovable, and always abounding in the work of the Lord, we will know that our labor is not in vain, and we will receive what He has for us. It doesn't matter our position; it just matters that we were chosen by Him to work in the kingdom of God. When God calls us, we should be ready to do our part and not worry about our place.

❧

Lord, thank You for choosing me and having a place for me in Your Kingdom. Thank You for unconditional love and for noticing that I needed to do my part in Your vineyard. I pray I walk in love and humility as I complete the work that You have put in my hands. In Jesus' Name. Amen.

AN ACT OF GRACE

For if by one man's offence death reigned by one; much more they which receive abundance of grace and of the gift of righteousness shall reign life by one, Jesus Christ.

ROMANS 5:17, KJV

In life there are times when we encounter trouble just because we were in a place. We really didn't have anything to do with the situation at hand, but because of the deed, we ended up getting punished. The punishment seemed unfair and unreasonable since we were not the initiator of the problem. The fact is we were associated with the wrong person at the wrong time. And because of this association, we needed someone to come and deliver us out of this trouble.

There are also times when we receive blessings because of someone's good deed or work. We didn't participate in the process. As a matter of fact, we came in at the end of it; but, because we were in the right place, we received recognition and the reward too. Wow! Just being associated with the project got us a promotion, visibility, and a move to a new location. We know we had done nothing to deserve it, but we still received the benefit because someone else included us in the project. Now that is love.

We were not there at the beginning when Adam disobeyed God and ate from the Tree of Life. But unfortunately, it caused us to be born into sin and in need of redemption. We cannot work our way into God's good graces, but He had a plan and it was for us to believe in His Son Jesus Christ and receive His grace. The same way one man's action of disobedience caused destruction on the human race, another Man's action of obedience brought redemption and life. If we only believe, we have the right to eternal life—not that we deserve it, but it is by the grace of God.

❧

Thank You, Lord, for Your obedience, Your sacrifice, Your love, and Your grace. Because of You, I can live. I am an heir to Your Kingdom, and I am blessed because You have blessed me in abundance with Your grace. Amen.

IT'S NOT GOING TO DESTROY ME

And we know that all things work together for good to them that love God, to them who are called according to his purpose.

ROMANS 8:28, KJV

A s Christians, we are going to have some ups and downs. We are going to be faced with all kinds of situations—loss of jobs, lack of income, foreclosure, bad relationships, and the list goes on. We don't see things as we are going through them, but it is all a part of the process.

The loss of a job seemed devastating, and we didn't know how we would bounce back; but it led us to look at our career choices and make a turn that ended up being profitable for us. If we had stayed in that situation, we would have never made the move. The lack of income is frustrating, but we have learned to trim the fat so that when we receive an increase we won't spend it all. Losing a home is life altering, and of course, we did everything to hold on to it. We called the banks to work out refinancing or to get a loan modification to no avail—nothing worked out. We couldn't see it then, but the neighborhood was getting worse and the home values were plummeting; if we would have stayed there, we would have faced another financial pitfall, but God delivered us and allowed us to revamp and rebuild. We have had friends who were depending on us more than God. We tried to help them and point them in the Lord's direction, but every turn got worse and so we had to dissolve the relationships. We didn't see that it was part of that person's healing; the break-up prompted them to rely on God and not us, and their lives were turned around.

At the beginning, difficult times can be devastating, but if we trust God, and believe on Him, we know that in the end it is working for our good. So we hold on to His unchanging hand, knowing the trials we encounter are not to destroy us but to make us stronger!

❧

Lord, thank You for turning even my bad situations around for my good. I love You because every step I take points me to a closer relationship with You. Amen.

CONSOLING GRACE

Now may our Lord Jesus Christ Himself, and our God and Father, who has loved us and given us everlasting consolation and good hope by grace.

2 THESSALONIANS 2:16, NKJV

Many of us can identify with suddenly and unexpectedly losing a dear friend. It is devastating, to say the least. Such losses are incredibly hard to bear, particularly when the individual is young. Although our loved one may be saved, and we know that friend is in the arms of the Lord, it is difficult to find any comfort from those well-meaning friends around us. *Enters God.*

God's everlasting grace supplies believers with whatever is needed for any and *all* situations. When we are afraid, He gives us the grace to be courageous; when we are in doubt, He graces us with direction in His still, small voice. When we experience pain through the unexpected loss of a dear one, He provides us with consolation that never ends. The everlasting grace of God is all encompassing and all inclusive. It is God who loves us and gives us "good hope." The Bible declares that our God is the God of *all* comfort (2 Corinthians 1:3), so true consolation is a grace-gift from our Father.

God displays His never-ending grace to us by not only comforting and consoling us when we suffer loss, but also by freely giving us grace for every part of our lives, for every situation and circumstance. In other words, no matter where we need grace, God willingly and lovingly supplies it in abundance—and it is ours eternally!

God has not just promised to be our comfort and to give us hope that we will overcome the things we suffer, but He makes us stronger by those experiences.

We would do well to remember God's everlasting grace toward us as we go through our daily lives, remembering that He is the God of all comfort, and through His comfort we have everlasting hope, which will give us courage to face whatever life brings.

❧

Beloved Father, thank You for Your everlasting consolation and good hope to overcome all adversity that comes into my life. Your grace affords me confidence to move forward, comforted with the knowledge that You supply grace to help in the time of trouble and distress. In Jesus' Name. Amen.

CALLED OUT

What then? What Israel sought so earnestly it did not obtain, but the elect did. The others were hardened.

ROMANS 11:7, NIV

Most childhood games begin by selecting teams. Captains are chosen and, player by player, teams are formed. For various reasons, each captain chooses the best player available that can help the team win the game.

What if God's election was based on how good we are, how hard we work, how much others like us, or the skills we have? We would all be concerned about our position and probably attempt, in our limited abilities, to influence God's decisions.

Thank God for His grace. God chose us to be a people to Himself entirely by grace, not our merit. That eliminates our pride and boastfulness and insures that the glory goes to God, not us. God's election also encourages our love for Him. God chose us and opened our hearts to receive His love and salvation.

Today's Scripture illustrates how God's favor and love saved one undeserving group and rejected the other. Even though one group was denied by God, it did not give them license to live a corrupt and evil life. We are all responsible and accountable before God for what we do, saved or not. God sees all people for all things, good and evil. We can only stand in awe of the wonderful works of our glorious, omniscient King.

As we reflect on His goodness, let us not labor on what could have been, but let us rejoice in what is and how the Lord our God has worked it all out for our good.

Father, I pray You will touch the hearts of family and friends who do not call You Lord and Savior. If it's in Your divine will, I ask for Your guiding hand to lead them to a life filled with Your favor. I thank You in advance. In Jesus' glorious Name, I render this prayer. Amen.

THE GOOD, THE BAD & THE CHOSEN

But before they were born, before they had done anything good or bad, she received a message from God. (This message shows that God chooses according to his own purposes.)

ROMANS 9:11, NLT

Sibling rivalry is a constant in many households with children. Each child wants the advantage with his or her parents and will push, distort, and use trickery to gain it. At times, we also think we can work or render service in the kingdom of God in order to gain favor and choice, but not so. God's mercy and freedom to choose are always apart, or separate from what we do, no matter how innocent the intent or how good we may believe the task is. It is God's election or divine choice that paves the road to our salvation and our service to Him. God has already woven the perfect design in life for us, even before we were born.

Today's Scripture makes reference to an Old Testament story of sibling rivalry. Jacob and Esau, the twins of Isaac (Genesis 25:19-27, 40), found themselves in a tale of deception, or in today's vernacular, a scam. Esau, the firstborn, was entitled to receive his father's blessing. As the story goes, Jacob and his mother were able to outwit Esau and trick his father, Isaac. Old and in poor health, Isaac innocently fell for the scam and blessed Jacob instead of Esau and gave the older brother's birthright to Jacob.

What Jacob and his mother chose to do did not alter God's plans and purposes. Unwillingly, they actually fulfilled God's exact intent. Why? Because God had already chosen Jacob. So it is with us. God had chosen us before we had done anything, good or bad!

So what is our responsibility now? We don't have to manipulate or use deception to gain favor. Instead, we are to grow stronger in faith and receive even those things we do not understand as part of God's eternal plan. Regardless of what we think, what we want, or what we feel, it is all about our God's sovereign will and His eternal promises, that we are who we are.

Bless His divine hand upon us.

Father, in the Name of Jesus, help me establish my affections on things in heaven and to trust Your hand on my life. Bless me according to Your promise. Amen.

WHAT GRACE!

But by the grace of God I am what I am, and His grace to me was not without effect.

1 CORINTHIANS 15:10, NIV

How often do we take personal credit for accomplishing a task? We can probably recall a time in our lives when we would not hesitate to boast about an achievement we did not earn. But now, as sons and daughters of the Most High, we understand that if it had not been for the grace of God, so much in our lives would be different.

The apostle Paul realized this wonderful gift of salvation he received was not because of some remarkable deed or amazing feat on his part. Paul knew it was God's grace alone that saved his life and filled his heart with humility, that led him to become one of the most prolific ambassadors for Jesus Christ. Paul humbly said, "Christ Jesus came into the world to save sinners; of whom I am chief. Howbeit for this cause I obtained mercy" (1 Timothy 1:15b-16a KJV).

It is imperative that we, too, reflect on our lives through the eyes of grace. All that we are, and will come to be, is based solely on God's grace. We are Christ's workmanship, and the Holy Spirit faithfully abides with us as He guides our steps and perfects our lives. Because we have received Christ as Lord over our lives, and He has blessed us with eternal life, let us not forget there is work to do in the Kingdom. Paul did not receive God's grace and then take a seat to watch what unfolded in his life. He realized how blessed he was to be a recipient of grace and dedicated his life to sharing the gospel message.

We, too, should thank and praise God for His grace. His grace covers us and opens new doors of opportunity. God never gives up on us, because He loves us with unconditional, everlasting love. We do thank God for His grace, for without it where would we be?

❧

Father, in the Name of Jesus, I thank You for saving me and blessing me with Your grace. I pray I will press daily to be an effectual example of Your grace. I pray my faith will grow stronger as I witness the magnificence of this great gift of grace. Amen.

KNOCKED OUT

So that, just as sin reigned in death, so also grace might reign through righteousness to bring eternal life through Jesus Christ our Lord.

ROMANS 5:21, NIV

We all know what a knockout punch is, right? It is the one punch that hits the target and floors the opponent, eliminating him or her from the battle. We relate it to boxing, but it is applied in many different instances. For example, upon completing a task, one may say, "I am glad I knocked that out," or feeling confident after an exam, say, "I know I knocked that test out." Whatever the situation, we have a mental picture of success, victory, and achievement with that one knockout punch.

As believers, that is exactly what Jesus Christ did in bringing salvation by grace through faith in Him. He looked sin in the eye and launched a huge knockout punch. Christ's punch was so powerful, it defeated death, set us free from our sins, and removed any scars the power of sin may have put on us.

Romans 5:21 showcases the matchless power of God's grace. No matter how much sin attempts to overthrow grace, our righteousness, or right standing with God, enables us to stand strong as believers and defeat its influence over us. That same righteousness gives us the right to stand with Jesus Christ, our Lord, and reign victoriously. In righteousness, we can withstand the blow of the enemy's punch, but he cannot knock us out. By grace, we commit to live a life of obedience and grow in our commitment to holy living, and the enemy has no influence on us.

The next time the enemy tries to sway our judgment or cause us to venture off the path of righteousness with his weak, lying enticements, let us invoke God's power! Then open our mouths and, in the name of Jesus, rebuke the influence of sin with a powerful thrust, knocking it out and replacing it with a renewed and continual journey of victory in righteousness through Jesus Christ.

※

Father, thank You for Your wonderful grace. Thank You, Lord, for the path of righteousness I follow day-by-day. I pray You will give me more faith to withstand the enemy's punch and bless me with victory after victory after victory in You and through You. In Jesus' Name. Amen.

No Greater Gift

But to all who believed him and accepted him, he gave the right to become children of God. They are reborn—not with a physical birth resulting from human passion or plan, but a birth that comes from God.

JOHN 1:12-13, NLT

Jesus' purpose on earth was to seek and to save those who were lost. In today's Scripture, John emphasizes the transformative power of the new birth. The new birth, receiving Jesus Christ in our hearts, is not just about the forgiveness of sins, but it is also about a change that takes place in our hearts that affects everything about us. It is a change we cannot make on our own. It is a gift from God. When explaining the new birth to Nicodemus in John 3:6, Jesus Christ said to him, "Humans can reproduce only human life, but the Holy Spirit gives birth to spiritual life."

That's right. We are saved, delivered from the clutches of the enemy, and joined together with all other believers. Verse twelve calls it the "rebirth," a new beginning, a new life in Jesus that is empowered by the Holy Spirit. We are changed from a life of doom and gloom and introduced to a life with the Light of the world.

What Jesus Christ offers the world is a far greater reward than the temporal things. Our faith and our focus are strengthened in Him. "We do this by keeping our eyes on Jesus, the champion who initiates and perfects our faith" (Hebrews 12:2). Our faith depends on Him from start to finish. He is the only One who blesses us with life eternal. Ephesians 2:8 tells us, "God saved you by his grace when you believed. And you can't take credit for this; it is a gift from God."

Can you think of a greater gift?

Father, I thank You for choosing me to receive this wonderful gift—the gift of salvation. I pray Your guiding light leads me to a life filled with Your grace and love. In Jesus' Name, I pray. Amen.

SALVATION SO NEAR

Victory comes from you, O Lord. May you bless your people.

PSALM 3:8, NLT

Today's key word is "victory." God provides victory in times of trouble. Psalm 3, written by David, illustrates his weariness and fear while fleeing from his son Absalom, who was out to kill him and take the throne. David cried out to God to be protected from the son who had become his enemy. In verse seven David cries, *"Rescue me, my God! Slap all my enemies in the face! Shatter the teeth of the wicked!"* When David needed help, He called on God.

We want and need the same kind of help David cried out for. Whatever our situation, no matter how desperate, we can know that our God is a warring God; He will go before us and save us from those daily troubles that are real in our lives. It doesn't matter whether we have many years in our Christian walk or are just beginning this journey; we have the assurance of God's presence and the hope of victory as we travel along the way.

Our confidence in Jesus Christ is based on our faith and trust in Him. He honors His Word to us. He strengthens us daily to trust and obey Him. He upholds us during difficult times, and He protects us and gives us peace. Jesus Christ is our all in all and gives us the assurance that He is with us to deliver us and to keep us. Our confidence grows stronger each day as we learn who we are in Him. His blessings are evident in the grace extended to us through His deeds, His guidance, and His protection.

It does not matter the circumstance. Whether the boss is harassing us, our relationship with a spouse is in discord, or our children have gone astray, let us find the assurance and comfort in knowing our God cares for us and the trials that befall us. He is with us to deliver us and to give us victory and protection as we grow in the confidence of being in His presence. God is closer than we think!

Father, today I sit in awe of Your Sovereign grace. I cry tears of joy because I have victory in situations where I have failed. I am thankful for the blessings of Your favor. Help me to keep my eyes on You. In Jesus' Name. Amen.

NOW IS THE TIME

For the grace of God that brings salvation has appeared to all men.
TITUS 2:11, NIV

During basketball season, a local professional basketball team comes together in a huddle just before they run onto the court and shout in unison: "What time is it? Game time! Woo!" It is this chant that helps the team become united in their goal of winning the game.

In most of our lives, it is not time with which we have the most difficulty; it is usually the management of time. We repeatedly convince ourselves that we still have time to make that appointment, complete that proposal, do laundry before nightfall. Who are we kidding? Most often, we end up looking back and taking inventory of the time wasted doing frivolous things.

God did not bless us with life to waste it, nor does He want us to miss the wonderful opportunities He has designed for us. In God's eternal framework, there is a "time for every purpose under the heaven" (Ecclesiastes 3:1-8). But, like that basketball team, our minds have to have a singular purpose.

Today's Scripture reminds us that God's grace has been extended to us all. Today is the day for God's children to walk in the newness of a journey called salvation. We will find that our past is represented by *justification*—we have been declared righteous before God and free from the penalty of sin. Second, our journey embraces our present through *sanctification* that freed us from the power of sin by the Holy Spirit. And third, our salvation journey prepares us for *glorification* when we are totally conformed to the image of Jesus Christ.

God's grace has been bestowed upon us. We do not have to waste time playing games with our lives. We should not have to remind ourselves that it is game time. The only way to win this game of life—the only way to victory, eternal victory—is to surrender our lives to Christ Jesus. It is game time! Let's go out there and win this thing!

❧

Father, I long to do all things according to Your divine purpose. I do not want to waste time pursuing things that keep me from You. Help me to use my time in worship and praise so that You can be seen in all I do. Amen.

SUFFICIENT GRACE

I always thank my God for you and for the gracious gifts he has given you, now that you belong to Christ Jesus.

1 CORINTHIANS 1:4, NLT

When we find that someone has wronged us or chosen a wrong path in life, we know we should pray for them, but that is not always easy. What can we do? The apostle Paul had the difficult task of addressing the Corinthian church when they were immersed in several problems of great concern. Rather than just chastising them, Paul chose to begin by reminding the Corinthians of what God had done in their lives and that they belonged to Him. He was doing more than just building up their confidence before addressing the problems that were tearing the church apart. Paul first reminded these Christians that God had sanctified them, setting them apart and calling them to be holy. Paul reminded them, too, that they were connected with other believers throughout the world. He reminded them of the plan God had for the church. In essence, Paul extended grace and love to a bickering congregation.

What Paul did is identical to how God guides us when we fall by the wayside. He wraps us in His grace and compassion, and whispers, "I know you did it, but I am going to honor My promise to you because you belong to Me through the sacrifice of Jesus Christ. Although you have erred and gone astray, I am going to uphold you in My righteousness." What favor! What a God!

While Paul extended love and grace to the wrongdoers of Corinth, God's blessings of grace reach far beyond that for us. So let us take heed to Paul's example and first pray for the individual who may be in the wrong. Prayer strengthens us and keeps our minds focused on God and not the shortcoming. Let's encourage one another with love and understanding. Remember that a hand extended in forgiveness and forgetfulness is better than a word spoken to berate and accuse. That is what sufficient grace can do.

※

Lord, I bless You and praise You for sufficient grace. I pray I will be more attentive of the times when I receive mercy and grace from You when I falter, so that I will grow and extend the grace of another chance to others. In Jesus' Name. Amen.

GOOD NEWS

This salvation was something even the prophets wanted to know more about when they prophesied about this gracious salvation prepared for you.
1 PETER 1:10, NLT

Carl Boberg, a nineteenth-century Swedish minister, penned the words to the anthem "How Great Thou Art." Although originally written as a poem, the song was amended and expanded over the years to finally become one of the most soul-wrenching anthems in Christendom. The third verse says, *And when I think that God, His Son not sparing, Sent Him to die, I scarce can take it in; That on the Cross my burden gladly bearing, He bled and died To take away my sin. Then sings my soul, My Savior God, to Thee, How great Thou art! How great Thou art!*[5]

What good news rings out in the words of that song! Each phrase represents an aspect of the plan of salvation purchased by God's Son, Jesus Christ, whose sacrifice was proven in His cleansing blood. Boberg's words proclaim the wonder of the sacrifice that Old Testament prophets proclaimed by faith but longed to understand.

Our Scripture today was written by the apostle Peter, who was a zealous follower of Jesus Christ. Peter embraced his position in Christ and shared, with passionate joy, the grace and expectation that salvation brings. He demonstrated strength in his writing, reminding early Christians of the favor they had in Jesus Christ. Peter counted believers as blessed, and declared that they had three reasons to rejoice. First, they were chosen as God's elect. Second, their faith would grow stronger as they held fast, endured hardships, and suffered for their faith. Finally, believers could rejoice because salvation was revealed to them through Jesus Christ.

Through the unconditional outpouring of His love for us, God chose us and blessed us with the gift of salvation. That is good news and gives us reason to rejoice. *"Then sings my soul; my Savior God to Thee."*

❦

Father, thank You for bringing forth the fulfillment of redemption's plan in Your Son, Jesus Christ. In Jesus' Name. Amen.

Solid as a Rock

In his kindness God called you to share in his eternal glory by means of Christ Jesus. So after you have suffered a little while, he will restore, support, and strengthen you, and he will place you on a firm foundation.

1 Peter 5:10, NLT

All around us today, we witness natural disasters and calamities. In certain parts of the world, people are rising up in protest against governments that have hindered their human rights or taken over their lives, possessions, and freedoms. Natural disasters seem to be commonplace. Lives have been lost, countries devastated, and government leaders brought down. It would appear that the enemy has won and the world is doomed, but we know better. Our Sovereign God reigns. What may appear to be the end on one hand, could be the beginning of something new on the other. No matter the circumstance in the world, or in our lives, we know and trust that God's sovereign hand never leaves us.

Today's Scripture is like a checkpoint on the road of life. We are reminded that God chose us to be His. The Scripture goes on to let us know that even when suffering, trials, and calamity come, we have confidence that we will be restored and brought out. Losing a job is difficult to handle. Foreclosure is unspeakable. Having savings dwindled to almost nothing is unthinkable. But God is faithful. He is our Rock and is watching over us. So we rest in the assurance that He will restore us and support us in the hard times.

We have a role, too. First, we have to know who we are in Christ Jesus. We have to remind ourselves that we are chosen by God to do great things; He did not save us just to leave us hanging. Second, we must recognize the enemy. He uses his trickery to blind us and get us off track. He wants us to think God's way is not helping, to doubt our position in Him, and to tempt us to sin in order to find solutions to our problems.

Although we are witnesses to so many catastrophic events around the world, we must not lose focus of God's intent for our lives. His Word is our strength. His foundation is everlasting.

❧

Father, I thank You for being the steady hand on my life. Amen.

INCREASE!

And they will pray for you with deep affection because of the overflowing grace God has given to you. Thank God for this gift too wonderful for words!
2 CORINTHIANS 9:14-15, NLT

Remember weekly allowance? Remember how special allowance day was? Sisters and brothers anxiously awaited hearing the sound of their parents' voices saying to come down to the table to receive their allowance. We readily made plans for the five dollars that would take us to the next Friday, but we miscalculated. Our parents had already subtracted the twenty-five cents for our Sunday school offering and fifty cents for tithes! Five dollars was quickly reduced to four dollars and twenty-five cents. "What a bummer," we thought, not realizing the timeless seeds of faith our parents were planting in our hearts. They became stepping stones in our growth and maturity. Tiny sprouts of faith and blessings grew into strong branches that did not break or splinter. We developed an understanding of one of the Bible's most important principles—tithing.

Our abundance is a blessing from God that is to be used to support and sustain the work and ministry of Jesus Christ. When we give, God is glorified and needs are met. The apostle Paul humbly told the Corinthian church to continue its obedience in sharing the Good News by supporting the needs of others. When God's people give, it is a reflection of God's grace, which was given so we might be an example of His goodness and grace.

Kingdom ministry goes far beyond the doors of the church. It reaches to the uttermost parts of the world to meet the challenges of spreading God's truth and bring spiritual life to a dying world. Sharing or giving is how we partake in kingdom building. We must continue to give, planting seeds of Christ's grace, love, and mercy for the world to see. It is our contribution to our covenant bond with Christ.

Father, thank You for blessing me. I pray, Lord, that You will continue to shape my heart to be more trusting and more giving. In Jesus' Name. Amen.

STANDING ON THE PROMISES

Now may our Lord Jesus Christ himself and God our Father, who loved us and by his grace gave us eternal comfort and a wonderful hope, comfort you and strengthen you in every good thing you do and say.
2 THESSALONIANS 2:16-17, NLT

As children, we wondered why our parents put so much emphasis on attending Sunday school. Every Sunday the household was up for grabs. We didn't want our Sunday morning sleep disrupted by a teacher who rambled on about Jesus and His disciples. But we knew if we didn't attend Sunday school, we would not receive the rewards or privileges our parents so enticingly dangled before us.

Christian parents know the importance of their children learning who they are in Christ Jesus. The fact is our parents knew the importance of being grounded in God's Word, and they wanted to set a godly standard that God is first, and His Word is key to understanding the life God wants us to live. That is why they started early preparing us for life's challenges and making us aware of the tests that would certainly come our way. They wanted our hearts and minds filled with hope, and strengthened in His power and grace.

Today's Scripture emphasizes how we, even in trying times, can be encouraged. With God before us, and His Word deep in our hearts, is there anything to stop us? No. The Lord expects us to be victorious in our pursuit of a life committed to Him. The Lord expects us to know we are eternally His, and we can rest on that blessed assurance. Calamity may be all around us, but we are vessels of hope, standing firm in His Word.

The song "Standing on the Promises" speaks of the assurance of hope and strength we have when we stand firm and hold tight to God's Word.[6] The fourth verse says, *"Standing on the promises of Christ the Lord, Bound to Him eternally by love's strong cord, Overcoming daily with the Spirit's sword, Standing on the promises of God."*

❧

Lord, I thank You for the hope and power that Your Word gives me day-by-day. I thank You for teaching me how to stand on Your promises. Amen.

GOD'S UNSTOPPABLE PLAN

Therefore I endure all things for the elect's sake, that they may also obtain the salvation which is in Christ Jesus with eternal glory.

2 TIMOTHY 2:10, KJV

In the last months of his life, Bishop Arthur Brazier showed what grace looked like under pressure. Through his behavior, he delivered the message that the work of God should continue, even under adverse circumstances. He continued to encourage others and to comfort them, even though he was on his way home.

Paul wrote his second letter to Timothy while he was in prison. Amazing was his ability to encourage others while he was in the direst of circumstances! In the waning months of his life, Bishop Brazier had that same supernatural ability.

In today's Scripture, Paul encourages his readers by letting them know he is able to endure imprisonment because he knows that God's work will continue to go forward. Paul knows that this work is effective because salvation is its foundation. God is continuing to move among His elect! Paul wants his readers to experience God in the salvation provided by Christ the way he had. Not by sharing his imprisonment experience but from the standpoint of seeing God's work go forth despite tribulations and difficulties. In other words, Paul's imprisonment in no way prevented God's work from going forth through him!

Although he seemed to be shut down, nothing could be further from the truth. Paul's imprisonment served as a catalyst for the spreading of the Word of God to bring about salvation even to those who were his captors. Though the enemy sought to still his voice, to curtail his efforts in the gospel, it had the opposite effect. It was promulgated because it was the will of God that salvation through the gospel should go forth!

This Scripture offers hope to us when we find ourselves in difficult situations. Here is truth: nothing, no situation or circumstance, prevents those who are predestined from coming to salvation through the Lord, Jesus Christ!

Mighty One, You have sent Your Word forth, and it will accomplish all that You sent it out to do. Let me understand my role in this plan and learn not to be deterred because I may find myself in difficulty. Thank You, Father. In Jesus' Name. Amen.

THE ULTIMATE SECURITY

Who has saved us and called us with an holy calling, not according to our works, but according to His own purpose and grace, which was given us in Christ Jesus before the world began.

2 TIMOTHY 1:9, KJV

More and more in the writings of the apostle Paul, we can see that he seeks to press deep into our hearts, minds, souls, and spirits that we are secure in Christ Jesus. God's plan from the very beginning was to bring us to Himself to become His own dear children.

In this passage, Paul reiterates, as he did throughout his writings, that God chose us *before* time began, *before* the world was created; and He did it because it was His own good purpose and sovereign will. We were not saved according to works—it is simply impossible for anyone to earn passage into heaven—but it is by the grace, the unearned, undeserved, immeasurable grace of God. No one person had any part in the saving of one's immortal soul. God called us and saved us in Christ Jesus *before* the world was founded, by His grace. Jesus Christ was, and is, the proof of God's grace toward us.

Paul tells us we were called with a holy calling, that is we are called to live a holy life. We have been given grace through Jesus Christ to emulate the holiness of God—*Be ye holy for I am holy.* It is not a request!

We can give our best to God with complete abandonment, holding nothing back because we have proof of His grace toward us in the person of Jesus, the Christ.

Serving the Lord with gladness, dedication, and commitment is possible because we have been assured of the never-ending, free-flowing love that God has for His eternal children. Hallelujah!

❧

Most honorable and exalted Father, You have given the Best for the worst! Thank You for securing my soul's place in eternity with You through the gracious gift of Your Son, Christ Jesus, before the world began, according to Your good purpose and will. In Jesus' Name. Amen.

THE GREAT GRACE OF GOD

But we believe through the grace of the Lord Jesus Christ we shall be saved even as they.

ACTS 15:11, KJV

Grace is the very essence of God's love poured out without measure for the benefit of humankind. Jesus Christ is the embodiment of that grace, the evidence that God not only wants us and loves us but provided the way to bridge the chasm—the abyss—that separated us from Him because of our sins. Christ's "cross-work" was God's desired effect in turning His *wrath from* us to *love toward* us!

In this Scripture we find Peter defending Paul's decision to spread the gospel to the Gentiles. Earlier in the chapter, Peter argued that a precedent had been set when God allowed Gentiles to receive the gospel through Peter's preaching. So in today's Scripture, Peter is saying these Gentiles who received the gospel of Jesus Christ unto salvation were going to be saved, just as the Jewish Christians would be saved because of the grace of God. It was God's grace that called the Gentiles into the kingdom of God, just as that same grace called the Jewish Christians into salvation.

The Jews were insisting that the keeping of the law was a prerequisite for salvation, but Peter was assuring the Gentiles the same grace that saved the Jews was available to the Gentiles. God's hand in the matter can clearly be seen because it was His design from the beginning that the Gentiles be included in His plan for salvation.

This Scripture records the last words of Peter in the book of Acts. The rest of the book shifts to Paul and his ministry to the Gentiles. Without that shift to bring salvation to the Gentiles, we would not be saved today. Thank God His grace is all-inclusive!

What a marvelous thing! We, who were not of the commonwealth of Israel are also recipients of the great grace of God unto salvation!

Father, thank You for showering Your grace upon me through the gift of Your Son, Jesus Christ. In Him the gates of salvation were thrown wide open to the Gentiles, and as a result, I am saved! For this, I will worship You, praise You, and serve You forever! In Jesus' Name. Amen.

THE POWER OF AN OPENED HEART

And a certain woman named Lydia, a seller of purple, of the city of Thyatira, which worshipped God, heard us: whose heart the Lord opened, that she attended unto the things which were spoken of Paul.

ACTS 16:14, KJV

L ydia was a seller of purple, a merchant, or what would be considered an entrepreneur of the first century. It is striking that the Bible describes her as one "which worshipped God." In other words, her work did not take precedence over her worship.

Lydia teaches us that when we as workers worship, we prioritize our relationships with the Lord such that we are then open to the things of God. Worship sensitizes our hearts to be touched by God. Worship sensitizes our hearts to be open to the Word of God.

Lydia, the powerful merchant—seller of purple dyes to the aristocratic elite of her day—would have been a woman of great influence. Yet her true power rested in her desire to worship God and to know God more fully. So it was, the Bible tells us, that when Paul and his company of missionaries came to the prayer meeting that Lydia attended, the Lord opened Lydia's heart to believe on the Lord Jesus. The Lord opened her heart to His plans and purposes for her—and that was to reveal Jesus to her as Savior and Lord! Lydia responded to Paul's teachings, and she and her household submitted to water baptism as a sign of their heart conversion!

From there, Lydia invited the apostle Paul and his missionary team to stay with her and her household while they remained in the region. God opened her heart, and she opened her home to become the base for Paul and his missionary team. From that gathering many more people came to Christ and the church of Philippi was born!

We can learn from Lydia. As God has opened our hearts to His matchless saving grace, we must make worship a priority. Worship will sensitize our hearts to God, and God will open our hearts to His plans and purposes. Making worship a priority will bless us as we bless God—and open doors for others to enter into relationship with our Lord.

Lord, thank You for opening my heart to believe You and trust You as Savior. Help me today to make worship my priority. In Jesus' Name. Amen.

GOT POWER?

And with great power gave the apostles witness of the resurrection of the Lord Jesus: and great grace was upon them all.

ACTS 4:33, KJV

Feeling powerless occurs periodically in the life of every believer. Isn't it great that feeling is not fact! The fact of the matter is—we have power! Our Scripture reading goes a great distance in reminding us that the Power that spoke the universe into being and that rose Jesus from the dead resides in us today.

In the first chapter of Acts, before His ascension, Jesus tells the disciples to stay in Jerusalem and wait for what the Father had promised—power from on high by the in-filling of the Holy Ghost. Today's Scripture is a witness to the power Christ spoke of in Acts 1:8. The disciples became witnesses "in Judea and Samaria, and even to the remotest parts of the earth" (NASV).

These renewed and empowered men did many miracles. Buoyed by their witness, new conversions abounded, giving birth to the Christian church. This is the grace of God at full throttle! Grace that empowers His servants to build His church by revealing who Jesus really was—the long-awaited Messiah, the Son of the living God.

The great grace that is spoken of is God's evidence that He is not only involved but orchestrating things. This grace rested upon the entire community. They shared their provisions with each other so that none would have lack. They put God first, each other second, and material things third. Additionally, this grace is God's favor upon them, His support of their efforts to put His grace on display to all kinds of people, to win them to Christ.

Being filled with the Holy Ghost empowers us to put God first, live holy, endure all things, stand victoriously against the onslaught of the enemy, and represent God excellently in the earth. The apostles majored in impossibilities because of the Holy Spirit, and so can we.

❧

Father, I thank You for Jesus, the evidence of Your marvelous grace toward humankind! Thank You for the Holy Spirit, Who empowers me to witness about Your Son with great power! In Jesus' Name. Amen.

RESCUED!

For he has rescued us from the kingdom of darkness and transferred us into the Kingdom of his dear Son, who purchased our freedom and forgave our sins.

COLOSSIANS 1:13-14, NLT

God has delivered us from so much! Although sin seems overwhelming, and we are surrounded by it daily, we can take strength in the knowledge that our sin-debt was paid in full at the cross of Jesus Christ. Sin no longer has a grip on us and we are free, indeed. The veil has been lifted from our eyes and now we clearly see what an absolutely incredible thing God has done for us!

We have literally been removed *from* the kingdom of darkness and placed into the kingdom of God. The word "from" in this verse is magnificent! It stems from the Greek word *ek*. It is a small preposition with huge implications. In this verse, *ek* is directional in that Jesus has removed us from the sphere or realm of Satan. That removal, in and of itself, is indeed a rescue. Yet *ek* is also qualitative in that Jesus has rescued us away from the power, or hold, of the enemy and his darkness. That Jesus has removed us from darkness reminds us that He rescued us from blindness, ignorance, hatred, and misery; and from persons for whom darkness has become visible and holds sway.

What else did Jesus rescue us from? He rescued us from the domination of our own sinful flesh as well. Being delivered from the devil and *ourselves* is something to shout about!

Yet, Christ didn't just remove us *from* the kingdom of darkness and the domination of flesh; He brought us *into* His Kingdom and its marvelous light! He brought us into the realm of the Spirit where we can now walk freely as His sons and daughters. Today we can rejoice because we have the assurance that we have indeed been rescued from a life of misery and brought into a life of freedom and forgiveness.

🌿

Beloved Father, You provided me with all that I need to walk in purpose and destiny. I am free from my worst enemy and his devices and from my own fleshly desires. And You have given me an eternal home with You. For this I give You praise. Hallelujah! In Jesus' Name. Amen.

QUICKENING GRACE

And you being dead in your sins and the uncircumcision of your flesh, hath He quickened together with Him, having forgiven you all trespasses.

COLOSSIANS 2:13, KJV

Do you remember how you felt the day you were saved? Did it feel as if the whole world was brand new? Did you see through the eyes of a freshly rejuvenated spirit? Do you remember the feeling? That was the day that Christ came into your life.

Before Christ came into our lives, we were dead. Not sick, but dead—dead in our trespasses. In the original Greek language, the word "trespass" means to cross the line, to step outside the boundaries, or to deviate from the path of truth and uprightness. Generally speaking, in that state, we are unable to live a godly life, knowing what God requires but unable to abide by the requirements—not alive with the power of the Holy Spirit. In Christ we are empowered to live godly lives because in His Spirit there is life.

In this Scripture, uncircumcision is used symbolically for a person in whom the corrupt desires of the flesh are still in charge— dead in trespasses and living by the dictates of the flesh. Such a person is a mess in the middle of a mess!

Our Scripture, however, assures us that we have been made alive in Christ and that all of our trespasses have been forgiven. The grace of God has made us alive and that grace should be spread throughout our community as we forgive each other as Christ has forgiven us.

All that we have received and now enjoy is due to the matchless and wondrous grace of God. How very blessed and privileged we are to be recipients of that grace!

Lord God, thank You for making me alive to You and bringing me into the knowledge of who You are and for providing me with the ability to live according to Your will. Thank You, Lord, for giving me a holy and righteous life on earth and eternal life with You in heaven! In Jesus' Name. Amen.

BACK TOGETHER!

To the praise of the glory of his grace, wherein he hath made us accepted in the beloved.

EPHESIANS 1:6, KJV

Being separated from someone you love can be a stressful, painful experience. Missing someone can cause you to experience a deep yearning for that person's presence, his or her touch or smell, the sound of the person's voice and the facial expressions he or she makes when pleased, angry, surprised, or awestruck. You cannot wait to see the person again. Maybe God felt those same things when we were separated from Him. But now, because we have been accepted in the Beloved, we can celebrate. Because of Jesus' sacrificial work we are now back together with God. Hallelujah!

Nowhere is it more clearly seen that we are accepted because of Christ's sacrifice than today's Scripture. "Accepted" is *highly favored* or *full of grace*. In other words, God accepted everything that Jesus did, and we are accepted because all of His works were accepted by God.

Jesus' death on the cross was ordained aforetime to facilitate the glorious reunion between God and His highest creation, humankind. It was always in the plan of God to redeem us from the clutches of sin and Satan. Because Jesus was willing and obedient to the will of His Father, God's ultimate purpose was achieved— bringing His people back into right fellowship with Him.

The depth of God's love for us is indescribable and unfathomable. Who among us would sentence to death our only son to cover the sins of people who neither knew Him nor loved Him?

Being born again is a great privilege at the expense of a great sacrifice. We are accepted, so today let us walk out our purpose and destiny. In doing so, we will demonstrate our gratitude, appreciation, and thankfulness for the greatest display of the grace of God: the sacrifice of His only begotten Son, Jesus the Christ.

❦

Lord God, help me understand the tremendous price You paid for me to be in right relationship with You. You gave Your only Son so that I might live and, through that life, come to know and serve Him with a grateful heart. Thank You that I am accepted in the Beloved! In Jesus' Name. Amen.

FREE AT LAST

For sin shall not have dominion over you for ye are not under the law but under grace.

ROMANS 6:14, KJV

Jesus' sacrifice freed us from the captivity of sin and provided us with the power to live godly lives. By grace, we have been saved! The enemy of our souls had plans to enslave us through the law, but the plan of God laid out in today's Scripture superseded the plan of the adversary.

The law was created to put a glaring spotlight on humanity's inability to refrain from sin. It was designed to show us our need for a Savior. Herein is found a beautiful paradox, in that, as believers—recipients of the grace of God—Christ *fulfilled* the law we could not keep, and then counted us as righteous through the blood of Jesus. We have been freed from the power, the grip, the influence of sin. We are free at last!

It is interesting to note that this Scripture doesn't say that sin won't be a factor, but rather, it won't have *dominion* over us. Though we struggle with all manner of sin, the promise is victory—not that sin won't exist in us. That is why we are told to mortify the flesh and its deeds (Romans 8:13), to put the flesh to death because it is enmity against God. We are told to walk (live) after the Spirit and not after the flesh (Romans 8:11), which represents any stance against the will of God, whether in thought, word, or deed.

Sin has absolutely no power over us; we have to willingly yield ourselves to it. Nothing and no one can take our power. Through the power of the indwelling Spirit, we *choose* righteousness. Christ's unselfish sacrifice completely freed us from the *dominion* of sin; we have been made capable to resist it and maintain the righteous stance His blood purchased for us.

So today, there is no need to fear death, nor life, or angels, nor principalities (Romans 8:35); there is no need to fear that sin will enslave or have dominion over us. Rejoice! We are free—free at last!

✣

Lord Jesus, thank You for freeing me from being dominated by sin, for not leaving me defenseless and helpless against its onslaught. Thank You for lifting me to a place of righteousness by Your grace! In Jesus' Name. Amen.

SAVING GRACE!

And I will pour upon the house of David, and upon the inhabitants of Jerusalem, the spirit of grace and of supplication: and they shall look upon Me whom they have pierced, and they shall mourn for Him, as one mourneth for his only Son, and shall be in bitterness for Him, as one that is in bitterness for his first born.

ZECHARIAH 12:10, KJV

The amazing grace of God is unstoppable and unalterable! It's effective to all that are destined to receive it. We who have received the grace of God will rejoice with those who open their hearts to it in the latter days. Thank you, Jesus!

The nation of Israel is in view in this passage of Scripture. The Spirit of grace is the Holy Spirit, who will bring revelation regarding the true identity of Jesus—their long-awaited and long-hoped-for Messiah. The Holy Spirit will convict them about their unwillingness to accept Christ and about their forefathers' treatment of Him. They will fall into sorrow and into a deep and profound sense of regret. However, in the last days, the Holy Spirit will cause the Jewish nation to turn to Jesus in faith and receive the grace of salvation through His blood.

Just as this is good news for the Jews, it is also good news for those who have unsaved friends and family members. As in the last days with the Jews, God will hear the pleas of those who long for Him and want to give their lives to Him. The good news is they do not have to wait until the last days. God stands with arms wide open to receive them right now. Spread the news! There's hope in Jesus. They can become partakers of eternal life with Him. No one has to wait to experience the saving grace of Christ Jesus; it is readily available to all that will avail themselves of it. We know not the day nor the hour, so spread the Good News today!

※

Almighty God, Your grace is sufficient! How magnificent it is to include those who rejected You in Your plan of salvation. What a cause for rejoicing! Thank You for Your saving grace! In Jesus' Name. Amen.

BLOOD-BOUGHT GRACE

In whom we have redemption through his blood, the forgiveness of sins, according to the riches of his grace.

EPHESIANS 1:7, KJV

Webster's *New World Dictionary, 3rd College Edition* defines redemption as buying back; to recover, as in paying a fee; to convert into something of value, as into gold or silver coin or bullion.

As children of God, our redemption is by something of far greater value than silver or gold. It's through the precious blood of Jesus that we have been, and continue to be, redeemed. Scripture tells us that there is no remission of sin without the shedding of blood (Hebrews 9:22). Blood—Jesus' blood—was the price, the instrument, the propitiation for our freedom. Through His blood our sins have been forgiven, and we are no longer slaves to sin. Our redemption comes from the abundant generosity of God's amazing grace.

There is no sin that God's grace cannot cover, no situation or circumstance that can stand against it, and no evil that can successfully oppose it. God's grace is effective to bring all who are predestined to receive it into a right relationship with Him, regardless of any sin we may have committed, or will ever commit. We have been made alive and righteous through this grace that God has so kindly lavished upon us.

And, as blood-bought children of God, we can be confident in the knowledge that we "are a chosen race, a royal priesthood, a dedicated nation, [God's] own purchased, special people, that you may set forth the wonderful deeds and display the virtues and perfection of Him who called you out of darkness into His marvelous light" (1 Peter 2:9, AMP)

As recipients of this glorious grace, let us let our light so shine that those we encounter during our day will see our good works and glorify our Father in heaven.

Father, thank You for sending Your Son to ransom me from enslavement to sin, from being held in the grip of the enemy. In His selfless sacrifice, Christ shows forth the riches of Your abundant grace, which has established me and made me to be steadfast in Your love. It brings me to rest in eternity with You. In Jesus' Name. Amen.

FROM MISERY TO MERCY

But God, who is rich in mercy, for his great love wherewith he loved us.

EPHESIANS 2:4, KJV

Misericordia is Latin for "mercy." It literally means *wretched heart*. The word "misery" is clearly related, and initially, it may seem curious that misery is linked to mercy in this way.

On second thought, maybe not, for mercy is sometimes characterized as forbearance or leniency granted to an offender (Hint: We were those offenders before God).

God's mercy is divine, plenteous (Psalm 103:8), and incomprehensibly kinder than that of human magistrates. He not only saw our sin, but He also saw our wretchedness, our misery, and it aroused His compassion. One commentator wrote, "the mercy of God was awakened by the misery of man."[7] It is absolutely theologically correct that misery and mercy are linked.

You see, God's mercy is much more profound, far-reaching, and abundant than that of merely granting clemency. It is a transformative mercy. God didn't just want us forgiven from our sins—He wanted us to be forever delivered from the oppressive genesis that led to sin in the first place. He wanted all imprints of cruelty and spiritual death the enemy had inflicted upon us to be eradicated.

But beyond that, God desired fellowship and communion with the ex-offenders. Christ forgave you and me so He could have relationship with us! Our partnership with Christ—our presence at His table—is so valuable to Him that He died on a cross and took our punishment.

In short, the Lord Jesus wants you and me, the ex-offenders, in His social sphere. No wonder the writer penned: Love so amazing, so divine, demands my soul, my life, my all![8]

Father, thank You for Your exceedingly rich mercy, which has transported me from misery and eternal death to victory and eternal life. May my testimony always give You praise. Amen.

MARVELOUS GRACE

Even when we were dead in sins, hath quickened us together with Christ (by grace are ye saved).

EPHESIANS 2:5, KJV

Attending a funeral is the least favorite thing for many of us. Seeing a lifeless body inside a casket can be unnerving. A body without animation seems so unnatural. That is the way we were to God before Christ came to rescue us—dead, without spiritual life, and unable to please God in any way, because we were void of His Spirit.

In today's Scripture, the apostle Paul juxtaposes the horrendous state we were in as unbelievers with our current state of being made alive to God through Christ. As God quickened Christ (from the dead), so have we been made alive from death. Christ's death was physical, but ours was spiritual. Romans 6:5 tells us that "we were planted in the likeness of His death and resurrection." Jesus experienced a literal bodily resurrection, but we experienced a spiritual resurrection. When we were baptized, we were buried with Him (submerged in water as a symbol of sharing His death). As He was raised from the dead, we have also been raised (lifted from the water of baptism) to walk in the newness of life (Romans 6:4). Christ shared our death so we could share in His resurrection in eternity to come: this is the marvelous grace of God!

We we spiritually dead, spiritually lifeless. One cannot raise from death that which is already alive. So, we were prime candidates to receive God's grace of salvation.

We have been saved by grace and grace alone. There was no way to earn this grace. There was no way to "Bogart" our way into it, and we possessed no merit that allowed us to play a part in obtaining it. It was simply the marvelous grace of God toward us.

God did not wait until His grace had made us lovable, but He loved us to life through grace! God alone rescued us from spiritual death, and we should glory in Him for making us alive. *Hallelujah!*

❧

Most Highly Beloved God, thank You for saving my immortal soul! Thank You for calling me from spiritual death to spiritual life—being made alive with Christ, empowered to walk in the newness of life. Thank You for Your marvelous grace! In Jesus' Name. Amen.

BORN TO BE RICH

That in the ages to come He might show the exceeding riches of His grace in His kindness toward us in Christ Jesus.

EPHESIANS 2:7, NKJV

If we're honest, many of us (even as God's children) have fantasized about winning the big one. We sometimes toy with the what-ifs of gaining such instant wealth because we often operate from a premise of what we lack from a worldly perspective. We would pay off our debt, share some of the wealth with family, and donate a bit of our windfall to our favorite charity—all, of course, after we've given the Lord His ten percent. Many of us would even quit our jobs. *If only we were rich.*

Oh, but we are! And we didn't have to choose the right combination of numbers to become rich.

We are rich because God is rich in mercy and grace toward us. We are rich because God saved our souls, calling us to be His sons and daughters before He set in place the foundations of the earth. With our salvation, we have inherited spiritual blessings such as holiness (being set apart to serve God), adoption (becoming part of God's family), acceptance in Jesus Christ (being able to call Jesus our Lord), redemption (being forgiven of our sins), and discernment (knowing the mystery of God's will). Those blessings—not our material assets—are what really matter in the grand scheme of life. For us, earth is not home; heaven is.

God saved us and bestowed His spiritual riches upon us to equip us to live victoriously on earth and to prepare us to live an eternity with Him. That's why we live with an eternal perspective, not just for the here and now. In many ways, our redeemed lives are part of the riches that bring glory to God on earth and will do so when we arrive in heaven. We are spiritually rich because we have been redeemed and set free by the immeasurable grace of God, so let's live like it.

Thank You, Lord, for being rich in mercy and grace toward me. Thank You for preparing a place for me to live forever with You in glory—and to Your glory. From now on, I pledge to pursue a life that brings honor and glory to Your holy name. In Jesus' Name. Amen.

THE CHOSEN ONE

But when it pleased God, who separated me from my mother's womb, and called me by his grace, To reveal his Son in me.

GALATIANS 1:15-16A, KJV

Have you ever been the last one picked? The gym teacher separated your class into two teams and picked captains who were to build the teams. The captains often picked the strongest people first: the ones who could run fast, leap high, or dribble a ball well. Sometimes they picked the popular people. Neither athletic nor popular, you're picked dead last—not by choice but by default. If that's not your story, you know that person, have felt sorry for that person, or did not pick that person.

In this life, even the most talented and popular among us will experience rejection. Yet, we can rejoice in knowing that, as believers, we have been chosen to be part of a special team by a special captain. We have been chosen by God. He knew from the time we were in the womb (and beyond) what or who we would turn out to be (good and bad). The awesome thing is that His choosing was not based on any good we did.

In the beginning of his letter to the churches at Galatia, Paul emphasized that he was not preaching a gospel he made up and that he was not moving in his own authority but that God chose him (and was pleased to do so!). God chose Paul to reveal Christ in him and to spread the gospel message before Paul was even born. He did that despite knowing Paul would grow up to become a Pharisee who persecuted Christians. By God's grace, Paul was saved, set free, and chosen to do a great work for the Kingdom.

God doesn't choose us because we're good and strong and pure. On the contrary, He chooses us because *He* is good and strong and pure. He chooses us because He loves us. And He doesn't pick us begrudgingly; He rejoices in choosing us to do a special work for Him.

🌿

Lord, I am humbled that You chose me to represent Your Son. Thank You for seeing beyond my shortcomings to adopt me into a great family of believers and to be a part of a great team that carries and delivers Your gospel message to a dying world. In Jesus' Name. Amen.

No Strings Attached

And if by grace, then is it no more of works: otherwise grace is no more grace. But if it be of works, then it is no more grace: otherwise work is no more work.

ROMANS 11:6, KJV

Let's say a friend gives you a car. It's used, but it's no lemon. Only several years old, it's clean inside and out. All your friend asks of you is to accept the keys and take care of the car. You feel compelled to return the favor somehow, but you are strapped. Your friend saw a need, and the Lord blessed him to be able to bless you; but you have a hard time accepting the gift without a "proper" thank you (a simple thank you won't do). So you buy your friend a budget-busting hundred-dollar gift card to repay the favor.

Many of God's chosen people (the Jews) rejected His gift of salvation when they rejected Jesus as the Messiah. Some Jews (a remnant) were "being saved as a result of God's kindness in choosing them" (Romans 11:5, NLT); however, even some of them had a difficult time letting go of the Mosaic Law, attempting to abide by its rules while following Christ. It's as if they received a generous gift from a friend but felt compelled to pay for it—to earn it—somehow. They were turning to works to earn their salvation.

There are times when we feel undeserving of God's gift of salvation. The truth is we're not good enough on our own to earn it; there's nothing we can do to deserve it. It is what it is: unmerited favor. The awesome thing is that God gives it willingly; He doesn't regret giving it to us, even when we struggle to take care of it. We can never lose our salvation (John 10:28), but we can (and should) safeguard our relationship with the Lord against the enemy, who seeks to erode it. We do that by seeking God's heart daily, praying, and reading the Word to learn how to live for Him.

Dear God, I cannot thank You enough for blessing me with life that is mine forever. While I can never repay You, I don't want to take such a wonderful gift for granted. So each day I will strive to live for You in word and deed. In Jesus' Name. Amen.

WHEN THE GOING GETS TOUGH

Let us therefore come boldly unto the throne of grace, that we may obtain mercy, and find grace to help in time of need.

HEBREWS 4:16, KJV

When the going gets tough, where do you go? When a trial seems unending despite our crying out to God, we sometimes stop crying out because we think He doesn't care. When we mess up, we sometimes shrink in shame and fear instead of falling before His throne in repentance because we think He won't hear us. Whatever our struggle, when the going gets tough, instead of running toward God, we sometimes run to what feels safe and certain (e.g., old ways of solving problems).

The Hebrew Christians found themselves wanting to return to what was safe and familiar to them (Judaism) when what was new and transforming (Christianity) proved to be challenging. They were being persecuted for their newfound faith. No matter our struggle, we sometimes forget to take it directly to the Lord in prayer. Yet, to Him is exactly where He wants us to run.

When we go before the throne of God (whether to seek His forgiveness or ask for His protection), we'll discover that God's grace is not only for saving souls but also for empowering us to live for Him. Thus, when we go to God, we will find grace (His favor) to endure our trials and mercy (His compassion) for the times we've messed up.

Have you messed up and feel bad about it? Our compassionate God understands our struggles, so go to Him. Are you suffering persecution because of your faith? Jesus knows exactly how that feels, so you can take every concern to the One who not only cares but also knows. Are you struggling to hold on and feel like giving up? Cry out to God who has enough mercy and grace to see you through. When the going gets tough, we can always go to God.

Father, thank You for being an ever-present help in times of trouble—even when I am the cause of my trouble. When I mess up, You are there. When I'm being pursued by the enemy, You are there. You are always there. Amen.

GIFTS IN DISGUISE

Every good and perfect gift is from above, coming down from the Father of the heavenly lights, who does not change like shifting shadows.

JAMES 1:17, NIV

Have you ever heard a person declare that being diagnosed with cancer was the best thing that's ever happened to them? Say what!

To claim what's obviously bad—disease, layoff, financial ruin, foreclosure—as something good defies human logic. Most people would call us crazy if we ran around jumping for joy at the announcement of bad news. Yet James admonished us, as the body of Christ, to "count it all joy" when we face adversity (James 1:2).

Trials prove our faith and mature us spiritually; they draw us closer to the "Father of the heavenly lights." God does not cause our trials, just as He does not trigger the temptations to which we sometimes fall victim (we can blame the enemy and our sinful nature for that). Yet He allows trials to come to show others our faithfulness, as well as to bring glory to His name and His character. Thus, some of our challenges are gifts. James teaches us how to embrace them as such and, subsequently, how to overcome them. He shows us that the way to survive our trials is to never forget God's character when we're tempted to blame Him for our struggles and to look to the Lord, who directs our steps by the light of His love and truth (the Word).

Unlike humankind, there is nothing fickle or double-minded about God. He never changes (Hebrews 13:8). That means He will never change His mind about us; if God saved us, He will keep us. He doesn't just plop us on life's course and leave it up to us to find our own way. He guides us. He illuminates the path before us, giving us direction by His Holy Spirit and His Holy Word. So, there's no reason for us to be double-minded, teetering between the wisdom of a dying world and the wisdom of a living God.

❧

Dear God, thank You for being my light and my salvation. With Your love and Your truth anchoring my life, I can endure any trial and resist any temptation. I love You, and I thank You for loving me. In Jesus' Name. Amen.

THAT LITTLE MEMBER

*Let no corrupt communication proceed out of your mouth, but that which
is good to the use of edifying, that it may minister grace unto the hearers.*

EPHESIANS 4:29, KJV

Imagine this scene: it's recess and two kids are going at it on the
playground. One has her small, balled-up fists planted firmly on
her hipbones, rolling her neck as she slays the other with insults.
Her opponent stands defiantly, steely eyed with arms folded,
awaiting her turn. Then, when there's no greater insult left to hurl
at the one who's gotten the crowd to go "Oooh, she told you," she
throws down her trump card—"Sticks and stones may break my
bones, but words will never hurt me"—and walks away determined
not to say another word.

All grown up and no longer working out our differences
between monkey bars and swings, many adults have come to
realize that words do hurt. A lot. Even after coming to Christ,
some of us still bear the scars of certain words spoken to us as
youth. They are scars that often reveal themselves in the forms of
low esteem and lack of confidence. Sometimes they show up in
our tendency to snap without thinking; when upset, we release a
barrage of lethal words to protect our fragile egos and keep our
enemies in their place. The problem is we often attack the wrong
enemy. We do that when we try to fight our own battles. Whenever
we rely on our strength in the heat of a verbal battle, we can count
on saying the wrong thing. "[T]he tongue is a small thing, but what
enormous damage it can do" (James 3:5, NLT).

As recipients of God's grace, we are empowered to extend
loving kindness to others through life-affirming words, whether
the hearers deserve it or not. That means we can speak life into
those who have hurt us, persecuted us, or betrayed us because
that's exactly what Christ did for us. With our words, we can let
others know how much the Lord, who is full of compassion, loves
them.

❧

*Dear Lord, I confess I've used my tongue to hurt others, but I want my
words to minister truth, love, and grace to everyone who hears them. Help
me to first examine my heart and then season my words with the salt of
Your love and grace. In Jesus' Name. Amen.*

The Gift that Keeps on Giving: Part 1

And from his fullness we have all received, grace upon grace.

JOHN 1:16, ESV

Job's trials hit him one after another. He could barely recover from one announcement of bad news before he received another one. When the trials of life visit our doorsteps, often that's how they arrive: one after another. Imagine God's blessings showing up in our lives the same way. One day it's a financial blessing, the next day it's a promotion, and the day after that it's an unexpected gift. Well, we don't have to imagine God's blessings showing up that way because they already do.

The string of gifts we receive from God is immeasurable. It begins with Jesus Christ, through whom we have received eternal life. The gift of eternal life cannot be revoked or returned; it is ours for keeps. We are the recipients of His grace and mercy every day (Lamentations 3:22-23). We also receive wisdom and faith, and the list goes on. So, from His abundance, the Lord gives us gift after gift, spiritual blessing after spiritual blessing, and favor after favor. No material gift can top that.

Material or spiritual, it is because of Jesus that we have anything good that we have. Jesus said, "I have come that they may have life, and have it to the full" (John 10:10b, NIV). Our salvation isn't just about living in heaven with Jesus forever; it's also about living a fruitful life on earth. That fruitful life is not necessarily about having the perfect job, living in the perfect home, or earning the ideal income. It speaks more to experiencing the overflowing joy and peace—gifts—that come with being a part of God's Kingdom.

The next time we're tempted to believe we're not being blessed because we lack "things," let's be reminded of a stanza from the song "More Than Enough": *Jehovah Shamma, You are with me and You supply all of my needs; You are more than enough, You are much more than enough, You are more than enough for me.* [9]

❧

Father, You alone are everything to me. Sometimes I get caught up in viewing things as a measurement of how much You've blessed me, but from this day forward, I declare that You alone are more than enough for me. In Jesus' Name. Amen.

THE GIFT THAT KEEPS ON GIVING: PART 2

For the law was given by Moses, but grace and truth came by Jesus Christ.
JOHN 1:17, KJV

How many times have I told you not to do that?" If that line sounds familiar, either you've said it to a child or it was said to you when you were a child—and probably more than once. When we find ourselves constantly doing what we strive not to do and failing to do what we know we ought to do (Romans 7:14-25), it's easy to suppose that God might be saying something like that to us.

Parents know their children. They know which ones will get in line after one good chastisement and which ones seem to be gluttons for punishment. Likewise, God knows us. That's why He sent Jesus Christ to rescue us from ourselves.

The Law, given through Moses, reveals the justice and righteousness of God. It also reveals how much we need God's grace because it is impossible for us to keep the Law. With the Law only, we were doomed. But Jesus Christ came to earth and lived out the Law to perfection. He not only kept it, but He also became the perfect sacrifice, taking our sins upon Himself and laying down His life so that God's grace and mercy might be revealed.

Now when we fall, God's grace allows us to go directly before His throne and seek His forgiveness (1 John 1:9). Does God's grace exempt us from pursuing holiness, from seeking to live a life that's informed by the standards of His Word? Absolutely not! Living under grace doesn't allow us to willfully disregard the Word and live any way we want. It doesn't work that way because God knows our hearts. Even with the weakness of our flesh, we strive to follow God's law (His Word, His precepts for living). The more we do, the more we mature spiritually and the less we need to seek His forgiveness for the same crimes. So let's never take God's grace for granted.

※

Dear Father, thank You for Your grace. Thank You for always making a way of escape from the habits and things that tempt me. Thank You for every time You've forgiven me when I gave in to my flesh. Thank You for Jesus Christ. Amen.

GO TO THE SOURCE

And now, brethren, I commend you to God, and to the word of his grace, which is able to build you up, and to give you an inheritance among all them which are sanctified.

ACTS 20:32, KJV

One day, a young pastor told his congregation that he would be shutting his phone off after 8 p.m. Newly married with a growing family, he felt that at some point in his day he had to turn his attention toward his wife and children.

Some may ask, "What kind of pastor isn't available to his or her congregation twenty-four hours a day, seven days a week?" Perhaps the kind of pastor who realizes God alone is more than able to protect and keep His sheep. But definitely the kind of pastor who leads in such a way that the flock knows where to turn (the Word) and to Whom to turn (the Lord) whether or not he or she is available.

Sometimes we look to our pastors to be everything to us spiritually. If we're honest, we sometimes feed strictly off of what they teach and preach, forgetting that God has given us the same responsibility He gives the pastor to read, meditate upon, and apply the Word to show ourselves approved (tried and true to our personal confession of faith). Although the pastor delivers God's message and teaches the lessons that should encourage us to want more of God and to know God for ourselves, his or her work alone cannot build us up. Thus, we have a role in nurturing our faith that our pastor cannot fill.

When we personally build up our faith by seeking to better understand and apply God's Word, we ensure that we receive everything we need (our inheritance) among those whom God has set apart for Himself. And we consecrate ourselves for the specific work God calls us to do (reaching others for Him). After all, what kind of witnesses would we be if we could only say, "The pastor said" instead of "God says"?

Dear Father, thank You for giving me Your Word, which guides me, comforts me, and corrects me. Whatever answer I need to overcome life's challenges, I can find it in Your Word. In Jesus' Name. Amen.

A DONE DEAL

All that the Father giveth me shall come to me; and him that cometh to me I will in no wise cast out.

JOHN 6:37, KJV

When we share the gospel with someone who rejects it, we sometimes take the rejection as a personal failure. Were we not convincing enough, did we fail to make the message clear, did we add too much of ourselves (our philosophical meandering) when we should have stuck to the script? When our efforts to witness fall on deaf ears and closed hearts, questions abound. But here's the truth: salvation is God's job, and we're to trust He knows how to do His job well.

God knows who will readily receive Jesus, who will flat out reject Him, and who will need more time to decide. He knew it from the beginning of time. For those who take a little time to respond to Christ's call, Jesus will receive with open, loving arms and hold nothing against them.

It's difficult to think or know that someone we love may be among those who have encountered Jesus with a hardened heart. Either the person is not ready to make the commitment, is unwilling to lay down his or her life, or has a difficult time accepting that Jesus Christ is the only way. However, when a friend or relative rejects our invitation to try Christ, we cannot allow feelings of frustration, doubt, failure, or even disappointment to sidetrack us.

That may seem easier said than done, but once we've shared the Good News (however we share it) with a person who doesn't readily embrace it, we're to commit the person to God and pray. It's like casting our cares (our burdens, our worries) on God, leaving them there, and trusting Him to handle them. Our job is to plant the seeds of the gospel message, whether we do it by telling people about Jesus and what He has done for us or by living like it. How others respond is up to God.

❧

Father, thank You for reminding me that closing the deal on salvation is Your job. While I can plant the seed of truth, it's You who changes hearts and transforms minds. In Jesus' Name. Amen.

GROWING UP

And the child grew, and waxed strong in spirit, filled with wisdom: and the grace of God was upon him.

LUKE 2:40, KJV

M ost parents want their children to grow up to be successful, mature adults. Jesus' parents—despite knowing who He was—were no different. They took great care to raise Him according to the customs of their faith and to ensure He had a normal childhood. They even worried when a 12-year-old Jesus went missing for three days. Here's what we can learn about growing up in our faith from the few scenes of Jesus' childhood:

Follow the Leader (Hebrews 13:17). After Mary and Joseph found the missing Jesus, they took Him home to Nazareth, where He "was obedient to them" (Luke 2:51). Jesus knew He was the Son of God, yet He never said to Joseph, "You're not my real father." Children are to obey their parents in all things. Likewise, we must obey God in all things, and that includes obeying those who hold positions of authority over us.

Seek Understanding (Psalm 119:34). Jesus may have occasionally played with the boy next door, but one thing is clear: He sought the heart of God. When His parents found Him, He was hanging out with religious scholars who were amazed by His knowledge; it was clear Jesus spent meaningful time with the Father. Thus, as children of God, the time we spend with Him is paramount to our spiritual maturity. The better we know God, the wiser we'll become and the more we'll choose His way over ours.

Walk in Humility (1 Peter 5:6). Jesus' birth was a sign of humility. Soon after entering the world, the Wonderful Counselor, the Mighty God, the Everlasting Father, the Prince of Peace was placed in a trough. Jesus demonstrated humility throughout His earthly journey. From the manger to the cross, empowered by God's grace, He subjected Himself to the will of the Father. Likewise, in every moment of our lives—even as we take our last breath—we must yield ourselves to the will of God.

※

Dear God, Forgive me for the times I have succumbed to childish rebellion and failed to obey You. I'm ready to grow up and subject every area of my life to Your will. In Jesus' Name. Amen.

OUTSIDE THE COMFORT ZONE

Thou therefore, my son, be strong in the grace that is in Christ Jesus.

2 TIMOTHY 2:1, KJV

Because of his shy and reserved nature, it's probably safe to say Timothy at times questioned his ability as a church leader. Imagine him saying something like this to the apostle Paul: "I can't do this. They won't listen to me like they listen to you." Paul was not only Timothy's colleague in the faith, but he was also Timothy's mentor. And it was in his relationship with the more assertive Paul that Timothy often found encouragement to preach the gospel, especially in a hostile environment.

Some of us are like Timothy—not necessarily shy but quick to seek the encouragement or validation of a faithful friend when we need a push. Like Paul, those friends will not always be around, but God will. In his last letter before he was executed, Paul told Timothy he would be leaving soon. He also told Timothy that he had to find strength in God's grace to carry on the work. It was God's favor and spiritual blessings upon Timothy's life, Paul wrote, that would enable Timothy to do it well.

God's grace equips us to do things for Him we cannot do within our own strength. Yes, some of us are blessed with a natural ability to lead; but, the rest of us must walk strictly by that saying *If God brought you to it, He'll see you through it.* Either way, it's all God all the time empowering us to do a work for Him.

In a hostile environment, a timid person seems like the last person to lead a church, but that's exactly the kind of person God chose in Timothy. Thus, we should never determine we can't complete an assignment for God because we're not naturally suited for the task—even when others say we're not cut out for it. By God's grace, we can complete any task He places before us.

❧

Father, I often look at my shortcomings and determine I'm not cut out for the task, but You always remind me that I can do "it." You not only encourage me, but You also equip me to do "it." Thank You for being all I need to accomplish Your work. Amen.

It's Coming

For the LORD God is a sun and shield: the LORD will give grace and glory:
no good thing will he withhold from them that walk uprightly.

Psalm 84:11, KJV

Life can hurt. The more life-jarring events we experience, the more we long for the reprieve only heaven can bring. When we're worn out emotionally and spiritually, we often want to abort the journey. We become so focused on escaping our desert moments that fighting a good fight, finishing our course, and keeping the faith are far from our minds. We just know it hurts—"*bad.*"

Psalm 84 was written during a time of captivity. The Jews were in exile, away from their homeland and unable to go to the Temple, the one place they knew God dwelt (imagine being in a hospital or at home for months on end and unable to go to church). They discovered, however, that they could experience the peace and joy that God's presence could bring right there in their valley experience. They learned to praise Him, and thus invoke His presence, in the midst of their tears. They realized that they wouldn't be in that place always because their gracious and merciful God promised to deliver them despite their disobedience. Finally, they learned that trusting God and following Him even while in captivity were vital to experiencing true freedom.

In our relationship with the Lord, we can find everything we need to survive our valleys and experience the kingdom of God while we are going through dark times. God lights our way in darkness. If we're not sure what to do, or we can't see our way out, all we have to do is turn to His Word and submit our hearts to prayer. He protects us from the harsh elements of our fiery trials.

God promises to see us through our journey on earth, with its mix of triumphs and failures, and to make it worth our while when we reach heaven. That's where true living begins.

❧

Dear God, because victory is mine, I can praise You now. No matter what's going on in my life, I will keep my mind set on You and on things above. I am determined to live a resurrected life. In Jesus' Name. Amen.

Don't Get it Twisted

What shall we say then? Shall we continue in sin, that grace may abound?
God forbid. How shall we, that are dead to sin, live any longer therein?

ROMANS 6:1-2, KJV

You know how some questions are posed to cause you to ponder a particular reality? They are asked either to make you think or challenge what you're doing? Paul asks such questions to challenge the idea that Christians would continue to live a life of sin once they've come into a saving knowledge of Jesus Christ. He poses yet another query to solicit understanding from those who had been saved by the grace of God. Like Paul, we struggle to untwist the knots of our spiritual understanding. We wrestle not with God's truth regarding sin but with our knowledge of ourselves and our propensity to give in to our own will instead of God's.

Paul answered his rhetorical questions with a resounding, "God forbid." Over and over again we see Paul respond emphatically when the issue of sin came up. He answered with another question that struck the heart of a committed follower of Jesus. The carousel of questions is asked and answered—live in Christ or die in sin! Try as we might, those two things cannot be twisted together. As Christians we make the decision to not practice sin because we are obligated to follow God's moral law, not in spite of grace but because of it. While the law cannot conquer sin, the grace we receive allows us to triumph over it. Sin's power has been broken, but we have to decide not to play with it. That decision starts with a committed heart that is grateful for all that we have in Jesus Christ. C. H. Spurgeon said n unchanged life is the mark of an unchanged heart.[10] When we're made right with God through faith, our hearts are changed to go His way instead of our own.

Our lives in Christ demand obedience, and our march toward holiness puts sin to death in our lives. Commit to never again twist the freedom in Christ with license to sin (1 Corinthians 6:12). You have been freed from the bondage of sin; don't get tangled up again.

※

Father, I am so grateful that I am free from the power of sin and death. You have made the way for me to live victoriously through Your Son. Amen.

ACCESS GRANTED

Through whom we have gained access by faith into this grace in which we now stand. And we boast in the hope of the glory of God.

ROMANS 5:2, NIV

Have you ever come to a door that you thought was open and upon closer examination you found it was bolted shut? You watched as others went through the door, but every time you attempted to enter—nothing! You couldn't get in. It was probably a miserable experience riddled with frustration and pangs of rejection. How wonderful to know that, as the sons and daughters of God, we have access that can't be altered by just anyone because *Someone* has brought us to this new place of immeasurable grace. That *Someone* is Jesus, whose finished work justifies us and allows us to stand in the favor we find in God.

Our access was secured when the veil was rent from top to bottom making provision for our Father's love to reach beyond our sin through the blood of His Son all the way to us. No human hand could rend the tapestry as thick in width as the palm of a person's hand, yet welcoming us into a place that previously only admitted the high priest. Now because of Jesus Christ, our High Priest, we can enter the presence of God boldly and fall humbly before our God. No longer are we kept outside of His presence; we enter in the hope of the glory that is revealed through faith.

This grace access is one of the great honors of being a Christian. Through Christ, we are introduced to the realm of God's riches. By His sacrifice, we have the freedom to come into His presence and we are given the privilege of standing secure in His love. We see the glory of God in the life of His Son. Others will see the glory of God when they observe our lives because the same faith that gives us peace with God allows us to live in the peace of God as we stand in the favor of God.

Father, thank You that I have access to You through the shed blood of Jesus Christ. His death brought me life, and I am able to stand before You because of what He has done. Thank You that your glory is revealed in Your Son and will be seen in me as I live for Him. In Jesus' Amazing Name. Amen.

RELIC OR TREASURE

And Isaiah boldly says, "I was found by those who did not seek me; I revealed myself to those who did not ask for me."

ROMANS 10:20, NIV

It would be wonderful to discover what you thought was an old relic in the corner of your basement was a priceless treasure that was waiting to be discovered. Even more so, the previous owner of the house just threw it in the corner assuming it was of no real value—simply left it for you to do with whatever you will. The discarded thing becomes the treasured thing.

Our treasured thing is the gospel that was once hidden and is now revealed to us. It was revealed when our eyes were made open to see Jesus for who He really is. The treasure is revealed when we receive Christ by faith and cease our striving to do it on our own. It was revealed to the Jews but found too insufficient for their self-righteous hearts that counted more on the Mosaic Law than the grace of God. It wasn't enough that they could be saved by grace through faith; they clung to their acts of righteousness. In caring more for the Law than the finished work of Christ, they heaped the judgment of God upon themselves. He judged their blindness, their arrogance, and their stubbornness all the while reaching out His hand of love while they clung to the laws of their fathers. In our text, Paul recounts the words of Isaiah that illustrate the simultaneous responses to the message of salvation—acceptance by those whose hearts are open and submitted to the revelation of Christ and judgment for those that reject it.

We all face the choice of discarding things we haven't prized in the way we should. Make a point to examine the place Jesus has in your life. Are you living in the reality of your faith in Him or are you still trying to earn your way? Commit today to be one of the grateful ones who has found the True Treasure!

Father, I marvel at Your provision for me. Thank You for the gracious way You have revealed Yourself in Your Son. He is my treasure, and I pray He remains in His rightful place—center stage of my heart not relegated to the corner of my life. Amen.

DANGEROUS TERRITORY

I do not set aside the grace of God, for if righteousness could be gained through the law, Christ died for nothing!

GALATIANS 2:21, NIV

How would you like to dance on the side of a cliff? Today many people go rock climbing with all the wildlife paraphernalia to rescue them if they should lose their footing and slip. With all the fancy equipment available, one could easily put his or her trust in making sure he or she has all the tools—chalk, harness, helmet, carabiners, backpack—check, check, and triple check. The trouble is invariably something doesn't work or something was left behind and you need to depend on the person who is with you.

Likewise we tread on dangerous territory when we mix keeping the law with the abiding grace of God. The intermixing mocks what Jesus has done on the cross and leaves us striving to do what Christ alone can do. God's grace surpasses our human efforts. Our penchant for mixing the law with grace threatens to nullify what Jesus did on the cross because if we are made right with God by keeping the law, Christ died in vain. The apostle Paul makes the point that our righteousness comes through faith in Jesus Christ, not though the law.

The immeasurable grace of God rushes into our lives with the treasures of heaven, wound up in the atoning work of Jesus Christ. It manifests itself in His goodness and love. It is the vehicle through which our lives are transformed. Paul reminds us that we are not made right because of our strict adherence to the law but by our faith in Jesus Christ. If we hold to rule-keeping more than the grace we now stand in through faith, we render the grace useless or ineffective. Jesus corrected Peter's erroneous behaviors that waffled back and forth between following Mosaic ritual, and the law of love fulfilled in Christ. Like the climber on the cliff, we are on dangerous ground when we think we can get to God because we have the right equipment instead of depending on the Person of Jesus Christ who is with us.

Lord God, I bless You that You are always with me. I don't have to fear unchartered waters or dangerous territories because You said You would never leave me nor forsake me. My life in You is not based upon what I may not do but on what You've already done. Amen.

WE'VE BEEN CLEANED UP!

And all are justified freely by his grace through the redemption that came by Christ Jesus.

ROMANS 3:24, NIV

Sometimes children run indoors, dirty from playing in the muddy backyard and think they are clean enough to trample through the house. With dirt all over themselves, they reach for, and touch, everything in sight. They could be turned away by an angry parent, frustrated with the filthy mess they bring, with or be greeted with loving arms and cleaned up to join the dinner feast.

Such is the case with us. We are the dirty children running in to our God with all the filth from our sin upon us. We have our sins washed as a gift of our Father's love, which comes to us through the blood of His precious Son. Jesus' sacrifice on the cross canceled the debt we owed. Someone aptly said, "Jesus paid a debt He did not owe because we had a debt we could not pay." We who were at one time held hostage had the ransom paid by a faithful Savior. We are no longer captive but freed by love. Jesus steps in and through His shed blood declares us right before God, freely justified by grace.

Something about that disturbs our sensibilities, even regarding our salvation. Oswald Chambers said, "There is a certain pride that causes them to give and give, but to accept a gift is another thing."[11] Our egos can't handle it. We believe we should work for it. We would go around bragging about how good we are and look at what we did to be worthy of it. Paul says *no!* We can't earn it (Ephesians 2:8-9), so there's no reason to brag—we can't save ourselves! We enter into this great salvation through the magnificent grace, and it is the absolutely free gift of God.

We who were once filthy from the dregs of sin are washed up, cleaned up, and filled up by God's grace. We no longer run through life slinging mud everywhere. We have received the greatest clean-up of all, and it's free!

❧

Father God, thank You for Your amazing gift of grace that cleans me up through the blood of Your dear Son. Help me to live in a way that honors You and demonstrates my gratitude for what Jesus did for me. I pray it, in Jesus' Name. Amen.

HE KEEPS HIS PROMISES

Therefore, the promise comes by faith, so that it may be by grace and may be guaranteed to all Abraham's offspring—not only to those who are of the law but also to those who have the faith of Abraham. He is the father of us all.

ROMANS 4:16, NIV

What have you believed God for even when it seemed impossible? What ridiculous thing was impressed upon your heart that nobody but God could have put there? Have you had a "stop playing" or "are you kidding me" moment with God? Some things come like that. Impossible…ridiculous…stop playing!?!

No, He's not playing. God puts big dreams into our hearts, some to show us His love and all to show His glory. He wants our expectation to be of Him and not of ourselves. Otherwise, we would be off bragging about what we did and how we got it done. He wants it clear that all we have come as a gift of His grace. It isn't earned because of who we are but rather Who we know. Moreover, we see the promises of God fulfilled by grace through faith as did Abraham.

Even after God told Abraham he would be the Father of many nations (Genesis 17:4), Abraham still had no sons! Despite the ages of his wife and him, God made Abraham a promise, that he would have that son. When it seemed hopeless, God put hope in Abraham's heart. Long before he saw a son, Abraham believed God. (Genesis 15:6) God proved to Abraham that He "calls into being things that are not" (Romans 4:17). He called us as the offspring of Abraham by grace through faith. It's not because we deserve the gift we receive when we embrace Christ by faith; it's because God wants us to have it!

While faith and grace are inextricably tied together, when it comes to salvation, *faith and works* are polar opposites. Believe God keeps His promises. Trust Him for the things He alone can place in your heart including responding in faith to His Son. Thank Him for the unmerited blessing of His grace in your life and embrace it by faith afresh today.

❧

Lord, I thank You for giving me a heart to believe You for the promise I have in Jesus Christ. I bless You for the way You still speak in my circumstances. Amen.

No Comparison

But the gift is not like the trespass. For if the many died by the trespass of the one man, how much more did God's grace and the gift that came by the grace of the one man, Jesus Christ, overflow to the many!

Romans 5:15, NIV

Compare apples and oranges, or PCs and Macs, Adam and Jesus. Comparisons abound in things that are similar in purpose, in function, or in essence. Apples and oranges are both fruit but have their own distinctions. PCs and Macs are both computers aimed at assisting our ability to communicate and function in our high-tech twenty-first century world. Adam and Jesus were both men, but that's where the comparison stops and the study in contrast begins. The comparison is blurred by the fallible man, Adam, and in the infallible, incomprehensible God-man, Jesus. While there was similarity in the sense of what they did, they did completely different things.

The devastating impact the world experienced as a result of Adam's sin is only surpassed by the abundant grace God has provided through His Son. Jesus came to do the impossible and forgive the unpardonable. It took the unparalleled work of Jesus to bring restoration for us from the spiritual wreckage caused by sin. Jesus came doing for us what we couldn't do for ourselves, bearing our sins and covering our shame. He came as the One who would bruise the head of the serpent (see Genesis 3:15) that came to beguile Adam and Eve and have the garden disrupted with sin that threatened our eternal expulsion. He came rescuing us from ourselves and our propensity to go our own way.

Jesus is God's gift of grace. He is the gift that keeps on giving and receives all that would come to Him. He redeems us from the pit and will triumph over every evil that comes before and against us. Let's make it our goal today to honor Jesus as God's grace to us and live knowing nothing is compared to Him!

❧

Lord God, thank You for rescuing me from sin and death and reversing the curse that I was under because of Adam. Help me to live a life of obedience to You every day as I look forward to reigning with You forever one day. I bless You for it, in Jesus' Name. Amen.

THE DISTINCT DIFFERENCE

For if by one man's offence death reigned by one; much more they which receive abundance of grace and of the gift of righteousness shall reign in life by one, Jesus Christ.

ROMANS 5:17, KJV

We need only look as close as our own family to see the ravages of sin. We have seen and felt its impact in our own lives. Born under the penalty of Adam's choices, we look for a way out of the mess that sin offers. But when we look to Jesus, we see the new reign that is life and is fulfilled in His obedience to the Father. Once we understand the reign of death through sin versus the reign of life through Jesus Christ, we can comprehend Paul's exhortation to "not let sin reign in your mortal body so that you obey its evil desires" (Romans 6:12).

There is a stark contrast between the act of Adam and the action of Jesus. Adam's kingdom reigned for a short time, while Christ's kingdom will last forever. Adam disobeyed God, and his disobedience brought us death. Christ obeyed God, and His obedience brought us life. Because of Adam's disobedience in the garden, we were condemned to eternal death; but through Christ's obedience on the cross, our salvation was purchased with His blood and we have the gift of eternal life. Adam got the opposite of what Satan promised (see Genesis 3:5). We get more than we deserve through Jesus Christ. In Adam we had no hope, but in Jesus we have eternal hope. So as we were condemned through one, we are justified through One—Jesus Christ, the Righteous. Through His grace, we are made righteous and will reign with Him both now and forever (2 Timothy 2:12).

While comparisons may be made to the first-man Adam and the God-man Jesus, there is a distinct difference. In spite of the depth of the sin, God's abundant grace reaches farther and makes us righteous. Hallelujah! Let the reality of this distinct difference lead you to praise God for the indescribable gift He has given us in His Son.

❧

Father, I am grateful Jesus' blood reaches farther than my sin! I thank You He reversed the curse I was under because of the sin of Adam and because of His obedience, I can live for You. Amen.

THE SANCTIFIER

And now, brethren, I commend you to God, and to the word of his grace, which is able to build you up, and to give you an inheritance among all them which are sanctified.

ACTS 20:32, KJV

Television, Internet, self-visualization, the gym—where do you go to grow? What builds you up—others, your own ego, the latest and greatest whatever? Where do you go for strength?

Luke records Paul's encouragement to the church at Ephesus as he prepares to leave them for the final time. After reminding them of his love and devotion, Paul goes on to tell the Ephesians he is now entrusting them to the Lord and the revelation of the gospel of Jesus Christ. He wants them to understand what we know; we are saved by grace and made the children of God. With our faith in God firmly established, we follow with obedience to His Word. Once secured in His love and saved by His grace, we begin the process of being set apart as God's own. It's as we continue on in our salvation in obedience to the Word of God, that we are built up. The reality is we are being built up in Jesus Christ through the Word.

This *building up* process is the great sanctifier! We learn to turn to God's Word for our instruction and strength and, in turn, get stronger on our daily journey. Sanctification is the process God uses to make us like His Son. It causes us to be made holy in our hearts and lives in increasing measure. We are made partakers in Christ's inheritance because we are given a new hope in Him. God will bestow blessings upon His people both now and forever (1 Peter 1:4). Our inheritance is preserved in heaven for us and like an account with compounding interest; it only grows as we grow in the knowledge of our Lord and Savior, Jesus Christ.

The Word will be a guide in all our situations and difficulties. Whatever situation we encounter, God has made provision with answers in the Word of His grace. Let Him lead you like sheep that are led by their shepherd, and our great Shepherd will guide you into green pastures.

❧

Lord, thank You for using Your Word to sanctify me. I pray it is becoming the rejoicing of my heart more and more each day. Amen.

We are Born of the Spirit

...and that which is born of the Spirit is spirit.
John 3:6b, KJV

Puberty. High school. Some things we wouldn't re-live for anything. Yet there are many of us who would turn back the clock and do "it" all over again if we could reverse that one decision that changed our lives forever, or take back the "thing" that marred an important relationship. Of course, there's no turning back the clock; there are no do-overs. But being born again of the Spirit is better than a do-over. The moment we repented of our sins and confessed Jesus Christ as Lord and Savior, we received the Holy Spirit—and all things were made new. Our slates were cleaned. Our minds were transformed. With the Holy Spirit residing in our hearts, we received power to do life differently and much better than before. We can love others as God loves them—unconditionally and eternally—for love is the hallmark of the Spirit-filled believer. Both the fruits and gifts of the Spirit are manifested by love.

From April through June, you will walk through what it truly means to be a new creation in Christ—born of the Spirit. As winter fades and spring dawns, be inspired to fully embrace your new self and let go of the old you once and for all.

WATER AND SPIRIT BORN

Jesus answered, Verily, verily, I say unto thee, Except a man be born of
water and of the Spirit, he cannot enter into the kingdom of God.

JOHN 3:5, KJV

How miraculous it is to see new babies, conceived with their
parents' DNA and birthed from their mother's womb, enter
this world. Once they enter this world, the babies have access to
their parents' resources and exposure to their parents' environment.

About 2,000 years ago, a religious leader and government
official, Nicodemus, pondered if he would have to enter his
mother's womb a second time because Jesus told him he must be
"born of the water and of the Spirit." What does that mean and
what are its implications?

To be born of the water and of the Spirit is to receive the "life-
giving and purifying activity" of the Holy Spirit.[12] It means we are
born of God, through the presence of the Holy Spirit, and are given
exposure and entrance into God's Kingdom.

The kingdom of God is the "realm of God's authority and
blessing."[13] When we receive the Holy Spirit, we have exposure and
entrance into that authority and blessing of God. Like a newborn
child, we become part of God's family. We belong to Him, and the
Holy Spirit is God's assurance that He will assist us in the process
of becoming more like Him.

When observing our children, we notice our own mannerisms,
personalities, and character traits through the influence of our
DNA. Similarly, as the Holy Spirit purifies our lives through the
process of sanctification, we look more and more like God. Our
character and convictions confirm that we are born of the water
and of the Spirit.

Now that we are born of the water and of the Spirit, we can
face the day with boldness because we have the assurance that we
are under God's authority and blessing.

❧

Father, thank You for Your Holy Spirit who gives me exposure and entrance into
Your kingdom. Strengthen me to face my fears with courage as I am purified by
Your Spirit. In Jesus' Name. Amen.

UNPREDICTABLE

The wind bloweth where it listeth, and thou hearest the sound thereof, but canst not tell whence it cometh, and whither it goeth: so is every one that is born of the Spirit.

JOHN 3:8, KJV

The paradox of life is we prefer unpredictable endings in our movies. Even if we know the hero will rescue the damsel in distress, not knowing exactly how he will do it creates enough suspense to maintain our interest.

Yet, when it comes to the role of the Holy Spirit in our lives, we prefer to know exactly what He is doing and where He is going. The truth is God is as much into surprise endings as we are, but, unlike us, He already knows how the movie ends.

When we are born of the Spirit we receive the presence of the Holy Spirit into our lives. He is an invisible guide as we try to make sense of living life, as children of the Spirit, in an ungodly world. The Holy Spirit leads us where He pleases. He knows the path we should take, He knows the traps that await us, and He knows the destiny we have in Christ. We can confidently follow His lead.

The Holy Spirit sometimes speaks to us as we read God's Word. Other times He speaks to us through the pastor or minister. And, at times, He speaks to us in our times of prayer and devotion. Our responsibility is to listen for His voice.

The Holy Spirit cannot be predicted. There are moments when we will have no clue what God is up to. It is during those moments that we rely on the faithfulness of God and know that He still is at work.

We all like watching the damsel in distress being rescued, but none of us like being the damsel in distress. The suspense of when and how the Holy Spirit will move in our situation can sometimes be overwhelming. We are born of the Spirit and, although we may not be able to predict when and how the Spirit will move, we can still confidently predict that He will.

❧

Father, thank You for the Holy Spirit, who leads and guides me every day. Increase my faith to trust His leading, even when I cannot predict where He is leading me. In Jesus' Name. Amen.

WE ARE ONE

One Lord, one faith, one baptism.

EPHESIANS 4:5, KJV

American politics has become extremely divisive over the past decade. Today, we see the constant battles of Republicans vs. Democrats, Conservatives vs. Liberals, and Fox News vs. MSNBC. With the political climate as it is, we could easily forget that we have pledged allegiance to be "one nation under God."

In America, we are united by the same law, liberty, and land. In the Church of Jesus Christ, we are united by the same Lord, faith, and baptism. Sadly, similar to American politics, the Church is sometimes divided.

Through the baptism of the Holy Spirit, we are united as members of the body of Christ (1 Corinthians 12:12-13); therefore, it is critically important how we treat our brothers and sisters in Christ. In Ephesians 4:4-6, there is no ambiguity about our relationship with one another. The word "one" is mentioned a total of seven times. Beginning with our being "one body" and ending with us having "one God" as our Father. Scripture assures us that we truly are one family.

We share Jesus as our Lord because He is the head of our lives; we share a common faith that is lived out before the world each day; and we share a common baptism by the Holy Spirit, who baptizes us into the body of Christ. What we share through the Spirit's baptism is also shared through the Spirit's fruit. When we recognize that we are one, we treat each other with humility, gentleness, and patience. We also accept each other with love and work hard to keep the unity of the same Spirit who baptized us.

On September 11, 2001, there was no concern about political parties and ideologies. Americans stood before the world as one nation. The world is watching how we treat our brothers and sisters in Christ. Will we stand before them as one body, boldly declaring the one Lord, one faith, and one baptism in which we believe? After all, it is what our Lord expects, our faith expresses, and our baptism embodies.

❧

Father, thank You for the baptism of Your Spirit, which makes all believers one in Christ. Teach me to keep the unity of the Spirit as I demonstrate love and patience to my brothers and sisters in Christ.

WE ARE HURTING SOMEBODY

What? know ye not that your body is the temple of the Holy Ghost which is in you, which ye have of God, and ye are not your own? For ye are bought with a price: therefore glorify God in your body, and in your spirit, which are God's.

1 CORINTHIANS 6:19-20, KJV

The modern mindset for some is that we can do whatever we want as long as no one else is hurt by our actions. That way of thinking suggests that if we want to get drunk or high, or if we engage in illicit sex, it is absolutely acceptable if our fellow humans are not harmed.

Paul wrote this epistle to remind Spirit-filled believers that our sin does hurt someone, even when we are alone. Our bodies belong to the Holy Spirit, who indwells us and makes us His personal sanctuary, or temple. Therefore, our lifestyle must be consistent with honoring His continuous presence in our lives.

A sanctuary is where God voluntarily chooses to reside. When His presence occupies a building, it becomes the house of God. Because of the presence of the Holy Spirit in our building (bodies), we have become the house of God. That means our bodies now belong to God. He purchased us through the crucifixion of Jesus Christ, and He dwells in us.

The indwelling of the Holy Spirit, and the price of Jesus' death on the cross for our bodies, leads Paul to a "therefore," which means "because of" or "as a result of." Paul is saying that because of God's purchase of and presence in our bodies, we are to bring honor to Him through our living. We do that by avoiding worldly behaviors including sexual immorality, worship of anyone or anything other than God, stealing, lying, drunkenness, and more! It is not enough to avoid cursing, fighting, or getting drunk in the brick building. God is also interested in the buildings that have no pulpit or choir stand—the buildings we call our bodies.

Contrary to modern thinking, we do hurt someone when we sin—we hurt God. Our bodies belong to Him, and He expects us to know it and live like it.

✣

Father, thank You for making me a sanctuary for Your presence. Continually remind me that my body belongs to You and my lifestyle is to be consistent with Your holiness. Amen.

IN WITH THE NEW!

If anyone be in Christ, he is a new creation; the old has gone, the new has come!

2 CORINTHIANS 5:17, NIV

Springtime is one of the most beautiful times of the year. Buds begin to appear and blossom; tiny leaves burst into blushing colors and vibrant fragrances. Earth smells fresh as gentle showers tease out tender blades of grass. The atmosphere is full of new hope and promise as a winter-weary landscape gives way to a brilliant new portrait of life.

This cadence of spring provides a visual glimpse of the newness of life afforded by salvation in Christ Jesus. But the miracle of the new birth is even more startling and gracious than spring's awakening. When a person receives the Lord Jesus Christ, a marvelous event occurs by the majestic operation of the Holy Spirit—he or she receives a brand new nature. One Bible translation says "...if a man is in Christ, he has been created all over again" (Barclay's New Testament).

By God's love and grace, we are born of the Spirit and grafted into the body of Christ (Ephesians 5:30). We are no longer the slaves of sin; sin no longer has dominion over us (Romans 6:14). This is remarkable, because we were born in sin and destined to serve it well. But something wonderful happens when we receive Jesus Christ: we have a new Lord, a new heart, new assignments, and a new destiny (Ephesians 2:10).

However, God doesn't give us a new mind when He saves us. Our mind is still programmed to operate from an old and defeating set of values. The only way to allow that new nature to blossom is to be transformed by the renewing of our minds (Romans 12:12). We have to pluck up the old entangled roots, so that new concepts can flourish. Shedding old habits takes time and consistency, but we can do it because we've been redesigned in Christ Jesus precisely to walk in the newness of life. So out with the old and in with the new!

Father, thank You that I am a new creation in Christ. Grant me daily grace to shed my old ways and walk in the vibrant newness of life that You have so richly provided. Amen.

A NEW YOU

Not by works of righteousness which we have done, but according to his mercy he saved us, by the washing of regeneration, and renewing of the Holy Ghost; Which he shed on us abundantly through Jesus Christ our Saviour; That being justified by his grace, we should be made heirs according to the hope of eternal life.

TITUS 3:5-7, KJV

The chorus of the song "My Soul's Been Satisfied" by George Jones contains the words *"I looked at my hands, my hands looked new, I looked at my feet and they did too."*[14] What Mr. Jones is referring to is the work of the Holy Spirit in changing the behavior of those who receive Jesus as their Savior.

When our hands are no longer used for sin and our feet no longer take us to ungodly environments, they figuratively become new. Only the Holy Spirit can make this happen, because the new birth brings about new behavior. We are saved by God's mercy, and our behavior is made new by the presence of the Holy Spirit in our lives.

Those of us who have been saved for any considerable amount of time can sometimes forget just how sinful we were. We have been renewed by the Holy Spirit transforming our inner nature to be open to God's law. We no longer lust after the things of the world. We even experience days when we feel joy for not having committed a sin. Yet, we can occasionally become judgmental of those who have not received the new birth.

It is good to be reminded that we were once "foolish, disobedient, deceived, serving divers lusts and pleasures, living in malice and envy, hateful, and hating one another" (vs 3). It was only through the kindness, love, and mercy of God that we were rescued from that behavior to now produce good works.

Now that we are wise, obedient, and understanding, we share God's love for those who still serve their own pleasures. Who better to tell about what our hands did, where our feet went, and how God can also make them new?

❧

Father, I thank You for the renewing power of the Holy Spirit. Give me the compassion to remember the life I once lived, so that I may share Your love for those who have yet to be made new. In Jesus' Name. Amen.

DON'T STOP THE FLOW

In the last day, that great day of the feast, Jesus stood and cried, saying, If any man thirst, let him come unto me, and drink. He that believeth on me, as the scripture hath said, out of his belly shall flow rivers of living water. (But this spake he of the Spirit, which they that believe on him should receive: for the Holy Ghost was not yet given; because that Jesus was not yet glorified.)

JOHN 7:37-39, KJV

At the Chicago Children's Museum, there is a water works exhibit, complete with raincoats, boats, and a steady flow of water. The exhibit also has pieces of plastic that serve as dams—open the plastic and the water flows through, close it shut and the flow stops.

The Holy Spirit is the river that flows in the life of believers. He is present in our lives to satisfy our desire for intimacy with Christ. A steady flow of the Holy Spirit is received when we invite Christ to satisfy our spiritual thirst (John 4:10). Just as we ask the store clerk for water when we are naturally thirsty, we are to ask Christ to satisfy our spiritual thirst when we need to refresh our fatigued spirits.

Our verses today refer to events at The Feast of Tabernacles, which was one of three important Jewish feasts. During this feast, the priests would bring a vessel of water each day from the Pool of Siloam and pour it out at the base of the altar in Jerusalem. This displayed their dependence upon God to satisfy their natural thirst.

As Jesus attended that feast, He spoke of satisfying spiritual thirst through belief in Him. We have received this river "of living water" through the indwelling of the Holy Spirit. It is our continued invitation for Christ to refresh our spirits through devotional practices, such as prayer and meditating on Scripture, that keep us drinking from the unending flow of the Spirit.

When we are not consistent in establishing daily and weekly devotions, we erect dams that stop His flow. We can reopen the flow of the Holy Spirit by being intentional in establishing consistent devotional practices.

❦

Father, thank You for Your Holy Spirit, who satisfies my thirst. Help me to enjoy the endless flow of Your Spirit by establishing consistent devotional practices. In Jesus' Name. Amen.

BORN OF GOD

Which were born, not of blood, nor of the will of the flesh, nor of the will of man, but of God.

JOHN 1:13, KJV

It is amazing to know that God actually cares about us. Though He exists in eternity, He picked a moment in time to present Himself to us on earth, so that we could present ourselves to Him in heaven.

Even more incredible is that God accomplished His plan by making us His children. It is precious to know we can call God our Dad, and it brings joy to His heart to call us His children.

When we receive Jesus as Savior, we experience the new birth, and we become God's children through the new birth. We receive Jesus as Savior by believing He's God's Son, who was sent into the world to save it.

Jesus came into the world with a mission—to present God to us so that we could know God. During His tenure on earth, the Creator came into contact with His own creation. Yet, His creation rejected Him (John 1:11).

Yet countless people across the globe have received Jesus, who "was in the beginning with God." We believe He is the Light in whom all men are to believe (John 1:7); and as a result, Jesus granted us the right to be God's children, born of God's Spirit.

We did not become God's children through our family lineage, our parents' love, or man's will, but through the indwelling of the Holy Spirit, who confirms that we belong to God (Romans 8:16).

Our responsibility is to live like God is our Father and we are His children. We have been given the right to do so; it is, therefore, expected of us. Furthermore, we understand that our behavior reflects on our Father, because we are born of God.

※

Father, thank You for sending the Word to be a Light unto the world. It is because of Jesus that I have the right to be Your child, and it is because of the indwelling of Your Spirit that I am born of God. May my life reflect that I am Your child. In Jesus' Name. Amen.

TRANSFORMERS

And be not conformed to this world: but be ye transformed by the renewing of your mind, that ye may prove what is that good, and acceptable, and perfect, will of God.

ROMANS 12:2, KJV

The *Transformers* cartoon has made it to the big screen. Understood to be "more than meets the eye," because they are "robots in disguise," the *Transformers* look normal on the outside—that is until we see what they are really made of on the inside.

When we join a new workplace or relocate to a new neighborhood, our new co-workers or neighbors may notice nothing different about us: we drive the same cars, walk the same dogs, and cook on the same grills. Yet, overtime, they come to realize that we are *Transformers*. The believer is transformed from the present culture's lifestyles and desires by the Holy Spirit's aid in developing a new way of thinking.

A conformer is a "carnal" Christian whose way of life patterns those who do not know Christ (1 Corinthian 3:3). A *Transformer* is a Christian whose life is changed on the inside and is displayed on the outside. Both have the Holy Spirit, but only one invites Him to work the process of metamorphosis—change from within.

We become *Transformers* by submitting to the Holy Spirit, Who transforms how we think. The way we view the culture in which we live is new. Instead of applauding debauchery and drunkenness, we denounce it. The way we view God's will is new. Instead of insisting that God's law is restrictive, oppressive, and outdated, we conclude that His will is good for us.

Being a *Transformer* is not always easy. Peer pressure and the desire to fit in can sometimes inhibit the work of the Holy Spirit in transforming us from the inside out. However, because of the mercies of God, we make a conscious effort to allow that work to take place.

No matter where we live or work, let us always remember that we are *Transformers,* who are more than meet the eye, because the Holy Spirit is in our lives.

Father, thank You for Your Spirit, who makes me a Transformer. Give me the courage to not conform to this world, the commitment to allow Your Spirit to transform me, and the obedience to prove Your will is perfect. Amen.

RICH AND RESPONSIBLE

In whom we have redemption through his blood, the forgiveness of sins, according to the riches of his grace.

EPHESIANS 1:7, KJV

There are countless stories about people who have squandered their riches: the inheritance of a parent spent in less than a year, the lottery winner who now has to apply for a minimum wage job at retail store, and the infamous Prodigal Son, in Luke's Gospel, who wasted his premature inheritance partying in a far country.

The first chapter of Ephesians reveals just how rich we are. This great wealth we have is the grace of God. Through the riches of God's grace we receive salvation and through the presence of the Holy Spirit we are to live accordingly. These riches go beyond the cattle on a thousand hills (Psalm 50:10), and the earth being the Lord's (Psalm 24:1). God's grace is so rich that it is inexhaustible and inexplicable. God's grace is in such plentiful supply that if every person who ever lived could be saved, it would not experience any depletion.

The death, burial, and resurrection of Jesus Christ set us free from the power of sin and from the punishment that corresponded to a sin-dominated life. Through Jesus, we are declared the Children of God. That was always God's plan, and He did it because He loved us. He did it because of His grace. From the moment we are freed from sin and its punishment, we receive the Holy Spirit, who leads us into a holy life and its corresponding reward.

Because we are rich, we are responsible for how we manage God's grace. We can squander it, with the attitude that we may live any kind of way, or we can submit ourselves to the presence of God's Spirit and live like responsible children who have been accepted in the Beloved. It is our obedience that demonstrates how rich God is and gives Him praise and glory for His grace.

What we have received is not a family fortune or a winning lottery ticket. We have the riches of God's grace sealed by the indwelling of the Holy Spirit.

Father, thank You for Your grace, which You have poured out upon me richly. Teach me to appreciate the privileged position You have given me and to live like a responsible child of God. In Jesus' Name. Amen.

BELIEVING WITH THE HEART

For with the heart man believeth unto righteousness; and with the mouth confession is made unto salvation.

ROMANS 10:10, KJV

Have you ever spoken from the head and not the heart? Perhaps you know people who say they love you, but their actions reveal that they do not mean it. Perhaps you have said some things that were intellectually accurate but not truly from your heart.

Some people are confused about the heart because they think it is the same as the mind. The prophet Jeremiah said, "the heart is deceitful above all things...who can know it?" (Jeremiah 17:9). Jesus goes on to say, "out of the heart proceed evil thoughts" (Matthew 15:19) but also commands us to love God with all of our heart, soul, and mind (Matthew 22:37). Paul then completes that thought by saying "the peace of God, which passeth all understanding, shall keep your hearts and minds through Christ Jesus" (Philippians 4:7). The fact is there is a distinct difference between the heart and the mind although they work in harmony with each other. Yet God is looking at the heart, as He did in calling David a man after His own heart (Acts 13:22).

When we come into the saving knowledge of Jesus Christ, the first thing God changes is our heart. God wants this very core of our being to totally embrace Him. The way we communicate, whether verbally or non-verbally, is impacted by the condition of our heart. Therefore, when we receive the Holy Spirit, our hearts are energized to live right by the power of God. It is then that we understand what it means when the psalmist said, "Trust in the Lord with all thine heart and lean not on your own understanding" (Proverbs 3:5). We must determine today to trust God to the very end and that, whatever we say and do, we will live for Him from the heart.

※

Heavenly Father, I thank You for creating in me a clean heart. Help me to continue to say and do the things that would please you. I honor and thank You each and every day of my life. In Jesus' Name, I pray. Amen!

A FRESH START

That which is born of the flesh is flesh; and that which is born of the Spirit is spirit.

JOHN 3:6, KJV

There is nothing better in life than having a fresh new start after things have gone wrong. Just think about it. For example, if someone is burdened with debt and suddenly that debt is wiped clean, having a fresh start with a fresh new mind, attitude, and perspective would be amazing. Think also about this: Jesus offers us a fresh start.

In today's Scripture, one night the Jewish teacher Nicodemus secretly admits to Jesus that He must have come from God. Nicodemus concluded that nobody could possibly do the miracles Jesus was doing unless God was with him. Jesus gets straight to the heart of the matter and says, "You must be born again." Now the plot thickens and the subject matter shifts. Since Nicodemus only knows the things of this world, he can't begin to fathom what Jesus is talking about. Jesus lets Nicodemus know that unless you are born again you can't see or enter into the kingdom of God.

To show the necessity of this change, Christ redirects Nicodemus' thinking to the natural state of humans. As a teacher of the Jewish law, Nicodemus understood that the nature of humans was corrupt, defiled, and sinful. In that condition, it is impossible for any human to come before God and do what God expects, let alone doing supernatural works. Therefore, Jesus teaches the teacher that the born-again experience is essential in order to please God.

John 1:13 states that Jesus Christ was born "not of blood nor of the will of the flesh, nor of the will of man, but of God." Flesh and blood can neither do the miracles that Jesus did, nor enter into the spiritual realm where God is. Mankind needs a fresh start and the only way it can be achieved is by being born-again and submitting to the Holy Spirit.

What has gone wrong for you? It may be time for a fresh start in Christ!

🦅

Everlasting Father, without You, I can do nothing; but with You I can do all things. Thank You for saving me from eternal destruction as I give my life to You and live in the grace of Your fresh start. Amen!

PAY DAY SOME DAY

For the wages of sin is death; but the gift of God is eternal life through Jesus Christ our Lord.

ROMANS 6:23, KJV

Don't you just love it when payday comes? After putting in your hard-earned hours, you get a check for the work you did. What if your employer gave you a check and said, "Here, take this check as a gift from me" Or said you didn't get a check because "You didn't work hard enough"? You would quickly wonder what happened to the wages you worked for! Ah, but there is something that you cannot work for, or earn…it is eternal life.

Believe it or not, when Jesus comes back, we will all be held to accounting for what we do on earth. If it were like a regular payday, some would receive checks for all they did for Christ, while others would receive checks that could only be cashed in hell. What a thought! But Jesus reckons payday differently; because Christ has always been there extending His hand asking each of us to take His gift of eternal life.

Some people think that offer is too good to be true; because we have been conditioned to work for what we want. Nevertheless, eternal life is a gift. If you have to do anything to get a gift, it is no longer a gift but something you received by works. All Jesus ever asked us to do was to simply, truly believe in Him. He promised to never leave us nor forsake us. He is not like people who make all sorts of promises and then break them. He is so good to us that the Bible says He cannot lie (Titus 1:2).

God wants to take our heavy load and prepare a great future for us, yet people can be eternally lost because they hear the Word and reject it. We cannot earn salvation, but one day everyone, whether saved or lost, is going to be judged by the Lord for the things we have done in this human body based on our decision to accept or reject His offer. Let us make sure our "payday" is spent eternally with the Lord.

Heavenly Father, I receive You today as my personal Lord and Savior. Thank You for Your gift of eternal life. I will forever honor and worship You. In Jesus' Name. Amen!

REBORN...FREE!

Knowing this, that our old man was crucified with Him, that the body of sin might be done away with, that we should no longer be slaves of sin.

ROMANS 6:6, NKJV

Many people in the world see Christians as hypocrites who push their intolerance on others. Some non-Christians (and even some Christians) have a tendency to think we are supposed to be perfect in everything we do. Unfortunately, that isn't possible. We are human and we mess up! That is the message the apostle Paul gave to the Romans. They needed to be aware of this inner conflict because they, like us, were experiencing it.

Our old nature was dominated by sin, which held us in slavery to the world system and all its indulgences. Whatever our old manner of living wanted, we embraced. But when we committed ourselves to following Christ, we agreed to be identified with Christ. Ultimately, that means we will struggle sometimes with living holy and making decisions that please God.

Our old nature, and the mistakes of our past, will never be used against us by the Lord. God used the cross as the means to bring new life for all who believe in Jesus Christ as Savior. When we submitted ourselves to Christ, our old nature was put to death and made powerless by the cross. Although we know we are not perfect, we know that He that began a good work in us shall perform it (Philippians 1:6).

Our new manner of living is empowered by the Holy Spirit that transforms and renews us daily, so that the struggle to live in the new life might be accomplished. We must keep in mind that, despite our struggles, we will be victorious in living for Him! The new man, our new nature, is free from sin's embrace and power. We can live out God's will because we are liberated and free to do so.

❧

Father, as my Lord and Savior, You put my old nature to death and brought me out of darkness into Your marvelous light. Thank You for rescuing me from a life of slavery to sin and making me free. Forgive me for my sins because I want to follow You, Lord, and not my sinful desires. In Jesus' Name. Amen.

New Life in Christ

Therefore we were buried with Him through baptism into death, that just as Christ was raised from the dead by the glory of the Father, even so we also should walk in newness of life.

ROMANS 6:4, NKJV

Many of today's popular teachings say that if we follow God, we will prosper materially and be successful. Of course, God may bless His people materially, but few can make this claim in third world countries that, despite limited resources, are growing in the number of new Christians who love the Lord. Wealth can sometimes be a by-product of a Christian's life, but it is never the goal. The real goal of the Christian faith is death.

When Jesus died on the cross, it was an act of obedience to the Father. It did not gain Him popularity, or a life of leisure, or fortune. His obedience gained Him death on the cross. This is the same goal Christ has for each of us—death of our old nature so that He might live through us. The Christian life is paradoxical—the first will be last and we die in order to live.

God requires obedience. Jesus' obedience gained Him the cross. Although our old nature and mistakes of our past are buried and never used against us by the Lord, we have to choose to live an obedient life of faith in Christ. Because God operates from a different set of values than we have been accustomed to in the world, we must change our thinking to God's system. Let death work in you to produce a life that only God can raise up.

※

Father, teach me to follow Your ways. I confess I have followed my ways instead of Your ways sometimes, and I ask for Your forgiveness. I want to obey You, Lord, because You know what is best for me. Thank You for reminding me of my real goal in life: to die so that I can live for You. Help me to walk in newness of life through praying and reading Your Word daily. In Jesus' Name. Amen.

LOVE IS BORN

But God demonstrates His own love toward us, in that while we were still sinners, Christ died for us.

ROMANS 5:8, NIV

L ove is all about relationships. Relationships are vital in life because they promote the sharing of ideas, express care and concern for someone other than yourself, and provide a genuine acceptance for who you are. Love is expressed in many ways. For some of us, just thinking about someone we love brings an instant smile to our faces and joy to our hearts. Some people express love by saying kind words that affirm the love they have for another. To others, love is an action that is expressed through giving time, doing special deeds, and sacrificing what is important to them for someone else. As love is nourished, the relationship grows and flourishes; therefore, no matter how love is expressed, it is easy when it is reciprocated. But how easy is it to love someone who doesn't love you back?

The apostle Paul reminded the Christian church in Rome that God showed His love in an unusual way—by loving those who were His enemies. In this, His love surpasses all that has ever been demonstrated among people. Jesus willingly submitted Himself as a sacrifice for others. There are many people who wait a lifetime to hear someone say, "I love you." But Jesus has already shown His love for each of us. Through Christ's sacrifice of death on the cross, He saved us from eternal death. His love was expressed through His willingness to do what no one was willing or able to do— sacrifice Himself for those who did not know Him and did not love Him back. Jesus, who knew no sin, took our place as sinners. His loving kindness and generosity to us, who were born in sin, now makes it possible for us to be born again. What love!

Lord, I thank You because, as the great Shepherd that You are, You love and care for me every day. I am grateful that You showed Your love for me through the sacrifice on Calvary's cross. Thank You for Your acts of kindness and grace when I didn't even know You. Help me to live my life in a way that pleases You. In Jesus' Name. Amen.

HAVING A SAVED HOME

And they said, Believe on the Lord Jesus Christ, and thou shalt be saved, and thy house.

ACTS 16:31, KJV

Many times our children and other family members never realize the sacrifices made by our forefathers or our parents. Blessings have been bestowed upon a family lineage simply because one person made a decision that had a domino effect upon that family. For example, Henry Ford made a decision to make the automobile in the 1920s, which continues to effect generations of the Ford family. Likewise, a similar opportunity came upon the jailer in this story.

When Paul made a decision to follow Christ, it altered his whole life. In this Scripture passage, Paul and Silas were locked in prison because of their preaching of the gospel. The jailer heard them singing praises to their God in the midst of their trials, felt an earthquake open the prison cell doors, and witnessed the stocks and chains that bound them be loosed. The jailer recognized something miraculous had just happened. Not only were Paul and Silas miraculously set free, but all the prisoners were also freed. However, the jailer knew he would be held responsible for the jailbreak, so he started to kill himself until Paul stopped him. He must have wondered what kind of God is this that cared so much for His own that He would not only loose them but everybody else that was locked up with them (Acts 16:26).

He was so impressed that he asked the question that has been asked down through the annuls of time: "What must I do to be saved?" Paul shared the answer—simply believe on the Lord Jesus Christ. It is Christ, and Him alone, who saves the sin-sick soul. That is the bottom line. If the jailer trusted Christ for his salvation, this same Jesus would save his whole house if they, too, trusted in Him. Your household can be saved when we share Christ with them and trust in the living God to do the rest.

❧

Blessed Lord, I make a decision right now as Joshua once said, "As for me and my house, we are going to serve the Lord." Keep Your hands upon me and my house this day. In Jesus' Name, I pray. Amen!

OBEY GOD'S RULES

Can any man forbid water, that these should not be baptized, which have received the Holy Ghost as well as we? And he commanded them to be baptized in the name of the Lord. Then prayed they him to tarry certain days.

ACTS 10:47-48, KJV

The uniqueness of sports is that they allow everyone the opportunity to excel without bias. Because sports have rules, they apply to everyone equally. For instance, if you hit a home run, it is not worth more than someone else's home run; or to score a touchdown, everyone must cross the goal line. Additionally, each rule of every sport can only be applied to that particular sport. One cannot apply the rules of soccer to a baseball game. And, if you begin a new sport you have never played before, you cannot change the rules at will. Likewise, one cannot arbitrarily come into the Christian faith and begin to change what God has ordained from the beginning of the world.

Many people try to say that baptism is not important. But whoever heard of an unbaptized Christian? Although water baptism does not save you all by itself, it is an external conviction of an inward decision. In this passage, this group of Gentiles believed on Jesus and were then saved exactly as the Jews who first believed in Jesus. They received the Holy Ghost and were baptized in the name of Jesus, just like those first Jewish believers. As these new Gentile converts obeyed the command, they were born again. This highlights that the ways of our Lord are mysterious, "And without controversy great is the mystery of godliness…" (1 Timothy 3:16). Salvation did not start in the mind of man but in the mind of God.

Almighty God has done all of this without our permission and input. He set the standards we are to live by, therefore we need to trust everything He says and not pick and choose at our own leisure. God promises that if we do what is right before Him, He will honor our commitment.

❧

Heavenly Father, I bless Your holy name. You are my King and my Lord. Help me to obey the Spirit of God and follow Your will through Your Word. Then, surely goodness and mercy shall follow me all the days of my life. In Jesus' Name. Amen!

SOMETHING MONEY CAN'T BUY

But Peter said unto him, Thy money perish with thee, because thou hast thought that the gift of God may be purchased with money.

ACTS 8:20, KJV

There is not much in this world that money can't buy. Money is used to buy supplies, food, art, houses, trade secrets—even people. But when it comes to the spiritual things of God, money has no power at all. We pay the best instructors and life coaches to help make us more charismatic, more attractive, or even more business savvy, so we can imitate famous people. But, when God has empowered us to demonstrate the supernatural, others may envy us and try to buy what we have for their own personal fame and gain. But one can't buy what God gives.

Today, the writer tells us that God and His power is not for sale. Simon the sorcerer tried to imitate great power until the "real" power showed up in town. When Simon saw the supernatural power of God come upon the people by the laying on of hands by the apostles, he wanted to get involved. But he did not want to come under the subjection of Almighty God. He wanted to buy the power that was conferred upon Peter as a gift from God. He, much like people today, wanted to demonstrate the anointing of God but did not want to submit to God to obtain the anointing.

Isn't it interesting how people will reject God's ways but want the benefits He has to offer? Peter expresses his righteous indignation with Simon's offer. Simon was already well on the road to destruction, and Peter said let your money perish with you as well. Imagine the thought that money could buy the extraordinary influences of the Holy Spirit. It is absurd to think that what God has could be purchased by worthless silver or gold. The earth is the Lord's, and the cattle on a thousand hills belong to Him (Psalm 24:1; 50:10). The thought of trying to bribe the One who owns everything is preposterous. Nor can we now buy a blessing from God. We must realize it is He that made us for His purpose and glory, and money can't buy that.

※

Father, I honor You as my Lord and King and I thank You for Your grace and mercies every day. Keep Your mighty hands upon me, I pray. In Jesus' Name. Amen!

THE CHOICE IS YOURS

And he said unto them, Go ye into all the world, and preach the gospel to every creature. He that believeth and is baptized shall be saved; but he that believeth not shall be damned.

MARK 16:15-16, KJV

Have you noticed in this day and age that a lot of people do not want to take responsibility for their actions? Some want to blame their troubles on "the absent father"—even though other men have stepped into their lives and given them godly examples. Or some want to suggest that because their mothers didn't hug them enough—even though she worked two jobs and always kept their clothes clean and food on the table—they weren't loved. Or, if some do badly in school, they want to blame the teachers, though they are the ones who cut classes.

In today's Scripture, Christ clearly holds each person responsible for his or her actions. After Christ's resurrection, He revealed Himself to the disciples and commanded them to preach the Word of God everywhere. If those who heard the gospel believed, they were saved. If they rejected the gospel, they were damned. One writer said it this way, "For unto us was the gospel preached, as well as unto them: but the word preached did not profit them, not being mixed with faith in them that heard it" (Hebrews 4:2).

You see, the reason many of our blessings are held up is due to the fact we choose not to believe in the One who makes all things possible. When we do not believe God, and try to do things on our own, we receive the fruit of our own labor and decisions. We cannot blame anyone but ourselves. The answer to this dilemma is to choose to believe God. We trust everyone one else, but we refuse to believe in the only One that has the absolute power to do exactly what He said.

Father, thank You for giving me access to Your promises in the Bible. You are the way, the truth and the life, and I choose to believe You for every need in my life. In Jesus' Name, I pray. Amen!

PROMISE KEEPER

The Lord is not slack concerning his promise, as some men count slackness; but is longsuffering to us-ward, not willing that any should perish, but that all should come to repentance.

2 PETER 3:9, KJV

We should all be in anxious expectation of the return of our Lord and Savior. In the Old Testament, the prophets talked about how the Messiah would suffer and die and return to deliver His people. Even when Christ was born, many of His chosen people (Israel) did not recognize Him as the King of kings. The Bible says, "he came unto his own and his own received him not" (John 1:11). Before Christ went home to be with the Father, His disciples wanted to know when He would restore the kingdom to Israel. Christ began to tell them about the power of the Holy Spirit and the work they must do. At Christ's tomb, two angels spoke to the disciples saying, "this same Jesus, which is taken up from you into heaven, shall so come in like manner as ye have seen him go into heaven" (Acts 1:9-11). So, for generations people have been waiting for God to keep His promise to come back for His people.

The writer in this passage, Peter, addresses the scoffers who question "Where is the promise of His coming?" (2 Peter 3:4). In other words, they had heard this talk long enough. Since their forefathers, nothing had changed.

Although it seems to take a long time, God keeps His promise. God is not like humankind. He deals in eternity, while we deal in time. The real issue is that God is giving people the opportunity to accept Him as Savior before He returns. So, when He returns, we can all go back with Him. Starting today, if you haven't already done so, ask God to forgive you for all of your wrongdoings and receive Him as your Lord and Savior. If you don't, will you be ready when He returns?

Father, thank You for getting me ready for Your return. I ask that You would forgive me as I forgive those who have wronged me. Thank You for keeping Your promise. In Jesus' Name, I pray. Amen.

THE BEST FLIGHT YET

But now in Christ Jesus, you who once were [so] far away, through (by, in) the blood of Christ have been brought near.

EPHESIANS 2:13, AMP

Pat had a dear friend who lived many miles away in another country. The friends maintained their relationship through periodic correspondence. Since the advancement in technology, the two could not only make phone calls to each other, but they could also see each other through the video chat function on their computers. Yet, at the end of those calls, Pat seemed even more aware of how far away they really were, in spite of the technology, which aimed to bring them closer.

Finally, after one of Pat's phone calls with her dear friend, she knew they needed to close some of the distance between them. Pat knew they needed some time in one another's presence. So Pat flew to be closer to her friend, and it was just what she needed!

Before we surrendered our lives to Christ we, too, were afar off from God. We were separated—estranged from God. We needed to be brought close and in relationship with Him. Thank God, He called for us and closed the gap that sin had created. The thought still comes, how were we who were dead fulfilling our own desires, allowed anywhere near the most Holy and Righteous Savior?

The only way we were able to come to God was through the blood of Jesus! It was because of the shedding of blood that we are no longer afar off. Just as distance kept Pat away from her friend, sin drew us further from God. This passage serves as a reminder to all the saints of where we were, and what God has not only brought us from but of what God has brought us to!

It is the wonderful workings of His shed blood that we are carried right into His presence. In His presence are joy, peace, and contentment! As we reflect on what God has done for us, surely we can say this certainly has been "The Best Flight Yet."

Dear Jesus, help me to always remember not only what You've done for me but to enjoy where I am in You—and to look forward to where I am headed with You. Amen!

NOT JUST WASHED, BUT DRESSED

For as many of you have been baptized into Christ have put on Christ.
GALATIANS 3:27, KJV

How wonderful to see a brand new baby—so cute, so cuddly, so dependent, needing help for everything (eating, bathing, and dressing). As time goes on the baby becomes less so, even though these rudimentary activities continue to be a part of everyday existence. Eventually, children will feed, bathe, and dress themselves. They learn to do so in accordance with what has been demonstrated to them. A pattern is set for them to observe and then stick to from that point on.

In ancient Roman society, when youths became adults they literally changed their clothes. They went from the clothes of children to togas of adults, which represented not only full rights but full responsibility. Baptism marks the point at which we change the clothes of sin and death and dress in righteousness *for life*. When we're baptized, like Christ's baptism we're consecrated to God. At His baptism, Jesus identified with us—taking on our sinful state—while He, Himself, remained sinless. At our baptism, by faith we exchanged the rags of wretchedness we once wore for robes of righteousness we now wear.

Our faith brings us into a wonderful place of privilege because of the power of the gospel. We now can put on something we had not been able to wear before—the righteousness of God, which is found in Christ. "Putting on Christ" means we put on a new life and new purpose. It unites us in love and relationship with God. We can no more change our ways on our own than a baby can change his or her clothes on its own. We need the Holy Spirit in us to help us live the life we have committed to in Christ. Along with being washed in the waters of baptism, we who put on Christ are dressed to live our lives in the Spirit.

Plunge into life today, knowing your sins are washed away and you are dressed to live for Jesus.

Father, I thank You for all I have in Your redeeming Son. I have been baptized into Him and desire to put Him on daily so that I can live the way You want me to. I realize I can't do it by myself, but I can do it through the Holy Spirit. Amen.

GET THE PICTURE

Know ye not, that so many of us as were baptized into Jesus Christ were baptized into his death?

ROMANS 6:3, KJV

Sometimes it is hard to understand a thing without a visual depiction of it. An empty canvas, with brushes and paints to the side, doesn't quite help us see the splendor of a vibrant, towering vase captured by an imaginative artist. It can be described so you hear how the colors are combined, but seeing is believing. Seeing a thing adds to our understanding and solidifies what words attempt to convey. God has purposed it so that we would hear the truth (faith comes by hearing, Romans 10:17) and respond. It is His plan that, once we come to faith, we are baptized because of what we have heard, and now believe, about Jesus Christ.

Paul goes on to give us an illustration of what it means to be baptized into Christ. He says we are baptized into His death, so we die to or turn our backs on anything that hinders our life in Him. We give up our old way of doing things and submit to the will of God, just as Jesus submitted to it and died in our place. We then, are placed *in Christ* in baptism and, thereby, united and identified with Him. What's done in the water paints a picture of what is done in the Spirit. The one gives us a picture of the other. Baptism then is a picture of our death to sin and our resurrection to a new life in the Spirit. It is the public declaration of an outward physical expression of the inner work that has been started in our hearts by the Holy Spirit. It isn't optional for those that place their faith in Jesus, and neither is submitting to the work that He has begun.

The picture is clear. We go from death to life and from sinful to righteous because, like death, sin has been defeated. Can you see yourself getting up from the things that have tried to hold you down? Get the picture of this inner work showing up on the outside. What a picture!

Lord, You have given me a wonderful picture that reminds me that I am dying to sin and living in Christ. Help me live in this reality every day. In Jesus' Name. Amen.

INSIDE OUT

Therefore, if anyone is in Christ, the new creation has come: The old has gone, the new is here!

2 CORINTHIANS 5:17, NIV

The change that takes place as the caterpillar morphs into the beautiful butterfly is an amazing one. Who would think the puny, writhing, wormy thing slithering around on the ground would become a picture of such splendor? The reality of the latter is not lost on the former because, before the beautiful flutter is ever seen, everything needed for it is already in it. So it is with us. When we receive Christ, God puts in us everything we need to live out our purpose in Him. We may still be in a state of becoming, but the seed of what we're to be is on the inside waiting to come out.

Paul repeatedly talked about being *in Christ*. The thought captivated his heart and mind. Why? Remember, Paul went from being a persecutor to a proclaimer of Christ on the way to Damascus (Acts 9). He went from being self-righteous to made righteous by the revelation of Christ. He had been an antagonizer and now he was a Christ follower. He was compelled because of Christ's love on the cross. Imagine your life being turned upside down and then made right side up again. This was Paul! That's why he talked so much about being in Christ. He realized that all he thought he had apart from Jesus was junk compared to being in Him.

Like Paul, we are made a new creation in Christ and our lives are turned right side up. God redeems our lives and restores us to Himself through His Son. His purpose is fulfilled in us as new creatures, who have yielded our lives to Jesus Christ. When we are renewed from the inside out, a spiritual transformation takes place. This transformation, which started on the inside, eventually changes not only our hearts and minds but also our actions. Because we've been made new by the Holy Spirit, we put away our old ways and embrace the new thing that God wants to do in us. Let Him do it today from the inside out!

❧

Lord, thank You for making me a new creation. Work in me and help me to fulfill my purpose as a new thing that will bring You glory and honor. In Jesus' Name. Amen.

GOING PUBLIC

Peter replied, "Repent and be baptized, every one of you, in the name of Jesus Christ for the forgiveness of your sins. And you will receive the gift of the Holy Spirit.

ACTS 2:38, NIV

Today, everyone wants to wave the banner of their "rights" or pick up a cause. As human beings we tout basic rights and freedoms afforded to everyone, regardless of who they are, where they come from, or what their status is. Different affinity groups champion their respective causes. Everything from children's rights, to women's rights, to veteran's rights, to worker's rights points to our desire to be liberated from some imposing oppression. Those who know the contradiction between what is presumed and what is gained don't hold back when they gain it. They stand confidently, going public with what they've received.

Peter boldly answered the question that was posed by the Jewish hearers. They were asking what they should do in response to what they had just heard about the lordship of this Jesus. Peter responded with a call to a radical change from the presumed rights that they thought they held, to the fundamental freedom that would only be found in Jesus Christ. He let them know this change wasn't for a few, but for everyone. Each person would have to make a shift as decisive as a military "about face" regarding sin and turn to Jesus. Only then would they be positioned to receive the gift of the Holy Spirit that is reserved for them.

The rights they thought they had were set aside for the privilege of knowing and being known by Christ. The hearers, once proud in their ancestral heritage, were cut in their hearts and knew that what they had once felt entitled to could only be attained through trusting the One God sent. They embraced, by faith, what they had rejected with mocking. Now in this Jesus, they receive the gift of forgiveness and the gift of the Holy Spirit. Two gifts are given to one heart at the same time. The same is being done today when our hearts are changed by Jesus' power. Now that's something to go public about!

❧

Lord, thank You for the gift of the Holy Ghost. I thank You that You alone give good gifts to us and I will live letting the world know that I am Yours and You are mine. Amen.

SAFEST PLACE I KNOW

And this water symbolizes baptism that now saves you also—not the removal of dirt from the body but the pledge of a clear conscience toward God. It saves you by the resurrection of Jesus Christ.

1 PETER 3:21, NIV

One maddening Monday, Hurricane Katrina hit the streets of New Orleans with brute force. Although warned of impending danger, there were natives that met the caution with a nonchalant repose that contradicted the threat. The city was sacked with a category four eruption that blew through it, hurling torrents of rain and leaving hard times behind for everyone in its wake. It threatened to carry away anything that wasn't riveted to the strongest foundation. As the winds howled and sheets of torturing rain fell, only the massive erected structure seemed to hold the promise of safety from the ensuing devastation.

Another historical storm reminds us of the need for refuge from nonstop torrents. That storm illustrated a man, his obedience, and the need for salvation. As the obedient builder, Noah built an ark that would save his family from the flood waters that God had promised would come. Noah was saved from the flood because he obeyed God, built the ark, and, when the time came, went inside. Just as water didn't save Noah, it doesn't save us but illustrates the work of salvation that comes when we are in Christ.

Our text tells us we are saved by the resurrection of Jesus Christ. He is the ark of safety that we come into. When we place our faith in Him, we pass through the waters of baptism into salvation, just as Noah and his family passed through the waters of the flood to safety. Our submission to submersion makes us clean before Him and gives us a picture of the spiritual reality that occurs in baptism—not of water but of Christ.

While the Superdome became an imperfect makeshift place for those seeking shelter from the pounding rain, there is a perfect safety for those that seek shelter in the arms of our Supernatural God. No storm of life can snatch us from the safety we have in Jesus!

※

Father God, thank You that You have made a way of escape throughout history for Your people to find safety. I am thankful for the safest place I know, and that is in You. Amen.

MORE THAN A DEAD MAN WALKING

I am crucified with Christ: nevertheless I live; yet not I, but Christ liveth in me: and the life which I now live in the flesh I live by the faith of the Son of God, who loved me, and gave himself for me.

GALATIANS 2:20, KJV

Susan Sarandon played Sister Helen Prejean in the movie *Dead Man Walking*. The film was about a nun who found herself transformed and fighting for issues of social justice in an impoverished community. Her work led her to take up the cause against capital punishment, and that led to her providing spiritual direction for men headed to death row. The movie is all the more compelling when we witness people being put to death for crimes they didn't commit. Then we remember that we were spared from the penalty of sins we did commit!

Paul said that we have been put to death with Christ, Who died to fulfill the sentence that would be imposed upon us by the law. While Christ was crucified under the law, He is Lord over the law, and He invites His followers to a new way of life beyond the law. This new way of living makes us dead to the law, to sin, and to the world. Like Paul, who was crucified with Christ, we aren't dead! But we *are* dead to our own way and our own plans. Our lives are now hidden in Christ and we are to be eager, energetic, and enthusiastic in our love and service to Him. Paul had been vigorous in his pursuit of following the law and he became even more vigorous in following Jesus Christ. The Holy Spirit led, directed, and empowered him to do what was needed to bring God glory.

Christ lives in us, so when we're crucified it means the end of us as sinners. Christ didn't die for us to live any kind of way. Our sinful ways were put to death with Christ as He took on our sin. Our lives aren't lived in the flesh but in the Spirit because while we are not sinless, we *are* free from sin's power. We are so united with Jesus that our natural tendency to sin is put on death row. The power of Christ lives in us!

❧

Lord, You have brought me to life through Your death. Thank You for loving me and living through me. I bless You now and forever. Amen.

MEMBERSHIP HAS ITS PRIVILEGES

And if children, then heirs; heirs of God, and joint-heirs with Christ; if so be
that we suffer with him, that we may be also glorified together.

ROMANS 8:17, KJV

One of the best known slogans in the world of advertising is the American Express mantra, "Membership Has Its Privileges." It left every young, up-and-coming futurist pining to receive the coveted card known by travelers and financiers around the world. The slogan suggests that one will receive better treatment—even the choicest offerings—because he or she is a bearer of the card. We are reminded that we are bearers of something much more precious and enduring than a card that touts privileges. We are bearers of the name of Jesus Christ, and everything He has we have.

What God has reserved for us is much greater than the possession of a plastic card emblazoned with the prized logo reserved for advantaged people. It is greater than the inheritance provided under Jewish tradition for the first-born son. Jesus is the first-born of many brethren (Romans 8:29), and when we are in Him we become joint heirs with Him and we receive the full inheritance as sons and daughters. While we are joint heirs with Christ, we are different heirs— He by His nature and we by adoption—into the Father's love. We are recipients of spiritual blessings of peace and favor now and eternal life to come. An heir inherits the father's estate. Even though the heir doesn't take possession of all the father has, it is his, and the heir can ask for what he needs, because of the relationship he has with the father. As believers, we are heirs of God (Matthew 25:34). We are heirs of His promise and eternal salvation.

We go from being enemies of God to being His children. Children experience security when they know their place in the family. God has called us His children, and we have all that our Father has. We are members of the body of Christ, and that has definite privileges. We don't just get riches and earthly treasures. We get *the* treasure; we get God!

❧

Father, You have given me riches beyond measure. Thank You for the treasure I have in You. I am a joint heir with Christ and I bless You that I have all spiritual blessings in Him. Amen.

From "If Then" to "Now Therefore"

There is therefore now no condemnation to them which are in Christ Jesus, who walk not after the flesh, but after the Spirit.

ROMANS 8:1, KJV

Growing up, children learn the reality of consequences. They learn that if they do what is asked, things will often go well. But they also learn if they don't do what's asked, in all likelihood, things won't go as well for them. Like children, we have the desire to do the right thing, but somehow we lean to the side of doing what we want instead of what we ought—our desire over what our Father has expressed, our sin over His command. Paul recognized the conflict in our will and obedience. He also recognized the resolve of our God to make a way for us to leave Condemnation Island for Grace Place, and that way is in Christ.

Therefore gives us the sense that something has taken place and must be considered to come to the right conclusion. Paul's declaration that we who are in Christ are not condemned comes on the heels of his assertion that condemnation awaits those under the law. He recognized and experienced that an imperfect people would not be able to keep a perfect law. Paul realized that striving to keep the law left him bound up in a prison of blame because he was powerless to do so in his own strength. Once he embraced the freedom that came in Christ, he was able to live in the boundless grace that was found there.

Try as we might, our very best efforts will still fall far short of the expectation of a Holy God that demands and deserves holiness. It's only when the Holy Spirit is operating in our lives that we are able to live out the salvation we have received. We go from the tyranny of the law, and our inability to withstand its demands, to the sanctifying walk the Spirit leads us on. If we understand our insufficiency to do it on our own, then we recognize our need for the Holy Spirit. We can therefore trust Him to do it through us!

❧

Father, I thank You that I am free from condemnation through the power of the Holy Spirit. Help me to live like it and walk in the Spirit today. I pray this in Jesus' Name. Amen.

The King is Coming!

I indeed baptize you with water unto repentance: but he that cometh after me is mightier than I, whose shoes I am not worthy to bear: he shall baptize you with the Holy Ghost, and with fire.

Matthew 3:11, KJV

Do you know the excitement and anticipation of waiting for something that you've heard about and even longed to see? Have you experienced the pounding of your heart for a promise to be fulfilled? The clarion call of the messenger who spoke pointedly to the religious leaders turned to anybody and everybody that would listen because many within earshot had also waited and longed for the Promise to come.

Can you imagine John the Baptist's zeal as he anticipated the coming of the Messiah, whom he had heard so much about and waited for? From the womb, he had been called to herald the coming of the Lord. As babes still veiled in the wombs of their mothers, John, who became the baptizer, leaped in proclamation of the presence of the King (Luke 1:41). The excitement that started then continued, as the flames of devotion grew within him. He understood his calling. He pointed beyond himself to Jesus. John understood that, while the spiritual process had been started as people were called to repentance and baptized in water, Jesus would baptize them with the power of the Holy Spirit. As they gave an outward sign of commitment to follow God, the Holy Spirit would give them an inward sign that they would have power to obey and follow God's leading. While he gripped the reigns as forerunner of the Lamb of God, he counted himself not even worthy to hold the sandals that clung to His feet from the dust of the world He had come to save. John the Baptist had baptized many, but now he baptized the Son of God!

Jesus came for many, and now He comes to you. What is your response to the presence of our King? While your feet may be planted beneath your desk or table, let your heart leap because the King has come into your heart now and forever.

❦

Father, how I thank You for Jesus! You sent Him to save me and bless me with His abiding presence in the Holy Spirit. I bless You that He is with me forever! Amen.

WE HAVE A REASON TO HOPE

Blessed be the God and Father of our Lord Jesus Christ, which according to his abundant mercy hath begotten us again unto a lively hope by the resurrection of Jesus Christ from the dead.

1 PETER 1:3, KJV

The second decade of the twenty-first century ushered in unprecedented hardship for families in this country. Like never before, we witnessed banks on the verge of collapse, natural disasters from coast to coast, oil prices at an all time high, and human atrocities of the worst kind afflicted on the most vulnerable—from the very old to the very young. Yet, in spite of those things, we have a hope that supersedes the events and casualties that surround us. Our hope is not found in the things of this world, nor is it fueled by the waves of them but by the sovereign Hand of God who turns hopeless situations into hopeful ones.

Such was the case when Peter encouraged saints who were spread throughout parts of Asia to remember what they had in Christ and remain hopeful. They had experienced hardship and persecution, and they had no hope, except for death, apart from Jesus. While Peter suggested that even the apostles' hope faltered when Christ was crucified, their hope was resurrected when Christ rose from the dead. His resurrection is the foundation of our hope because it is a promise of what is to come. Peter gave God thanks and praise for the great salvation we've received and the explanation that it is not because of our goodness but His—His mercy, His grace. We are not saved because of who we are, or what we've done, but because of His abundant mercy.

The saints of old, like today, faced difficulty and yet their hope was firm and their faith unshakable. They hoped in the good that was to come through Christ. We, too, have a reason to hope because we have received the gift of hope and redemption through God's own Son. Thank God that our hope is secured by the resurrection of Jesus, and that is a gift of His grace!

✒

Father, I thank You for the hope I have in Jesus Christ. You have made a way for me through Your mercy and grace. Remind me of Your abundant mercies and help me to receive it as a brand new gift today. Amen.

WE'RE GETTING UP!

*Buried with him in baptism, wherein also ye are risen with him through the
faith of the operation of God, who hath raised him from the dead.*

COLOSSIANS 2:12, KJV

L earning to swim is a life-saving endeavor and the more you
do it, the more empowered you become. When you first start,
the water temperature can be a little jarring until you settle into
the swirl of liquid ripples that surround you. Pretty soon, you're
practicing strokes that demonstrate your advancing skill, and
before you know it, you're ready for the diving board. You jump in,
going down deep but rising again, wet with the water of an eager
diver who has plunged beneath a waiting flood.

Our baptism reminds us of the swimmer who dives in, goes
down, but rises again. The major difference is that we don't just
rise up from water but up from sin. Our submersion in water
represents our supernatural immersion into the Spirit of Christ.
When our hearts are pricked with the truth of the gospel, our
response of being baptized in Jesus' name unites us with Him.
Baptism illustrates our identification with Jesus Christ in His
death, burial, and resurrection. It also illustrates our parallel death
and burial to a life of sin, as well as resurrection with our Savior.
Our death to sin is more than mental ascent; it is a commitment to
the work of God that began in us and a rejection of the sinful works
that prevailed before the revelation of Christ came. That revelation
started with God and continues through the Holy Spirit, as we die
daily to our sinful desires and choose to live in the resurrected life
that is provided through Jesus!

We live in the resurrected power of Jesus Christ. Our faith
reminds us that we are raised above the sin that would try to hold
us and we will be raised from the dead with Him. Rejoice in the
reality that in Christ we live both now and forever. Our baptism
reminds us that, just like we went down, we are getting up!

🦅

*Lord God, thank You for the resurrection power I have in Jesus! Today, I
dive into the glorious riches found in Your death, burial, and resurrection.
I bless You that I have the power to say no to sin and yes to living for Your
glory and honor. Amen.*

A WHOLE NEW WAY

That ye put off concerning the former conversation the old man, which is corrupt according to the deceitful lusts; And be renewed in the spirit of your mind; And that ye put on the new man, which after God is created in righteousness and true holiness.

EPHESIANS 4:22-24, KJV

Not so long ago, you could find the unspeakable horror of racism down the back roads of many country towns. Its shadow was cast widely where segregation and fear drew the line between the privileged and the enslaved. Long after freedom was announced, slavery hung on and fought bitterly to live in the hearts of people that clung to the way they knew. It took then, and takes now, the deliberate action of moving toward the thing we now know to live in the freedom we are called to.

Paul spoke pointedly to the believers at Ephesus concerning how they were to live. Like those that reveled in the muck of racism enjoying the exploits of their transgression, Paul told them they needed to stop living like heathens doing anything they felt they wanted to do. After he reminded them that they should be increasing in spiritual maturity and living like they know Jesus as the Christ, he encouraged that they should not continue to live the way they had before they came into the saving knowledge of Jesus. They were to behave differently, do things differently, and it all started with their thinking. Truth revealed a whole new way of thinking and being.

Whether people lived as perpetrators of atrocities or those that had been subjected to them, whose spirits are broken and heads bowed and dejected, it matters not. When truth and freedom finds you, you either drop your chosen weapon or lift your enlivened heart because truth has come. You now see and know that things are different. Similarly, the grip that sin had over us is gone when our minds are transformed. Transformed minds don't go back to the old way and dabble in the filth of sin. Remember, we put away that old thinking and doing because we have a whole new way!

❧

Father, thank You for Jesus Christ. Because of what He has done I can live in victory, free from the sin that tries to ensnare me. I thank You for a whole new way today. In Jesus' Name. Amen.

Is Your Mind Set?

Since, then, you have been raised with Christ, set your hearts on things above, where Christ is, seated at the right hand of God.

COLOSSIANS 3:1, NIV

We are a world that pursues any number of things—some good and, sadly, some bad. There's the gymnast pursing victory on the balance bar, the swimmer finishing the lap with dolphin-like ease, the scholar dozing by the lamplight of predawn study to achieve the highest test score, or the poet languishing over every line of prose. All have laudable goals before them. Then there are those that don't run after anything at all except your distraction, even your destruction. Their focus is on getting you off your goal and the thing that is set before you. While there are great goals and feats to reach for, none are more rewarding or praiseworthy than the unending pursuit of Christ.

Paul writes to remind Christians at Colossi that, while they are here on earth, their thoughts are to be on things above. They weren't to be weighed down with giving their affection or attention to needless concerns that had no eternal purpose. He reminded them that their spiritual experience was based upon who they were in Christ.

Paul encourages a deep knowledge of Jesus and all that goes with living and belonging to Him. This pursuit is living worthy of His name and seeking His kingdom. Paul's admonishment to the Colossians was to set their minds on Christ and make a decision to focus on Him. He was challenging them to have a new mindset and a recalibration of their own will.

As Christians, we won't seek what we haven't made up our minds to seek. Like a factory reset button, we have to have our minds set for Christ. A new mindset has to be established, so, as we are alive to Christ, we can understand spiritual truths, grasp previously hidden realities, and know the will of God.

Whether gymnast, swimmer, academic, or poet, we pursue our goal with our mind set on Christ. We determine to have our affection and mind set on Christ because He is our life.

Lord God, I am so thankful for the many opportunities to pursue goals that will make me a better person. Let me chase after none more than You. Bless me with Yourself. In Jesus' Name. Amen.

MIDNIGHT MIRACLE

And they said, Believe on the Lord Jesus Christ, and thou shalt be saved, and thy house.

ACTS 16:31 KJV

These are the times we find ourselves in situations that we have no control over. Not only have we had our midnight experiences, but we have also walked alongside people who are in the same space as we are. Weather it is sickness, sorrow, suffering, or trials and tribulations, we have had "the midnight hour" occurrence. But, there is one thing we are aware of: there is a "morning" after a midnight. God will show up and make a pivotal shift, just in time.

Can you imagine how Paul and Silas felt in jail after experiencing that great quake? What made it a great earthquake is that the prisoners were released and yet restrained. The doors opened and the chains fell off, but nobody left. The jailer just knew that everybody was gone. When he saw the doors open he drew his sword, ready to take his own life. The cost and punishment for losing a prisoner was that his life was supposed to be taken. And rather than go through all the drama, he decided to kill himself. To his surprise, Paul said, "do thyself no harm; we are all here." And it was at that time that the jailer realized that there was a greater power at work in that jailhouse. It was the awesome power of God that kept every man in his cell. And the jailer cried out, "Sirs, what must I do to be saved?"

Now, one of the things about midnight experiences is that oftentimes God does some of His best work when we think it's too late. When we've given it all up as gone, God has a way of showing Himself strong. Even in our darkest hour, God will turn around the gloomiest situation to show us His power and His might. For some it will be salvation and being set free. For others it may be the midnight jolts of the vicissitudes of life (e.g., calamity on our jobs, in our homes, in our wallets, in our bodies) from which God will release us. Whatever our circumstance might be, we know to believe on the Lord Jesus Christ, "and thou shalt be saved" (Romans 10:9).

❧

God, help me to walk through my midnight phenomenons knowing that, through them, You are in control, and that, from beginning to end, You will make a way of escape. In Jesus' Name. Amen.

Power Packed

But you are not controlled by your sinful nature. You are controlled by the Spirit if you have the Spirit of God living in you. (And remember that those who do not have the Spirit of Christ living in them do not belong to him at all.)

Romans 8:9, NLT

Control—to be in charge of, to direct, to lead or guide, to be in command of. "Control" is not a word we like to hear when it pertains to relationships. We, for the most part, like to think we have control and authority over the matters of our lives. We are not too receptive of someone else leading us through the ebb and flow of daily living. But for those of us who are in Christ Jesus, we love that He kindly and lovingly brought salvation to us, changed us spiritually, and blessed us with the Holy Spirit. He is the One in charge, guiding us through the ups and downs of life. The Holy Spirit—Spirit of God, Holy Ghost, Spirit of Life, or Spirit of Christ—has the authority and the guiding hand. He is the One who glorifies Christ through us and is the internal witness of our salvation, enlightening our understanding and changing our lives.

Verse 9 illustrates the importance of the Holy Spirit in our lives and confirms the work of our Savior, Jesus Christ. Christ came that we might have an abundant life. No longer are we led or ruled by our sinful nature—that is our past, which has been defeated, dethroned, and cast down. Jesus Christ, our hope of glory, sealed our victory by sending the Holy Spirit to lead and guide us to all things true.

The Holy Spirit's presence seals our position in Christ. The Holy Spirit steps in and draws a line in the sand. Either we are with Him, who is Life, or we remain disconnected, defeated, and lifeless, being controlled by our carnal nature. Our carnal nature points to death, spiritual death. The only thing that can change that is a submitted heart yearning to be set free. If you have Christ, you have the Holy Spirit dwelling in your heart packed with power!

In the Name of Jesus, I praise Your glorious name. I rejoice in knowing the Holy Spirit, whom You promised, abides in me. Thank You, Lord! Amen.

RELEASED!

Because through Christ Jesus the law of the Spirit who gives life has set you free from the law of sin and death.

ROMANS 8:2, NIV

Romans 8 is one of the most pivotal and theologically rich chapters in the entire Bible. It bestows upon the believer a plethora of blessings. Beginning with having the shackles of condemnation (guilt, shame) released, being filled with the Holy Spirit, and set free from sin's power, we are adopted into Christ's family, leading to the fullness of the expectation, or hope, of His love and promise. Summarily, the chapter closes with our embracing His ever-present goodness and faithfulness. Through God's love and Christ's sacrifice, which positioned us to receive the righteousness of God, we are made not guilty; and we can apply this reality when situations or circumstances try to condemn us.

Verse two of today's Scripture declares we are no longer being held captive with the guilt and shame of our past sins. We now have the right and desire to hold fast to the Spirit's leading. We are no longer tangled with Old Covenant sacrifices that ceremoniously atone for our sins yet have to be made over and over again. We are free from the rules and ordinances of the Law. By our faith the Holy Spirit takes command of our thoughts, our heart, and our actions. The Holy Spirit instructs us to move outward and onward in Christ Jesus. He empowers us and guides us through every storm, every heartbreak and every letdown. We have been released from the sin. We have been released from the shame. We have overcome death through Jesus Christ and have been released from its power.

We are an army of Christian soldiers that has gained access to the key that unlocks the door to our freedom. Reverend Sabine Baring-Gould from nineteenth-century England was inspired to write a hymn that galvanized children who walked to a neighboring town for Sunday school. The children were newly baptized believers, and he wanted to give them a marching song, the result, "Onward Christian Soldiers" was penned.

Like the little children in 1865 England, go onward Christian soldiers! You have been released!

❧

Father, I thank You for the power and authority of Your Word. I praise You for releasing me and planting my feet on the path of righteousness. In Jesus' Name. Amen.

FREEDOM, FREEDOM

"In the same way, count yourselves dead to sin but alive to God in Christ Jesus."

ROMANS 6:11, NIV

Life, and all that it encompasses, is filled with wonderful, engaging lessons that teach us, shape us, and, on occasion, knock us down. Life in Christ is like the journey of a man called Christian in the timeless book *Pilgrim's Progress*, by John Bunyan. Each encounter he experienced on his journey taught him more and more about himself, his life, and the Christian walk. Although some instances along the way caused moments of hesitation and contemplation, the characters he met mirrored life as we know it. From his guide, called Evangelist, to a companion named Faithful, Christian trekked on passing Worldly Wiseman, another called Ignorance, following the path named Wall of Salvation. Christian was not the most faithful believer, but he journeyed on to his destination, the Celestial City called Mount Zion.

Although somewhat far-reaching, Christian's mission was to reach heaven. His life was fueled by his faith and conviction that, whatever the cost, he would press on, conquering all that resisted him and reaching a heavenly life with Christ Jesus. Sin swayed him from time to time, and it challenged him to his core, but his faith endured.

The apostle Paul taught us this same lesson. Highlighted today is verse eleven; with us now dead to sin and resurrected with Christ. What now? We act or live out this victorious life we have in Jesus. So Christ has really set us free. Now let's make sure that we stay free and do not get tied up again in slavery or sin (Galatians 5:1, NLT)

What kind of freedom is this? Free to be part of God's family; free to obey God; free to be alive in Christ, rejoicing in the spiritual experience; and free to face life knowing Jesus Christ conquered sin and death so we may have a life abundant in the richness of His grace. Thank God for being free.

❧

Lord, I pray the power and authority that conquered sin and death be with me as I journey through this life. Thank You for victory so I, too, can proclaim, "Free at last! Free at last!" Thank God Almighty, I am free at last!

MOVING FORWARD

Well then, should we keep on sinning so that God can show us more and more kindness and forgiveness? Of course not! Since we have died to sin, how can we continue to live in it?

ROMANS 6:1-2, NLT

Some lessons learned in life can prove to be challenging. A child having touched a hot stove, is unlikely to touch it again. A teen anxious to learn to drive a car will not be so motivated after driving the family car through a garage wall. A saint most often will not tread the deep waters of sin if caught in the rough undertow of the transgression. That is how we live and learn. We take steps forward navigating through the twists and turns that come our way. Sometimes the choices are great, and they propel us upward and onward, reaching goal after goal. Then, on the other hand, sin and bad choices can send us around and around in a dismal cloud of guilt and confusion.

The book of Romans illustrates the profound vastness of Christ's power bestowed in us. Today's key verses open with two questions. Do we continually sin and live in it because we can? And, if we have died to sin, why would we go and dig it up again?

By God's grace, and our right standing with Him, our hearts are following a road of grace that is paved with His love. We have died to the ruling power of sin because God's grace transformed us. Sin is no longer our master. We are united with Christ and have been raised up to a new life in Him (Colossians 3:9-11). Our life is now hidden in Christ (Colossians 3:3). We are set apart (sanctified) and desire to move upward, growing closer and closer to Him.

So, having died (turned away from it) to sin, why would we want to continue to live in it? No one who is united with Christ, would consider taking a step backwards. We are *pressing upward, gaining new heights every day.* Just as the baby and the teen mature, so do we grow in God's grace.

Father, I thank You for Your grace. Help me to grow upward in You. As I move forward, may Your Word continue to permeate my heart. In Jesus' Name. Amen.

MORE THAN ENOUGH

For since we were restored to friendship with God, by the death of His Son while we were still His enemies, we will certainly be delivered from eternal punishment by His life.

ROMANS 5:10, NLT

Family reunions are great. We get to see relatives we have not seen for a long time. It's a great time of fellowship and sharing. The unfortunate thing is, like many families, we may have left last year's reunion with an unresolved conflict with a relative. We have not spoken to that relative since last year, and now we feel awkward about it. Too much time has passed and we need to right this wrong. Should we be loving and ask for forgiveness, or should we spend the weekend ducking and dodging making both of us miserable? This is a great time to ask ourselves *What would Jesus do?*

Today's Scripture explains that through Christ's death we have friendship, therefore fellowship, with God and we gain even more in His life. It is through His life that we receive peace and forgiveness of sins and escape the wrath that awaited us apart from Christ's death on the cross. Jesus Christ's life is the blueprint we use in building our lives. With Christ as our cornerstone, imagine using bricks to build our lives, with each laid brick representing one attribute of Christ's life. The brick of forgiveness reminds us of what we've received in Christ and what we can extend to others (like the relative at the family reunion). We demonstrate Christ-like love with the brick of peace and harmony, to those with whom we come in contact. Another brick is our commitment to live a sanctified or holy life, growing in the grace and knowledge of Jesus. As we continue to build, our lives illustrate an understanding and appreciation of what we have been spared and what we have.

So, what did Jesus do and what is He presently doing? By His shed blood, He reconciled and restored our fellowship with God. By Christ's life, He continually gives us much more grace, much more mercy, much more love that enables us to build our lives according to His standard. Can we ask much more than that?

❧

Lord, I pray for Your grace as I strive to live according to Your likeness. Let me mature in the image of You and not myself. In Jesus' Name. Amen.

AN UNEXPECTED OCCURRENCE

And they said, "Believe in the Lord Jesus Christ, and thou shalt be saved, and thy house."

ACTS 16:31, KJV

Have you ever been going about your regular, everyday activities and something unexpected occurred? How did you feel? How did you react? Well, in this often recited passage, Paul and Silas were placed in the dungeon and under surveillance of a guard. The guard was going on about his normal daily routine—watching prisoners. The guard may not have even been fully aware of who these two new guys really were, but he would find out.

The guard, while tending the prisoners, asked a pivotal question. Today's text highlights Paul and Silas' answer, which gives the backbone of salvation—that if we believe, we will be saved. What a great response, right in the midst of what could have been considered an inopportune time. They didn't let false accusation and imprisonment get in the way of sharing the Gospel of Jesus Christ. This is a wonderful lesson—we must always, no matter the situation, be ready to offer Christ.

This ordinary day proved to bring several jarring events that would give the guard much to be concerned about, but it ended with an unexpected promise for him and his family. He witnessed an earthquake, prisoners' bands loosed, and prison gates opened. Thinking prisoners would run away, the guard despaired to the point of taking his own life. But he experienced the grace of God through Paul and Silas, which provoked his question about salvation. Today's Scripture was his answer. It shows that even in some of our weakest moments, hope is just around the corner.

We need to just ask and wait for the response. The guard assumed all was lost but found hope in the Christ of Paul and Silas. The day turned out to be not so regular after all; it led him to the ones who would answer his question about what he needed to do to be saved.

When we answer the call of salvation and grow to trust God in everything, unexpected blessings and, yes, miracles can come our way.

🌂

Father, help us to look for You in the unforeseen events of our lives. I pray that we won't be manipulated by our circumstances but look forward to unexpected blessings in our walk with You. Amen!

POWER OF THE GREAT I AM

Jesus said unto her, I am the Resurrection and the Life: he that believeth in Me, though he were dead, yet shall he live.

JOHN 11:25, NIV

The story of Lazarus' death and miraculous resurrection is probably one of the most well-known stories in the Bible. It reveals how our Savior uses even the most trying circumstances to teach us biblical truths. It demonstrates Jesus Christ's omnipotence over life, death, and the grave. Jesus reached beyond the natural and did the supernatural.

As the days passed after Lazarus' death, his sisters, Mary and Martha, did not understand why Jesus had not returned to comfort them. But, we know that His thoughts are not our thoughts neither are our ways His ways (Isaiah 55:8). Jesus wanted to use Lazarus' death as an opportunity to glorify God, and to demonstrate His power over death and the grave. Jesus wanted Mary and Martha, and all those present, to understand that physical death is not the final word in the Christian's life and that He has all authority over every circumstance, every crisis, and every defeat.

Today's verse illustrates one of the seven great I AM affirmations of Jesus Christ. Jesus declared that He had all power over all who died and all who live. This is an example for us. Jesus has power over every situation in our lives, even the grave. When we are faced with tragedy, even death, let us not lose hope but remind ourselves of Jesus Christ's love for us. Jesus said He will never leave us nor forsake us, and we know His Word is true. He has the power to do all things, even fix the situations that seem impossible to us. He is God.

Let us remember He *is* the Resurrection and the Life. We do not have to experience tragedy and death alone, but we can rejoice with renewed hope, knowing Jesus Christ is the great I AM. We live in the power of Jesus' resurrection. He is the great *I AM* of our lives!

Lord, I honor You for the majesty and power of Your miracles. I rejoice in knowing with assurance that I have a blessed hope in You. I bless You in Jesus' Name. Amen.

JESUS, I COME

*If we confess our sins, He is faithful and just and will forgive us our sins
and purify us from all unrighteousness.*

1 JOHN 1:9, NIV

A well-known hymn titled "Just As I Am" was written in the late
1800s. The writer was not someone we would recognize as
the composer of such a personal and dynamic hymn to God. She
was an embittered lady who blamed her maladies and disabilities
on God. Her intolerable character drew the attention of a minister
who took time to talk with her, minister to her, and to share the
love and goodness of God. That lady, Charlotte Elliot, questioned
the minister about God and the proposed cure he presented to
her—faith in God, forgiveness of her sins, and hope in Jesus Christ
as her personal Savior.

Miss Elliot could not quite grasp the thought of such a Savior
who would forgive her and forgive every misstep and every negative
thought and deed she committed. As her heart began to soften, the
tender words the minister shared continued to penetrate her mind
and heart. Miss Elliot received Christ into her heart and marveled
at the miracle she witnessed as she was received by Him just as she
was![15]

In today's Scripture reading, once we identify our sins we must
then humbly confess them. We must recognize God's faithfulness
and know He will forgive us. His forgiveness brings a cleansing
that can't be understood apart from the mystery of His love.

Just as the composer of the song noted, we can be beaten
down, angry, stubborn, and defiant in receiving God's grace and
peace through salvation—but praise to the King, who washes away
all of our sins and leaves them covered in the sea of forgetfulness.
We don't have to get cleaned up. We don't have to do anything
to get God's attention. The only thing He desires of us is that we
come—just as we are, without one plea. But that His blood was
shed for us. He bids us to come to Him. Let your heart say, "O
Lamb of God, Jesus, I come, I come!"

✨

*Oh Lamb of God, I bow my head and worship You. In Your majesty You
receive me still, and I bless You for Your cleansing blood. Thank You, Father,
for allowing me to come just as I am. In Jesus' Name. Amen.*

REDEMPTION'S PROMISE

He personally carried our sins in his body on the cross so that we can be dead to sin and live for what is right.

1 PETER 2:24, NLT

Most parents tend to raise their children to not make the same mistakes they did growing up. They want to order their children's steps around life's obstacles to keep them from making mistakes and to keep them from suffering. Their logic: why confront something harmful that will hinder your growth when you don't have to. If you do that, or go that way, this is what can happen. Parents share what happened to them, but are we hurting or helping their growth as they adapt to life? The answers vary and depend on how we were raised.

Today's Scripture has a different approach to assuring our life in Christ Jesus. From the beginning, our limitations in following the biblical precepts laid down by God have affected our fellowship with Him. We have stumbled and have fallen over and over again. We have made sacrifice after sacrifice attempting to maintain our right standing but hopelessly failed. But Christ humbly substituted for us. We have God's Word in our hearts and we are filled with His Spirit. Christ has laid down His life so that we can live in Him. Jesus Christ took our sins, and all of our shame and suffering, when He shed His blood on the cross. His life-changing, healing blood did not just cover our sins; but it washed them away, setting us on higher ground and sealing our fellowship and our covenantal relationship with God. That certainly warrants a shout!

Looking at the Scripture even further, Christ's blood healed us spiritually. All of the gaps in our lives that were/are filled with guilt, shame, doubts, and transgressions, were filled with His love, grace, and mercy. He committed Himself to us so that in Him our lives would be complete.

Jesus promised He would never leave us nor forsake us. He promised us a life more abundant. He promised to lead us on the path of righteousness, and He did it. Glory to our Holy and Glorious Savior!

❧

Father, in the precious Name of Jesus, I thank You for the promises of Your Word. I bless You for the price that was paid on Calvary. Hallelujah! Amen.

THE PERFECT EXAMPLE

And once made perfect, He became the source of eternal salvation for all who obey Him.

HEBREWS 5:9, NIV

We can all attribute much of our maturity and wisdom to lessons learned in our lives—some from childhood that made a lasting imprint and others from recent and present day mistakes. Some were painful lessons, but we adapted, grew, and matured. In hindsight, we probably would choose to avoid those hard lessons and move forward with no more than a ripple in the smooth waters of life. It sounds wonderful, but experiences like pain, suffering, and disappointments help us grow and can even give us a measurement of our spiritual maturity. Through Jesus Christ, who has set the standard for our lives, we can judge what is right and wrong, good and bad. He sets things in order, and He is our Mediator before the presence of God.

Today's verse identifies Jesus Christ as High Priest. But He became even better. Jesus Christ humbly wrapped Himself in flesh, was made in our likeness, and became the perfect example for us. He was divine and human, priestly and obedient. Christ became that better example—that better offering, that better peacemaker for us—and was the foundation and the Chief Cornerstone of this great salvation.

It is because of Jesus that we are saved. It is because of Jesus that we have eternal security. It is because of Jesus that we live and move and have our being (Acts 17:28). It is because our Lord and Savior became the guarantor of this everlasting covenant sealing it with His blood so that we can now grow in wisdom and have the right to come boldly unto the throne of grace, so we may obtain mercy and find grace to help in time of need (Hebrews 4:16).

Let us rejoice in knowing our Lord and Savior, Jesus Christ, is the source of our salvation. Let us, by faith, follow in the path of righteousness He has set before us because He is the only One who can lead and guide us.

❧

Lord, thank You for teaching me not only by experience but by Your example. Help me to be an example to others of how to live a life that brings You honor and glory in all things. In Jesus' Name. Amen!

A LOVING GOD

Since now we have all been justified by His blood, how much more shall we be saved from God's eternal wrath.

ROMANS 5:9, NIV

One of the most powerful forces on earth is love. Why? Because God, the Almighty, Sovereign, Covenantal God, so loved the world that He gave His only begotten Son (John 3:16). God gave; we received. With God's love, the vast breach that once separated us from Him in fellowship is now filled. By faith we are justified, or made righteous, by Jesus Christ. Sealed in Christ's righteousness, we endeavor to live a holy life. This life of holiness, or sanctification, delivers us from the power of sin and strengthens us day-by-day to be more like Christ.

Today's Scripture is taken from one of the most powerful chapters in the Bible. Earlier, in chapter 5, the apostle Paul speaks of our peace of God, the security or gratitude in experiencing Christ's blessings. He adds that we also have peace with God, the fellowship we share with God through reconciliation. Reconciliation, the restoration of our broken fellowship with God, was made possible by Jesus Christ. In turn, our relationship with Christ becomes the barometer for love, peace, and harmony with one another.

When we see ourselves with just an old rough exterior and give up on ourselves, remember that God sees our value and our potential. That's why He sent Jesus in the first place, to do for us what we couldn't do for ourselves. His desire is that we give Him consent to do His work in our lives—to justify us and bring us into right standing with God—and to draw us closer to Him through sanctification.

Think about the ship the Titanic. As the boat began to sink, it broke into a myriad of pieces. There were people who drowned, and then there were people who couldn't see but hung onto a broken piece of the boat. Those people who hung on were saved and made it to land. God does the same for us through Jesus' blood. When we can't see our way, He makes the way of escape for us.

❧

Father, I bless You for the remarkable love and gift of Jesus Christ. I bless You for the miraculous work You have done on our behalf to bring us back to together in unity and in love. Amen.

We are Children of God

*And because we are his children, God has sent the Spirit of his Son
into our hearts, prompting us to call out, "Abba, Father."*
Galatians 4:6, NLT

In storybooks and movies, orphans are often depicted as children yearning to be cute enough, sweet enough, good enough, or fortunate enough to be picked by a loving couple. Many of those young protagonists are often overlooked because they aren't *enough* of something until the "right" couple comes along. Well, God didn't read a profile, look at a picture, or observe us at life before He made His decision to pick us. Because of His inexplicable love, we didn't have to be enough of anything to be chosen by Him. Every person orphaned by sin who believes in his or her heart that Jesus Christ is Lord and was raised from the dead has been adopted into God's family. Now we are joint-heirs with Jesus Christ—no longer in fear of not being good enough.

As you look toward the hot, summer days to come, bask in the warmth of God's love for you and the new relationship you have with Him as a result of that love. For the next couple of months, turn your attention toward your identity as God's child and an heir of the promise who has moved from bondage to freedom, from fear to courage (Romans 8:15).

THE GIFT OF PREDESTINATION

Having predestinated us unto the adoption of children by Jesus Christ to himself, according to the good pleasure of his will.

EPHESIANS 5:1, KJV

Some parents are blessed to work with a birth mother before her baby is born. As the adopting family, they get to choose their baby even before the baby is born, sight unseen. Before personality is shaped or habits developed, adopting parents choose their child before birth.

That is what God did for us. He chose us in love before we were born. He predestined us, setting forth our destiny in Him even before our birth. What a glorious reminder—one filled with strength and confidence, that gives courage for life's journey through this world.

Understanding elements of adoption in ancient Rome can help us truly appreciate today's Scripture. Children adopted during that era were given all the rights and privileges of a child born into a family, had all rights to the old family completely eliminated, and had any debts or other kinds of obligations erased, considered never to have existed.

Is that not the perfect picture of what God has done for us in Christ Jesus? God has given us all rights and privileges of a child born into His family. Through Jesus Christ, all rights (and penalties) of the old family—Adam's family—have been completely eliminated. All debts, or obligations to sin, have been eradicated.

God always knew we would be His—that is the beauty of predestination. The criteria for making the choices He has made will forever remain a mystery. We were picked out beforehand, chosen out of many. Seriously meditate on what Christ has actually done for us. It is nothing less than mind-blowing! God's incredible love for us, and His determination and yearning to bring His creation back into right fellowship with Him, can clearly be seen in the gift of predestination.

❧

Faithful Father, I bless You for the incredible provision of predestination. I am encouraged by this knowledge, which gives me the courage to live life on purpose—to find out why it was Your good pleasure and Your will to choose me—so that I can live out my destiny in the earth. For this, I give You praise and thanksgiving. In Jesus' Name. Amen.

FROM GOOD TO GREAT

If you then, being evil, know how to give good gifts to your children, how much more will your heavenly Father give the Holy Spirit to those who ask Him!

LUKE 11:13, NKJV

What a privilege we have to go to God in prayer, to pray not just for good things but for the great. Jesus, when asked by one of His disciples to teach them to pray, taught three critical lessons about prayer and moving from good to great (Luke 11:1-13).

First He taught them the *purpose* of prayer. His followers were to go to the heavenly Father, asking for God's Kingdom to be expanded, for their daily bread, for forgiveness, for protection from temptation, and deliverance from the evil one. In other words, every aspect of a follower's life was to be the subject of prayer. Our heavenly Father is concerned about all that concern us, and prayer is the vehicle through which we express our needs to God.

Next, Jesus taught His disciples about the *process* of prayer. His followers are to pray with persistence, expecting answers. Using the audacity of an urgent midnight caller, Jesus taught His followers to persevere in prayer.

Finally, Jesus taught His disciples the *promise* of answered prayers. Just as human parents meet the needs of their children, our heavenly Father will meet our every need. In fact, Jesus used the illustration of good gifts (bread and fish) that earthly parents give to their children to prepare His disciples for the great gift— the Holy Spirit—that the Father would give on the Day of Pentecost.

So it is we are assured that our heavenly Father supplies our needs. By giving us the Holy Spirit, the great gift, He assures us that He can also give us the good gifts we need. Our heavenly Father cares for us and provides what we need according to His will. Isn't it great to know that as children of God, we are assured that through the presence of the Holy Spirit, we have moved from good to great?

❧

Heavenly Father, I come to You with the confidence that You supply my every need. Thank You for the Holy Spirit and for every good gift that comes from You. I pray for Your kingdom to come and Your will to be done in my life. In Jesus' Name. Amen.

ADOPTIVE BENEFITS

For ye have not received the spirit of bondage again to fear; but ye have received the Spirit of adoption, whereby we cry, Abba, Father.

ROMANS 8:15, KJV

Today's text gently reminds us of one of the many blessed benefits we have as born-again believers: we have been adopted into the family of God and we are now joint-heirs with Jesus Christ, the only begotten Son of the Father!

Before receiving the Holy Spirit, we were much like orphans—alone and unconnected to our spiritual Father. We were also without hope of eternal life, living our lives steeped in sin, and we were slaves to our fears. To illustrate this point further, consider orphans and how they live unconnected and in fear. They feel unconnected because they don't have a sense of family, a sense of belonging. Such was the state of our souls prior to being filled with the Holy Spirit; we suffered from being unconnected to God the Father. Then Jesus came, and with Him came the love and protection of His Father. God's love has been given without measure; it has brought peace to our lives and satisfaction to our souls. No longer do we live in fear as others who have no hope! Instead, we rejoice in the fact that we are children of God and joint heirs with Christ; we share the privilege of calling His Father our Father.

All the intimacies that come with this parent-child relationship have been given to us as children of God. So much so that God entreats us (Spirit-filled believers) to cast "the whole of your care [all your anxieties, all your worries, all your concerns, once and for all] on Him, for He cares for you affectionately and cares about you watchfully" (1 Peter 5:7, AMP). The beauty of it all is that, like an adoptive parent, God chose to love us as His own. There was nothing we did to deserve His love, nor could we ever earn it. So today let's praise God our Father for adoptive benefits.

❧

Father, thank You for the benefit of adoption that enables me to rest in the security of Your endless love. Help me bring glory to Your name, to walk worthy of Your love, and to share that love with everyone I encounter today. Amen.

GOD'S CHILD

Beloved, now we are children of God; and it has not yet been revealed what we shall be, but we know that when He is revealed, we shall be like Him, for we shall see Him as He is.

1 JOHN 3:2, NKJV

Mara never knew her father. When she was three, her mother abandoned her. She went through many foster homes. In some, she was terribly abused. At nine, she didn't have a favorite color. She was too anxious and nervous to sit down. She didn't trust anyone. She didn't know herself.

She went to live with kind people who cared for her. She began to heal, slowly. The kind people told her that God knew her and loved her. Still her pain was overwhelming. One night, doubled over in grief, she cried out, "How can you know me when my mother doesn't know me?"

It was true that Mara's mother no longer knew her. As sad as that was to Mara, the fact was that Mara was changing, slowly but steadily, because she was loved. By fourteen, she was a joyful, vibrant girl who encouraged other children that they could make it through. She knew that she was lovable and worthy of having a favorite color. She graduated from eighth grade surrounded by her pastor, friends, and her foster mother, who loved her dearly and told her that she was a valuable child of God.

Love changes us. God loves us as His children, and His love transforms us, slowly, steadily, from what we were to what He wants us to be. As we continue in relationship with Him, we grow, we heal, and we deepen. Whatever the heartache, He is able to comfort. Whatever the situation, He is able to bring us through. We don't know ahead of time what the change is going to be. Some day we will look up amazed at what God has done with us. Furthermore, a greater change is coming, for when we enter into heaven we will see Jesus and we will be like Him—glorified, pure, spotless, whole.

❧

Jesus, I pray for all the motherless and fatherless children. I pray that they will seek You as their Parent. I thank You for being my Father and for transforming me. Today, give me a heart to let others know of Your transforming love, grace, and power. Amen.

SPEAK TO US HOLY SPIRIT

For his Spirit joins with our spirit to affirm that we are God's children.

ROMANS 8:16, NLT

There are turning points in our lives: events that change us, jobs that give us a new perspective, people that change us. Before life was one way. Now it is different.

When the Holy Spirit comes into our lives, the change is drastic—"transformation," Paul calls it, a "renewing of your mind" (Romans 12:2). Old things pass away; everything is new (2 Corinthians 5:17). What is new is the presence of the Holy Spirit, right there, all the time. He joins with us; He hooks up with us. As we make decisions, the Holy Spirit shows us direction that we had not seen before. As we look at ourselves, the Holy Spirit opens up new possibilities, a new perspective. He whispers in our ears, "You are God's child."

Previously we would yield to temptation. We would cheat, or lie, or take the selfish route. Now the Spirit pulls us back. "Look at it this way," the Spirit says, "See as a child of God ought to see." Previously in the midst of struggle, we would go into a rage, sure that our circumstances were "unfair." Or we would close ourselves in, be depressed, escape, get a drink, run away. Now we cry out to God, "Father, Dad, I need help. I know You can handle this" (Romans 8:15).

The Holy Spirit produces new characteristics in us: love, joy, peace, long-suffering, gentleness, goodness, faith, meekness, temperance. "Fruit" Paul calls these (Galatians 5:22-23). Fruit starts popping up inside us. Previously, we would have laid into that person, blown up, cursed. Now we take a step back; we choose different words. Something opens up inside us, an insight, a sensitivity. We are amazed at ourselves. The Holy Spirit lays the fruit out so that we see the evidence that we are God's children.

It's a different life—a life where we know grace and peace, reassurance and belonging. The Holy Spirit speaks to our spirits, whatever the circumstances, to let us know that today God is there, taking care of us, guiding us, lifting us up, settling us down.

※

Holy Spirit, speak to me. Let me feel Your presence. Whatever I face today, let me respond as a child of God. Strengthen me. Humble me. Give me a mind to trust You. Amen.

TESTIMONY

Behold what manner of love the Father has bestowed on us, that we should be called children of God! Therefore the world does not know us, because it did not know Him.

1 JOHN 3:1, NKJV

On September 11, 2001, Genelle Guzman-McMillan was on the stairs at the thirteenth floor of the World Trade Center when the tower fell. She was trapped in the rubble; her leg was crushed, but she was alive. She was rescued after twenty-seven hours—the last person to be pulled out alive. Later, she testified at her church, Brooklyn Tabernacle, of her miraculous survival, her miraculous recovery from her injuries, how God sustained her during those twenty-seven hours, and how God drew her close during her recovery. A year later, *Time* magazine did a story about her. The writers had a difficult time with her testimony: "We scarcely have a vocabulary for these people." They grappled with how to "fully register people" like Genelle. Her friends said that she was not depressed, but *Time* searched for signs of post-traumatic stress disorder. She told about getting married and how she and her husband had come to the Lord in the months after 9/11. She talked about a profound sense of purpose and peace. *Time* asked, "How does Genelle Guzman-McMillan find herself again?"[16]

We each have a testimony of God's loving kindness: how He has cared for us and brought us through. The world may not get it. The world may give us the credit for our success. The world searches for signs that it wasn't really a miracle. But we know. It didn't have to be that way. God carried us, blessed us, comforted us. We ought to be traumatized, bitter, depressed, and anxious. But God made a way for healing, forgiveness, joy, and peace. There are things about us that people in the world cannot understand because they don't know Who we know. We can tell whoever we meet, and some will hear the power of our testimony. But they will understand only if they, too, know Jesus.

❧

Jesus, there are times I struggle. There are times I am in the midst of trouble on every hand and side. I thank You for Your love. I know that I can turn it all over to You. Let me see Your miracles in my life, that I may praise You with all my heart. Amen.

WHO BELONGS?

For you are all sons of God through faith in Christ Jesus.

GALATIANS 3:26, NKJV

There were rifts years ago in Janet's family. One brother had angered another. One sister married a man from a race their aunt didn't like. The separations were most apparent on Christmas and Thanksgiving. Some were invited; others were not. The children grew up without knowing their cousins. Everyone had a reason why they couldn't get along. No one forgave; they hardly remembered what needed to be forgiven. Their father tried to get them to reconcile, but no one would listen. Then he died violently, hit by a drunk driver. His death shocked them all into forgiveness and understanding.

Similar riffs can occur in the body of Christ. Who belongs to the family? Who is excluded from the family? Who belongs to our churches? Who is excluded? We decide every day who belongs. Or doesn't. Let's get down to the basics, Paul told the Galatians. We who love Jesus are all children of God, brothers and sisters, belonging to the same family. Whatever our background, our socioeconomic level, our race, our neighborhood, we belong in God's family because we believe and love Jesus Christ.

It may take some patience to include one person. It may take a lot of understanding to include another. We may have to lay aside a few stereotypes. We may have to lay aside our pride. We may have to get past some hurt. We may need to forgive or be forgiven. Yet Paul challenges us to include each other, whatever effort we have to make. The core, Paul says, is faith in Christ Jesus. Don't expect to look alike. Don't expect to agree on everything. Expect that we all love Jesus. When our differences get in the way, Jesus will show us the way to love and include each other. Jesus paid a heavy price for us to be family, a violent death that should shock us into finding a way to love one another. This is how much it mattered to Him that we invite each other in.

❧

Oh Lord, You have sent many believers into my life. Help me to recognize them as my brothers and sisters. Soften my heart. As I go through this day, give me the discernment and courage to include those who love You. Thank You for including me in Your family as one of Your children. Amen.

No Cross, No Crown

And if children, then heirs; heirs of God, and joint-heirs with Christ; if so be that we suffer with him, that we may be also glorified together.

ROMANS 8:17, KJV

Most of us are wired in the flesh to avoid pain. We don't want to suffer. We don't want heartache. Yet the paradox of the Christian life is that the pain of suffering for the believer ultimately results in glory with God.

As born-again believers, we are heirs of God and joint-heirs with Christ. Being an heir to something, or someone, denotes an inheritance, basically something for nothing. The inheritance is left for the heir as an act of extended love. Leaving an inheritance tells the inheritor, "I love you so much I want to give you a reminder of me." What love! God has done that for us—His children. He's given us an inheritance of eternal life. As born-again believers, we are part of His spiritual family. Being joint-heirs with Christ, we are covered, protected, and taken care of.

Ironically, when we think of the inheritance, we may mistakenly limit our thinking to the promises of life, joy, peace, and victory. And, yes, we inherit these as joint-heirs with Christ. Yet today's passage teaches us that we also inherit the privilege of suffering with Christ. Christ suffered and died to secure eternal life for us. Before His death and resurrection, He let His followers know that they too would have to take up their cross and follow Him (Mark 8:34), and they too would suffer tribulation (John 16:33). But today's passage assures us that we not only suffer with Christ, but we will also glory with Him. We will receive our crown of glory when Jesus returns for us (1 Peter 5:4).

Be encouraged today. Though we suffer with Christ, we shall receive a crown. God is faithful!

Dear God, my Father, in the name of Jesus I come telling You thank You for loving me. I thank You for the suffering and, for one day, being glorified together with Christ. Knowing this helps me to overcome any challenge that comes my way. I can get through it and keep moving forward. I love You and thank You. Amen.

GOD KNOWS US

Before I formed thee in the belly I knew thee; and before thou camest forth out of the womb I sanctified thee, and I ordained thee a prophet unto the nations.

JEREMIAH 1:5, KJV

How many of us have uttered the words "I can't do it", only to be told, "Yes, you can; I know you can do it"? We wonder how this individual can be so confident in our abilities to perform a particular thing when we are equally apprehensive about what is before us. Could it be that his or her confidence is based on what he or she knows about us?

God knew Jeremiah because He created him. Jeremiah's name means "whom Jehovah has appointed," and his ministry spanned forty years. When he was a young man, Jeremiah received the Word of the Lord concerning the call on his life. Right away Jeremiah expressed his inability to accept the call, stating that he was too young. However, God let Jeremiah know that before he was conceived in his mother's womb there was a plan for his life: he was to be a prophet to the nations. While the Scriptures do not tell us whether Jeremiah had any other apprehensions after that revelation, we do know that Jeremiah accepted his call and became one of the greatest prophets that ever lived.

Isn't it wonderful knowing that God knows His children so well? He knows everything about us because, like Jeremiah, He created us. God has equipped His children with awesome gifts, and there is much to do in the kingdom of God. While we may experience anxiety when God calls us to service, the Bible lets us know that He is always with us. And with this assurance we know that we can do anything God wants us to do. When we consider that God knows His children, it is humbling. What a blessing it is to be known and loved by such an awesome God!

❦

Thank You, Father, for Your infinite wisdom. You know everything about me because You created me. You have given me the ability to accomplish what You have called me to do, and I have full assurance that You will be with me every step of the way. In Jesus' Name. Amen!

THE OVERCOMER

He that overcometh shall inherit all things; and I will be his God, and he shall be my son.

REVELATION 21:7, KJV

John recorded the Revelation from the Holy Spirit during a time when the people of God were under extreme persecution. They were faced with beatings, torture, even death. Imagine the emotional and mental turmoil they experienced. Imagine how they felt as they were threatened with defeat.

Yet the message John received was to encourage the people of that time, and all believers since, that they would not be defeated. He let them know (and us as well) that the ones who overcome will actually inherit the eternal blessings of God. The sons and daughters of God will be the ones that overcome. In fact, God saves us by His Son and seals us through His Spirit; in His infinite wisdom and mercy, He causes us to triumph (2 Corinthians 2:4).

John wrote not just to the saints of his time but also to saints in the end time. The days are growing darker and darker. Sin tugs at our spirit, old habits haunt us—bitterness, negative communication and relationships try to wedge their way back into our lives, openly and in disguise. But it is when we persevere, and fight against the evil and overcome, that we attain our promised inheritance.

We will confront many issues and circumstances that may tempt us to act out of the will of God—pressure, shame, pride, the world's standards, and false expectations. However, let us remember today's Scripture, "He that overcometh shall inherit all things!" That word is given to encourage us to stay strong through our trials. That word is given to remind us that the Lord is our God and we are His sons and daughters.

We overcome because our heavenly Father has ordained us to overcome. God has already planned our victory. God has already orchestrated our breakthrough. We will make it. We will win!

🦅

Heavenly Father, full of grace and mercy, thank You for making me an overcomer so that I will inherit Your promises and dwell in Your blessings. In Jesus' Name. Amen.

LINING UP WITH GOD

In this the children of God and the children of the devil are manifest: Whoever does not practice righteousness is not of God, nor is he who does not love his brother.

1 JOHN 3:10, NKJV

Mommy, I want a baby brother," the little girl said. Then the brother arrived. He sat in Mommy's lap. He took the little girl's toys. He ate a lot. It was hard for her to remember why she wanted a little brother.

Brothers (and sisters) are challenging. John tells us to love our brothers and sisters in Christ. What was he thinking? Didn't he know how hard this would be? Plus, he draws a line in the sand: love them or forget about being aligned with God. No need to make a list of all the reasons why they cannot be loved. Just love them. Not because they deserve it. Not because you find them lovable despite their faults. Love them when they don't feel lovable. Love them when they have done wrong. Love them when they have wronged you in ways that are impossible to forget and unreasonable to forgive.

How can such love be attained? It is not humanly possible. Yes, God replies, these things are not possible for us, but with God all things are possible (Matthew 19:26). Furthermore, God set the example when He gave His Son for us, not because we were lovable, not because we were faultless, not because we deserved it; He just loved us. Because of His love we are capable of loving our brothers and sisters, whoever and whatever they are. We can love them because God loves them. We can love them enough to face their faults and to face their sorrows. We can be lovingly honest. We can be helpful and yet tough enough to challenge them to be better. We can lift them up in prayer and cry out to God for them. When we run out of love (as well as patience, understanding, and compassion), God will fill us back up, and give us more love to give.

Oh Lord, thank You for loving me. Thank You for loving my brothers and sisters. Let me see them in the light of Your love. May I lean on Your wisdom and understanding, that I may respond to them in love. Amen.

THE GREATER ONE LIVES IN US

Ye are of God, little children, and have overcome them: because greater is he that is in you, than he that is in the world.

1 JOHN 4:4, KJV

Have you ever felt like you were up against someone or something bigger than yourself? Maybe it was regarding a special cause for which you were fighting, or a personal issue significant to you but seemingly unimportant to others. Once we realize that we are on the right side, it strengthens us. The support of others encourages us even more!

As children of God we have an inherent position of victory in Christ that is not diminished by antagonists or "haters." The Holy Spirit is our strength. When we have this understanding of ourselves as believers, we can face this world.

The Bible teaches us that we will encounter opposition to our faith. That opposition is prompted by the spirit of what the apostle John called the anti-Christ. This spirit had begun to show up in the church as false prophets and false teachings. It was represented by those who spouted doctrines that were against Christ or who substituted other ideas for the Truth of God. The apostle John encouraged the church not to fear but to realize it possessed the greater Spirit within.

The anti-Christ spirit might show up in bold or subtle ways. Either way, we have within us the ability to discern and recognize it in the workplace, social circumstances, and the various world systems. We can stand for Truth, however and whenever we encounter falsehood.

We don't face it alone. The Greater One is within us. The Spirit of Truth is greater than the spirit of the anti-Christ. He's greater than the spirit that says there is no God, denies the power of Christ, or teaches false things about Him. The victory that Jesus has over this world is the same victory we have in it. The opposition might be fierce, but He has overcome and so have we in and through Him!

✺

Father, thank You for the Holy Spirit, which dwells in me. Your Spirit enables me to discern what is false and what is true, and it fortifies me to walk in Your Truth. Help me to have the mind of an overcomer from day to day, for You are great in me. And so it is!

THE TRUE ANOINTING

And as for you, the anointing which you received from Him abides in you,
and you have no need for anyone to teach you; but as His anointing teaches
you about all things, and is true and is not a lie, and just as it has taught
you, you abide in Him.

1 JOHN 2:27, NASB

There is a change in our lives when we receive the Holy Spirit.
It's hard to explain to someone else. All we can tell them is that
the Holy Spirit is amazing, wonderful, and every other superlative
we can come up with.

A very important thing we can tell others is that the Holy Spirit
is *for real.* The Spirit of God has truly come to abide in us. Like the
wind, we feel God's presence. He opens up our understanding. We
see things differently. The fruit of the Spirit grows in us—love, joy,
peace, longsuffering, gentleness, goodness, faith, kindness, self-
control (Galatians 5:22-23). As the fruit grows, we see our lives
and our surroundings differently. We prioritize what God values.
Superficial distractions fall away. It's not us. It's the Spirit of God in
us, showing us what is right and valuable and true.

John recognizes that others may doubt the anointing of the Holy
Spirit, and we must be wary that others' doubts and deceptions do
not sway us. We ourselves may be perplexed at the changes we see
in ourselves. In times of discouragement, we may even question
whether God continues to abide in us. So John reassures us. God
is abiding in us. This is true and not a lie. Certainly, there are many
difficulties in this life. We are not yet in heaven. But God is with us
constantly. We can depend on Him. We can seek His guidance. We
can trust His strength and His wisdom. We must not let anyone
tell us that God is an impersonal higher power. He has made our
relationship with Him very personal. He sent His own Spirit to
abide within us personally.

Oh Lord, thank You for making it personal. Let Your Spirit speak to me so
that I will not be discouraged, so that I will live true to Your Word. Help me
to be conscious of what You are teaching me. Thank You for Your constant
presence in my life. Amen.

I STAND CORRECTED!

Furthermore we have had fathers of our flesh which corrected us, and we gave them reverence: shall we not much rather be in subjection unto the Father of spirits, and live?

HEBREWS 12:9, KJV

Do you recall being a child and when you did not follow the instructions of your parents you would receive correction from your parents? During the process of receiving correction, we would sometimes wonder if they loved us anymore or if they really enjoyed seeing us unhappy because of the correction. As we matured we would come to an understanding that the correction was not for our parents' benefit, but it was for our good.

Now that we are children of God, from time to time we come under correction from our heavenly Father. He wants to remove errors from our life through His correction to improve us, not to destroy us! The trouble we may find ourselves in is not to punish us but to train us. Training is a process by which we learn to walk in His ways. If we delight in His ways, we will discover that the training improves our walk with Christ. What are you willing to go through to improve?

If we can be corrected by our earthly parents, whom many of us respect(ed), how can we not even the more be subjected to our heavenly Father's correction? There are certain things we must endure in order to develop into full mature Christians. Let's decide today that we are going to make the proper changes.

❧

Heavenly Father, I call out to You, asking that You help me to walk in Your ways and under Your authority. I know that You know the end from the beginning, and I truly trust You have my best interest at heart. Lord, have Your way in me. In Jesus' Name. Amen.

TOUGH LOVE

If ye endure chastening, God dealeth with you as with sons; for what son is he whom the father chasteneth not?

HEBREWS 12:7, KJV

Isn't it strange that things we were chastised for when we were children are all of a sudden cute to the grandparents of our children? For some strange reason a different set of values emerge as we get older, and what seemed punishable when we were children is now deemed as minor or insignificant. If we model this pattern, we miss the initial lesson of disciplinary action that our parents sought to teach us, which are honesty, integrity, and respect. Can't we hear those words now, "This is going to hurt me more than it is going to hurt you."

The Bible tells us that as children of God we are to expect correction. We are not to shun being corrected because it is an act of God's love toward us. For whom the Father loves He also chastens. Chastening means to nurture, correct, and instruct by disciplinary action. Isn't it great to know that God loves us enough to correct us when we are doing things against His will or are heading in the wrong direction? What parent would allow his or her children to play with matches or be disrespectful toward other people without correcting them? As such, the Father deals with His children in a way different from the harsh treatment of the world. The Father deals with us in love.

The world system of correction is punitive, but our Lord deals graciously with us. Though there are times when we may feel as though His hand is heavy, we know we are covered by His amazing grace as He lovingly corrects a multitude of sin. The world may deal with us according to wrath, but the Father deals with us in love. The world will send us to jail, and we may return the same; but when the Father corrects us, we return with changed hearts, minds, and lives. If we remain steadfast in being disciplined, it shows the faithfulness of God as Father and our commitment as children of God.

Dear Lord, I thank You for loving me enough to correct me when I work contrary to Thy Word. Continue creating in me a clean heart and renewing me in You. In Jesus' Mighty Name. Amen.

LOVE GOD

Love the Lord your God with all your heart and with all your soul and with all your mind and with all your strength.

MARK 12:30, TNIV

We think of love as a feeling, an emotion that comes beyond our control. Yet God commands that we love Him. The implication is that love is under our control and is even our choice. We can decide. We can choose to love God, with all that that means—we want to know what He wants, we want to please Him, we follow His commands, we do His will—even when our desire is to head in another direction. We can choose to not love God and ignore His love for us.

We stand at a crossroad—love God or don't love God. We take that first little step toward Him, maybe because we trust Him, maybe because we really need some help. That first little step, and we find that He is lovable. He is goodness itself, gentle and kind. In our worst stress, He eases the burden from our shoulders. In our sorrow, He wraps His arms around us. He gives us clarity of thinking, nudging us toward the wise, good way to go. He helps us see others in a more complex, honest light, so that we love others better. He makes demands, yet He helps us fulfill those demands. We experience the most awesome, most satisfying, most comforting peace that could be felt or imagined.

Now the choice seems obvious. How could we have chosen the other way? We are grateful for His command to love Him. It brings us joy and fulfillment. It is not an onerous command but one of those parental commands born out of love. It is the *greatest* commandment, the most critical decision of our lives: to love God with all our hearts, souls, minds, and strength—with everything we've got. So let's step out and come to know the most Glorious, the most Wonderful, the Most High.

❧

Jesus, I hear Your command. I feel Your command. I know it is good for me. Without this choice I cannot have a relationship with You. Without that relationship I am miserable and lost. I choose to love You with all my heart, soul, mind, and strength. Bless this choice. Perfect my love for You. Thank You for loving me. Amen.

GLORIOUS FREEDOM

Because the creature itself also shall be delivered from the bondage of corruption into the glorious liberty of the children of God.

ROMANS 8:21, KJV

Some years ago a beautiful, caramel-brown puppy was born. After six weeks, it was placed in an extremely small cage. Over time, the puppy began to chase its tail, becoming more aggressive and violent as it did so. One day the puppy was taken out of the cage and placed in the arms of an adopted family. Almost immediately the pup gently laid its head on the new owner's shoulder and happily wagged its tail realizing that it was finally free.

Romans 8:21 refers to the bondage of all creation, which is destined to death and decay. The hope of a new destiny for all God's creation is bound to the plan of deliverance God has provided for humankind. Only when we live eternally with Christ will we be freed from the destiny of death and decay.

As we await the Lord's return and eternal life in Him, we realize that here and now we have been delivered from the caged bondage of sin and made free through the sacrifice of Jesus Christ. We are no longer plagued with running in circles, chasing our own misguided notions of what life should be. We are now children of God; we are free in Him. Life's challenges will always attempt to lure us back to bondage, and unless we pay attention, we will treat those temptations like old friends and find ourselves picking up where we left off. But we are no longer bound; we are bondage-free through Christ Jesus. And all of creation awaits the day when the Lord will return and they, too, will enjoy eternal freedom.

Today, no matter what happens, we can trust that our God will guide us. Today, we pray for His direction and move forward as He leads. As children of God, we are free, and one day we, with all of His creation, will enjoy eternal life in Him.

❧

Lord God, thank You for being all I need. You are my Jehovah-Jireh, the One who provides my strength in the realization of Your deliverance. I love You and thank You for everything. In Jesus' Name. Amen.

GLOWING IN THE DARK

That ye may be blameless and harmless, the sons of God, without rebuke, in the midst of a crooked and perverse nation, among whom ye shine as lights in the world.

PHILIPPIANS 2:15, KJV

Years ago, marketers inundated us with advertisements related to glow-in-the dark products. Gradations of glow-in-the dark paint, jewelry, fashion sunglasses (if you can believe it), and so on, could be found in many average households with children. These products would fascinate the minds of the young as they played with these ingenious gadgets. The gadgets had to first be charged with *a* source of light; otherwise, they would be of little use for which they had been created.

Likewise, we have to be charged with the light of the Lord Jesus, our Christ. We can glow in the dark places of a world that seek to pull us into their clutches by their mesmerizing devices. As children of God, our purpose was outlined by Jesus in Matthew 5:14-16, when He tells us to be the light of the world, so that others may see us shining and glorify God. The writer of Philippians expounds upon this concept by telling us to be blameless, innocent, and faultless— lights shining and, yes, even glowing in the midst of a crooked and perverse generation (2:14).

Know that the crooked and perverse will create seemingly bright, shiny things that will attempt to lure us; they're not the true light but those generated by deception. However, staring into it and playing with it can leave us feeling the pangs of remorse because we failed to be charged by the presence of the light of the Lord Jesus. We can recharge from the true source of our power. We will stand blameless and innocent in the midst of a generation that charges itself by imitations of *the* light. Let's recharge daily so that our lights are seen in a dark world that so desperately needs our glow.

❧

Father God, it is in Jesus' Name that I come before Your presence. I seek to be recharged with the light of Your presence so that I may stand blameless and innocent before a crooked and perverse generation. As I go through this day, let the light from Your presence within me glow and shine brightly, so that others may see the good works that bring You glory. Amen.

WE BELONG TO GOD

And it shall come to pass, that in the place where it was said unto them, Ye are not my people; there shall they be called the children of the living God.

ROMANS 9:26, KJV

Sorry, which group are you with? Whom are you representing? Are you sure you belong in this place? Is your income bracket right for this group? Do you have enough education to be with us? Where is the love? Not in people who "tag" us with what they think is an *in* or an *out*. Because of the focus of others, we may not be in their vibe: the type that belongs. Not fitting in can become depressing and make some feel as if they are failures.

How great is our God to provide us with His love, His grace, His Son! Being part of God's family, we needn't be depressed nor feel as if we are failures. He tells us that we're His. Many may have questioned to whom we belong or why we even came around, but now we belong to the one and only God—our living God. How great is His love for us!

It's wonderful to know that God has received us and will receive those who believe in Him and believe that Jesus is His Son, who died for our sins. We may go to various places where we are treated as if we do not belong, but God accepts us just as we are—His children. No matter our past—drugs, fornication, lying, or gossiping—God receives us as His own, accepting us as His children. He then covers us and allows us to represent Him. Through testimonies, we are able to share what God has done for us and what He's delivered us from. Let us go forth and represent the One who loves us the most—let us represent God well.

❧

God, accepting me as Your child is the greatest thing I can imagine, yet You are much more. You accept me when others don't, no matter my past. You continue to provide for me, and because of that, I can only say "Hallelujah!" My soul rejoices because of You. I love You and thank You in advance for Your love, Your forgiveness and Your joy. In Jesus' Name, I pray. Amen.

BECAUSE OF FAITH

For ye are all the children of God by faith in Christ Jesus.

GALATIANS 3:26, KJV

Every day a middle-aged, married couple prays to God for employment; both are out of work. Every morning they go their separate ways and hit the pavement job hunting. Door to door he goes. He's told the same thing each time: you're a bit older than we expected. Let us phone you about the position. The wife is told the same thing. The bills pile up, and suddenly they find themselves homeless and living in a shelter. A stranger sees their Bible laying on a cot and asks, "So, you really believe in all that stuff? Well, if God loves you so much why are you here?" What makes a person believe and follow God when it appears the bottom has fallen out? The couple replied, "Our faith is in our risen Savior, Jesus Christ. Knowing that we are children of the King, we will make it with whatever God supplies." Each day thereafter, the couple continues praying and seeking employment. No matter what, they are determined to trust God for His open door.

Sometimes our lives are like the couple's—we pray each moment we get, and our faith never waivers. Yet our bottom may appear to have fallen out. It may seem as if we're not reaching God. Keep the faith in Christ and know that once a child of God we are always a child of God. God is our Father, our provider, our keeper, our way-maker and our God. He knows what is to come, what is happening, what happened and all of the reasons why—He even knows the situation we are in right now. Keeping the faith will get us through.

Remember when we were children and asked something of our parents? We begged and cried; yet it seemed that particular request wouldn't be granted. We didn't decide to disown the family and move somewhere else. We just waited until our parents decided the moment was right.

So, too, our Father God knows when the moment is right. And, as His children, we know that God's timing is perfect for His children.

❧

My God, my Father, I love You and thank You for Your perfect timing. In Jesus' Name. Amen.

GOD'S MANIFESTO

In this the children of God are manifest, and the children of the devil: whosoever doeth not righteousness is not of God, neither he that loveth not his brother.

1 JOHN 3:10, KJV

In this brief but very powerful passage of Scripture, the apostle John breaks down the Christian walk for us into its simplest form: if we choose daily to live righteously and we consistently show love to those around us, we then manifest to the world that we are children of God. In other words, it's what we do that confirms whose we are!

Merriam Webster's Collegiate Dictionary defines manifesto as "a written statement declaring publicly the intentions, motives, or views of its issuer." In this Scripture, the apostle John tells the born-again believer that he or she is commissioned to be God's manifesto in the earth.

God wants to use us to prove that He alone has the power to save and to change lives. When people around us—people who knew us before we received the Holy Spirit, those who saw the kind of lives we led and knew the kind of people we were—see the change in our lifestyles, they know that our lives have been changed for the better, and they witness the life-changing power of Christ. Interestingly, John chooses here to highlight the positive by pointing out the negative, "whosoever doeth not righteousness is not of God, neither he that loveth not his brother." He ascribes this person to be a child of the devil. From this we can infer that whosoever doeth righteousness is of God and he that loveth his brother is also of God. Also interesting is the tense of the verbs used, *doeth* and *loveth*. They are in the present tense (third person singular) of the verbs do and love, which suggests a continued state of doing and loving. So then, we are expected to always do righteousness and to always show love because in so doing we become God's manifesto in the earth.

My God, thank You for placing within me, through the gift of Your Holy Spirit, the ability to declare in the earth Your intentions, Your motives, and Your views. Now reign in me and work through me that I might be Your manifesto, a vessel that brings glory to Your name. Amen.

RECEIVING CHRIST

But as many as received him, to them gave he power to become the sons of God, even to them that believe on his name: Which were born, not of blood, nor of the will of the flesh, nor of the will of man, but of God.

JOHN 1:12-13, KJV

Today, let's focus on the idea of receiving Christ. It was the sainted Bishop Arthur M. Brazier who brought to our attention the idea of "receiving Christ" as opposed to accepting Him. The difference in wording is small, but the difference in meaning is monumental.

This notion of accepting Christ goes contrary to the teachings of Scripture, which always refer to our receiving the Holy Spirit. When we become cognizant of receiving versus accepting, there is opened up to us a whole new revelation of just how precious both the Gift and the Giver are. When we consider the great sacrifice made by Jesus Christ on the cross and all He gave up to ransom our souls from eternal damnation, accepting Him becomes a ludicrous thought. To crystallize this point, Bishop Brazier would often paint a word picture of the triumphant Christ—resurrected from the dead, with all power of life and death in his hands—standing or pacing, rubbing those nail-pierced hands, sweating from the brow that wore the crown of thorns, waiting for a lowly sinner to accept Him. The very idea is shamefully laughable, isn't it? Instead, it is we who are accepted in the Beloved, or so says the Scripture in John 15:16, "Ye have not chosen me, but I have chosen you, and ordained you, that ye should go and bring forth fruit, and *that* your fruit should remain: that whatsoever ye shall ask of the Father in my name, he may give it you."

Oh, what a blessing to know that we were chosen of God to receive Jesus, His Son, the propitiation for our sin, and that we (through Him) have received power to become sons of God! This is not something that will happen later. No, we already have the power to become children of God.

❧

Lord, keep me mindful today of the supreme sacrifice You made on the cross to purchase my salvation, opening for me a way to receive You into my heart and giving me power to become Yours in the earth. Amen.

LOVE ANYWAY

But love ye your enemies, and do good, and lend, hoping for nothing again; and your reward shall be great, and ye shall be the children of the Highest: for he is kind unto the unthankful and to the evil.

LUKE 6:35, KJV

A group of individuals were participating in a charity event competition. Although there was tension in the group, they pulled together and won the competition. Later, when they talked about how it felt to work side-by-side with those with whom they had experienced tension, one of the individuals shared, "I have learned to love folks anyway, even when I am not loved by them." While there was some humor in the statement, the perspective was commendable.

Our Scripture is a continuation of Jesus' Sermon on the Mount, also found in Matthew 5-7. Here Jesus instructs His disciples to love their enemies. Their enemies were those who opposed the teachings of Jesus. He also tells them to do good and to lend to those enemies, not expecting anything in return. To some, Jesus' teachings do not make sense. Why would anyone be expected to love and do good toward an enemy? But, the disciples would comply because of their love for Jesus and because they wanted to please Him. It was easy to love, give, and lend to someone they liked, but the challenge was to do the same to those that opposed them.

Isn't it a blessing knowing that we are the children of God and that He loves us? Just as He instructed His disciples, He encourages us to love our enemies. But, why would we want to love someone who seems to be against us? God knows and understands our feelings, yet He says to love anyway. The more we walk in God's love, the easier it will be to love others—even those who are our enemies. And while it may seem as if we are not getting anything in return, loving our enemies will render a far greater reward than anything man can give us.

※

Thank You, Lord, for Your great love. Your love encourages me to love those I don't easily regard. When I demonstrate Your love, people are drawn to You, and my reward is far greater than I could have ever imagined. In Jesus' Name. Amen!

YOU ARE MY "SONSHINE!"

Then shall the righteous shine forth as the sun in the kingdom of their Father. Who hath ears to hear, let him hear.

MATTHEW 13:43, KJV

Y*ou are my sunshine, my only sunshine. You make me happy when skies are gray. You'll never know dear how much I love you. Please don't take my sunshine away.*"[17] Oh, the memories that flood my mind when I recall this song. I learned it in kindergarten and I still have that "happy" feeling when I sing it. The melody is sweet and the lyrics speak to how someone felt about a special somebody.

In our Scripture, Jesus speaks of the righteous and their future state. He had just taught the parable of the wheat (good seeds) and the tares (bad seeds) and was now explaining the tares of the field to His disciples. The good seeds represented God's children and the bad seeds represented the children of the wicked one (the devil). Jesus explained to His disciples that at harvest time (the end of time) the tares would be gathered together and burned in the fire. At that time, God's children will "shine forth as the sun."

In other words, God's children are going to share in His glory and future kingdom (Romans 8:18-19). Jesus admonished His disciples saying, "Who hath ears to hear, let him hear." It was important that His disciples heard and understood His sayings and, thereby, bore good fruit.

We are the light of the world, and one day we are going to shine forth! What a privilege it is to know that we will share in God's glory and His future kingdom. But, what are we reflecting? Can others see the light of Jesus Christ shining through us? As we hear the Word of God and show forth His light, people will be drawn to Him. What a blessing it will be when they sing to the Lord, "You are my 'Sonshine!'"

Thank You, Father, for calling me Your righteous. It is a blessing knowing that one day I am going to share in Your glory. As I hear Your Word, show me how to let Your light shine through me so that others are drawn to You. In Jesus' Name. Amen!

DEMONSTRATE GODLY CHARACTER

That ye may be the children of your Father which is in heaven: for he maketh his sun to rise on the evil and on the good, and sendeth rain on the just and on the unjust.

MATTHEW 5:45, KJV

How many of us have been told to "just take the high road"? Many of us have, and have often concluded that what was really being said is that, since the other individual might not change his or her stance, we should consider changing ours. While that might not be a popular position, it is the one that will honor our Father.

In our Scripture, Jesus addresses His disciples concerning their role as His followers. Jesus was preparing them for ministry and He wanted them to be mindful that they would face all kinds of tribulation. Even though they would face adversity, they were expected to act in love because they were children of the Father. Jesus said bless them that curse you, do good to them that hate you (Matthew 5:44). The disciples were to demonstrate God's love despite how their enemies treated them.

Jesus makes it clear that He had no respect of persons. The text reads, "he maketh his sun to rise on the evil and on the good." So if Jesus didn't make a difference between those who were evil or good, then the disciples could not. They were expected to love their enemies, no matter what.

We are excited to be part of God's family and are also mindful that God expects us to demonstrate His love to others, especially our enemies. Godly character dictates that we take the high road. Since God has no respect of persons, we are encouraged to do the same by loving others, without making excuses as to what they have done to us. In the end God always looks to us to display the characteristics of a child of God, no matter what.

❧

Father, You are a loving God! Teach me to love like You, even my enemies. Thank You for the privilege of being called Your child. May I always do those things that honor and draw others to You. In Jesus' Name. Amen!

FIGHTING FOR PEACE

Blessed are the peacemakers: for they shall be called the children of God.
MATTHEW 5:9, KJV

The war between the Spirit and our flesh is a daily dilemma. We pray for guidance from the Holy Spirit to help us navigate the pitfalls and minefields of our day's journey. Our day starts with a barrage of multimedia, from television, radio, billboards, and social media. Far too often, these messages reinforce a mentality that contradicts Jesus' command to treat others as we would want to be treated (Luke 6:31). The call of "make war, not peace, as long as you don't mess with my 'piece' of the pie" is a philosophy of this world and not of God.

Jesus understands the spiritual fight we face. He gave us His Word as our rule book and sent the Holy Spirit as a Comforter and Guide. Armed with both, we become spiritual referees, setting the record straight, fighting the good fight for the Prince of Peace.

The Bible is filled with references of war, yet the word "peacemaker" is mentioned just once—"Blessed are the peacemakers: for they shall be called the children of God" (Matthew 5:9). Jesus is the ultimate peacemaker. It is our connection with Jesus that gives us peace with the heavenly Father. Jesus understands the importance of God's children bringing peace to communities filled with chaos and crime.

The pursuit of peace is an active endeavor that requires specific qualities. Peacemakers are spiritual referees, holding their peace and letting the Lord fight their battles. Peacemakers show compassion when faced with ridicule. Peacemakers are courageous when faced with seemingly overwhelming odds and peacemakers have charity for those who the world says deserve no love.

We are called to promote peace in a world of war and pain as our reasonable service. Producing peace has its challenges, but its rewards are far greater. Fight for peace.

❧

Heavenly Father, guide me in the path of peace. Let my actions bring peace to shattered souls. Let me understand that the greatest reward of a peacemaker is to be called a child of God. Amen.

In God's Hands

*They shall come with weeping, and with supplications will I lead them: I will
cause them to walk by the rivers of waters in a straight way, wherein they
shall not stumble: for I am a father to Israel, and Ephraim is my firstborn.*
JEREMIAH 31:9, KJV

The end of the work day has finally arrived and it's off for home.
The comfy chair awaits and relaxation mode is setting in.
Turn on the news and the end of the day appears dampened by the
barrage of events. Instead of feeling pity, prayer requests go up to
God for deliverance of people who cause harm to others.

Watching and listening to the news reports may leave one
feeling as if there's no hope, no love, and no peace. But as children
of God we are comforted and protected by Him, and we come to
Him not only for His continual guidance but on behalf of others.
We're in God's hands and are led by Him. Whatever the condition,
He cares for us and listens to us. We have a wonderful and cherished
position, where we can communicate with God, whether through
tears, prayers, or being still.

As in ancient times, the world is filled with doom and judgment.
Despite the reports then and now, the people of God have a hope.
Our hope is in the sovereign King who rules righteously. So we can
be strong in the Lord, knowing He knows all and is in control of
all. Through God we can make it, because it is His strength we rely
on. We can go to God with prayers, and our fervent tears lead us to
a place in Him that renders peace, love, and comfort. We can go to
our Father for everything—seeking His wisdom and guidance no
matter the situation. We can call on Him, and He will lead us forth
in joy and bring us to a smooth path. We are in God's hands.

❧

*God, my Father, my strength comes from You. I desire to be like You and
what You would have me to be. Help me to remember to pray for others
as things in the world become more desolate. Remind me that You are the
supplier of my needs and that You protect and guide me as my Shepherd. In
Jesus' Name, I pray. Amen.*

FULLY EQUIPPED

Blessed be the God and Father of our Lord Jesus Christ, who hath blessed us with all spiritual blessings in heavenly places in Christ.

EPHESIANS 1:3, KJV

In the mid 70s there was a series of commercials for a spaghetti sauce called Prego. The hook for the commercials was "Prego: it's already in there," suggesting that everything needed for spaghetti sauce like your grandmother made from scratch was in this jar all ready to go—just heat and serve. Well, in today's passage we find the apostle Paul writing to the saints of the church at Ephesus reminding them that they have already been fully equipped by God, "who hath blessed us with all spiritual blessings," with everything they need to fight the good fight of faith.

From time to time we find ourselves faced with new struggles and challenges in life, struggles and challenges that seem insurmountable. It is in those times that we can gain strength from God's Word by using Scriptures like today's passage to remind us that we are fully equipped (it's already in us) with everything we need to be more than conquerors over anything that comes against us on our Christian journey. Perhaps in those times we should even shout "Prego!" in hopes that it will spark the memory of those old familiar commercials and we'll connect that memory to this Scripture and others like it—Scriptures like Philippians 4:13, which says, "I can do all things through Christ which strengthens me" or Romans 8:37, where Paul writes, "Nay, in all these things we are more than conquerors through him that loved us," reminding ourselves that whatever we need to be victorious is already within us.

The enemy loves to use our struggles and challenges to thwart the work of the Spirit in our lives, but if we can stay focused on our goal and use the arsenal we have in the Word of God, his plan of attack will become like so many other things we read about in the Scriptures: "and it came to pass." Think about it—you are fully equipped!

❧

Dear Lord, help me remember that there's nothing that will confront me today that You have not already fully equipped me to conquer. And if I need one, You have already provided a way of escape for me. Thank You, Jesus!

JUST CALL ON YOUR FATHER

In the fear of the LORD there is strong confidence, And His children will have a place of refuge.

PROVERBS 14:26, NKJV

When walking down a church corridor, a saint overhead a conversation between a little girl and a young teen. The little girl said, "I'm gonna tell my daddy," to which the young teen replied with a sarcastic tone, "Who is yo' daddy?" The saint smiled and kept walking, thinking to herself, "Somebody's gonna get it now!" That little girl believed that if she told her daddy what the young teen did to her, that "Daddy" would come to her rescue and make everything all right. That spoke volumes about how she felt about her daddy.

In our Scripture, Solomon begins by saying, "In the fear of the LORD." "Fear" in this context means "reverence" or "respect," and Solomon encouraged the people to honor and respect the Lord. He wanted them to know that as they lived lives that honored God, they could be confident that God would protect them. Again, living honorably was the key to having this confidence. How comforting it must have been for them to know that they could live a life of abundance and that God would take care of them whenever they called upon Him.

Isn't it wonderful having a Father who knows everything about us? We are His children and when we honor God it pleases Him. But, how can we honor God? One important way is to have confidence that He will take care of us. Just as that little girl believed that her daddy would be there for her, God wants us to have that same confidence in Him. He is Jehovah, the self-existent God. As we live godly lives, we can have confidence knowing that when we call on our Father He will be right there to take care of us. Just call on Him!

❧

Thank You, Father, for Your loving protection. It's comforting to know that You will be right there when I call. Please show me how to put You first in every circumstance of my life, for when I do I will live a life of abundance that will draw others to You. In Jesus' Name. Amen!

DON'T GO BACK

My little children, of whom I travail in birth again until Christ be formed in you.

GALATIANS 4:19, KJV

How would you feel if you spent a great deal of time teaching someone how to do something and, after you left, he or she reverted to doing it the old way? You wouldn't feel very good about it, would you? You each knew the old way was not effective, which is why time was spent teaching the person how to do it differently. But now you're back, willing to show him or her again and wondering if he or she will stay with it this time.

Paul experienced this with the Jews and Gentiles at the churches of Galatia. In his letter, he expressed sorrow over them reverting to their old ways. For the Jews, they had been under bondage to the Law before they accepted Christ. For the Gentiles, they had been under bondage to the moral law of nature before they had accepted Christ. Moreover, because of false teaching, they had reverted to the Law of Moses.

Paul writes *My little children,* which shows his affection for the Galatians. Paul had spent a great deal of time teaching on the doctrine of justification by faith, and now they were deceived by false teachings concerning the works of the Law. Although he could not be present with the Galatians, Paul wanted them to know that he was willing to labor with them, like a woman who travails in childbirth. He wanted to make sure that this time Jesus Christ was a reality in their lives.

Jesus died for our sins, and we are justified by faith alone. How unfortunate it would be if we reverted to our old ways after receiving Jesus Christ. We were freed from the bondage of sin when the Holy Spirit came in and we now have an opportunity to live victoriously through Him. While we know there are false teachers looking to deceive the very elect, we can stand firm on the Word of God knowing that our salvation in Him is sure.

❧

Thank You, Father, for the privilege of being justified by faith. I do not have to "work" in order to be right with You. I have been freed from the bondage of sin and now I can live victoriously through You. In Jesus' Name. Amen!

IF MY PEOPLE…PRAY

If my people, who are called by my name, will humble themselves and pray and seek my face and turn from their wicked ways, then will I hear from heaven, and I will forgive their sin and will heal their land.

2 CHRONICLES 7:14, NIV

There was a popular saying a while back that went something like this, "Prayer changes things." In actuality prayer changes people. Prayer changes us. Prayer is the way that we, as God's children, go to Him and talk about anything—absolutely anything. And God will not turn us away. In fact, God wants us to come to Him.

From the time of the first temple in ancient Israel, King Solomon set aside a place specifically for the people of God to be able to go to Him in prayer. After seven years of building, Solomon completed the temple. During the dedication, King Solomon prayed the temple would be a place to hear and listen to God. God affirmed for Solomon and God's people throughout the ages that He hears our prayers.

But we cannot go to God just any old way. We must approach Him with a humble heart—an attitude of humility. The God we pray to is sovereign, all powerful, and mighty. Yet years later, the writer of Hebrews taught that we can come boldly to the throne of grace to find help in the time of need (Hebrews 4:16). Yes, boldly but humbly, that is the posture of the praying child of God. We approach God with confidence that He hears us, yet without arrogance or entitlement that God owes us anything. In fact, today's passage reminds us that the very pride that could keep us from hearing from God is the very thing we must turn away from when we seek God's face.

As children of God, called by His name, we are promised forgiveness of sin. We are promised healing of our land, or that which we possess. We are God's people, and God wants His people to pray!

❧

Father God, I start this day in repentance, prayer, and meditation. Help me to trust You and Your promises. Allow me to realize that worldly riches are not a part of my eternal inheritance. I thank You for allowing me to be an heir to Your throne of grace and mercy. In Jesus' Name. Amen.

FOLLOW THE LEADER

Be ye therefore followers of God, as dear children.

EPHESIANS 5:1, KJV

Across the country a common game played by young children is Follow the Leader. The premise is basically the same—someone is in charge, providing directions, and someone else is following, whether in lock-step or imitating the action. To successfully continue in the game, you have to follow the leader.

Much of our Christian life is like that. We have to be in hot pursuit of God's will, which is revealed in His Son, our glorious leader. God has given Him the authority over everything and every answer to every problem. Our goal is to follow closely behind Him, stay in step with Him, and be led by Him. Like the games mentioned above, we can lose our footing when we don't pay close attention to the One who is guiding. We can miss a cue and move out of sync with the Leader. We may have our attention diverted, which causes us to neglect a critical direction that will advance us to the next level.

We are called to be imitators of God as His children (Ephesians 5:1). That means we look to His example. How do we do that? We do it by looking to His Word to guide us on what we are to do in the situations we encounter. We do it by looking at the lives of His servants and how He strengthened them in times of adversity, as well as in times of triumph. We do it by continuously examining ourselves, in light of what is revealed in His Word and spoken into our hearts; then we do what it says.

Who are you following? Are you listening attentively, staying keenly alert to His directions, or are you drawn away by other voices that don't want you to win the game or race that you're in? Make sure you don't get derailed, sidetracked, or pushed back because you weren't *following the leader* or doing *what He says.*

Eternal Sovereign God, I want to have the obedience and excitement of a child when it comes to following You. Help me to follow the leader every day by Your grace. I pray in Jesus' Name. Amen.

GOD LOVES AND ACCEPTS US

To the praise of the glory of his grace, wherein he hath made us accepted in the beloved.

EPHESIANS 1:6, KJV

Acceptance can be a major issue in our lives, as children and adults. We often wrestle with feelings of inadequacy and the need to belong. As children of God, the Father has made us accepted in His family. We are a part of the "beloved" to the praise of the glory of His grace! If we should ever feel unworthy or forsaken, we can rest assured that there is One who approves of us.

Encounters of rejection on different levels—unrequited love, a rejected job application, or an ignored friend request—are all part of the human experience and challenge our self-esteem. We crave affirmation from others, and when approval doesn't flow quickly and easily to us, it can get us down. However, as we experience the love of God, and His acceptance, we come to know our true value. It's a value determined by God that doesn't decrease and that cannot be lost. It is an acceptance based on the Giver of Life and His goodness, not our own.

God wants us to know His love for us as His children, created in His image and after His likeness. He wants us to know that as those who had once gone astray, our sins are forgiven and we are heirs of His heavenly kingdom. By His Spirit within, He draws us closer into relationship with Him and assures our merit in Christ Jesus. The Father's love and acceptance is to be increasingly enjoyed from day to day!

We can become instantly lifted when we consider God's love and acceptance toward us.

We don't have to concern ourselves with what others think about us, or seek any outside approval. God accepts us and goes even further: He helps us become all that we can be as we receive and walk in His love!

❧

Father, it is so good to know that You love and accept me. It brings peace to my mind to know that You delight in me and that I belong to You. Thank You, Lord, for choosing, saving, and empowering me to receive Your love. Your grace reveals my true value and worth as a child of God! Amen.

GOD'S LOVE GIVES US LIFE IN CHRIST

For God so loved the world, that he gave his only begotten Son, that whosoever believeth in him should not perish, but have everlasting life.

JOHN 3:16, KJV

There have been many great spiritual leaders throughout world history; subsequent religions were formed and practiced in honor of those leaders, or as a result of their spiritual enlightenment or practices. However, the Bible teaches that there is one Savior for humankind: Jesus the Christ, God incarnate and we have life in Him.

Many people think of God as a supreme being who seeks to punish and condemn humankind for sin. They consider Jesus to be one who separates rather than the One who reconciles all things unto God. Scripture teaches us that it was because God so greatly loved and prized the world that He provided the way of redemption through His Son, Jesus the Christ. The fact that Jesus showed up is an example and expression of the Father's love and not any vindication we attribute to Him.

The Bible teaches that those who do not receive Jesus stand condemned, not because Jesus condemns them but because they do not receive salvation and, by choice, remain outside of God's love. They reject salvation because they like the darkness—a spiritual place where self-will supersedes the will of God. They don't come because they don't want to change their thoughts or ways. In essence, denial of Christ is not just a denial of God but a denial of our own soul's salvation.

However, the believer's testimony is one of receiving God's plan of salvation through faith in Jesus the Christ. In coming to Christ, we come to live, not to be condemned. We come to learn His ways and lose our own. We come to be loved and to love. We come to gain strength and shed weakness.

God's love is amazing, for it bears eternal life. We rejoice knowing God's plan for our ultimate good here and now, and throughout eternity!

❧

Father, You have no desire that I perish, fail, or meet any demise. Your will for me is only good, a reflection of Your divine nature. Thank You for salvation through Jesus Christ, my Lord. Through Christ, I experience Your love, power, and blessings. In You I have life! And so it is!

POWER OF BELONGING TO GOD

But as many as received him, to them gave he power to become the sons of God, even to them that believe on his name.

JOHN 1:12, KJV

One day after working, a timid young woman needed to attend a workshop and she was running late. Upon arrival at the training session, she was met with the limits of time and a clash of demands. Greeted with a "Hello, glad you made it," she looked nervously around for the information that was needed to participate in the training. One final packet was labeled for someone else and set aside to be picked up. Knowing her need for the information, the timid young woman prayed for the favor of God to rest upon her as she asked God to make a way for her to get the packet she needed. Out of nowhere came, "Here's a packet for you. It's the last one." Reaching out to shake the attendant's hand, the shy young lady boldly looked up, thanking him, *and Him,* for the packet.

The young lady didn't rely on her ingenuity to get what she needed; she relied on her God. She quickly acknowledged her need, bowed her head, and received the help that came through prayer. She demonstrated the kind of trust that comes from relationship. She expressed the confidence of one who had seen prayers answered before because, when presented with an obstacle, her first inclination wasn't to use her human understanding but to look to divine intervention on her behalf. She bowed her head to her heavenly Father, who heard her and answered her plea for help. When we open our hearts to receive Christ, we receive all that He has for us—even extraordinary power in ordinary moments.

When the workshop ended, participants came to the young lady after noticing she had garnered the last packet, wondering what kind of power she had. Someone asked, "How did you get that? She confidently remarked, "My Father looks out for me."

Let's walk in faith, favor, and power today as children of God. We belong to His family. We can come to Him as sons or daughters.

❧

Father, thank You for looking out for me in all things. I'm grateful to be Your child and appreciate the relationship I have with You. Thank You for always caring for me. Amen.

IN WITH THE NEW!

Therefore, if anyone is in Christ, the new creation has come: The old has gone, the new is here!

2 CORINTHIANS 5:17, NIV

Springtime is one of the most beautiful times of the year. Buds begin to appear and blossom; tiny leaves burst into blushing colors and vibrant fragrances. Earth smells fresh as gentle showers tease out tender blades of grass. The atmosphere is full of new hope and promise as a winter-weary landscape gives way to a brilliant new portrait of life.

This cadence of spring provides a visual glimpse of the newness of life afforded by salvation in Christ Jesus. But the mechanics of the new birth are even more startling and gracious than spring's awakening. The flowers that bloom in spring wither again in fall, only to reappear another season according to the encoding of that species. By contrast, when a person receives the Lord Jesus Christ a marvelous event occurs—he or she receives a brand new nature. One Bible translation says "…if a man is in Christ, he has been created all over again."[18]

By God's love and grace, we are born of the Spirit and grafted into the body of Christ (Ephesians 5:30). We are no longer the slaves of sin; sin no longer has dominion over us (Romans 6:14). This is remarkable, because we were born in sin and destined to serve it well. But something remarkable happens when we receive Jesus Christ—we have a new Lord, a new heart, a new assignment, and a new destiny (Ephesians 2:10).

However, God doesn't automatically give us a new mind in salvation, for our mind is still programmed to operate in the old, defeating set of values. So the only way to allow that new inner self to blossom is to be transformed by the renewing of our minds (Romans 12:12). We have to delete those old corrupted files and learn the new operating system. Shedding old habits takes time and consistency, but we can do it because we've been redesigned in Christ Jesus precisely to walk in the newness of life. So out with the old and in with the new!

Father, thank You that I am a new creation in Christ. Grant me daily grace to shed my old ways and walk in the vibrant newness of life that You have so richly provided. In Jesus' Name. Amen.

A NEW HEART FROM GOD

A new heart also will I give you, and a new spirit will I put within you: and I will take away the stony heart out of your flesh, and I will give you an heart of flesh. And I will put my spirit within you, and cause you to walk in my statutes, and ye shall keep my judgments, and do them. And ye shall dwell in the land that I gave to your fathers; and ye shall be my people, and I will be your God.

EZEKIEL 36:26-28, KJV

There are many movies that center around a person with a hardened heart. Such characters are mean, inconsiderate, cold, and callous. They don't give anyone a chance and they don't give handouts. Then, after hurting many people, something drastic (and heartbreaking) happens and a change overcomes them. In life, too, we come across stone-hearted people, and they can be challenging. They may be our boss, co-worker, neighbor, or family member. Sometimes those people are us! Unlike the movies, we have to ask, "What, if anything, can happen to change these hearts?"

God, in His grace, gives us a new heart. Here's what is so wonderful about it: with the new heart God gives us, we also get His Spirit, and with His Spirit we are able to be in sync with Him. We are able to follow His ways, His rules—Him. We will face challenges even with our new hearts, but our challenges become the steps of our prayers so that we get direction about handling our problems as we go through them. There is no longer a need to grumble, to be mean, or to complain. We are now part of God's family and the proof is our new hearts. Now we can pray through our challenges. Now we can call on our Father freely because God loved us so much that He really did make a way for us. He gave us new hearts!

❧

Dearest God, I thank You. I love You and appreciate You for giving me a new heart that enables me to get through my challenges. Knowing that You are always there makes my day, my life go easier. I love You, Lord. Amen.

ONE FATHER

For though ye have ten thousand instructors in Christ, yet have ye not many fathers: for in Christ Jesus I have begotten you through the gospel.

1 CORINTHIANS 4:15, KJV

There was a time when the father's faith was the family's faith, but today's statistics show that many American households are fatherless. While the current data can seem depressing, there is good news: we are under grace and are able to seek God through Jesus for ourselves. It's through the grace that God has for us that He has become our Father, and we have become His children. Being God's children hinges on the fact that we believe in the Gospel of Jesus Christ, our Savior, who died for our sins. As a result, we have eternal life and we belong to God.

As we go through our daily routines, as Christians and believers of the Gospel, we still come upon life's challenges. We are still faced with choosing between right and wrong, and sometimes we get briefly entangled with the wiles of the enemy. In some really challenging situations, when we find our nerves knotted, we can rest assured that, in Christ, we have the Father and can call on Him at all times. It is through God that we will get through every situation. No matter what's going on in our lives, we can call on God to get us through all things.

Though many households don't have a father or a father figure, Jesus is always in our hearts and minds so that we can go to our Father for all things. If you happen not to know God, there is always an opportunity for you to get to know Him and to become His child. In fact, you can call out to Him right now.

❧

Dearest Father, my God in Heaven, oh how I love You. I seek forgiveness for those times when I have tried to handle things on my own and not come to You, my Father. In Your kindness, mercy, grace, and love, I find all I need to get through each day. Father, Your Word comforts me and guides me so that I know I can make it. Help me to know You as my Father even more deeply than ever. In Jesus' Name, Amen.

PROTECTED BY GOD

We know that God's children do not make a practice of sinning, for God's Son holds them securely, and the evil one cannot touch them.

1 JOHN 5:18, NLT

We all have bad days. You know, days that begin with sour milk in our cereal and end with a situation that makes sleeping difficult that night. We all have bad days, but we can all be grateful that bad days don't define our lives.

It is our reaction to our bad days—as well as to our everyday triumphs—that really tells who we are. Because we are born-again Christians, our response cannot be the same sinful one we showed in our old lives. In our unsaved state, perhaps anger and payback were the ways we made our disdain known, but now we have the power to show love. Perhaps we used to tell someone off or throw a fit, but now God has delivered us from sin, given us power over our enemy and our old selves. We no longer make a practice of sin because that's not who we are anymore. We belong to Jesus Christ, and He protects us through it all.

The apostle John was an old man when he wrote the letter recorded as 1 John. He had been through quite a few bad days. He had been persecuted for His faith in Jesus Christ and sentenced to death in boiling oil, but John did not die. John was finally banished to an island called Patmos. During his life, John wrote to help the saints who were struggling in the face of some pretty bad days.

John's words are still right and true. We will have bad days—even pretty bad weeks—but we don't have to lose our tempers, our minds, or our testimony. We just have to remember that God's only begotten Son, Jesus Christ, was crucified for our sins. His resurrection saved us, and He holds us secure in His love. The evil one cannot touch us, no matter the scheme or the plan—no one, nothing, can keep us from God, take us from God, or pull us from His protection.

God, I thank You for loving me enough to protect me from all hurt, harm, and danger. It is in the Name of Jesus Christ I pray to You. Amen.

LIVING GOD'S WAY

God forbid. How shall we, that are dead to sin, live any longer therein?

ROMANS 6:2, KJV

A man knowingly practices a sin each day and each night goes to God in prayer seeking forgiveness. Is he right or is he wrong? In Romans 6:1, Paul speaks to us about sin and grace posing the question, "Shall we continue in sin, that grace may abound?" He immediately tells us No! "God forbid!" Being a child of the King, we are prompted to live a life worthy of God rather than prone to sin because we have a new nature. We are not like we were before having Christ in our lives. We are no longer sinners—though sometimes we do occasionally sin. Moreover, if we sin, we have an advocate with the Father (1 John 1:9). It's not our practice; we work hard at not making it a first choice.

Once we are born-again Christians, we become dead to sin and can't fathom living in sin as we did before Christ. However, we know that if we do sin, when we repent, God is there to forgive us and get us through the aftermath. He will still love us, care for us, and protect us.

Our human condition tends to shed a bit of doubt our way, God strengthens and brightens our life and we focus on living His way. Jesus Christ is our Comforter, and He has promised to never leave nor forsake us. He's our way-maker. If we find ourselves in a sinful situation, we must get out of it by walking away and calling on God to provide us a way of escape. Keeping our focused on Him, will help us live God's way.

Dearest God, I come to You thanking You for Your grace, mercy and deliverance from sin. I thank You for Your Word that strengthens me each day. God I thank You for Your protection and comfort. God, forgive me please for any sin I've committed against You and all You represent. I ask that You make me whole again, make me right with You again, and let me focus on all that is of You. In the Name of Jesus Christ, the soon coming King, I pray. Amen.

THE POWER TO PLEASE GOD

The Lord our God has secrets known to no one. We are not accountable for them, but we and our children are accountable forever for all that he has revealed to us, so that we may obey all the terms of these instructions.

DEUTERONOMY 29:29, NLT

Everything today seems to have a diminishing return. Housing values are so low that properties are worth less than owners paid. The Euro and the dollar have lost global value. College costs are increasing at a rate that job placement can't match.

Yet in Jesus Christ we get much more than we ever dared to expect. God's grace can never be fully known. His mercies are unsearchable because they are new each day. The secrets of what God has for those who love Him cannot be fully known. Yet, as with Israel, God doesn't hold us accountable for more than He has revealed to us. The children of Israel knew this.

In Deuteronomy 29, Moses rehearsed before the nation all that God had done in leading them out of Egypt and through the wilderness for forty years. All the Lord demanded was that they and their children be accountable for what He revealed to them in His Law. Unfortunately, the prophets record that Israel was never able to keep the Law. Time and again, they failed to honor God before hostile nations and to raise their children to know and obey Him.

The Lord makes the same demand of us, but with an added provision, because "God so loved the world, that he gave his only begotten Son, that whosoever believeth in him should not perish, but have everlasting life" (John 3:16). When we place our trust in Jesus as Lord and Savior, we gladly submit to baptism in His Name and are born again by His Spirit.

It is the Spirit of God that gives us the power to live for Him and to love Him with all of our hearts, soul, and strength. Through Jesus a way has been made for us to do all He commands, to live for Him, and to share the Good News of the Gospel with our children and all who will surrender to Him.

❦

Thank You, Lord, for the great secrets of Your love. I praise You for the richness of Your grace toward me. Amen.

ACCEPTANCE OF FATHER AND SON

Everyone who believes that Jesus is the Christ is born of God, and everyone who loves the Father loves his child as well.

1 JOHN 5:1, NIV

Over time, a widower of a teen son met and became enamored with an attractive single woman. They began to meet regularly after work for dinner, at church during worship services, and on weekends for matinees. From time to time they would go to the movies with his son to watch the latest show. One day, during dinner, the man broached the subject of marriage with the woman. The woman hesitantly admitted that, though she loved him, she didn't want any children and didn't seem to have the patience for his teen son. Perplexed by her answer, he asked, "How can you love me and not my son, who is a part of me?"

Today, Christians have to ask that very same question. How can proclaimed Christians love the Father and not love the Son? It's not plausible to have one without the other. Scripture reminds us that if it were not for the Son, we would not have a connection to the Father (John 14:6); it's through the Son we get the benefits of the Father. However, some people decide to choose the Father over the Son. They say, "I believe in God, but I don't know about this Jesus."

First century believers faced comparable issues that the apostle John wrote to address. At that time false teachers denied the incarnation of Christ and taught that the true God did not become flesh and blood. Spirit, they taught, was not compatible with material or flesh.

John became the defender of the Lord and proclaimed that "in the beginning was the Word, the Word was with God and the Word was God … and the Word became flesh and dwelt among us (John 1:1,14).

To believe that Jesus Christ is the Son of God, who died for all of our sins, is an act of faith and evidence that one is truly born again. Today, we celebrate what the Father has done in and for us, through His only begotten Son, Jesus.

My God, I love You for everything You've done and provided to me. I am so grateful for Jesus. Thank You for my salvation. I pray in Jesus' Name. Amen.

CHILDREN OF PROMISE

Now we brethren, as Isaac was, are the children of promise.

GALATIANS 4:28, KJV

In this day of the "world wide web," we are inundated with communication venues that allow anyone to "preach" his or her beliefs. If we read the Bible for ourselves and listen carefully, however, we discover that not everyone "preaching" from the Holy Bible is holy and not everything being taught is right. How do we discern the difference so that we can do the right thing? In Galatians, the apostle Paul reminds us of who we are in Christ.

Paul beautifully uses the birth of the two sons of Abraham to compare the new birth of the believer with the "old" life of the sinner. Paul equates our old/flesh man with Abraham's first born son, Ishmael—who was born to him by a bondwoman—to our new/spirit-filled believer represented by Abraham's second son, Isaac, who was born of his wife Sarah. Isaac's birth was the fulfillment of the promise God made to Abraham—that despite their ages, Sarah would bare him a son who would be blessed of God. Neither Abraham nor Sarah worked for or deserved God's blessing. God had preordained that Abraham and Sarah would be blessed with a child and they were! Isaac was the child of promise.

Paul takes his discourse further by comparing us to Isaac. We, too, are born of God, making us children of promise. As born again believers we are not shackled to the old ways of keeping the Law of Moses, but are free through the shed blood of Jesus Christ to worship God in the beauty of holiness. We are to be completely reliant on the Grace of God and we are no longer bound by the Law.

So let's be selective of the teachings and teachers we allow into our homes and our hearts. As children of Promise, let us remember that we live and thrive in the Grace of God. Our destiny is secure in Christ; we have eventual victory and we have inherited the promise of God just as Abraham, Sarah and Isaac did. We are indeed children of promise.

❧

Lord, thank You for the peace of knowing that "the old man" won't reign over me. I can place my confidence in You because I'm a child of promise! Amen.

Clusters of Priceless Diamonds

For ye were sometimes darkness, but now are ye light in the Lord: walk as children of light.

Ephesians 5:8, KJV

God is incomprehensible. The words we use cannot describe His majesty, His power, or His love for humankind. Try to think of an image that might attempt to describe God. Of course, we can't; but imagine for a moment that we could glimpse into God's heart, the center of His love for us. If we could see God's heart, it might look like a diamond with such transforming light that its undefinable brilliance would astonish the world. Imagine, too, that if we could look into the innermost being of God's heart, we might find the nuggets of salvation through Jesus Christ and the power that resides in the Holy Spirit. If we could look into God's heart we would glimpse the Divine Jewel that existed before the heavens and earth—unblemished, flawless, indestructible.

Perhaps if we could look into God's heart, we would realize that we are His foreordained and adopted children. Perhaps, then, we would appreciate that we, too, are hidden in our Father's heart. Perhaps, then, we would be ever conscious of walking as children of light, facets of brightness reflecting the light of God's favor, filled with His love and empowered with courage to be lights for the world. Perhaps just realizing that, through the sacrifice of Jesus Christ, we possess the luxuriant, illuminating identity as God's children would embolden us to always reflect God's love.

The light of God's love calls us to increase in knowledge, revelation, and understanding. Because we are His, our lives are to reflect honesty and faithfulness, as we willingly follow Christ, with fortitude and perseverance. As we mature in holiness, our lights will shine even more brightly for Him. Our testimony must be presented to the world as a beacon of peace and unity. As born-again believers, we remember that we reflect Christ at all times. It is almost as if our hearts, too, are like we might imagine God's to be: diamonds of love that shine brilliantly toward all humankind.

❧

Eternal Sovereign God, thank You for allowing me to be among the cluster of diamonds set in the amazing glory of Your light. Amen.

No Fear Here

For God hath not given us the spirit of fear; but of power, and of love, and of a sound mind.

2 TIMOTHY 1:7, KJV

Today's Scripture is one of many "memory Scriptures" from the days of our youth. Other verses include: "In the beginning God created the heaven and the earth." (Genesis 1:1); "Then Peter said unto them, Repent, and be baptized every one of you in the name of Jesus Christ for the remission of sins, and ye shall receive the gift of the Holy Ghost" (Acts 2:38); and, "For God so loved the world, that he gave his only begotten Son, that whosoever believeth in him should not perish, but have everlasting life" (John 3:16). These "memory Scriptures" bring comfort to our souls and are foundational cornerstones for our faith. But, as we periodically ruminate on them, God will give a fresh word, a revelation heretofore unseen. Such is the case with today's Scripture.

The apostle Paul, writing to Timothy, his son in the Gospel, admonishes Timothy to hold fast to the doctrine of faith that Paul taught him. Paul informs Timothy that "God hath not given us the spirit of fear." It's interesting to note that Paul refers to fear as a spirit, as in a living thing. Interesting also is the fact that fear (or the spirit of fear) is not what God gives us. Instead, Paul proclaims that God has given us the spirit of power, love, and a sound mind! These three can be seen as symbolic of the Father, Son, and Holy Spirit at work in our lives. We experience the power of the Father, because "in the beginning God created the heaven and the earth." We can celebrate the love of the Son because "God so loved the world that he gave his only begotten son." And finally, we can live with a sound mind because the Holy Spirit "guides you into all truth" (John 16:13). Praise the Lord for Paul's reminder that we have no need to fear because God has given Himself to us fully and completely.

❧

Lord, thank You for gifting me with power, love, and a sound mind. Help me to walk in those gifts and to remember what You didn't give me, I don't have. No fear here! In Jesus' Name. Amen.

GOD CHASER

And be not conformed to this world: but be ye transformed by the renewing of your mind, that ye may prove what is that good, and acceptable, and perfect, will of God.

ROMANS 12:2, KJV

A young adult man came bounding into the kitchen of his home with wild new body art and several piercings. His parents looked at him in amazement and asked, "Son, what did you do?" "I was looking for a way to express myself," he explained. "There's nothing wrong with them! Many of my friends have tats." Calmly, his mother asked, "If everyone were chasing squirrels, would you chase them, too?!"

Her point was well taken. We are sometimes swayed by the people around us, letting the whims of the world influence us. It becomes less about personal decision, or a set of convictions, and more about what others are doing. Today's world offers many departures from the mainstream—some good and some downright evil. *You may not see the rabies in the flitting squirrel, but it's there, and you might get bitten.* Don't be swept into a decision that is less your own and more the following of others, like the myth of the lemmings, who follow each other off a cliff and into the sea.

In today's text, the apostle Paul gives a cautionary word to believers to not be conformed to the world. Another way of looking at it is to determine not to be stretched or shaped by the things around you, but to be intent on having your mind shaped by God. Making a decision to be in pursuit of the things that are going to bring us into a closer relationship with Christ is the thing to chase after. What activities are God using to push you to be better, for His purpose and His Kingdom? Maybe it's Bible reading, meditation, or prayer? Those *are* the things, as followers of Jesus Christ, we *are to run after.* Get into His Word, and His glory will mark out a path for you as you pursue Him.

Live your life in obedience to God because He gives us power to pursue Him. Pursuing Him will yield the peaceable fruit of righteousness that belongs to a God chaser!

✎

Father, I am committed to following You with my whole heart. I won't chase trends, people, or things, but I will chase after You every day. Amen.

GOD KEEPS HIS PROMISES

For when God made promise to Abraham, because he could swear by no greater, he sware by himself. Saying, surely blessing I will bless thee, and multiplying I will multiply thee. And so, after he had patiently endured, he obtained the promise.

HEBREWS 6:13-15, KJV

I promise. Yes, I'll be there, I promise. Of course, no problem, I promise. How often we hear those two words, "I promise?" When someone tells us, "I promise"—we expect it to happen. Bill collectors call, *I promise the payment will be in by.* A best friend is having an event when we really can't go but declare *I promise I'll be there.*

To make a promise connects your word with your name. However, we quickly learn we can't fulfill all of the promises we make. Life happens; we meant well, but we just didn't come through. Thankfully, God isn't like us. He *always* keeps His promises.

In today's passage, the writer of Hebrews recounts the promise God made to Abraham that he would be the father of many nations. The writer goes on to talk about the immutability of God's counsel—that is the unchanging nature of God's character and God's Word. God's promises are connected to His name and His unchanging nature. We now are the seed of Abraham (Galatians 3:29), and just like Abraham, we can trust God's promises.

God promised we are joint-heirs with Christ. God promised that we are His children. God promised that we will be glorified together. What does that have to do with now? *Everything.* Trusting God's promises gives hope and that hope anchors our soul—our very mind and being in the most troubling of times.

That seems easier said than done, but it's true—as we are on earth, things and events are temporary. We continue day-by-day until our service to God is done here. We live to draw others to Him. We then become glorified together with Christ. We make it each day knowing the best is yet to come, assured that God keeps His promises!

❧

God, You are indeed a promise keeper. I am grateful for Your promise of eternal life. I am grateful for Your abundant life. Amen.

HEART CONFESSIONS

That if thou shalt confess with thy mouth the Lord Jesus, and shalt believe in thine heart that God hath raised him from the dead, thou shalt be saved. For with the heart man believeth unto righteousness; and with the mouth confession is made unto salvation.

ROMANS 10:9-10, KJV

The sermon ends and the preacher opens the doors to the church saying, "Confess with thy mouth and believe in thy heart…" Many will get up and walk toward the altar. Many others will remain seated. They want to go up, but… What does it all really mean?

What is the heart? Physically, it is muscle, tissue, and blood: the human's lifeline. Spiritually, it is the very thing that connects humans to God. Our natural hearts were designed and created by God so that one day our spiritual hearts would believe that God raised Jesus from the dead and, as a result, we can have eternal life. When we confess Jesus Christ as Lord, we are responding to the call of God that started in our hearts.

That sounds so simple, doesn't it? It is not always so easy. There are people who go through their daily routine trying really hard to be "in Christ." They attempt to be "perfect" in their actions and relationships. Yet, each time there's an altar call, they squirm. Their heart skips beats and beads of sweat appear. They fight to remain in their seats. They don't want to be seen by others, to be "found out" as not already saved or already baptized. And each time they find a different excuse, thinking they can hide.

In Romans 10, Paul expresses his yearning for the salvation of the people of Israel, the people who were resisting God's call on their lives. He reminded them of Deuteronomy 8:12, as he explained that the faith to believe God is not far off. It is right on our tongues. If you have been resisting the call of God, now is the time to surrender. Whether you feel the call to be baptized, to receive the Holy Ghost, or to make a deeper commitment to God, you have but to confess with your mouth!

❧

Father, I love You. Thank You for Jesus Christ, my Savior. Please strengthen and guide me this day. In Jesus' Name. Amen.

GOD'S WORK

And we know that all things work together for good to them that love God, to them who are the called according to his purpose.

ROMANS 8:28, KJV

Non-stop rain falls rapidly, then eases. The driver stays below 30 mph, following the curved road crossed hundreds of times. Suddenly, a lightness is felt at the wheel and the control of the car is lost slightly. Heading south, the car wobbles across the painted median and spins into the northbound lane, still headed south. The car hits the curb, pops up somewhat, and lands, facing north, in the grass. Despite a bent tire rim and a flattened tire, the unafraid, but shaken, occupants look in amazement as they realize they have just witnessed "the hand of God."

God will take all things and put them together for our good—His children's good, His children who love Him and are called according to His purpose. Why? Because God's grace intervenes for us; God has a plan and a purpose for each of us. His plan began with creating all things (Colossians 1:16), and His purpose is to have us glorify Him (1 Corinthians 6:20). Accidents, bad choices, good choices, working in a stress-filled or stress-free environment will all eventually show themselves as coming together for good. At times we can't see the "forest because of the trees." We can't see the good God intends because of the things that happen. We just have to know that God's word is true.

In life "we have to go through to get to" and when we "get to," it's for our own good. Each breath we breathe, each step we take, each encounter we have, and each thing we do come together for good because we love God and are the called according to His purpose.

God, you are my strength and my joy. Thank You for never changing and always caring, for providing me with peace. Thank You for taking everything that happens concerning me and bringing it together for my good. Your strength and promises see me through. I ask that You continue to keep strengthening me and fulfilling Your promises in a clear way for me. I love You, God. In Jesus' Name. Amen.

PART OF A PLAN

For whom he did foreknow, he also did predestinate to be conformed to the image of his Son, that he might be the firstborn among many brethren. Moreover whom he did predestinate, them he also called: and whom he called, them he also justified: and whom he justified, them he also glorified.

ROMANS 8:29-30, KJV

A flower seed is planted in a garden with other unknown seeds. The immature gardener isn't fully clear on what exactly to do. She knows that somewhere in the process water, sunlight, and nutrients are needed. She's naïve and doesn't know that the flowering process begins with water. Then there is germination, sprouting, leafing, budding, and a flower—a beautiful delicate thing. She looks in amazement. The flower seed cannot become anything else but the flower.

We, the children of God, are much like the flower seed. Our lives are predestinated, determined before they ever began. We are foreknown, predestinated, conformed in the image of Jesus, justified, and glorified, meaning we are of a righteous people: children of God.

God knew us before we became. In knowing us, He devised a plan for our lives—He placed us in specific gardens nurturing us in various ways. Where we are, and what we go through, is part of our path that gets us to where God planned for us to be. Our right now is what it is. No matter what we will do differently, it's what it should be for now. All of our challenges and hurts make us stronger in Christ. We are justified, declared right, and will one day be glorified.

So like the flower seed we are planted; then we germinate, sprout, grow buds, and begin to grow in God. We grow stronger and more reliant on God. We become a flower in His garden because that is part of His plan.

My God, how great is my love for You. I know You are my strength and have set forth a plan for my life. At times, I may be a bit uncertain and not totally rely on You. Forgive me, God. I thank You for my life plan. I thank You for Your guidance. I ask that You continue to strength me, guide me, and set godly people on my path who will help keep me focused on You. In Jesus' Name. Amen.

THAT'S LOVE

But God commendeth his love toward us, in that while we were yet sinners Christ died for us.

ROMANS 5:8, KJV

Who was it that said, "Love is what love does?" Today's Scripture puts flesh on this colloquial expression. We could also paraphrase this Scripture and say that Jesus proved His love for sinners when He died on Calvary for us. Why is this so significant? As the Son of God, Christ was sinless and shared perfect communion with God. It was because of this sacred communion that He sacrificed His life to redeem our souls from hell's eternal damnation. This meant that, during His time on the cross, covered in our sin, Jesus was, for the first time, separated from God the Father. This is significant because Jesus was God made flesh or, as one Scripture declares, "in him (referring to Jesus) dwells the fullness of the God Head bodily" (Colossians 2:9). If so, then it is clear that His sacrifice cost Him dearly. The fact that Christ freely took on the sin of all humankind to reconcile us back to God makes His sacrifice even more substantial! Here we have God in the flesh laying down His deity, relinquishing His position—all to redeem fallen man. When you think about it, it truly is the perfect example of love!

The fact of the matter is that, since God is omniscient (He knows all things), He knew that Adam would fall prey to sin in the garden. And because God loved us so, He also knew that He would send His Son into the world to reconcile us back to Him through Jesus' horrible death on Calvary's cross. God did all of that because He wanted to prove His love for us. We are indeed blessed people of God, created to serve Him with everything within us! No wonder the songwriter penned these words in an old hymn of the church, *"No one ever cared for me like Jesus ; There's no other friend so kind as He; No one else could take the sin and darkness from me. O how much He cared for me!"*[19] Now that is real love!

Dear Jesus, thank You for Your eternal love for me as evidenced on the cross of Calvary. Help me remember Your supreme sacrifice of love. In Your mighty name. Amen.

THE GREAT EQUALIZER

For as many of you as have been baptized into Christ have put on Christ.
There is neither Jew nor Greek, there is neither bond nor free, there is neither
male nor female: for ye are all one in Christ Jesus.

GALATIANS 3:27-28, KJV

Here we find the apostle Paul writing to the Galatians, reminding them that their salvation came through faith in Jesus Christ, and not through works of their own. The apostle is concerned that they might slip back into their traditional religious beliefs that were centered around things that were made inconsequential to us as born-again believers by the shed blood of Jesus—such as works and pedigree, instead of faith and trust in God. He cautioned the Galatians to remember that in Christ it doesn't matter who you are, what you do, or where you come from. It's not important where you live or where you work, what you drive, and how you look.

The apostle wanted them then, and us now, to know that our salvation is wrapped up in our faith in Jesus Christ, the risen Savior. Paul said that "baptized into Christ," we "have put on Christ." These phrases, at first glance, could seem redundant when, in fact, they complement each other beautifully. To be "baptized into Christ" refers to our salvation, while "putting on Christ" speaks to our daily walk and our taking on Christ's character. It is not until we receive Christ that we can put Him on. When we put on Christ, we become His witness in the earth, and there is no separation among the children of God. We are all one in Christ! Gone are the class discriminations—the big I's and the little you*s*, the Jews and the Gentiles. When we received the Holy Spirit, we were stripped of everything that wasn't like Jesus and given a new image, one in which we are all equal. The Holy Spirit came into our hearts and made us all one in mind, one in purpose, and one in destiny. Praise God for His Holy Spirit, for He is the Great Equalizer!

Oh God, thank You for Your equalizing power. Help me to put You on in every situation that arises today; get the glory out of my life. In Christ's name. Amen.

THE PROMISED SEED

And if ye be Christ's, then are ye Abraham's seed, and heirs according to the promise.

GALATIANS 3:29, KJV

In the history of African Americans, it is true that our yesterdays have highly affected our today. Hundreds of years ago, African-American people struggled to gain respect, equal opportunity in housing, employment, education, politics, and citizenship. Many nationally and locally famous African Americans, such as Frederick Douglass, W.E.B. DuBois, Shirley Chisholm, Dr. Martin Luther King Jr., and Dr. Arthur M. Brazier, dedicated large parts of their lives to paving a way for African Americans. Today there are better housing, employment, and educational conditions, as well as evidence of opportunities in the political arena. It is a great thing to see something come to pass and even receive something waited for.

It is indeed wonderful to eagerly await something you've longed for. This must have been true of the people of God who longed for the Messiah to come. We know that when He finally came on the scene, it was not in the manner many had supposed. And yet come He did, and respond we did. We are now the sons and daughters of God and heirs to the promise. We didn't do anything to be part of God's family, earn our salvation, or pay our way into heaven. We are heirs because of the promise God made to give us eternal life when we receive Jesus. Individually, we are saved by the grace of God, but we have an inheritance together as the saints. Through God's love, we are connected as a community of faith and heirs to the promise of things to come. Imagine the realization of the inheritance of the promise from thousands of years ago. Can you imagine yesterday affecting not only our today but also our tomorrow? God has paved the way for us to receive the promise through His Son. Who are we that God thinks about us enough to pave the way for us? We are heirs to the kingdom—that's who we are—God's children!

❧

God, I love You for everything You have done for me. Out of all of the people in the world before me, here today, and after me, You've allowed me to be Your child, an heir to Your promise. I thank You for it in Jesus' Name. Amen.

Body and Soul

What? know ye not that your body is the temple of the Holy Ghost which is in you, which ye have of God, and ye are not your own? For ye are bought with a price: therefore glorify God in your body, and in your spirit, which are God's.

1 Corinthians 6:19-20, KJV

Some think the body and the soul to be two distinct entities that coexist, one with the other; when, in fact, the truth of the matter is this: the body was originally designed to be the dwelling place of God's Spirit in man. It can neither live nor have life without the soul. This is confirmed by Scripture in Genesis 2:7, "And the Lord God formed man of the dust of the ground, and breathed into his nostrils the breath of life; and man became a living soul." Important to note also is the fact that Adam was God's only creation designed in His image/likeness (Genesis 1:27) and yet, until God breathed into his nostrils, Adam was only a brilliant design without life. It was the breath of God (or the Spirit of God) that brought forth life within the body of Adam. That breath also instantly connected Adam to God and to the world around him.

Upon Adam's fall in the garden, humanity lost that connection. And it was the work of Jesus Christ, through His death, burial, and resurrection, that reconciled us back to God (2 Corinthians 5:18). Today, the unregenerate person, the person without the indwelling of the Holy Spirit, is like Adam in the garden…just a beautiful pile of dead dust, unconnected and unreconciled to God! It isn't until we receive the life-giving Spirit of God that we become alive and truly connected to both God and the world around us.

Considering that, is it no wonder the apostle Paul seeks to remind us that within our mortal bodies dwells the Spirit of the living God? He admonishes us to treat our bodies and conduct our lives as if we are aware of this fact. So let us serve the Lord both in our body and soul/spirit, living lives that exhibit the indwelling of the Almighty God's Spirit.

Lord, thank You for entrusting me with Your Holy Spirit. Help me to live a life within my mortal body that honors Your presence within me. In Christ's name. Amen.

In God's House

And Moses verily was faithful in all his house, as a servant, for a testimony of those things which were to be spoken after; but Christ as a son over his own house; whose house are we, if we hold fast the confidence and the rejoicing of the hope firm unto the end.

Hebrews 3:5-6, KJV

When people move into a new home, there's usually a housewarming. Then gifts are brought and guests compliment the hosts on making a great selection of a home. The owners smile, and their happiness is seen as they express gratitude to their friends. The scene is familiar because we have either attended a housewarming or hosted one. Some may even have served hors d'oeuvres to satisfy the palates of feasting guests.

The servant, although in the house, is not the host but serves at the behest of the owner of the house. Everyone present is there by invitation, whether as a guest or one who serves. We have a Savior who is both building the house and welcoming us into it.

The house that Jesus is over is still being built today. Christ is building a house that is greater than all others because it is made of the Children of God. This house will be greater because the builder is greater. He is greater than the servants of the house. Colossians records that all things were made by Him and for Him. They were created for God's purpose and His glory. We have the glorious privilege of being *in* God's house for these reasons, but it is His only begotten Son that is *over* His House.

Blessings abound to the faithful. Moses was faithful as a servant. Jesus is faithful as His Son. We are to be faithful as His sons and daughters, who will faithfully serve Him until He calls us home. We will stand firm on who He is and who He has called us to be. Be grateful today that you have a place in God's great house.

Lord, I praise You that You have provided a place for me in Your great house. I come as Your child and am grateful for the privilege of serving You with my life. I look forward to the feast that will be given one day for all who belong to Your great house. Amen.

ADAPTING OR ADOPTING

I am crucified with Christ: nevertheless I live; yet not I, but Christ liveth in me: and the life which I now live in the flesh I live by the faith of the Son of God, who loved me, and gave himself for me.

GALATIANS 2:20, KJV

With whom do we identify? Even though youth are being reared by their parents in a particular way, there is a tendency to be influenced by their friends and sometimes not for the best. Some maturing adults will even connect with a popular personality and adapt their particular style. Adapting to what's around us can become a tad expensive emotionally, financially, and spiritually. The bottom line is that human beings tend to adapt to their surroundings.

The Old Testament (Law) paints a picture of sacrifices that had to be made. The land was filled with sacrifices to pagan and foreign gods. But only the ones made to Yahweh, the LORD Jehovah, could fulfill the law that was given to God's people. In the New Testament (Grace) we see a picture of intimate relationship emerging from the sacrifice of God's own Son. Under the Law, every commandment had to be followed, along with certain sacrificial ordinances, to be right before God. Under Grace, God's only Son is the single acceptable sacrifice for us. Under the Law, the head of the household's religious choice applied to the entire family. Under Grace, we respond personally in order to stand together in His body.

As Jesus died on the cross, so did we to sin! We live in faith—crucified, or dead to sin, so that Christ is alive in us. While outward appearance may be the same, we are not the same on the inside because Jesus lives there! While we live in this world, in these bodies, our hearts are fixed on living for Him and not adapting to everything around us. Let's live in a way that we are adopting more and more to what Jesus Christ wants for us.

God, You are so good to me. You have showed me the amazing way You love me through Your Son, and I am grateful. Teach me to die to the things that don't matter so I can more fully give myself to You and glorify Jesus Christ. I pray this in His redeeming name. Amen.

PRECIOUS TO GOD

Behold the fowls of the air: for they sow not, neither do they reap, nor gather into barns; yet your heavenly Father feedeth them. Are ye not much better than they?

MATTHEW 6:26, KJV

It's said that when the eaglet is born, it does not immediately have the inclination necessary to become that great bird. It takes time, precision, and the imprinting characteristics of the parent. So it is that the eaglet learns to fly by watching its parents. To encourage flight when the time is right, a mother eagle may fly in circular motions above the nest without food. Then at other times she dangles it for the young eaglets to reach for. The eaglet may eventually lose a small amount of weight as it languishes for nourishment, but soon enough, it takes its first flight. About forty percent of them are successful on their first flight, yet God continues to provide for them. He takes great care of His creatures by providing them with what they need, and He does even more for us.

God has given us charge over the fowl of the air and He cares for us as His own. We are made in His image. We bear His name and care for His world. We know that, just as He cares for the birds of the air, He cares for us. Today's Scripture reminds us that these gracious creatures of flight don't plant, gather, or store but God cares for them. They make it through inclement weather and uncertain conditions, and God takes care of them. Will we not make it through trying times and uncertain markets, when we have the certainty of our God?

Know that we are precious to God and He is with us. We can't give in to the temptation that makes us feel we are alone, or that God isn't listening—not there for us or just plain ole left us. He hasn't. Like the eaglet, our situations are the baby steps that move us to maturity—it is to soar in the sky; ours is to soar in Christ. The eaglet doesn't focus on where it is—it focuses on where it is going, and it survives that first flight.

🕊

God, thank You for caring for me much more than the birds of the air. I love You and am happy to be Your child. Amen.

LIVING IN THE LIGHT

Ye are all the children of light, and the children of the day: we are not of the night, nor of darkness.

1 THESSALONIANS 5:5, KJV

On summer evenings, in years gone by, children could be found playing hide-and-go seek. One of the fun things about the game was the sense of adventure that accompanied looking for someone hiding in darkened, obscure places. It was easy to see those playing as they moved around in the light of day, but it became more difficult as the evening wore on and darkness fell. Playing after dark brought antics and escapades that only increased, as the night grew dark and the light grew dim. Searching became harder in the dark while hiders welcomed the cloak of darkness that overtook those searching for them.

So it is, as we are the children of light. The darkness tries to overtake us, but it can't if we stay in the light. Jesus, Himself, told His followers to walk in the light so the darkness would not overtake them (John 12:35). How might it overtake them? Perhaps with fear of things to come—whether economic calamity or shrinking from violence in the streets. Or it might come in the form of arrogance brought about by too much confidence in oneself and not enough in God. Perhaps by focusing on who has what and our tendency to compare and covet what is not ours. Any of these could draw our hearts away, toward something other than the Sovereign Lord, whose light shines in our hearts and leads us in the path of righteousness.

The brightness of our God can easily be seen in us as we walk in the day. Prior to becoming saved, our life was that of sin. The sin that casts darkness upon us is dispelled in the light of who Jesus is. While we once walked in darkness and without wisdom, we now walk in the wisdom of God, revealed in Christ. Thank God today that we are in Him who is the light.

※

Father, how gracious You are to give us the Light of Your Son, which shines in our hearts and lights up the world to see how amazing You truly are. Help me to live in the light of Your love, reflecting Your radiance and Your truth. In Jesus' Name. Amen.

BEING REDEEMED

And not only they, but ourselves also, which have the firstfruits of the Spirit, even we ourselves groan within ourselves, waiting for the adoption, to wit, the redemption of our body.

ROMANS 8:23, KJV

A young widow, new in Christ, with three young children to clothe and feed, loses her job due to corporate downsizing. She tries desperately to make ends meet. She hesitantly takes her old engagement ring and wedding band to a pawn shop to exchange her possessions for financial gain. Recalling a Sunday school lesson she heard about trusting God, she prays. She struggles to get through another month. Once she has saved a little money, she returns to the pawn shop to redeem her rings. The pawn broker had displayed her rings in a shabby casing in the front window hoping for a quick sale, but that wasn't to be. Most felt the price too high, but the happy young widow was able to redeem her rings. What was too costly for some meant the world to her.

We have the promise of the Holy Spirit that God's work will be done. As His children, we anxiously await the fulfillment of those promises. We wait also as His heirs. We may go through challenges, and times may become difficult; we do so living in the tension between who we are now and who we will be. We have been adopted into His family, and one day we will be fully redeemed by Him.

Like the young widow who agonized over parting with something so precious, although for a short time, we feel the pain of the things that separate us from our God. Only He could purchase us with His own blood, and while the price seemed too high to others, it was not too high for Him. We were created for Him, and by Him, and will go through some things as we wait for what is to come. As we continue moving forward, we do so knowing we are part of God's family and soon will be transformed forever. Just as the widow returned to the shop for her rings, so will Jesus Christ return for us!

My God, my God, oh how I love You. I adore You and thank You for making me a part of Your family—being redeemed—In Jesus' Name. Amen.

GOD IS OUR FATHER

And because ye are sons, God hath sent forth the Spirit of his Son into your hearts, crying, Abba, Father. Wherefore thou art no more a servant, but a son; and if a son, then an heir of God through Christ.

GALATIANS 4:6-7, KJV

Falling from the high bar on the play lot, a young child cries out for a watching parent to come to his rescue. A broken-hearted teen falls into the waiting arms of a parent when she has been taunted by school-yard bullies. And a frayed spouse can't stop the tears from spilling from his eyes when his marriage is on the rocks, as he confesses the pain to a listening father. Each reaches for and receives comfort from the loving and willing parent that has been there for them. They receive what comes from close, intimate relationship. They don't look for the pain to be soothed or comfort to come from the hand and heart of a stranger or passing acquaintance, but from someone trusted and dear.

Even more, we as the children of God can come to Him as His dearly beloved children. We have the blessed consolation of knowing we can cry out to Him, and He hears us. He is not a stranger passing us by, but He is the God whose heart is toward us and whose ear is inclined to hear us, because we are His. We are His because we have received His Son, and His Son demonstrated for us the intimate relationship we can have with God as our Father. Jesus cried out to God, "Abba, Father" when He was in distress about the cross that was to come (Mark 14:36). Although God in flesh, Jesus threw Himself on the heart of His heavenly Father, who He knew would comfort Him and strengthen Him for what was to come. We too can cry "Abba, Father" and our heavenly Father comforts and strengthens us, not because we've been introduced, or met once or twice, but because He knows us and we know Him. He is our Father!

※

Lord God, I thank You for hearing me and coming to my rescue. Thank You that I am able to cry out to You as Your child and know that You are there. Thank You for being my Father. Amen.

ACCESS PASS

For through Him we both have access by one Spirit unto the Father.
EPHESIANS 2:18, KJV

A fter attending a Christian concert, a group of zealous fans had an opportunity to meet the singers and musicians backstage. Everyone was excited to see the musical artists, but only a few did what was necessary to get a purple access pass. Waiting in line for an hour, amid the backstage conversation, an announcement came across the airwaves—only those with a purple access pass would be allowed to meet and speak with the artists. Just five people had the purple pass, and off they went. The rest frowned and quietly walked away, missing the opportunity to spend time with those they had come to see.

When we think of access, consider what Christ does for us before our Father. Through Jesus we have access to God, and yet not everyone will respond to His invitation though He paved the way with His life. We can't even come to God except through His Son. Jesus said, "I am the way, the truth and the life" (John 14:6). He brings us into God's glorious presence, where we can experience the fullness of His love. Imagine, we make appointments to meet with people, even speak with them, but not with God. We will pull out calendars, smartphones, or small sheets of paper to use as a makeshift appointment book, but the same effort isn't always made to get in touch with God.

Stop, take a breath, and realize the One who has made all things possible needs no appointment; He is accessible by faith through prayer. As we go through our day let's remember, because of Jesus we have access to our Father. By God's grace, Jesus' death on the cross brings us before the Father.

Let's celebrate the access we have because our Father gave His Son just to have us. Because of that access, we now have relationship with our Father, who answers our prayers and empowers us by His Spirit!

Dear God, I honor and adore You because of who You are. I thank You for giving me access through Your Son, Jesus. Because of the access I have to You, I am able to come to You knowing I will be received and I belong! Thank you for that in Jesus' Name. Amen.

We are Connected

For by one Spirit are we all baptized into one body...
1 Corinthians 12:13, KJV

Believers are adopted into the same family. That means we're related—blood related, as a matter of fact. We are one in spirit because the Holy Spirit has baptized us into the body of Christ. We may have different roles to play, different gifts to use, and different assignments to carry out, but we need each other to meet one common goal: to glorify God, our Father. We don't always see eye-to-eye, but love overcomes our differences, especially when we live in love—and if we live in God, we live in love (1 John 4:16). We pray together, we serve together, and worship the Lord together. We seek forgiveness when we have offended and forgive those who have offended us. We help one another, we serve one another, and we intercede for one another.

You are part of a great body of believers, and it's the Holy Spirit who connects you. From July through September, the readings will encourage you to always strive for unity within the body, which comes by the Spirit, and to always choose love.

GOD'S SPECIAL GIFT

That the Gentiles should be fellow heirs, and of the same body, and partakers of his promise in Christ by the gospel.

EPHESIANS 3:6, KJV

How many of us have participated in a competition we did not win? However, by virtue of having participated, we received a prize. We walked away happy, feeling a sense of connectedness, because although we did not win the competition, we could boast that we received a prize, indicating that we were part of something special. As children of God, we can "boast" that we are His. We have God's gift of salvation, and we didn't have to compete to receive it.

In his letter to the church at Ephesus, Paul told the Gentiles that they were part of something special. In his prior journeys to Ephesus, Paul shared the gospel, thereby strengthening the church of Jesus Christ. Now Paul wanted the Gentiles to know that God's promise of salvation included them. God had a perfect plan whereby the Gentiles could share with other believers in His inheritance, and they did not have to compete to be partakers of His plan. What an awesome feeling they must have had knowing that they were part of something special and they didn't have to vie for this wonderful gift!

We are part of something special as well; God's promise includes us! When we accepted Jesus Christ, we became partakers of His grace through the Good News. Now we are part of His body, sharing in His blessings with other believers.

How wonderful it is to know that we do not have to compete to win a place in God's Kingdom. God had us in mind in His plan of salvation. All we have to do is receive Him as our Lord and Savior, and the gift of salvation is ours. We can now enjoy a wonderful relationship with an awesome God, who gives special gifts. He is perfect in everything, and His plan of salvation is sure.

Thank You, Father, for loving me and including me in Your plan of salvation. What a privilege it is to be a partaker of Your grace. I have received a gift that indicates I am part of something special. Please show me how to appreciate what You have given me. In Jesus' Name. Amen!

WE ARE FAMILY

Consequently, you are no longer foreigners and aliens, but fellow citizens with God's people and members of God's household.

EPHESIANS 2:19, NIV

Families adopt children for varying reasons. Still, there is one commonality: the love for the family unit. Often, when a young child is adopted, the family does all it can to make the child feel like a member of the household. This is necessary for the well-being and stability of the child. The child develops a sense of security as he or she understands his or her place in the family. We can relate to this in some way in that we have been adopted into God's family. Being a part of His family helps assure us of our place in the kingdom of God.

In Paul's writings to the Gentiles, he encourages them concerning their place with God. God saw no difference between them and other believers—and they needed to know that. Whereas many believers considered the Gentiles foreigners and aliens to the kingdom of God, the Gentiles were now fellow-heirs and members of God's household. God received them into His family, and they now had the same privileges that other believers had. What a privilege and a blessing that they could join with others and be part of such a great family.

Many of us come from different backgrounds, nationalities, religions, and the like. We were even once considered foreigners and aliens to the kingdom of God. While we were yet estranged from Him, God drew us. In His infinite love, God included us in His plan of salvation. Now we are joined with other believers, living our lives as fellow citizens in the kingdom of God!

What a privilege it is to be members of God's household. The more we learn of God, the more we can appreciate who we are in Him. While we can never thank God enough for receiving us into such a great family of believers, we can honor Him by living lives that please Him.

Gracious Father, I thank You for receiving me into Your family and making me feel at home. What a privilege it is to be joined with such a great body of believers. Help me to live a life that honors and appreciates You. And please help me to be mindful to always tell others about the family of God. In Jesus' Name. Amen!

WE BELONG TO GOD

If you belong to Christ, then you are Abraham's seed, and heirs according to the promise.

GALATIANS 3:29, NIV

All of us are tied to someone. For instance, when we were younger and did something wrong, an adult probably said, "Whose child is this?" Someone probably replied, "That's what-cha-ma-call-its child." Of course, the adult knew our parents, and we could probably expect a spanking for our misdeed when we got home. As Christians, we belong to God. If someone asks, "Who is he or she?", we can only hope that the response is "That's God's child."

Paul's letter to the Galatians sheds light on an important issue that developed. The Gentiles had enthusiastically received Paul's teachings of who they were in Christ, and then later received teachings that were contrary to Paul's. The Judaizers insisted that the Gentiles could not be true Christians until they submitted to the Jewish ordinance of circumcision. They also said that the Galatians had to adhere to the Law of Moses. Paul's letter attempts to disprove the Judaizers' false claims and prove that people are justified by faith through Christ's atoning work on the cross. Paul wanted the Gentiles to know that their identity was tied to Abraham through the shed blood of Jesus Christ. Moreover, every promise God made to Abraham was theirs.

What a wonderful feeling, knowing that we are also tied to Abraham through the shed blood of Jesus Christ. In addition, we are heirs of God's promise. As we spend time in God's Word, we have the opportunity to learn and understand what that promise means to us. Moreover, as we grow in His Word, we can shield ourselves from teachings that are contrary to God's Word. And when others look at us and wonder who we are, they can say with confidence, "That's God's child!"

✦

Heavenly Father, I thank You. I feel honored to belong to an awesome God who has a great plan. You had me in mind when You died on the cross, and everything I will ever need is in You. Please help me to learn and understand what Your promises mean to me so I might live my life in such a way that others know that I belong to You. In Jesus' Name. Amen!

Living a Life of Freedom

And it shall come to pass, that in the place where it was said unto them, Ye are not my people; there shall they be called the children of the living God.

ROMANS 9:26, KJV

America was now free! Historically, the country was connected to Great Britain. However, on July 2, 1776, the Continental Congress voted in favor of thirteen colonies declaring America's independence from Great Britain. Two days later, the Congressional delegates adopted the Declaration of Independence, a historic document drafted by Thomas Jefferson.[20] From 1776 until today, July 4th has been celebrated as the birth of American independence. As Christians, we understand being free because of the atoning work of Jesus Christ. God has called us out of darkness and into His marvelous light, and we are now free to live victoriously as His children!

In speaking to the church at Rome, Paul quotes from Hosea 1:10, where Israel was first called "not my people." Hosea later prophesied that Israel would be restored and called "the sons of the living God." Here, Paul wanted the Gentiles to know that while they were formerly considered "not God's people," they were now called the children of God because of His grace. God calls and chooses whom He pleases, and now the Gentiles could share in the good news of Jesus Christ with other believers. This knowledge brought freedom to the Gentiles.

While we were once considered "not God's people" because of sin, we are *now* called children of God. When we responded to the call of salvation, we received freedom and the opportunity to live a victorious life in Him. Now we can share the Good News of Jesus Christ so others may have the opportunity to be called children of God. The more time we spend in, and live according to, God's Word, the more we become independent of this world's system. As God's children, living victoriously with other believers will please Him!

※

Thank You, Lord, for Your death on the cross and Your great plan of salvation. I have been freed to live a victorious life in You. Hallelujah! As I study Your Word, please help me to understand and appreciate what being a child of God really means. I will always bless and honor Your Name. Amen!

WE ARE A FAMILY OF FAITH

There is neither Jew nor Greek, there is neither bond nor free, there is neither male nor female: for ye are all one in Christ Jesus.

GALATIANS 3:28, KJV

Sometimes we feel alone in our walk and service to God. The events of the day and the challenges of the times may cause us to feel alienated from others. Our lives and testimonies become *my* struggle and *my* journey, somehow separate from others'. We may even feel alone in our victories.

But we are not alone. We are each a part of the whole in Christ Jesus. We have a shared journey and destiny. It requires reworking the mind and reconditioning the heart to realize that we—male and female; Black, White, Asian, and Latino; rich and poor—are all one in Christ Jesus. Our differences don't have to divide us when Christ has come to unite us!

When we consider that we are not alone, we must also remember that we are not separate from each other. Sure, we might be divided by land and experiences, or we may have cultural differences, but we are a family of faith. What seems to separate us is but a call to learn more about and appreciate the diverse work of Christ!

There is one God and Father of all. As people of faith, we share the same heritage in Christ Jesus. It is the one Spirit that fills us. It's that one love that unites and harmonizes us. It is our one faith that moves the mountains in our lives.

When we feel alone or isolated in any way, let us remember that God has called many all over this world—from all cultures and languages—to salvation. If we should think that others are somehow better or worse than us, let's remember our kinship. Let us remember one another in our prayers and in our hopes and dreams. We are not alone; we are a family of faith in Christ Jesus!

※

Our Father, which art in heaven, hallowed be Thy name. I am so thankful that, although I have my own spiritual journey, I share in the faith of many who believe in and worship You. I celebrate this kinship today and honor the singleness of the diversity of Your ways! And so it is!

BY ONE SPIRIT

For by one Spirit are we all baptized into one body, whether we be Jews or Gentiles, whether we be bond or free; and have been all made to drink into one Spirit.

1 CORINTHIANS 12:13, KJV

We often sing "I Need You to Survive," which speaks to how we need one another and how important people are to us.[21] While we recognize our need for others, we cannot help but acknowledge that, from the time we were toddlers, we were encouraged to be independent. "You can do it" was the echo, and we did our best to operate independently of others. However, God has so connected us in the body of Christ that we cannot make it except we look to one another for help. No matter who we are or where we come from, we need each other to survive.

In our Scripture, Paul admonished the church at Corinth concerning its role in the body. All of its members were baptized into one body, and all would partake of the same drink (the Holy Spirit). Since they were members of the same body, Paul wanted them to know that they needed each other to operate effectively; they could not do so independently of each other. God's design was that they look to each other to help carry out matters concerning them and the church. They were members of the same body, and each of them were equal in God's eyes.

We serve a loving God, who is concerned about each of His children. When we were baptized, a spiritual transformation took place, connecting us with God and other believers. Now we are members of the same body and, like the church at Corinth, need each other to make it. As members of the body, let us support each other with prayer and encouragement, so we may operate effectively in the church. This will not only please God, but it will also bless those in the body of Christ.

❧

Thank You, Father, for connecting me with other believers. Your perfect plan of salvation has helped me see the significance of oneness in the body. Please help me to appreciate the value others play in my spiritual walk so that together we might bless You. In Jesus' Name I pray. Amen!

A Life that Honors God

Do you not know that your body is a temple of the Holy Spirit, who is in you, whom you have received from God? You are not your own; you were bought at a price. Therefore honor God with your body.

1 Corinthians 6:19-20, NIV

Some years ago, a professional basketball player was involved in a motorcycle accident. Because of that accident, he sustained multiple injuries. The player had violated the terms of his contract by riding a motorcycle and injuring himself. Eventually he was released by his team.

A player's life is not his or her own when he or she signs a contract. The player is expected to live up to the guidelines of that contract. In a way, Christians can relate to that. When we received the Holy Spirit, our life became that of Jesus Christ's. Consequently, there is the expectation that we represent God in a manner that brings glory and honor to Him.

In our Scripture, Paul addressed the Corinthians concerning how they were presenting themselves. Jesus made the ultimate sacrifice when He died on the cross. He sent His Holy Spirit to empower them because they now they belonged to God. However, the Corinthians were still living the same as they had lived before they received the Holy Spirit. Paul reminded them that they indeed belonged to God and that the expectation was that they live a life that honored God.

Jesus Christ has poured out His Spirit upon us, as well, and now we belong to Him. Because we have the Holy Spirit, we are equipped to live our lives in a manner that honors God. "It's not about me!" we always say, and that's true. However, it is all about God, and we can demonstrate that His ultimate sacrifice meant something as we live a life that honors Him. Spending time in God's Word and praying give us the opportunity to learn how best to bring Him glory, and He deserves just that!

❋

Thank You, Father, for Your Holy Spirit. My life is not my own, and I am reminded of this as I read Your Word. I pray that my life reflects an appreciation of Your ultimate sacrifice and that I always bring glory and honor to You. In Jesus' Name I pray. Amen!

FITTING INTO GOD'S DESIGN

From him the whole body, joined and held together by every supporting ligament, grows and builds itself up in love, as each part does its work.

EPHESIANS 4:16, NIV

Most of us have put together a jigsaw puzzle at least once in our lifetime. In order to make a complete picture, every piece of the puzzle has to fit into its respective groove. Once we have completed the puzzle, we are able to take in a beautiful design. Christians are a lot like a puzzle. God has uniquely created each of us, and we play a vital part in the body of Christ. When we come together to help build up the kingdom of God, we show forth God's love and the unity God desires we have in the body of Christ.

The church at Ephesus was gifted; God had given gifts to the church in order to equip the saints for ministry, and to help build up the body of Christ. While the gifts contributed to the growth of the church, it's possible that the Ephesians did not understand the significance of working together to promote that growth. Paul addressed that very issue in his letter, indicating that each part of the body had a purpose. As they worked together, not only would they promote unity in the church, but they would also build themselves up in love.

What a blessing it is to be part of God's design. God has purposed that Christians come together as one, which is vital to the health and growth of the church. God has gifted His people, and He expects us to work together to help build up His Kingdom. As we read God's Word and pray, we learn how we fit into His design.

Coming together to fulfill God's purpose helps promote unity in the church, and we will build ourselves up in love. This will not only bless the body of Christ, but it will also bring glory and honor to God.

Thank You, Father, for Your perfect plan of salvation. I know that I play a vital part in building up the kingdom of God, and I appreciate being a part of Your plan. Please show me how to work with other believers so that I can help promote unity in the church and build myself up in love. In Jesus' Name. Amen!

JESUS REIGNS OVER ALL!

And he is the head of the body, the church: who is the beginning, the firstborn from the dead; that in all things he might have the preeminence.

COLOSSIANS 1:18, KJV

More than ten years ago, our nation suffered a dastardly attack on the landmark twin towers in New York City. Because of that attack, the nation was on high alert. Many wondered what our next move would be, especially since there was so much at stake. We knew there had to be some form of response, and the only person who could make a critical decision concerning our nation was the President of the United States. Not long after the attack, our president declared war. While a president's authority is limited in scope, we serve a God who has supreme authority over all creation.

Paul wrote to the Colossians because of the false teachings that had spread throughout the church. Christians were being told that, while Jesus was superhuman, He was not truly God. Paul's response was that Jesus created all things and that He was all they needed. He was Lord and, because of His resurrection, made possible their salvation. Jesus was superior over everything, and those were the teachings Paul wanted the Colossians to embrace.

We are blessed to serve a God who reigns supreme over all creation. All things were created by Him and for Him, and He is to be praised! Jesus is the head of the church, and we look to Him for all things. What could possibly go on that we cannot tell God about? Moreover, what is going on that God does not already know? The answer to both of these questions is "Nothing." When we are faced with situations, let us look to God first; He knows how best to handle them and desires that we acknowledge Him. The more time we spend in our Word and pray, the more we will embrace God's preeminence. He is truly Lord, and He reigns over all!

※

Heavenly Father, You are the creator of all things and in You all things consist. You are concerned about every facet of my being, and I acknowledge Your preeminence. When I am faced with uncomfortable situations, please show me how to look to You first, for You know how best to see me through every one of them. In Jesus' Mighty Name. Amen!

THE POWER OF ONE

I therefore, the prisoner of the Lord, beseech you that ye walk worthy of the vocation wherewith ye are called, with all lowliness and meekness, with longsuffering, forbearing one another in love; endeavouring to keep the unity of the Spirit in the bond of peace. There is one body, and one Spirit, even as ye are called in one hope of your calling; one Lord, one faith, one baptism, one God and Father of all, who is above all, and through all, and in you all.

EPHESIANS 4:1-6, KJV

Throughout this Scripture text, there is an underlying theme of oneness. The writer wants us to live our collective Christian life in unity with God, as well as with our brothers and sisters. One sure way of becoming one with God is to experience Him through His Word. How do we do that, you might ask? By studying God's Word and becoming familiar with His character and His mode of operation. When we do this, we will inevitably make a connection to God by applying His Word to our lives and the many situations we find ourselves dealing with on any given day.

Here, the apostle Paul is promoting oneness within the household of faith. Although his letter was written to the saints at Ephesus, it is also applicable to us today because the message herein has withstood the test of time. We must still strive for oneness of mind and purpose amongst ourselves. When we strive as such, we position ourselves, as a body of believers, to do great things for the kingdom of God.

Cultivating a spirit of unity allows us to focus on what's good for the whole and not just its parts. He wants us (the church) to be of one body and one Spirit, even as we are called in one hope, considering there is one Lord, one faith, and one baptism. He then concludes by declaring that there is one God and Father of all, who is above all, through all, and in you all. Now that's the power of one, ya'll!

❧

Father, I long to be one with You and one with my brothers and sisters. Help me walk worthy of You. In Christ's Name. Amen.

SHEEP IN THE FOLD

And other sheep I have, which are not of this fold: them also I must bring, and they shall hear my voice; and there shall be one fold, and one shepherd.

JOHN 10:16, KJV

God has sent His great call to the whole world! It's a call that resonates in the hearts and minds of people of all backgrounds, cultures, and nationalities. It's a single call to salvation, love, and justice on the earth. It's a call to unity and peace, the kind of call that wakes us up and gives us sweet rest. It's the call to restoration and reconciliation in Christ Jesus.

We are all called from a "scattered" state to a unified assembly, led by the one Shepherd of the fold. We are all called to one field of green pastures and led to the same still waters. It is one Shepherd who shows us the way and inspires us to take the walk. This Shepherd brings us together and unifies us in His divine purpose unto a common destiny.

Who are we then to judge and divide ourselves? What gives us the right to create obstacles for one another in order to come to God? Why try to hinder anyone's hearing of the call of God? After all, it is the Lord's voice that does the calling. It is His place of plenty to which we are called. It is at His table that we sit to share the blessed meal. It is His oil of anointing that overflows each of our cups. We are overtaken by His goodness and dwell in His house.

It is the Lord Jesus who loves us and is the Shepherd to this wandering, weak fold strong only in Him. In love and faith, we welcome all whom the Lord calls!

Father, I rejoice that Your call is great and is heard by all who seek and listen for Your voice. I thank You that nothing can hinder Your will or purpose, and I rejoice in how You gather Your children together in Your Name. You are the good shepherd of my life and I am one of many in Your loving fold! Thank You, God. And so it is!

A TRADITION WORTH STANDING FOR

To which He called you by our gospel, for the obtaining of the glory of our Lord Jesus Christ. Therefore, brethren, stand fast and hold the traditions which you were taught, whether by word or our epistle.

2 THESSALONIANS 2:14-15, NKJV

Honoring family traditions is important to many of us. We hold them as special and do our best to keep them going. For instance, there are those who come together for family reunions. Others come together on the Friday after Thanksgiving for Christmas shopping. Still others come together for birthday parties and other social events. Regardless of the family tradition, it is a special, time-honored occasion and we look forward to each one. Traditions are important in the kingdom of God as well. Whenever someone shares the gospel of Jesus Christ, the tradition of bringing others to the kingdom is being passed on.

In our Scripture, Paul encourages the Thessalonians, who were enduring hardship, to "stand fast," despite their sufferings. Through Paul's teachings of the gospel, many had received salvation and were now experiencing persecution. Nevertheless, God had purposed from eternity past that the Thessalonians be saved, and it was important that they hold on to the teachings they had received from Paul. For sure Jesus was coming back and they would enter into the rest that God had promised them.

What a privilege it is to share the gospel with others. They have the opportunity to hear God's Word and receive Him as Lord of their lives. This is a tradition that we can pass on to others so that the gospel continues to be spread to as many people as possible. Even though there will be times our sharing of the gospel is rejected, and times when we will be persecuted, the rewards of doing so far outweigh any hardships we may endure. Christians can look forward to entering into Jesus' rest when He returns, and this is something worth passing on.

Thank You, Lord, for allowing me to hear about a tradition that has lasted for generations. The spreading of the gospel has continued, and many have been drawn to You. Please help me to continue the tradition of telling others about You, so they, too, can have the opportunity to do the same. In Jesus' Name. Amen!

THE TALK

Wherefore whosoever shall eat of this bread, and drink this cup of the Lord, unworthily, shall be guilty of the body and blood of the Lord. But let a man examine himself, and so let him eat of that bread, and drink of that cup. For he that eateth and drinketh unworthily, eateth and drinketh damnation to himself, not discerning the Lord's body. For this cause many are weak and sickly among you, and many sleep.

1 CORINTHIANS 11:27-30, KJV

How many of us, when we were younger, visited others' homes and were given "the talk" before we got there? "The talk" consisted of telling us how to act, and it was important that we did as we were told. Christians can relate to being given "the talk" as well. God's Word teaches us how we should conduct ourselves prior to receiving the Lord's Supper, and it is important that we do as we are told.

Paul addressed the manner in which the Corinthians were approaching the Lord's Supper. Some of them were drunk and others selfishly ate without any regard for those Christians who did not have food. Paul admonished them to examine their own lives to see if there was anything lacking, especially since how they received the Lord's Supper did not demonstrate their faith in His work on the cross. It was critical that they change their ways because the results of their selfishness had serious consequences.

How wonderful it is to partake of the Lord's Supper; Jesus encourages us to do so. Let us pray that God shines the spotlight on whatever is in our lives that is not reflective of His teachings so that we can repent of any sins before coming to the table. Just as when we were younger and received "the talk," shouldn't we first get "the talk" straight from God's Word before our next Lord's Supper? Doing so will allow us to right any wrongs in our lives, so that what God sees will bring glory and honor to Him.

※

Thank You, Father, for allowing me to participate in the Lord's Supper. You encourage me to examine myself so that I know what is lacking in my life. Please show me how to act so that when I come to the table what You see will bring glory and honor to You. In Jesus' Name. Amen!

FOLLOWING A GOOD EXAMPLE

Be ye followers of me, even as I also am of Christ. Now I praise you, brethren, that ye remember me in all things, and keep the ordinances, as I delivered them to you.

1 CORINTHIANS 11:1-2, KJV

The Bible lets us know that it's okay to follow the good examples of others in life. When we follow something or someone, we seek to "keep with, comply with, adhere to, pursue, or understand" it or them. There are several adages that speak to this, including "association brings assimilation" and "birds of a feather flock together." If we want to become like something or someone, keeping company with it in thought, word, and deed is the way to do it!

The apostle Paul wrote to the saints of the church at Corinth about their interactions with one another, and the examples they were setting and following. It was both a warning against participating in idol worship and a declaration of their right to exercise their liberty by keeping ordinances in Christ Jesus. This letter teaches us not to hinder or be hindered in our spiritual experience by the nuances of the practice of our faith. Paul said that whatever we do should be done to the glory of God and with a free conscious. As a result, our time of fellowship renders a time of honor and joy.

Former pastors and leaders passed many of our church traditions from generation to generation. Our goal as church leaders and followers is to adhere to biblical mandates. Our actions are to be those that spur one another to thanksgiving and the greater good.

Paul said to follow him as he imitated, or followed, Christ. He made clear the standard of Christian protocol. As we go along on this spiritual journey, it's commendable to admire our leaders. However, we must do so remembering the origin of our faith—Jesus Christ—and the example He set, which, above all, speaks to and directs our steps and all our affairs.

❧

Heavenly Father, You have set a standard for Your children. You have provided great leaders and examples of those who follow Your Truth. Thank You for leaders and peers who walk this walk and talk this talk. Together, we edify one another and glorify You in all that we do. Amen.

SOVEREIGN APPEAL FOR UNITY

I speak as to wise men; judge ye what I say. The cup of blessing which we bless, is it not the communion of the blood of Christ? The bread which we break, is it not the communion of the body of Christ? For we being many are one bread, and one body: for we are all partakers of that one bread.

1 CORINTHIANS 10:15-17, KJV

The cross is a powerful symbol of our relationship with God and our brothers and sisters. Our relationship with God is seen in the vertical line, while the horizontal plane extends outward to show how we are to be the reaching hands, the welcoming arms, the rescuing presence of Christ on earth. When examined together, these two components depict unity and strength held together by Christ's love. These relationships are what we cherish and celebrate when we take part in the Lord's Supper.

The saints in the Corinthian church had started taking their Communion gathering for granted. Instead of focusing on their relationship with Jesus Christ and one another, this congregation started partaking of a Communion meal without recognizing its purpose. They didn't give recognition to the sacrifice of Jesus. They didn't share with one another.

Paul reminded the Corinthian Christians that Jesus' invitation to eat the bread and drink the wine that symbolize the Lord's precious, chaste body and His purely innocent blood sacrificed for the remission of our sins is a privilege. Paul charged them to remember that Communion joins us to other believers in relationships that are not distant and indifferent. Communion requires that we have hearts filled with forgiveness and wrapped in the love and will of God.

Paul's words remind us today that we are one body in Christ, anchored in the hope of the work done on the cross when the Lord's body was broken and His blood was shed for us. Jesus' invitation to eat of His body and drink of His blood is His sovereign appeal for unity, a reminder that we are no longer children pushing one another away. As children of God, we must acknowledge Him with tear-stained hearts as we eat, sharing His love and peace.

✯

Eternal Sovereign Christ, thank You for Your body and blood given for me. I am grateful. Amen.

SINGLED OUT

And my spirit hath rejoiced in God my Saviour. For he hath regarded the low estate of his handmaiden: for, behold, from henceforth all generations shall call me blessed. For he that is mighty hath done to me great things; and holy is his name.

LUKE 1:47-49, KJV

Do you come from a large family or a small one? Do hundreds of people live in your neighborhood? How about your city? Do you sometimes feel like one of the crowd and think that your presence is lost or overlooked? If at any point you've wondered if your efforts make a difference, then today's Scripture—taken from Mary's song of praise for being chosen as the mother of Jesus—is for you.

Some religious artists depict Mary as angelic and god-like. The truth is that there was no notable difference between Mary and the other young Jewish girls of her day. There was nothing in her praise, thanksgiving, or worship that made her special. Even the words of her song admit that she was of low estate, a handmaiden, a servant of God. So why did God choose her to be the human vessel for the birth of the Messiah? It was God's grace—His unmerited favor—that made the difference.

Like us, Mary realized that God had singled her out. She recognized that since divine favor had found her in the crowd, she had to trust God even more. She accepted and obeyed the will of God even though she didn't understand it all. Mary sings of joy because God chose to use her life in a way that would impact the entire world for generations to come.

So what about you? What singles you out? God has chosen you from among the crowd to experience His love. God has filled you with His power and made you His servant. Like Mary, you must realize that His grace enables you to accomplish life-altering assignments for His Kingdom. So rejoice! Sing your thanks for the dreams and aspirations He has given you. Praise Him that He has counted you worthy to do spectacular works in His Kingdom.

❧

Eternal Sovereign God, my spirit takes pleasure in exalting Your Name. My soul sings in thanksgiving that You have chosen me to be a vessel that shows forth Your glorious splendor. Amen.

THE AUTHORITY OF JESUS

But that ye may know that the Son of man hath power on earth to forgive sins, (then saith he to the sick of the palsy,) Arise, take up thy bed, and go unto thine house. And he arose, and departed to his house. But when the multitudes saw it, they marvelled, and glorified God, which had given such power unto men.

MATTHEW 9:6-8, KJV

The life and authority of Jesus has often come into question by doubters and detractors of the Christian faith. They questioned if Jesus was who He said He was. They debated if He was who the people proclaimed. Jesus knew what the people were saying openly about Him, and He knew what was in their hearts.

The unfolding of Jesus as the Son of God came gradually. Through the miracles He performed, the wisdom He displayed, and the affirmation from the Father, the community began to see Jesus for who He was. As Jesus chose His disciples and they grew in their faith walk, belief in Jesus began to grow, as well.

Jesus knew His purpose. He let the people know that His reach and impact on earth was not limited to, or by, their lack of understanding or willingness to believe in Him as one sent by God. Yes, Jesus had power to heal, and He had authority to forgive sins. In our text, at the command of Jesus, the forgiven man took up his bed and returned to his own house, healed and forgiven. He returned to his own house knowing the love of the Father and the authority of the Son. He returned knowing that Jesus could address not just the symptoms of sin, but He could address the deeper issues of the soul!

We, too, know the authority of Jesus. We rest in His power to get to the core of our being and produce the healings, create the change, and bring the internal transformation we need. Even in a world of atheists, agnostics, and those who claim another, we acknowledge the authority of the One who is Lord of all and makes our lives brand new!

Jesus, You have come in the name of the Father. Sent by God, You have power and authority in heaven and earth. Through You, my life is transformed. In You are abounding grace, mercy, and great joy! Amen and amen!

WALK IN THE LIGHT

But if we walk in the light, as he is in the light, we have fellowship one with another, and the blood of Jesus Christ his Son cleanseth us from all sin. If we say that we have no sin, we deceive ourselves, and the truth is not in us. If we confess our sins, he is faithful and just to forgive our sins, and to cleanse us from all unrighteousness.

1 JOHN 1:7-9, KJV

The light of God is like a warm, fluorescent, beaming ray of light! It brings clarity to our path that we might more easily find our way. It glows like a burning fire through the darkest and coldest nights. It is the light of God that empowers us to walk in the ways of God.

Christian fellowship is not just a casual coming together of folks, but it is communion, partnership, friendship, and relationship. As a fellowship of believers, sometimes the most we have in common is Jesus, and our faith in Him. This is powerful in itself, but God is saying that to fulfill our purpose as the body of Christ, we need to learn to be in right relationship with one another.

Our text tells us that if we walk in the light—in understanding and Truth—then we have fellowship one with another, and the power of His blood sacrifice is effectual in our lives. It indicates that if on the other hand, we walk in darkness with hidden agendas, lack of spirituality, pride, and unconfessed sin, we walk as those out of fellowship with the Father, and this poses a problem for our coming together.

The text points out that we should walk in the light "as He is in the light." It says if we claim to have fellowship with Jesus, that this must be proved out in our fellowship with one another, otherwise we are living a lie! In walking in the light, our fellowship with God and one another is affirmed!

❧

God, You are light. In You is no darkness at all! I walk in the light as Jesus is in the light. This light shines forth from within me! I thank You that I have fellowship with You. This joyful fellowship with You produces healthy and happy relationships with others in my life. And so it is!

MADE BY GOD

For we are his workmanship, created in Christ Jesus unto good works, which God hath before ordained that we should walk in them.

EPHESIANS 2:10, KJV

We are creations of God—made in the image and likeness of God for good purposes. We are expressions of God and the work of His hands. By design, we were created for good. When we are open to the mind of Christ, we understand we were created to do good works.

It's great knowing that we have a good purpose for being here! As we look around and experience the not-so-good things of the world, it can lead us to doubt God's goodness, and our capacity for good as well. But, our text reference assures us that we are the work of God—no accident. We are the work of God—not of some extraterrestrial being, or the devil, or even ourselves. We are created from good, for good. We are God's workmanship (work of art) and masterpiece!

We can imagine ourselves as poetic expressions, picturesque paintings, dance movements, or erected sculptures of God. Our beings are illustrations of God expressing Himself in, and through, us. We are born out of God's divine creativity. Like the workmanship of any artist, we have His vibe and flair flowing in and through us as a mark of His creation. When people look at us, they see "Made by God" imprinted upon us!

By design, even through suffering, pain, and things gone wrong, we were made to become what God created us to be. We were created in, and are being conformed to the image of Jesus Christ. This is our eternal call and our destiny!

Our task is to yield ourselves as ready clay in the Potter's hands. As the Father had a plan and purpose for Christ Jesus, He has a plan for our lives, too. Let us express the masterpiece that we are!

Dear Heavenly Father, You are my maker and You are good. I praise You that I am created in Your image. You do good things and, through You, so do I. You think good thoughts and, through You, so do I. No matter the appearances, my life is a reflection of You, my God! And so it is!

SECOND CHANCE

For God says, "At just the right time, I heard you. On the day of salvation, I helped you." Indeed, the "right time" is now. Today is the day of salvation.

2 CORINTHIANS 6:2, NLT

Steve Jobs and Steve Wozniak were not the only founders of Apple computers. There was a third founder, Ronald Wayne, who pulled out long before Apple went *to* "big time." Wayne's story of missed opportunity causes us to reminisce about the opportunities we've missed and the bitter taste that surfaced once we realized that those opportunities would never come knocking again.

In 2 Corinthians 6:2, the apostle Paul cites Isaiah 49:8, where God told Israel about a time when He would send the Redeemer to reclaim them, despite the sins they had committed. In essence, God was saying that although Israel missed every opportunity to serve Him as He had instructed, He would send the Messiah to give them a second chance to glorify His name.

Paul found Isaiah's words appropriate for the Corinthians as he urged them to hold to their faith in Jesus Christ. The Corinthians had struggled with sinful behavior among their members. They found it difficult to stand strong for Christ in a city where pagan worship was the accepted norm and those who misrepresented Christianity were always busy distorting the truth of the gospel. Through Isaiah 49:8, Paul reminded the Corinthians that, while God told Israel the second chance was coming, through Jesus Christ God gave the Corinthians the opportunity and power to get it right.

Paul's message is timely for us as well. Despite being members of the body of Christ, we know that we have missed opportunities to glorify God. Our Scripture today reminds us that, despite our shortfalls, "at just the right time" God heard us. Despite our sinful past, "on the day of salvation," the Lord helped us. Because we have been sealed with the Holy Spirit, we have the power to act on today's second chance. We need not dwell on painful memories or regrets. Today we can know that "indeed, the 'right time' is now."

✷

Thank You, Lord, for today's second chance. Help me to remember that as part of Your body, I can cast my cares on You and take every opportunity to glorify You in my life. Amen.

THE TRANSCENDING POWER OF UNITY

Now I beseech you brethren, by the name of our Lord Jesus Christ, that ye all speak the same thing, and (that) there be no divisions among you; but that ye be perfectly joined together in the same mind and in the same judgment.

1 CORINTHIANS 1:10, KJV

Have you ever worked on a difficult task with a group of people who were unified? Yes, there may have been difficulties and the goals may have even seemed unreachable, but when people band together for a common cause, they are able to rise above the difficulties and achieve their common goals. Unity is more than an organizing principle; it is a spiritual force that connects us to one another through the Holy Spirit.

As believers, we are accepted in the beloved, according to God's good pleasure (Ephesians 1:5-6). We are now, and forevermore, a part of His family, sharing in the fortune of unity. Through our rebirth we possess the qualities of our heavenly Father. Unshackled, we willfully strive together toward a common cause: to obey God, proclaim the gospel, and love one another as Christ loves us.

Surely there will be upsets, but the Holy Spirit transcends all experiences, adversities, and challenges that are contrary to God's will. Our unity is the ironclad fact that we are of one body, one faith, and one baptism—serving our Lord, who is in us, and faithfully encouraging each other. Regardless of the challenges and constant changes in our lives, it is through Christ alone that we have the ability not to succumb to divisions, but rather seek solutions in peace, love, and growth within the expansion of our adopted family, which is filled with wisdom, empathy, and prayers.

The love of Christ, and our going forward in agreement to do His will, is the vantage point from which we settle all manner of conflicts. His Spirit of reconciliation is the superior conduit to successful relationships. We strive cohesively together in unity that transcends all differences—remaining steadfast, unmovable, always abounding in the work of the Lord.

❧

Eternal Sovereign God, You've fashioned me to be capable beyond my own reasoning, strengths, and love to move forward with my sisters and brothers in Christ with the transcending power of unity. Help us "to speak the same thing" as You. Thank You for my eternal family. Amen.

WE VALUE THE FELLOWSHIP

Not forsaking the assembling of ourselves together, as the manner of some is; but exhorting one another: and so much the more, as ye see the day approaching.

HEBREWS 10:25, KJV

Today we can find church services when we turn on television or listen to the radio. We can watch the "live streaming" of Sunday church services and Bible classes in real time. We get daily devotionals e-mailed to us or sent to our Twitter and Facebook newsfeeds. We are becoming accustomed to hearing spiritual lessons from various sources, often from the comfort of our homes, or from some electronic device, as we go about our busy day. Many of us even make our financial contributions online.

Having a number of resources to tap into the Word of God is a valuable asset. However, there is value in heart-to-heart and hand-to-hand connection in the body of Christ. While we want to stay in step with the times, we don't want to do it at the expense of following God's model for His church. God designed and desires us to be a family, connected to one another, learning from each other, and growing together. There is a blessing in the fellowship!

With all the technological advances, we may be tempted to give in to the feelings of fatigue and stress that make us say, "I'll just stay in this Sunday. We must guard against the distractions that magnify the sense of separation we may feel from time to time. God wants us to come together to know and to love one another.

When we come together we further declare and solidify our faith. We share in our joys. We help one another through our problems. We find greater hope for our lives.

Coming together is a design of the intelligence of God, who sees and knows all—past, present, and future. He knows what we need. When we come together, we follow His mandate and open ourselves to a corporate move of the Holy Spirit.

❧

Lord, thank You for the church! Thank You for the opportunity to come together with others of like faith, with one heart and mind to worship, praise, serve and hear from You. Bless our coming together Father, may it honor and glorify You. Amen!

AGÀPE

By this all will know that you are My disciples, if you have love for one another.

JOHN 13:35, NKJV

Words give insight into the significance of a concept in a given culture. In the English speaking world, we use the same word to talk about our affinity for inanimate objects as we use for humans. "I love pizza"; "I love my mother." Yet in the Greek language, in which the New Testament was written, there were at least four words that captured the nuances of what we call love.

Eros was used for a sensual or passionate love. *Storge* was used for the affection experienced and expressed between family members. *Philea* was used for friendship or the love for humankind.

Yet there is a fourth word that was in a class all by itself. *Agàpe* was the Greek word used to describe a true love. It came to be used to describe the love that God has for us and the love we are to have for God and for one another. Essentially, *agàpe* is a word that was adopted by and infused with special meaning in the Christian community.

Agàpe is the love that is shed abroad in our hearts by the Holy Spirit (Romans 5:5) and knits us together. *Agàpe* acts first and foremost for the good and welfare of another. *Agàpe* is self-giving. *Agàpe* is a sacrificial love that pours itself out for the sake of someone else.

Jesus stressed to His disciples that *agàpe* was to be the distinguishing characteristic of the Christian community. Notice it is not our political affiliation, race, ethnicity, gender and social status that are the true marks of our identity as followers of Christ. It is our devotion to a God who devoted Himself to our redemption. It is our commitment to care for others because God cares for us.

When the people around us look at us, can they see the love of Jesus expressed in our relationships? Can those in our home, at work, or in school see love in our actions? Can others hear love in our words, our tone—even when we are under pressure?

Today, let's commit to helping others see us as disciples of Christ by our love.

❧

Dear Lord, thank You for Your love for me. I want to be a witness of love and ask for Your help and grace today. Amen.

HAVE THE COURAGE TO FLEE

Flee fornication. Every sin that a man doeth is without the body; but he that committeth fornication sinneth against his own body.

1 CORINTHIANS 6:18, KJV

You're searching the Web for the best airfare to a certain destination. You click on a travel site when suddenly a lurid picture pops into view, arresting your attention for a split second. What do you do? Correct answer: You close the browser immediately. You pray: *protect my heart, Jesus; purge what I've just seen.* In short, you flee.

A Bible patriarch named Joseph did just that. Faced with intense sexual temptation, he fled (Genesis 39:12). Joseph was a Hebrew slave of a chief officer named Potiphar. Potiphar soon recognized Joseph's exceptional administrative skills and appointed him manager of his household. The only problem: Potiphar's wife had also taken notice of the handsome young Israelite. Daily she invited Joseph to commit adultery, but in his integrity, he refused. Finally, one day, when they were alone in the house, she grabbed Joseph by his garment. How did he handle that hot seat? There was no time to lose—he fled.

Why the undignified act of fleeing? Because immoral thoughts evolve quickly, and one has only a few seconds to resist. Fornication starts as a thought but, once entertained and not rebuked, evolves into an unholy action. Jesus declared if a man looks at a woman in lust, he has already committed adultery in his heart. An unchecked thought nourishes an unchaste plan, resulting in an unfit act. Worse still, the offender inflicts wounds to himself or herself even before the betrayal is exposed, which may take years to heal.

The key is to quickly cancel the thought by God's Word and physical relocation. We shouldn't feel guilty that the enemy tempts us, but neither should we dwell with the temptation, or it will trump our resolve. A great preacher once said, "You can't keep a bird from flying over your head, but you can sure keep it from building a nest in your hair!"

❦

Father, grant me the courage to stand for my convictions and flee from my temptations. Amen.

How Sweet the Sound

So then faith cometh by hearing, and hearing by the word of God.

ROMANS 10:17, KJV

Faith is the foundation of the Christian life. The Bible teaches us that without faith it is impossible to please God, and that to come to God we must first believe that God exists and He rewards those who diligently seek Him (Hebrews 11:6). Through Scripture we see great examples of the faith of the children of God—faith that produced miracles of healing, provisions of sustenance, deliverance from bondage, and favor with others. Faith was key in the lives of the people of God, and it makes the difference for us today.

Sometimes we are hard on ourselves because we don't seem to be operating in faith that's moving mountains, or producing the kind of life we desire (and know God desires for us). But what we must realize is that we often demonstrate our faith at our level of understanding God's Word for our lives. When we come to know that God heals, suddenly we begin to have faith in the power of God to heal us. When we understand that God desires that we have healthy relationships, our faith increases with thoughts of harmony and peace for one another. As we discover that God supplies all our needs, then we fret less over the little that seems to appear in the bank account, and instead see the expanse of riches in God! How does this happen? We heard about the love, power, and goodness of God!

Hearing is not only the physical sound that rings in our ears but includes all the things we perceive, pay attention to, learn and consider—naturally and supernaturally. When our life experiences support our faith—the music we listen to, friends with whom we associate, and habits we keep—our faith in God grows. Our whole lives should reflect our faith in some way. Yes, faith comes by hearing and it's a sweet sound in our ears!

Lord, my ears are attuned to the supernatural! I hear the sound of faith, and it's like music to my ears. It's a sound that resonates in my soul, vibrating in every cell of my body. It permeates the crevices of my heart and mind. I hear it, I speak it and I live it! And so it is!

The Abundant Life is Ours

The thief cometh not, but for to steal, and to kill, and to destroy: I am come that they might have life, and that they might have it more abundantly.

JOHN 10:10, KJV

There are times when we feel as though something is robbing us of the good in our lives. These are times when we feel that hope has slipped away, and that things will never get better. These, too, are the times to re-affirm our faith—to sit still and meditate on the goodness of God. As we do, the reality of it will flow back into our experiences, and we will be renewed in knowing the Father's love.

Sometimes we are unclear about the goodness of God, yet Jesus made a distinction between His godly purpose and that of the "thief." In this text, Jesus identified why He comes and why the thief comes. We see that Jesus came that we might experience life "more abundantly," while the thief came to "steal, kill and destroy." So, if we have an experience that is less than abundant (prosperous, productive, rewarding), then we know that's not the end of the story. God has a plan and will work all things together for our good (Romans 8:28).

Jesus came to realign our thinking with Truth. He came to remind us of the nature, power, and purpose of God. He came to help us see Him as the "Shepherd" of our souls —the rightful and good caretaker. He lets us know that if we are living a life that is robbing us of love, joy, and peace, or leading us away from the Father's care, that is an indication of a thief among us. It's a sign that we need to once again listen for the voice of the Lord and follow Him.

Jesus came that we might have life—eternal and abundant. We must affirm His purpose for ourselves. As we do, His purpose will be manifested and will be expressed more and more in our daily living.

❧

Lord, You are the Good Shepherd of my soul. I thank You that we commune together and You care for me. I thank You that I hear Your voice, and I follow You. In You is life eternal and abundant. I thank You that I share this abundant life in and through You. Lord, manifest Your good to me! And so it is!

REAL FELLOWSHIP

But if we walk in the light as He is in the light, we have fellowship with one another.
1 JOHN 1:7A, NKJV

The first decade this century may well be dubbed "the age of networking." Social media enabled people, who may or may not really know each other, to share photos, personal tidbits, career information, and opinions. Arguably, the connections facilitated by social media are superficial at best, and not the same as the deeper connections Christ intended for His community of believers.

The act, or process, for building deep, meaningful relationships among believers in the New Testament church was known as fellowship. Fellowship was a "coming together" to share life and the Lord. The significance of fellowship can be seen in the accounts of the earliest days of the church. After thousands of people received Jesus and were filled with the Holy Spirit, they "continued steadfastly in the apostles' doctrine and fellowship, in the breaking of bread, and in prayers" (Acts 2:42). Unfortunately, in the age of networking, many believers are tempted to settle for a pseudo-fellowship created by technology rather than the real fellowship needed to sustain a community of faith. So how do we participate in real fellowship?

Real fellowship stems, first and foremost, from fellowship with God, through Jesus Christ (1 John 1:3,6). Jesus went to the cross of Calvary to restore the fellowship between God and humanity that had been broken when Adam and Eve fell. Real fellowship requires a singleness of heart (Acts 2:46). It requires being in authentic relationships with fellow believers. Real fellowship requires walking in the light (1 John 1:7). It means being open and honest with God and self so one can be open and honest with others. There are no hidden agendas in the light or truth of God. There are no facades or false faces!

So today, think about it. Has church become another social network for you? Or are you really sharing in the real life of the community of faith?

Dear Lord, I thank You for restoring my fellowship with You. Today I ask You for grace to walk in the light and develop real fellowship with my brothers and sisters in Christ. In Jesus' Name. Amen.

BLOOD-WASHED CONSCIENCE

How much more shall the blood of Christ, who through the eternal Spirit offered himself without spot to God, purge your conscience from dead works to serve the living God.

HEBREWS 9:14, KJV

What does it mean to have a clean conscience, freed from the stain and guilt of the past and from the cruel oppression of sin? What does it mean to be constantly aware of Christ who indwells us? For believers, the joy of that liberation is inestimable, full of glory—and daily within our grasp!

You see, before Christ's sacrifice at Calvary, God instituted ritualistic offerings that served as a type of sacrifice He would ultimately make. However, those animal sacrifices only covered sin. They could satisfy a ritual but could not address the human conscience. They couldn't pay sin's price and redeem humankind.

But, praise God, Hebrews 9:14 declares the supremacy of the blood of Christ, which purged the very conscience held hostage by the wicked machinery that manufactured dead works. The blood of Christ alone could shut that factory down, once and for all! Now, with consciences freed from sin and guilt, our faith is no longer impeded—now we can draw close to God with the full assurance of faith (Hebrews 10:22). Empowered, we live conscious of Christ, committed to His principles, and daily striving to please Him.

How can we intensify Christ-consciousness? First, we recognize that it is a process requiring diligence and patience. Second, we agree that renewing our minds is just a reasonable service (Romans 12:2), realized by habitual prayer, Bible study, and occasions of fasting. Third, we embrace the importance of maintaining transparent and healthy relations with other believers. We commit to work at forgiving those who have offended us, keeping promises, and minimize, as best we can, hurting others.

As we exchange habits that produced dead works for habits that maximize fruitfulness in Christ and love for each other, we become true disciples of Christ, promoted from infancy to infantry. For now, the precious blood of Jesus has full recourse, and its almighty power progressively transforms us.

❧

Father, today, may the precious blood of Christ purify my conscience from dead works and empower me to better serve You. Amen.

THE SCENT OF THE SON

Know ye not that ye are the temple of God, and that the Spirit of God dwelleth in you?

1 CORINTHIANS 3:16, KJV

The city of Corinth was a socially, economically, and religiously diverse metropolis where both Jews and Gentiles lived. It was set at a pivotal point along the coast that brought in trade of all kinds—land, sea, and human. It had the smell of a city filled with worldly pleasures, drunk on itself. It was a city full of carnal passions that threatened the newly established church that was planted in this coastal city.

Paul recognized the negative influences of this bustling city, and he wanted to encourage spiritual fidelity in a land that was beset with all kinds of perversion and sexual sin. Paul knew the young church had been influenced by the things around it and sought to bring sobering light to the reality of living for Jesus Christ in the midst of the moral and spiritual chaos that was so heavily evidenced in the city. The wickedness of the day was so prevalent, the sinfulness of people was known as "acting like a Corinthian." Paul wanted them to understand that as believers they were the very temple of God.

This truth beat against the experiences of temple worship evident in the city. Every manner of evil was practiced and every passion indulged in Corinth. The ornate temples of the time were filled with individual pleasures, arguments, and division—yet Paul instructed faithful followers of Jesus to seek the holiness of God.

Paul reminded them that they were the very place where the Spirit of God dwelled. Christ would not, and could not, dwell in the depravity of moral corruption. They could not give in to the seduction of sinful behavior that would send up a stench before God.

We are to be the fragrance of His Son in a world that is perishing (2 Corinthians 2:14-16). Remember, we are to be mindful of the things we let into His glorious temple. Go about smelling like the sweetness of the Son!

❧

Lord God, help me to remember the privilege I have of representing You in the earth. I want to leave the sweetness of Jesus everywhere I go. I bless You and serve You with my life. In Jesus' Name. Amen.

WORKING TOGETHER AS ONE

For as the body is one, and hath many members, and all the members of that one body, being many, are one body: so also is Christ. For by one Spirit are we all baptized into one body, whether we be Jews or Gentiles, whether we be bond or free; and have been all made to drink into one Spirit.

1 CORINTHIANS 12:12-13, KJV

God has blessed us with amazing bodies that are unique in their own ways. Each part depends on another part. The brain is the supervisor! It is broken down into sections that function and coordinate with various parts of the body. It is always working—even while we sleep—controlling our feelings and emotions.

It is vital that we eat the right foods, exercise, and get the right amount of sleep. The misuse of alcohol, drugs, and tobacco will eventually destroy the cells in our brains, causing it to ultimately malfunction and perform below its capacity.

When Paul wrote to the church in Corinth, it was a church struggling to live in obedience. Paul described the church as Christ's body. As Paul admonished, Christians should work together in unity and oneness for the glory and coming of God's Kingdom. As believers, we may be unique in our own way, but we are also dependent on each other; like unified body parts.

Sometimes, as believers we have a difficult time assimilating into the body. By nature, we may resist being dependent on others or having others depend on us. Paul stated that "the eye cannot say to the hand, I don't need you," neither can anyone in the body of Christ say that to a fellow church member. In this way, Paul reminds us of our mutual dependence.

Our Father in heaven has provided each member with gifts and talents for the building of the body. All the members of the church are one in Him—serving each other, the world, and our Lord and Savior Jesus Christ.

Most Gracious and soon coming King, how excellent is Your name in all the earth. Help me to realize that I can do nothing without the aide and help of my fellow brothers and sisters in Christ. In Jesus' Name. Amen.

ALL FOR ONE AND ONE FOR ALL

Moreover, brethren, I would not that ye should be ignorant, how that all our fathers were under the cloud, and all passed through the sea; and were all baptized unto Moses in the cloud and in the sea.

1 CORINTHIANS 10:1-2, KJV

Paul was responsible for establishing the church of Corinth. While in Ephesus on his third missionary journey, he received disturbing reports of spiritual immaturity and sexual immorality in this church. The church at Corinth was plagued with division and partisan allegiances. Some members were bragging about being followers of Apollos, who was a great orator. Others were pledging their allegiance to Peter. Still others aligned with Paul.

Paul was compelled by the Holy Spirit to restore order to this church and remind them of the basics of the gospel and congregational life. He asked them: "Is Christ divided? Was Paul crucified for you? Or were you baptized in the name of Paul?" (1 Corinthians 1:13). In so doing he was reminding them that their factions were not in line with the unity that Christ intended for His body.

So it was in today's Scripture, Paul used the children of Israel in the wilderness as an illustration for the Corinthians to see the significance of unity and spiritual maturity. While escaping Egypt, Paul reminded them, all of the Israelites passed through the sea. They didn't hold a series of sub-committee meetings to debate the escape route. No, they all passed through the parted sea and out of reach of the pursuing Egyptians. Paul likened their passage through the Red Sea as a type of baptism, not unlike the common baptism that the Corinthians had experienced when they believed on Jesus as Lord and Savior.

So it is with us. As we have each received Jesus, and have been baptized, we become connected to each other through our common relationship with Jesus Christ. All-for-one-and-one-for-all is a call to solidarity. When one of us hurts, we all hurt. When one of us suffers, we all suffer. The Spirit-filled life is not a solitary journey but one we travel together through our cloudy days and sunny days, through our seas of sorrow and seasons of joy.

Dear Lord, help me to remain mindful of my common destiny with my brothers and sisters. In Jesus' Name. Amen.

Don't Major in the Minors

Endeavouring to keep the unity of the Spirit in the bond of peace.

EPHESIANS 4:3, KJV

Have you ever experienced friction over small, itsy-bitsy things? Have you witnessed conflict arise from the ashes of respective altars over which way is right and which is wrong? Can you think of a time when a stake was put in the ground around the wrong thing?

Such was the case in the church of Ephesus. Conflicts arose over how things were done—the liberties of some and the control of others. Paul aptly reminded them that God brought about reconciliation through the death of His Son, and we have a responsibility to strive to live in unity because of it. We cannot busy ourselves with major fights over minor issues, or allow something insignificant to become elevated to significance when there is no Christ or cross involved. Are there things we hold on to without reservation or hesitation? Yes! Is there someone we can release for the sake of peace with a brother or sister? The answer again is yes! Whether a Christian uses his or her Bible on a smartphone, iPad, or hard-bound book is a *minor* issue relegated to personal choice and the technological age we live in. Whether or not they use a Bible at all is a *major* issue when a community of believers can faithfully illustrate the need for it.

While they didn't face this particular challenge in Paul's day, they did have other challenges. They faced those that threatened the unity of fellowship and the peace that should be a hallmark of a body of believers. They faced issues of racial and class differences that may have kept them divided. Paul's encouragement was to maintain the unity that Christ's cross brought. Pursuing and walking in the Spirit of unity will help us focus on the right things. Just as they struggled with *not majoring* in things that Christ didn't, but rather majoring in the things that reflect His love and demonstrate humility, so, too, are we to major in them.

🌿

Father God, let me remember that walking in unity means that I should be willing to forgive all past transgressions of my brothers and sisters in Christ. Teach me to lift them up in prayer instead of tearing them down or focusing on the wrong things. In Jesus' Name. Amen!

To Know God is to Love God

Whoever does not love, does not know God, because God is love.

1 John 4:8, NIV

There have been many stories told about falling in love for the first time. Love is an emotion shared and deeply felt by two people. People often fall in love with those they find attractive and suitable for them, and they seek those who demonstrate that the attraction is mutual. Others have experienced falling in love after meeting someone for the first time—hence "love at first sight." Then there are those who find themselves falling in love with a friend they have known for years. Regardless of how it starts, falling in love is a pivotal point in a person's life, when all attention, focus, and heart go in the direction of the object of affection.

So it is when we come to know the Lord. Our attention, focus, and hearts are turned toward Him, and our actions follow where our hearts have taken us. Our relationship with God grows into intimate friendship. As we find ourselves spending more time with Him, we learn more and more about what He likes and dislikes.

Likewise, when our actions betray our verbal declaration of love, John says we do not know God. John implies that our knowledge of God will cause us to love Him. John was speaking about the kind of love that goes beyond our feelings and has its origin in God Himself. He was exhorting believers to love one another. "Anyone who loves their brother and sister lives in the light" (1 John 2:10), and "Anyone who does not love remains in death" (1 John 3:14).

John was encouraging them to love both "with actions and in truth" (3:18). God is love. He has always been love. In Jesus, we see what true love is. Love can overcome any obstacle; it can endure rejection, and bring peace, because God is the author of love. So next time we say we love God but refuse to exhibit His love with kindness, lets stop and recall Who the true origin of Love is.

🦋

My True and Sovereign God, to know You is to love You. Let me express my love for You by treating others with loving kindness and by living what I see in Your Word. In Jesus' Name, I pray. Amen.

STANDING ON LOVE

Let all your things be done with charity.

1 CORINTHIANS 16:14, KJV

What if we lived in a world where the only emotion displayed was love? We would never encounter divorce, abuse, hatred, divisions, revenge, retaliation, or getting even with our fellow Christians.

In today's culture, most people equate the word "charity" with giving money for some good cause. Paul specifically referred to charity as the love that we have toward men and women in Christ Jesus. Paul concludes 1 Corinthians with giving instructions and greetings to the church, and he encourages them to show hospitality toward one another. He wanted them to be generous, giving gifts for those who were poverty stricken in Jerusalem. Although Paul's eyesight was failing, his final instructions were written in his own hand, thus expressing the love he had for them. He advised them to be on guard. He wanted them to stand firm in the faith, be people of courage, and to do everything in love. Peter would echo the same as he told believers, "And above all things have fervent charity among yourselves: for charity shall cover the multitude of sins" (1 Peter 4:8).

The church in Corinth had problems related to spiritual immaturity and Paul wanted to correct their misunderstandings. He reminded them that they were to love God and love each other. He reminded them that they were not to tolerate sin. We, too, are reminded today that we are to love God, love others, and not tolerate sin. As we become more spiritually mature, we understand our need for God's love and grace not only in us but moving through us.

If we are to be the light of this lost world and the witnesses that God has called us to be, we have to base our Christian lives on the truth of God's Word and the love that is revealed. How else will we be able to witness to a watching world if what we do isn't done in love? Only God can help us commit to live out love and do good each day.

Most loving God, teach me how to be mature in my Christian walk daily. Help me to stop, pray, and look to You, so I can respond in a way that is pleasing to You and Your Kingdom. Help me to love. I pray these things in Jesus' Name. Amen.

LOVE NEVER FAILS

Charity never faileth: but whether there be prophecies, they shall fail; whether there be tongues, they shall cease; whether there be knowledge, it shall vanish away.

1 CORINTHIANS 13:8, KJV

What's love got to do with it? Everything! Remember, that's how it all started: "For God so loved the world, that he gave his only begotten Son, that whosoever believeth in him should not perish, but have everlasting life" (John 3:16). This Scripture of love is our greatest example of God's compassion for us, so much that He gave what was dearest to Him: Jesus Christ, His Son.

Perhaps there is a situation today that calls for extraordinary compassion or supernatural love that goes beyond what is deserved. When we reflect upon the ugliness of our sin, the cross that carried it away, and Christ's love for us, we know we don't deserve the grace that is extended to us. We are shown the magnitude of His love and compassion, yet it is this love that doesn't give up. It is the model for the kind of love we are to exhibit. It's the kind of love God had when He sent His Son to save the world. Paul reminds us that we are to so love that we don't give up but continue on in love. Our text says that other things—declaration of God's Word, speaking in other tongues, supernatural understanding—although great, will end. But not love! Realizing our own need for incredible, life-altering love causes us to walk in a spirit of humility, yielding ourselves to the power of the Holy Spirit so the love of God can be seen in us. We choose to take up our cross and follow Him out of love, to use our gifts, works, and knowledge as means of love to win the hearts of men and women that need Christ.

Our love will be tested against the gales of opposition—even hatred—to see if it is tempered and enduring. Can our love hold up to the fire of hostility? Can the image of Christ still be seen in us? Yes, because love never fails.

My faithful Father, teach my heart again how to love and respond in all situations. Let the power of love be renewed in me so that I can continuously give it away. In Jesus' Name. Amen.

No One has Ever Seen God

No man hath seen God at any time. If we love one another, God dwelleth in us, and his love is perfected in us.

1 John 4:12, KJV

Recently, a documentary aired that chronicled the lives of children at risk because the parents were absent. The program highlighted the children's grossly unfavorable social conditions and pointed to the challenges they faced, including identity crisis, anger management, and the fear of rejection.

One particularly heartbreaking story was that of a young girl who lived across the street from her father, but she never spoke to him. She had been abandoned by her mother, so her grandmother adopted her. That grandmother, and many others today, demonstrated the love the child needed. Yet, each day, when the girl would leave her grandmother's home and pass her father's house, her heart would break and she would become enraged. As she grew into a teenager, the girl continuously longed for her father's love.

Like many people today, the young girl ached for the love of someone who didn't reciprocate. While the circumstances may be different, God's answer is not. He will extend love and provide comfort to those who need it through His chosen ones. The presence of God is revealed in many ways and meets both the spoken and unspoken needs of a hungry heart. We saw God's love through the caring grandmother. We saw an expression of His goodness in her tenderness, and His love dwelling in the hands and heart of one generation to another.

How can we show a sign of love to someone today that will lessen his or her suffering or misery? Will we be like the parents of the girl, estranged from her life and her pain, or will we make a difference where we can? Through displays of love, others may come to know God because of what they see in us. May others see God by seeing us, and know that His love dwells in us.

Heavenly Father, give me a heart of compassion for those who need Your love to rise above their circumstances. Along my Christian journey, may those I encounter see the love of God that dwells in me because I walk in God's love. Amen.

IT ALL STARTS WITH HIM

We love him, because he first loved us.

1 JOHN 4:19, KJV

It's important to know how things start. The tallest building started with the laying of a foundation. The greatest teacher started as a young child in a classroom. The greatest marriage started with a young man and woman pledging fidelity to each other. The greatest love started with God. There's no need for proof of who you are, what you've done, how good you are, your net worth, or your rare intelligence…and your race doesn't matter. He doesn't care about your height or weight, and your educational level is a non-issue. God has decided to give you what He is: love. He loved us long before we would love Him. Scripture records, in Romans 5, that God demonstrated His love to us by sending Christ to die—even before we turned from our sins.

Rejoice in the fact that God's grace was extended to us because of His love, without any evidence of our worth. His love saw far beyond who we were, to who we would become in Him. So intent to rescue us from the pangs of sin that separated us, our Father sent the only One that could come for us, the purest expression of Himself: Jesus the Christ. Imagine the love of the Father, who would give His only Son for those who would later crucify Him.

All around, there is evidence of Him loving us first, with a response of gratitude from us that burst forth in love. The blind man exuberantly exclaimed, "I once was blind but now I see" (John 9:25). The woman of Samaria ran into the city declaring, "Come see a man…is not this the Christ?" (John 4:29). Love stopped and healed them. His unconditional love for us ignites our love for Him. His love is perfect and it anchors us.

Over and over, Jesus demonstrates His love and compassion in our lives to reassure us that He will never leave us nor forsake us. What a blessing to be loved first! What will you do to demonstrate your love for Him?

❧

Father, thank You for Your gracious love and how You loved me first. Grant me the courage to step up and love others first so they will see Your grace and experience Your love through me. Amen.

TOTALLY COMMITTED

And thou shalt love thy God with all thy heart, and with all thy soul and with all thy mind, and with all thy strength: this is the first commandment.

MARK 12:30, KJV

The Lord has commanded us to love Him with all our soul, mind, and strength. When we are totally yielded to Him, we live our best lives and are a blessing to the people of God. The Lord knows that true devotion comes from the heart. It is not merely lip service but an agreement between what we say and what we do. The Bible teaches us that, out of the abundance of the heart, the mouth speaks (Luke 6:45). Commitment occurs when our love and affection meet our allegiance. When Christ is our Lord, He will be the ruler of our hearts, the leader of our actions, and the director of our thoughts.

Just as the Lord wants our hearts, He wants our minds too! He wants to take control of our thoughts and lead and guide us into all truth. How do we get there? We get there with the map of God's Word, informing our thoughts and transforming our thinking. Like directions on a map, a clear route is marked out that shows us how to live in a way that moves us closer and closer to living out the first commandment. It reminds us to put God first in all things. Every day we make a decision, whether consciously or unconsciously, to align or turn our hearts and minds to the cause of Jesus Christ. A conscious effort to submit our minds (thoughts and decisions) to the Lord enables us to live a life of victory. We can do it by training our thoughts to think on good things, just as the writer of Philippians calls upon us to "think on whatsoever things are lovely, whatsoever things are just" (4:8).

Every part of us is to be committed to our King. Our commitment should not be in "fits and starts" but in a steady stream of intents and actions marking a life dedicated to our God.

❧

Heavenly Father, thank You that I am totally Yours. I am committed to love You, serve You, and honor You with my life. Amen.

No Fear

There is no fear in love, but perfect love cast out all fear, because fear hath torment. He that feareth is not made perfect in love.

1 John 4:18, KJV

There they were, sailing from the multitude, when a great storm arose and the boat was tossed to and fro. Jesus was asleep in the rear of the ship. The disciples awakened Jesus saying, "Master, don't you care that we are about to perish? And he arose, and rebuked the wind, and said unto the sea, Peace, be still. And the wind ceased, and there was a great calm" (Mark 4:37-39). Like the disciples, we may face storms that take us by surprise and cause us distress. The difference for them, as for us, is the Lord's presence.

No matter how much faith we have, situations arise that make us fearful while waiting for an answer, a solution, or understanding. "Lord if you love me, then why is this happening?" or "Lord, when will you give me an answer, a plan?" When our prayers appear to hit the ceiling, we feel alone; but God is there, ready to dispel our fears and assure us with His perfect love.

The Greek term for love today is *agápe*. It refers to a love that is unconditional and self-sacrificing. God's love is not to be confused with a feeling or an attitude. It bestows His peace and leaves no room for fear. Perfect love casts out fear. Fear expects punishment and tells us that, despite Christ's sacrifice, we are still helpless to stand against the evils and problems of this world. Fear is a sign that we are not standing in God's perfect love; but when we embrace the love of God, our love for Him and for others grows. As we abide in His love, we gain confidence in His promises and in our relationship with Him.

Fear may arise in a moment of despair or a situation that needs quick attention; but when we recall the love of God, we can cling to that love, which is able to remove all fear.

Heavenly Father, let Your love cast out the fear that tries to invade my life and keep me from the sweet state of grace and peace in You. This day help me to meditate on Your blessing. Amen.

FRUIT OF THE SPIRIT

But the fruit of the Spirit is love, joy, peace, longsuffering, gentleness, goodness, faith, meekness, temperance.

GALATIANS 5:22-23A, KJV

Ripe and juicy apples, peaches, grapes, and strawberries are absolutely delectable in their season. They ripen on the vine and are ready for the market and the consumer; the customer carefully selects the fruit with the best color, fragrance, and feel. But the ultimate defining moment is the taste test: does the appearance compare to what's inside?

What's inside of us? Each day as we walk this Christian journey, what we are is determined by our relationship with God and revealed in our interactions with others. Fruit in this Scripture refers to our character as followers of Christ. Christian character is not manifested in one area of our lives, but not another. Neither can we exhibit joy without longsuffering, or peace without love. The fruit we bear represents all that we are, and are called to be, in Christ.

What kind of fruit are we bearing? Is it something to be treasured and shared like peace and faith, or something that is unpalatable and to be discarded like anger or hatred? If we have been in the company of someone who seems to refuse to mature in Christ, we may notice that he or she seems to stubbornly resist help. Allowing the trials of life to build a destructive attitude is reflective of the person's character. Consequently, the fruit exhibited is marred with impatience, coarseness, confusion, negativity, and hatred.

Jesus said, "I am the true vine, and my Father is the husbandman. Every branch in me that beareth not fruit he taketh away: and every branch that beareth fruit, he purgeth it, that it may bring forth more fruit" (John 15:1-2). When we trust God, He prunes our attitudes and removes anything that inhibits our growth in Him. Today, let's celebrate because, as we remain in Christ and learn of Him, our lives will manifest a hearty, spiritual harvest of love, joy, peace, longsuffering, gentleness, goodness, and faith, meekness, and temperance.

Gracious Father, let Your perfect work be complete in me so that my life will manifest the fruit of the Spirit. People are looking for hope and genuine love. Let my life exemplify You. In Jesus' Name. Amen.

THE GREATEST IS LOVE

And now abideth faith, hope, charity, these three; but the greatest of these is charity.

1 CORINTHIANS 13:13, KJV

In his first epistle to the church in Corinth, Paul, with emphasis on the practical, explains the faith we have through Jesus Christ, the hope that is ours through the Holy Spirit, and the love that we are expected to show to one another. Near the end of the letter, Paul explains that, though there are many gifts in the body of Christ, the greatest gift is love. That is such an awesome idea that today's passage is one of the most beloved and often quoted in the Bible. But what would happen if we really took it to heart?

Consider what life would be if we just decided to embrace the love of Jesus then just give love away. We would become a mighty force in the body of Christ. This would be revolutionary love. This would be God-fortified love that would break every chain. Imagine life if we loved so sincerely, so openly, that not a single person in our presence would feel unloved or unimportant.

What if we came to every encounter with hearts and words ablaze with the compassion and the power of Christ. It would take away the gloom. We would be light-bearing, night-watching, gap-dwelling, breach-restoring servants of the Most High. We could be powerful intercessors praying on behalf of God's people everywhere.

Love is a powerful and miraculous force. Love caused Jesus to come and lay down His life for us. In following His path and likeness, we too, can lay down our love as an offering to God and a gift to others. Love can be demonstrated in many ways. Let's find a way to show the heart of God and revolutionize our communities with the love of Christ.

Heavenly Father, give me strength and grace to love as You love. Enable me to be revolutionary in my ability to extend love. Help me to operate in love so powerfully that I can help lift the gloom from someone's life and bring discipline and character to my own. Amen.

CONDUCT THAT GLORIFIES GOD

Finally, all of you be of one mind, having compassion for one another; love as brothers, be tenderhearted, be courteous.

1 PETER 3:8, NKJV

Today we have the teachings and opinions of religious leaders that can be played in our homes twenty-four/seven via television, radio, and the Internet. If we listen long enough, we will hear major differences on what proper Christian behavior is and what it is not in an increasingly angry and polarized world. We have to use prayer and discernment to determine if it is the speaker's interpretation or the Word of God.

In his first epistle, the apostle Peter writes a letter of encouragement to the early Christians who were scattered throughout the Roman Empire. At the time of this writing, it was dangerous to live in a society that was openly hostile toward Christians. Yet Peter tells them to live their lives in such a way that God would be glorified. Peter writes instructions on how they should act as citizens, masters, slaves, wives, and husbands. Then he says in 1 Peter 3:8, "Finally, all of you," regardless of your position in society and the suffering you may endure, you are still responsible for conducting yourselves in a certain manner.

Those principles serve as a guide for us—husbands, wives, employers, employees, co-workers. We should be uniformed in our beliefs about Jesus Christ as our Lord and Savior, His death and resurrection. We are called to have the kind of empathy that causes us to want to help others in their misfortunes. We are called to be passionate about the well-being of others, show kindness, be polite, and use good manners. This sets us apart from worldly behaviors and draws attention to God in our lives.

Today, ask God for grace to carry yourself in a way that pleases Him. Purpose in your mind to make sure your conduct glorifies God.

❧

Father God, thank You for the Holy Bible so that I can read and learn of You and know Your ways. Thank You for Your Holy Spirit that gives me encouragement in the struggles in my life. Help me to live in such a way that others will be attracted to You. In Jesus' Name, I pray. Amen.

Do Not Turn Aside

Now the end of the commandment is charity out of a pure heart and a good conscience, and faith unfeigned.

1 TIMOTHY 1:5, KJV

Timothy was more than a protégé of Paul's; he was Paul's son in the gospel. Paul writes this letter to Timothy to encourage him in his new role as the young pastor in the church at Ephesus. Timothy's task was formidable. False teachers were spreading incorrect doctrine and corrupting the faith of the saints. In this verse, Paul explains that his instructions to Timothy are designed to help the saints live in love. As *The Message* paraphrases it, this is "love uncontaminated by self-interest and counterfeit faith, a life open to God."

What might Paul's advice mean for us today? Paul would no doubt warn us against turning aside from the teachings and experiences that the Lord has brought into our lives to give us wisdom, hope, mercy, and fortitude. He might tell us to stand guard over the holy things that have been invested in us to minister an effective and fervent message to those in need and to build us up in the faith. Paul might even tell us to be watchful over the gifts the Lord has sanctified and sanctioned so that vanity, pride, and profane thinking don't corrupt the pure heart and good conscience the Holy Spirit is developing in us.

The Lord has counted us faithful and appointed each of us to be ministers in His body. There are so many needs to which God wants us to attend, but are we willing to go? Are we willing to carry the precious cargo of the Word of God? Are we willing to be vehicles for the Lord's miraculous power and grace? For the sake of God's commandment to love, we must be ready to move at His charge, with our hearts completely persuaded to carry forth the work with a pure spirit, a good conscience, and an authentic faith.

Heavenly Father, keep me spiritually fit to attend to the precious things that are Yours with a pure heart, a good conscience, and a faith unfeigned. Amen.

THE DONOR

For God so loved the world, that he gave his only begotten Son, that whosoever believeth in him should not perish, but have everlasting life.

JOHN 3:16, KJV

How does it feel to give away something that is precious? Heart transplant patients can only receive a heart if they have a donor; and of course, the donor must be deceased. Someone has to die for the transplant recipient to receive a heart. On the one hand, it requires a devastating loss for the family of the person whose heart is being donated. On the other hand, it is a miracle for the person waiting for renewed life.

God gave His only Son so that we could be redeemed by His death. Through His sacrifice and love, we were given a chance to live again; we are born again because of the death of Christ. The Lord knew that the Father's plan was to reconcile us to Himself. Jesus also knew that He had to die because only His blood could "purge your conscience from dead works to serve the living God". As a result of His sacrifice, we "receive the promise of eternal inheritance" (Hebrews 9:14-15).

In the Old Testament, many sacrifices of animals were offered, but none could take away the sins of the people. Those animals were only types, or examples, of what Jesus Christ would be as the worthy Lamb of God. Only the offering of the body of Jesus Christ could take away our sins.

Today, we can give thanks to *our donor*, our Lord and Savior, Jesus Christ, whose death provided the greatest gift of all: redemption through the forgiveness of sins. Like the person who receives a donor heart, we too, have been given new life. Because of God's love, we no longer have to be in bondage to our sins and addictions. Because of Jesus Christ, we can live righteously with dignity, courage, and hope. Through His death and resurrection we are the recipients of not just new life, but of eternal life in Him.

Heavenly Father, forgive me for ever taking Your miraculous sacrifice for granted. You are the greatest example of love: You laid Your life down for Your friends and enemies alike. Thank You for the blood that You shed for me on Cavalry. Amen.

LET THE MINISTRY GO FORTH

And this I pray, that your love may abound yet more and more in knowledge and in all judgment.

PHILIPPIANS 1:9, KJV

This is a portion of the letter written by Paul to the saints in Philippi, while Paul was imprisoned. The apostle sends these words of encouragement and thankfulness for their support of the ministry. Paul prays for the Philippians and exhorts them to stand firm in the faith.

Paul was not shaken by his circumstances. He had tremendous dedication to the work of the Lord, and he allowed nothing to deter him from ministry—not even prison. Paul moved forward with purpose and zeal to deal with the business at hand: the encouragement of God's people. Paul prayed that their love would abound toward one another, that they would increase in knowledge, and that they would have discernment regarding good and evil.

The church of Christ was under persecution, but the gospel was spreading around the known globe. Though Paul was imprisoned physically, he realized the importance of arming his fellow Christians for what they had to face. The church at Philippi was well organized with bishops and deacons to teach and serve the saints (Philippians 1:1). The saints in Philippi had stood by Paul when all others had abandoned him (Philippians 4:15). But Paul understood that, despite persecution, the work of the ministry must begin with love. As we love, we grow. As we love God more, we love the people of God more, we seek more knowledge of His Word, and we grow in our ability to distinguish His will from ours.

Paul's encouragement and exhortation were given in love. If we are to do the work of the ministry and support the work that others do, we must allow love to abound in our lives.

✣

Heavenly Father, make me to abound in love and grow in truth. Help me to discern good and evil, especially when good may be cloaked with deception. Arm me for the spiritual and natural battles I must face, and let me not neglect the ministry You have entrusted to me. Amen.

GRACE

Grace be with all them that love our Lord Jesus Christ in sincerity.

EPHESIANS 6:24, KJV

Ephesians 6:24 is the closing blessing or benediction from Paul's letter to the church in Ephesus. Paul's prayer or blessing was that God's "Grace be with all them that love our Lord Jesus Christ in sincerity." The most common definition of grace is the unmerited favor of God. Simply put, this defines grace as the blessings God gives us despite our having done nothing to deserve them. Modern phrases, such as "favor ain't fair," are based on this thinking and usually refer to material blessings. But grace is far greater than a phrase accented with the snap of a finger, a nod of the head, or an attitude that declares how special we think *we* are to the Lord.

The term "grace" embraces manifold treasures, abundant love, and unending extensions of God's mercy. God's grace has no bounds. It is so overwhelming that just when we think we have the definition comprehended, grace exposes itself on another level and exceeds all we can ask or think. Grace is so powerful that through it we were redeemed from sin, born again, and transformed into kingdom builders for Christ.

By God's grace we are made in His likeness and have a desire to live in a manner that brings glory to the name of Christ. By His grace, our actions and attitudes demonstrate our love for Him. And by His grace, Paul's prayer for the Ephesians can be embraced by us because we are among those who sincerely love the Lord Jesus Christ.

Paul wrote to strengthen and encourage the Christians in Ephesus, but his writing is an example for us as well. Just as Paul strengthened the saints at Ephesus, we must do the same for the household of faith. So today, know that God's grace is plentiful toward us, plentiful enough that we, too, can bless all those who love the Lord.

Heavenly Father, thank You for Your grace and the blessings of fellowship with the saints. Help me to encourage my brothers and my sisters in word and deed with sincerity of heart and humility. And I pray that my motives will be pure so that I may be an extension of Your love and grace. Amen.

MORE THAN A CONQUEROR

For I am persuaded, that neither death, nor life, nor angels, nor principalities, nor powers, nor things present, nor things to come, nor height, nor depth, nor any other creature, shall be able to separate us from the love of God, which is in Christ Jesus our Lord.

ROMANS 8:38-39, KJV

King David often wrote about the vastness of God. In Psalm 139:7-8 he wrote, "Whither shall I go from thy spirit? or whither shall I flee from thy presence? If I ascend up into heaven, thou art there: if I make my bed in hell, behold, thou art there." David was making the point that we are never out of God's reach. God has His hand upon us; He loves us and will not let us go.

Paul continues that theme in today's passage from Romans 8. This Scripture exudes an unshakable confidence that nothing can separate us from the love of God. When crises and trials storm our lives, and the intensity seems unbearable, God is there. When powers and principalities of darkness confer against us, God is there. Just as He stood with the Hebrew boys in the fiery furnace (Daniel 3:20-28), He will stand with us. At the height of our trouble and at the depths of our despair, if God is for us, it doesn't matter who opposes us.

Wherever we may find ourselves in life—whatever twists and turns, or forks in the road that might lead us to discouragement, failure, or bewilderment—we have confidence that we cannot be separated from God's love. God is able to raise us up and cause us to triumph over all manner of devastation. He is the author and finisher of our faith. He has the last word. Because nothing can come between us and God, we are more than conquerors!

Heavenly Father, restore that blessed confidence that nothing can separate me from You. Help me not to be shaken or be in terror of anything or anyone. Thank You for being my light and my Salvation. In Jesus' Name. Amen.

A HIDING PLACE

Most important of all, continue to show deep love for each other, for love covers a multitude of sins.

1 PETER 4:8, NLT

Can you imagine living in a society where your every movement might be reported to the authorities, and your life can be taken only because you follow the teachings of Christ? Imagine how difficult it would be to trust others or to sustain your momentum in pursuing the faith under such circumstances. This was the life that saints in the early church endured soon after the death of Jesus Christ. By writing this epistle, the apostle Peter affirmed their faith, despite their persecution, and encouraged their unity, despite their fears. Under the circumstances, what he did would seem impossible, but Peter explains that only God's love can enable someone to see past paranoia, pain, fear, and guile.

Peter's advice is also good for us, since our lives are often plagued by strife, raw ambition, rumors, anger, and fear. Our response to these encounters either marks us as believers in Jesus Christ or followers of the same sinful lifestyle we claim to have left behind. As Christians, we must encourage and strengthen each other, as we seek to live guided by the Holy Spirit. When we find someone who is struggling with sin, we should cover the person in love and resist gossiping. We must strive not to reveal faults and weaknesses, but to let the Holy Spirit drive us to love more deeply. We must not be easily offended, but we must be generous with grace.

It takes a mature saint to be discreet when society and pain are telling us to get even. It takes love to release a grudge and replace it with forgiveness, or to develop a lifestyle that produces fervent prayer rather than criticism. When we walk in the spirit of love and grace, we will handle each other with care and our love will become a hiding place for those in need of Christ's love. We must endeavor to love even the "unlovable," as Jesus Christ loves us, because "love covers a multitude of sins!"

✣

Heavenly Father, grant me the strength to be brave enough to love others as You love me. Help me to cover the faults of my brothers and sisters in love and discretion, because I, too, need Your mercy. In Jesus' Name. Amen.

WITH OUR ALL

Jesus said unto him, Thou shalt love the Lord thy God with all thy heart, and with all thy soul, and with all thy mind.

MATTHEW 22:37, KJV

A person with a divided heart or mind cannot fully serve the Lord and enjoy the fullness of His blessings. For instance, one's heart may yearn to carry out the ways of Christ, but if the mind is preoccupied with worries, cares, and distractions, we can miss the passion, adventure, and purpose of God for our lives.

The Pharisees challenged Christ, asking Him which commandment was more important to keep. Jesus responded with today's passage. In essence, he told them (and us today) that we are to love the God with the entire make-up of our being. He that created and redeemed us wants us to be fully devoted and faithful to Him. Our entire being belongs to God: our hearts *(the seat of our emotions and affections)*, our minds *(the part of us from and through which we perceive, think, and reason)*, and our souls. He has commanded us to love with our all.

You see, Jesus speaks of the wholeness that comes from a true relationship with the One who loves us unconditionally. When we love with all our heart, mind, and soul, we are loving with our all. The heart is unified with the mind, the mind with the soul.

The summation of the matter is that God wants our all. Christ has commanded that we love Him in totality. Why? We have given Christ complete Lordship over our lives; in filling every space of our being with Him, there is no room for idols. Out of submission to His authority and trustworthiness, we give Him our all, for He gave His life for us. There is no room to give the sacred away; we were created to worship (love) Christ with mind, body, and soul and to bring Him glory.

So today, let us consider whether or not we are giving God our all. Or are we divided and distracted in our service, worship, and love of God? Let's allow today to be the start of giving our all.

🕊

Heavenly Father, Help me yield to You completely. Let nothing divide my devotion to You as You have commanded me. Grant me strength to love You with all my heart, mind, and soul. Amen.

LOVE OF GOD

The commandment we have from him is this: those who love God must love his brothers and sisters also.

1 JOHN 4:21, NRSV

Kathy, a Christian woman, worked with a woman on her job who was extremely temperamental; she often threw fits of verbal rage with those whom she worked. On several occasions Kathy advised the woman about her behavior and how it alienated other workers from having more interaction with her. Kathy, at times, felt harassed and she prayed and asked the Lord how to handle the situation. With godly discernment and observation, Kathy felt the woman lacked genuine love from her family and others, and her outbursts were a subconscious test to see who would really love her at her worst.

Over the course of three months, Kathy was faithful and exhibited godly love under these difficult circumstances. The temperamental co-worker began to soften as a result of Kathy's example of love and patience. The co-worker soon shared some personal issues she was facing. She told Kathy, "I know you are a Christian by your life and the love you showed me when I behaved so disrespectfully."

It is a contradiction of faith to say we love God, whom we cannot see, and hate our sisters and brothers who we see each day. The Lord has given us the commandment to love, because God is love. We that follow after Christ must exhibit His unconditional charity with one another. Think about it, while we were yet sinners Christ loved us (Romans 5:8). That's right; He loved us before we loved Him.

It is a wonderful feeling to love someone who loves you, but quite often the real test is giving love with no return. But know that in our obedience to choose the path of love, God is glorified and we are identified in Him. So, today, let us commit to show the love of Christ in our actions, our words, our tone, and our attitude. Remember, love is patient and kind—love is Christ-like!

❧

Father, let me love my brother and sister as You have loved me. Give me the courage and grace to go beyond myself to build a godly bond of love. Let me be patient in my words, not quick to judge or hold a grudge. May I be first to offer the gift of love and compassion. Amen.

We're in This Together

Greet one another with an holy kiss.

2 Corinthians 13:12, KJV

In some churches, the preacher will tell the members of the congregation, "Turn to your neighbor and give them a high five." Others will ask members to "shake three people's hands and tell them how much you appreciate them." Still, in other churches, at a specified point in the liturgy, the congregants are instructed to "share or pass the peace," at which time they embrace fellow parishioners with a hug or handshake. All of these varying customs are means of connecting member with member, and perhaps have their roots in the New Testament practice of "greeting one another with a holy kiss."

For first-century Christians, the "holy kiss" was more than mere greeting. A kiss signified friendship and affection as was to be found among brothers and sisters in the Lord. In the context of the Christian community, a kiss was given to a person respected, reverenced, or as an act of forgiveness. That Judas kissed Jesus shows how deep his betrayal was, for only close confidantes greeted each other with kisses. The practice continued into the churches to which Paul wrote. So even when there was conflict that had to be dealt with, Paul admonished the members of churches to work through the conflict, and as evidence they were committed to remain in relationship, he encouraged them to greet each other in the love that comes from Christ and endures.

Today, in our fast-paced lives, we rush into church, sometimes waving to a fellow member, sometimes so preoccupied we walk right past other members without even speaking. When we get too busy to really greet one another—we are too busy! Greeting one another requires we slow down and intentionally acknowledge others, letting them know we are on this journey together.

So the next time you come to church, take a moment to connect with the worshipers near you. We come to worship the same God, sing the same songs, and listen to the same Word. A greeting, a handshake, a smile will let the person on your pew know we're in this thing together!

❧

Dear Lord, the Christian life is about relationship. I am grateful that You have placed me with other believers who worship You also. May we find peace as we worship and walk together in Your love. Amen.

Simon Says, "Submit"

Submitting to one another in the fear of God.

EPHESIANS 5:21, NKJV

Do you remember the game "Simon Says"? There was one person who was in charge and everyone else had to follow that person's commands; if they didn't, they were eliminated. The goal was to be the last person standing after completing all the commands. Everyone who participated had to listen carefully and obey the instructions. When we played this game as children, sometimes the moves would be difficult, and the instructions would be tricky. Yet we remained persistent and determined because we knew that if we stayed the course, we would win in the end. Even when frustration hit, very few people walked away because we knew that if we stayed long enough, we would eventually get to be Simon.

Well, submitting to one another is sort of like playing "Simon Says." We each have opportunities to be in charge of some situations and to follow in others. When we lead, we must display compassion, trust, and selflessness, because we care about the people who are following our commands. We want them to feel secure, with no fear that we would cause them to stumble or fall. And when we follow, we must let go of our own interests and surrender to the greater good.

Surrender is what Christ did for us. He submitted to the Father to complete His assignment of dying on the cross so the lost would be saved. Thank God He didn't give up or say, "This assignment is too hard." Because of His willingness to submit, we all have the opportunity for salvation. Submission can impact our lives in a very positive way. Submitting to one another allows us to help each other fulfill our life's mission. Simply put, it allows us to show our love for one another, and serve one another—just as Christ did.

Lord, I thank You for submitting to the pain of the cross so that I can live. Thank You for Your love and unselfishness and not giving up even when things became unbearable. Your obedience taught me that when love is at the heart of my submission, it can be powerful, and the rewards are great! In Jesus' Name. Amen.

THE APPEAL OF THE EYE

Love not the world, neither the things that are in the world. If any man love the world, the love of the Father is not in him .

1 JOHN 2:15, KJV

Today's advertisers are savvy as they create demand for products. They shape how people think and feel; they determine what's hip, what's sexy, and what's normal. Advertisers even try to determine what issues we need to worry about. They can be quite convincing with their appeal to consumers. Just turn on your new HDTV!

Their pull on us is not unlike that talked about by the apostle John in his letter to the churches of Asia Minor. John addressed the believers who were claiming a new life in Christ, yet were continuing to be pulled by the world. The pull was so strong that John likened it to loving the world and the things of the world.

In 1 John 2:16, the apostle explained why love for the world is incompatible with love for God—describing three elements that define worldly desires. First, "the lust of the flesh" refers to inordinate desires that appeal to our carnal nature and do not spiritually edify. Second, the "lust of the eye" is the tendency we have to be drawn to things that sparkle and catch our attention but have no eternal substance. And finally, "the pride of life" represents those things that we clamor for, such as status and fame, to build up our reputation but not our relationship with God.

Some of us have found it difficult to obey the call of full surrender to God because we are caught up in the attractions of the world and what it has to offer. There are some who claim to love Jesus—they read their Bibles, attend church every Sunday—but they still want to "fit" into the world. When we continue to indulge ourselves in the things of the world, we are not living in the love of God. We are living in darkness, and there will be no peace in our lives.

Today, let's examine our hearts and ask the Holy Spirit to strengthen our resolve to love God and not the world.

❧

Father God, help me to face the temptations that I encounter each day. I am praying for strength to stand up against these worldly desires. In Jesus' Name. Amen!

TREAT ONE ANOTHER RIGHT

And be ye kind one to another, tenderhearted, forgiving one another, even as God for Christ's sake hath forgiven you.

EPHESIANS 4:32, KJV

Getting into a "brothers and sisters in Christ Jesus" frame of mind can be hard. We are called upon to love people we don't know or, in some instances, don't like. We are challenged to be in relationship with folks who might have treated us wrong in the past, or are presently behaving badly toward us. How do we handle it? What can we do to move forward in a walk of love?

Surely we can connect, in thought, to the reality that we ourselves are beneficiaries of forgiveness. We can search our hearts for the unconditional love of God that fills it to overflowing. We can engage in performing "random acts of kindness" as we consider God's loving-kindness toward us, even in our disobedient and sinful state. In doing so, we connect to the Christ-consciousness and show ourselves also to be sons and daughters of God!

As with all families, we are often called upon to forgive one another. Media mogul Oprah Winfrey made popular this definition of forgiveness by Lilly Tomlin: "Forgiveness is letting go of all hope for a better past." It's a great definition in that it succinctly addresses the real issue. Often the lack of forgiveness is rooted in our desire to change something that has already happened. But it won't. Our only direction is forward.

As Christians, we have a great capacity for love and growth. When we yield our ways to the Spirit of God, we find a strength and ability we might not have known. We can be kind to one another. We can uplift one another. We can forgive. We can reflect the love and power of God within, even when challenged to do otherwise. God in us makes it so!

❧

Father, I am in tune with Your very presence within me. In touch with Your grace and mercy, I am kind and I forgive. I forgive others for perceived wrongs and things done against me. I forgive myself for not living up to Your highest and best for me. I have new joy. I go on in peace, relishing in Your love poured into my life afresh each day. Amen and amen!

THE VERDICT IS ... FORGIVEN

Now therefore fear ye not: I will nourish you, and your little ones. And he comforted them, and spake kindly unto them.

GENESIS 50:21, KJV

The case is that of Joseph against his brothers. The prosecuting attorney begins his opening statement, and everyone in the court is attentive. "We have here a case where my client Joseph was put in a pit, ultimately to die, because of jealousy. Joseph was young and eager to share his dreams and visions with his brothers, but, unfortunately, they couldn't handle it. They conspired together because they couldn't envision being under Joseph's authority. The brothers plotted to kill Joseph, but the oldest encouraged them not to kill him but to put him in a pit with no food or water. Another brother suggested, and the brothers agreed, they sell Joseph to the Ishmeelites. Once Joseph was sold they took his coat, killed a goat, and put blood all over it. They gave it to their father, asking him if he knew if that was Joseph's coat. The father replied yes and was devastated, thinking his son had been torn into pieces and eaten by a vicious beast

The defense attorney hangs his head and argues that the brothers were suffering from temporary insanity, and that the charges should be abated since they did not go through with their original plan.

In the midst of this intense family drama, Joseph stands up and says there is no need for a trial. "I forgive them. What my brothers meant for evil, God meant it for my good. They don't have to worry; I will provide for them and their families." Through every trial that Joseph encountered, from the pit to Pharaoh's house, he trusted God.

Forgiveness is an act of love, and God reminds us throughout Scripture that we need to forgive others of their sin against us so that the Father will forgive us. So if our Father is encouraging us to forgive, even when situations have been tough, like Joseph's experiences, we can choose forgiveness. Forgiveness frees us to love and give, just as Joseph did for his brothers.

❧

Lord, thank You for giving me the power to forgive those who have wronged me and mistreated me. Joseph proves that forgiveness is possible no matter the circumstance. Thank You for enabling me to forgive others. Amen.

SING YOUR HEART OUT!

Let the message about Christ, in all its richness, fill your lives. Teach and counsel each other with all the wisdom he gives. Sing psalms and hymns and spiritual songs to God with thankful hearts.

COLOSSIANS 3:16, NLT

A new show debuted last year that is an even higher stakes talent version of *American Idol* and its hybrid cousins. The show, titled the *X Factor*, scourers metropolitan cities looking for those with that "it" factor, that star quality. The premiere was practically a bust until one rousing rendition of Beyonce's "Listen" was belted out of the mouth of a beautiful young girl. She had the judges and the crowd up on their feet, with many singing and swaying to the song as she laid it down. She sang her heart out!

As the young woman moved others with her vocal veracity and passionate performance of the chart-topping song, we are to sing our hearts out about the love of the One who loves and listens to us. His message is to fill our hearts and abide in us. That message is to dwell in us richly and it does so by our studying, meditating on, and applying the Word. As early Christians finished many communal feasts, they would be invited to sing to the Lord in the presence of others. Often there would be spontaneous expressions sung that honored God. Some would recount the acts of God and praise Him for what He had done. Others might sing songs of celebration, while still others sang hymns confessing their faith in God. Some might even erupt into songs that brought correction and conviction.

Songs were sung because hearts were filled with the love of Christ and thankfulness overflowed. When we sing the transforming message of Christ, it finds a place in our hearts. Singing together, enjoying the fellowship of the body of Christ, the people of God share in the powerful convicting and life-giving work of the Holy Spirit. It happens as we are together, sharing and singing, building up and encouraging each other in His truth. Like the beautiful young girl who inspired the audience on the *X-Factor*, encourage others as you sing unto the Lord. Go ahead, sing your heart out!

❧

Father God, let Your Word dwell in me richly and let me sing it out boldly to bless You, me, and others too. Amen.

Go Ahead, Bless Somebody

And let us consider how we may spur one another on toward love and good deeds.

HEBREWS 10:24, NIV

A young woman with a vibrant smile was a faithful member of a Sunday morning Bible study class. She was always a pleasant presence, nodding politely to arriving class participants that slid into the row near her. She often reached across the aisle to squeeze the hand of a saint passing by. When service ended, she would make a beeline for the door, retreating as quickly as she had come. One Sunday, smiling widely as she headed toward the door, a kind usher said, "Sister In-a-Hurry, you would be great for the Greeting Ministry. Why don't you think about that."

We can see the burgeoning gifts and talents of God's people all around us. Some may be prevalent—out in the open and apparent for all to see. Others may be lying dormant, not quite tapped or revealed. We see the effervescence that is so needed to refresh the weighty sadness that seems pervasive today. Every now and then we might catch a hint of a hungry heart that belongs to open hands, just waiting to serve and meet a need. Are we not to inspire and encourage action that flows from love for God and love for His people? Can we not consider ways that we care for and motivate each other to engage in God's work?

The writer of Hebrews captures the idea of inspiring each other, stirring each other, and encouraging each other to serve others. This characterizes the commitment of followers of Jesus Christ. We recognize our responsibility to each other, as well as to help others. Sister In-a-Hurry was a virtuous woman whose warm smile moved beyond her small class into the vestibule of the church. On a bustling Sunday morning she can now be seen warmly extending her hand and touching hearts as she smiles encouragingly to all who arrive to worship. The encouragement she received inspired her to serve, bless others, and use her gifts in the body of Christ.

When we encourage others, we are, in fact, living out what the writer suggests. It is an act of love, and the fruit of the good work blesses others.

Lord, I thank You that You have given us people to encourage us and spur us on. Help me to do the same for someone today. Amen.

COME TOGETHER

And let us not neglect our meeting together, as some people do, but encourage one another, especially now that the day of his return is drawing near.

HEBREWS 10:25, NLT

Yesterday's devotion encouraged us to spur one another on, but in order to be encouraged in that way, we have to come together. It will be difficult to inspire others from afar, over the long haul. Oh, it can be done when it's needful, if circumstances prevent meeting together, but the truth is we receive encouragement and strength, and we experience fellowship, when we meet together as a body of believers. Likewise, we can grow weak and discouraged when we don't come together as a community of faith, allowing the enemy of our souls to wreak havoc on us when we are in isolation.

Today's text was written at a time when Christians were being persecuted for their faith. They were met with unimaginable brutality and ferocious hostility as they sought to worship their God. Their courage was found *not* in retaliation, but in provoking one another to pray and worship the Lord *through* their difficulty. They did not shrink back or isolate themselves in the face of opposition, but rather came together to worship their King. They gathered as a community of believers and grew in faith, godliness, and relationship with Jesus Christ. They welcomed God in their midst and experienced the blessing of being together.

Today, you may be tempted to withdraw because someone disappointed you, or maybe you disappointed someone. The feelings of hurt, embarrassment, and shame can threaten to drive a wedge between you and the church to which God has called you and purposed you to be connected. A small wedge can seem like a chasm, causing us to become weaker and leaving us more susceptible to deception and tricks of the enemy.

We gather as a body of believers coming together to grow in godliness, community, and love; we find comfort, joy, strength, nourishment, and peace when we come together. Be encouraged today for the blessing of coming together as the family of God. Remember, He dwells in the midst of us when we come together.

❧

Dear Father, how can I not take joy in gathering with Your people knowing You are in the midst? Thank You for being so mindful of us that You come in to us whenever we gather. Amen.

LOVE'S IN THE DOINGS

My little children, let us not love in word, neither in tongue; but in deed and in truth.

1 JOHN 3:18, KJV

Our elderly grandmother, who has now gone on to be with the Lord, had many sayings that her grandchildren heard many times; but they didn't know what the sayings meant until much later on in life, when her words began to make perfect sense and they realized just how wise their grandmother really was. One such saying of hers was, "I hear whatcha saying, but I'm gonna watch whatcha do; many times the two are as far apart as the day is from the night." Sounds funny, doesn't it? But if you stop and think about this one in particular, it's powerfully true and it ties into the Scripture for today.

Here, the writer admonishes us to love in deed and in truth rather than in word, or by giving lip service to love. For if we love in deed, we will surely love in truth, because true love is in the doing. Love is always action, and action supports love. The Scriptures back this up over and over again. In 1 John 4:8, we are told that God is love. And we know from our own experience with God that He is always doing something for us. John 3:16 declares "that God so loved the world that He gave His only begotten Son, that whosoever believeth in Him should not perish, but have everlasting life". Here God expresses, or proves, His love for us by doing something for us...the giving of His only begotten Son. Real love requires action in order to exist. Show me a man or woman in love, and I'll show the same man or woman doing something to show it.

So we can conclude that love is what love does. It's not enough for us, as Christians, to only speak of love, quoting the Scriptures with whimsical prowess; no, we must show love, and our actions will speak much louder than any words could. And our love will be confirmed by those on the receiving end of it. So let us be about the doing of love rather than the speaking of it!

Lord, let me act out my love rather than talk about it, so that those whom I love know it by the things I do and not the words I speak. Amen.

Choosing the High Road

That goes for all of you, no exceptions. No retaliation. No sharp-tongued sarcasm. Instead, bless —that's your job, to bless. You'll be a blessing and also get a blessing.

1 Peter 3:9, The Message

Is there anyone better to relay the message of not retaliating or seeking vengeance than the apostle Peter? After all, he was the one who drew his sword and cut off the ear of one soldier when they came to take Jesus by night. Was it not Peter who also denied that he was ever associated with Jesus? Yet, at this point in his apostleship, he had grown deeper in his walk with the Lord and was carrying out his call to feed the sheep of God. His message in this text is for those suffering for the faith to endure the hardness and remain faithful by taking the high road.

This text speaks to the heart of every Christian suffering for Christ's sake. Our example in Jesus is full of hope when it comes to suffering. Yet His desire was to forgive and not punish. As we live, we may be despitefully used—even persecuted. Peter's epistle was written to Christians dispersed among different nations; and it holds true today, as Christianity spreads around the world. Peter's message is as pertinent now as it was then. It reminds us that when we suffer for the sake of righteousness, we are called to bless them that treat us poorly.

As Christians, we may experience suffering at the hands of others, but our suffering will keep us connected to Christ. The challenge is to avoid the temptation of a worldly response by seeking revenge. While others seek vengeance or retaliation, we are encouraged to bless or speak well of our antagonists. When others speak to us in a demeaning and degrading manner, we are to return a kind, soft word and pray for them. You may feel the strain to bless those that have hurt you, but imagine the joy of the Father to see His children walking in obedience to His Word and choosing the high road, a road often seen but not often traveled.

🌿

Dear Father, I thank You for keeping me during times of mistreatment at the hands of others. May I extend to them the mercy You have extended to me when I mistreated You. In Jesus' Name. Amen.

Love Revealed

This is the very best way to love. Put your life on the line for your friends.

JOHN 15:13, THE MESSAGE

As children we played a game call "Hide-and-Go-Seek." At times we could spend more than ten minutes trying to find playmates before finally conceding and begging that they reveal themselves. It is great to know that when it comes to love, God revealed His love through His Son, Jesus Christ.

A look at the key words "love" and "life" will help us grasp the reality of love. The Greek word for love is *agápe. Agápe* means love, as defined in the July 23 devotion. The second key word in this text is the word life. In Greek *psuche* (psoo-khay) means "the seat of feelings, desires and affections."[22] We begin to reread this text with a different twist as such: this is the very best way to show love and good will. Put your feelings, desires, and affections on the line for others.

Observe Jesus and the terminology used to define God's love. Jesus exposed His love for us by dying for us while we were yet sinners. But let's not leave it at His death. Look at everything Christ gave up as an expression of His love. His desire that "not my will, but yours be done" (Luke 22:42, NIV) was revealed as part of this love, as was His affection toward His disciples. As we examine our lives and our desires, to whom have we revealed love and for whom are we giving our lives? We don't simply die to ourselves in order to love someone; we offer all that we have in Christ.

Look at Christ's crucifixion and become acquainted with the fellowship of His suffering as love. He didn't hide it. We didn't have to ask Him to come out of the shadows to reveal it; He freely gave Himself for us. Through His public shunning, beating, mocking, and death, His love was revealed. When we know how Jesus endured the cross, what will we endure? When people experience our love, will they see God's heart revealed?

Dear Jesus, thank You for exposing Your love to connect me with the Father above. May my life ever be a living testimony of love to expose the power of Your grace and the depth of Your love. In Jesus' Name. Amen!

LOVING HIM

"The most important one," answered Jesus, "is this: Hear, O Israel: The Lord our God, the Lord is one. Love the Lord your God with all your heart and with all your soul and with all your mind and with all your strength. The second is this: Love your neighbor as yourself. There is no commandment greater than these."

MARK 12:29-31, NIV

We must love God with every part of our being. Love for the Father should be shown through our studying His Word and giving our time, talents, tithing, devotion, offering, and service.

Jesus then encourages us to take the focus off ourselves and love our neighbor just as much as we do the reflection in the mirror. Let us strive to make a daily effort to use our God-given gifts, talents, and resources to help our neighbor. What is God asking us to do today? Perhaps this:

> *My child, do you love Me above all as I love you when you fall?*
> *Do you seek Me day-by-day and feel the love of my grace?*
> *Do you trust me when it's inconvenient*
> *and words of praise do you really mean them?*
> *Is your joy so easily replaced when you gaze upon another?*
> *Is your love for Me greater than mother, sister, father, or brother?*
> *Have you seen your fellow man so poor and full of need*
> *And never shared a dime as your heart was full of greed?*
> *Have you seen the homeless cold and provided him no home?*
> *Have you seen your friend so broken and left them all alone?*
> *Has your love grown yet so full you seek to share no more?*
> *Have you given all you have, yet kept sealed a secret door?*
> *Have you seen your neighbor haste for destruction*
> *and never warned him so?*
> *Then consider the possibility that My love you do not know.*

❦

Dear Father, as Your love has been shed abroad in my heart, may I also walk in the same manner of love for others, but toward You first. When I truly love You, loving others becomes easier. Help me realize that loving You allows me to love others. As Your love passes all knowledge, lead me into Your truth. In Jesus' Name. Amen.

RECEIVING THE MESSENGERS

Whoever welcomes a prophet as a prophet will receive a prophet's reward, and whoever welcomes a righteous person as a righteous person will receive a righteous person's reward.

MATTHEW 10:41, NIV

Have you ever been rejected? Have you ever offered advice to someone, but it was totally ignored? There was a time when we did the same at the call of our Lord and Savior, but one day we submitted. We finally heard the gospel message and joined the great body of believers known as Christians. It wasn't until we gave our lives to Him that we finally began to see the purpose of listening to those called by God to deliver His message of salvation.

This text provides insight into the benefits of those who hear and receive the message from the child of God sent as the messenger. At one time, when Jesus sent His disciples to witness, He instructed them to keep moving if anyone rejected them. But those that did receive the prophet—the ones who proclaimed God's Word—would also receive a reward. This receiving is more than just two strangers passing in the night. It is an intentional focus on the message of the Lord. The reward is a relationship with God and blessings from God. The reward is a renewed mind, body, and soul focused on God.

In the Old Testament, kings generally listened when they sought or received counsel from the prophets. In order to stay connected as a community, it is important that we tune in to the Word of the Lord delivered by His teachers and preachers. When we are connected to God's Word, we have the ability to hear clearly from the messenger. If we find ourselves feeling distant from God, be assured He is there. He said He would never leave us nor forsake us. Let's prepare for the methods in which God sends His people to shed light into our hearts. We never know what God is doing. We just might entertain angels sent by God.

❦

Dear Lord, Your Word is ripe for the ear and fresh for the plucking. May I be in a place to receive from those You send to encourage and lift me up. In Jesus' Name. Amen.

HEARD IT THROUGH THE GREAT VINE

I am the true vine, and my Father is the husbandman. Every branch in me that beareth not fruit he taketh away: and every branch that beareth fruit, he purgeth it, that it may bring forth more fruit.

JOHN 15:1-2, KJV

The Lord Jesus always revealed who He was to His disciples. At times He spoke to inspire them to think critically. On this occasion, He used the familiar element of the farming culture to help them understand the importance of relationship with Him. Farming was a common practice, understood by most, so it made sense that Jesus would take something occurring in their everyday experience to highlight a profound truth. While the people of God had previously been cared for and tended by Him, God was making a new provision through Jesus Christ.

Jesus told them He is the *true* Vine and His Father is the Vinedresser. He was illustrating the intimacy of relationship with the Father, and letting them know that relationship with God required grafting in Him. God tenderly and attentively takes care of those that are His own. As the Vinedresser, the Father meticulously attends to every branch on the Vine. It is watered, trimmed back, and cleared of things that hinder its growth in order for it to flourish. Buds peeping through the shoot of the branch are a clear sign of growth, while a branch that is ripe with color but unattached cannot produce anything because its nutrient source has been cut off. Jesus makes it clear that in order to grow spiritually, have fruit produced in our lives, and godly character realized, we are to remain in Him. He said, "I am the way, the truth, and the life" (John 14:6). We can't do it apart from Him, but His life in us produces more life.

Remaining in the Vine will help us be branches that produce lush fruit—ripe for the picking and feeding of those who are hungry. Our lives will have much fruit when we stay connected to the Great Vine!

❧

Dear Lord, prune me daily that I may be a living epistle and example for You. May the life I lead, the truth I share, and the testimony I bare plant seeds of righteousness that will surely bring forth more fruit ripe and fit for Your kingdom. In Jesus' Name. Amen.

LOVING MY BROTHER AND SISTER

Be kindly affectionate to one another with brotherly love, in honor giving preference to one another.

ROMANS 12:10, NKJV

Okay, Jesus: You ask a hard thing!
    In a world where taking care of "self" is routinely not only the number one law but the mantra by which one lives and moves, how can brotherly love and honor for one another come to fruition?

Paul writes to us to deeply love one another and put others in higher esteem than ourselves. Is it hard? Yes! Is it possible? For the blood-bought, born-again, Holy Ghost-filled Christian—a child of the Most High—the answer is a resounding *yes!*

Sometimes it appears that Christ asks us to do the impossible, as today's Word of reflection seems to suggest. We are being asked to be "kindly affectionate" toward each other and "in honor" to give preference to one another.

The phrase "kindly affectionate" means family love. We Christians are the family of God, and the Scripture asks us to treat our sisters and brothers in Christ as we would those in our own biological family.

We, in our own strength and will, do not have the tools to necessitate the extension of brotherly love and honor. However, the good news is that Jesus, through His catalyst—the Holy Ghost— has armored us with all essentials to walk in obedience and bring these things (and all things) to realization.

Before Paul, Jesus said in John 13:34, "A new command I give you: Love one another. As I have loved you, so you must love one another" (NIV). Because of the love of Christ that is shed abroad in our hearts by the Holy Ghost (Romans 5:5), we have the wherewithal to "be kindly affectionate" and to "honor" as we are commanded.

Lord Jesus, You have commanded me to do a hard thing. In my own strength I cannot do this, so I ask that You come into my heart and re-fill my heart with Your love so that I can love my brothers and sisters with Your love. In Jesus' Name. Amen.

What's Love Got to Do with It?

This is my commandment, That ye love one another, as I have loved you.

John 15:12, KJV

A twentieth-century blockbuster film (and concomitant rhythm and blues song) *What's Love Got to Do with It?* inundated the headlines and subsequently became a mantra for many relationships. The big screen attempted to make this four-letter word, l-o-v-e, appear to be overrated and unnecessary in the whole scheme of things. The results seemed to offer an escape, to relinquish accountability, and to minimize the significance—the need, the call—to love.

Jesus, why do You keep telling us to love one another as You have loved us? Is it that You know how difficult it is to love a spouse, a child, a co-worker, or friends? Are You at all acquainted with stiff-necked, hard-hearted people? Yet You command me to love them as you have loved me.

Contrary to what any blockbuster film or rhythm and blues song proclaims, love has everything to do with "it." So significant is love that it ultimately motivated Jesus to go to a cross to die for our sins. So significant is this love that we now have a right to eternal life. Yes, love has everything to do with it, and Scripture reminds us that if we *really* love Him, we will keep His commandments (John 14:15). So the question is, *Do we really love Him?* If so, how will we respond to His commandment? We respond by turning from our own way toward His. We respond by acknowledging that apart from Him we can do nothing, but through Him we can do all things—including love! We respond by allowing Him to express love through us to the unloved, the unlovable, and the hard-to-love. Let's thank Him for those around us, mindful that it is a joy to reaffirm our commitment to love them as Christ has loved us.

Father, I yield myself to You. You have commanded me to love and some days it's a hard task. Lord, I admit I cannot do this within my own desire, strength, or will and I ask that You forgive me for the times when I thought I had a right not to love others. I open my heart and receive Your love, which will transform my heart and help me love others. In Jesus' Name. Amen.

"Me, Me, Me…!"

And the second is like, namely this, Thou shalt love thy neighbour as thyself.
There is none other commandment greater than these.

MARK 12:31, KJV

Who wants to go first?" is the question a zealous teacher poses to a group of excited students—a question to which several eager students reply enthusiastically, "Me, me, me…!" Some students are eager to go first, while others hear their parents saying, "Let them go ahead of you."

For some of us, loving ourselves is a tall order, indeed. Yet today, it seems that Jesus is teaching the ideological concept of "me, me, me," saying, "You must go first!" By this, it is meant that yes it is true that in order to love my neighbor I have to love "me, me, me" first. Perhaps it seems a bit contradictory to be commanded to love yourself first when in fact we are also told to honor others and put them first (Philippians 2:3). But on a fundamental level, the way we treat others is a direct reflection of how we feel about ourselves.

The passage of Scripture that we're examining today not only requires that we love ourselves, but it also infers that it is okay to do so. We live in a society that, frankly, frowns on self-love, labeling it narcissistic or egotistic. And we understand that the world thinks opposite of what the Word of God says we must do—love ourselves.

Accepting the love of God is the beginning of learning to love ourselves. Because His love is totally unconditional and given freely, we begin to understand that we are love-worthy. The Bible teaches us that it was in God's great love for us that He gave His only begotten Son for our sins. In our acceptance of Christ's sacrifice, we also accept His great love, which serves as the foundation for us loving ourselves and consequently, loving others.

❧

Lord, help me to love me the way You created me to be before I was formed in my mother's womb. Help me to receive the love You have for me and allow me to extend that love to my brother and my sister. In Jesus' Name. Amen.

LOVE BEYOND THE CIRCUMSTANCE

But I say unto you, Love your enemies, bless them that curse you, do good to them that hate you, and pray for them which despitefully use you, and persecute you.

MATTHEW 5:44, KJV

The call came in the middle of the night. The sound of tragedy filled her ears, and her heart became mixed with hurt and revenge. It was hard enough to realize that her only child was killed, but killed at the hands of the one she came to love as a son-in-law? Love, bless, do good, and pray for someone who has become an enemy? Surely God must be mistaken to require such a difficult task of those He created from dust.

Yet Jesus says, *that you may be children of your heavenly Father, this is required.* How? This task is not humanly possible! What a grand discovery. God has waited for us to realize that what He requires must be done through His power and not our own. How does one look an enemy in the face and love, bless, do good, and pray for him or her? The dust must rely upon the strength of his Creator to re-shape the heart and the mind to aspire to seemingly insurmountable tasks.

The type of love commanded by Jesus is not predicated on circumstances. This love is solely dependent on the love of Christ that is in our hearts and is not birthed out of our desire to avenge any wrong-doing inflicted on us or on our loved ones. This type of love is humanly impossible but possible through Christ who gives us strength (Philippians 4:13).

Lord God, I have made You Master of my life. I am willing that You re-shape my heart and my mind to conform to the task of loving, blessing, doing good, and praying for my enemies. Take control of my heart and saturate it with Your love, Your mercy, and Your grace, so that I may do what it is that You require of me. I thank You in advance and I receive Your love for me. In Jesus' Name. Amen.

CAN YOU HEAR ME NOW?

Hear, O LORD, when I cry with my voice: have mercy also upon me, and answer me.

PSALM 27:7, KJV

There is an automatic assumption that if one's name is called, if the telephone rings, if there's a knock on the door, a response of some sort is required.

This notion of call and response beleaguered the airways with cellular phone commercials asking, "Can you hear me now?" The impression was to show the importance of retaining the connection between a caller and recipient with a particular cellular phone company. Responding to a call of any sort is considered common courtesy and not to be deemed rude and inconsiderate.

A recent conversation with two new mothers expressed that the common challenge for the new mother is the thought of not being able to hear her newborn when he or she is in distress. This dilemma may have even prompted an increased readiness to respond to the faintest cry. Yet many of these mothers retrospectively recall that they always heard their infant's cries. It was an automatic and innate response to their babies.

Similarly, God, as El Shaddai, whose name is associated with being the breasted one (Genesis 49:25), automatically, and in His inherent ability, hears us when we call out to Him. Long before the advertisers could ask, "Can you hear me now?" He told Jeremiah, "Call unto me, and I will answer thee" (Jeremiah 33:3). David, in his praise to the Lord, says the Lord is near to all who call upon him in truth (Psalm 145:18). So today we *will not* fear. God is near, and He will hear us when we call upon His name. Not only will He hear, but He will also have mercy upon us and answer.

Father God, I thank You for the privilege of calling on You. I am grateful I don't have to ask, "Can you hear me now?" because I am assured that You always hear me. Just as the mother always hears the cry of her infant, I am confident that You, Father, hear my cry. Thank You for never ceasing to extend Your hand of mercy to me and for always answering me. In Jesus' Name. Amen.

A CHURCH OF HOSPITALITY

Offer hospitality to one another without grumbling.

1 PETER 4:9, NIV

Peter admonished early Christians not to think it strange that they would be shunned by the world (4:12). Instead, the world will think it strange that Christians do not join them in their worldly excess. Peter reminds us that there will always be tension between the world and the church, and we shouldn't think it odd that unbelievers think us strange! Instead, because believers will be treated as strangers in the world sometimes, we are to make sure we show hospitality to all by opening our hearts to fellow parishioners and visitors.

Hospitality was a deeply embedded value in ancient Israel and the early church. Because Israel was at one time treated as a stranger among other nations, God instructed Israel to extend hospitality to the stranger (Genesis 15:13; 17:8; 28:4; 37:1). For instance, "thou shalt not oppress a stranger: for ye know the heart of a stranger, seeing ye were strangers in the land of Egypt" (Exodus 23:9).

Used in today's text, hospitality is derived from a Greek compound-word, *philoxenos*, which means "love" or "friendliness to strangers." It translates as "hospitable" or "generous" to guests. Because God's people are often accustomed to being treated strangely or as strangers, God admonishes His people to understand what it feels like to be considered an outsider, and not treat those who come into our midst as strangers. Instead, God asks us to welcome guests and make them feel at home.

We are called to be a church of hospitality, one that, through God's grace, embraces members—old and young, male and female, rich and poor—as one body. We are called to be a church that welcomes guests, strangers, and visitors alike with love. We are called to extend God's grace to each other and to our guests.

Today, commit to doing your part to help our church become a church of hospitality.

Lord, thank You for placing me in the body of believers. I am grateful for my church. Give us Your grace to always welcome guests and allow the love of Christ to be evident among us. Amen.

SERVE ONE ANOTHER

As every man hath received the gift, even so minister the same one to another, as good stewards of the manifold grace of God.

1 PETER 4:10, KJV

At age 40, Roy suffered a mild stroke. An avid fitness instructor in top physical shape, he bounced back from the stroke in record time. Roy's recovery amazed his doctors, yet they had to acknowledge the handiwork of God's design of the human body—everything Roy needed to heal was already in his body. A healthy body has all it needs to fight infection, disease, and other maladies.

So it is in the body of Christ. A healthy body has all it needs to ward off the attack of the enemy and ensure the growth of the body's members. Through the Holy Spirit, God endows believers with spiritual abilities. These spiritual abilities—or gifts—are an outflow of God's grace to us. We are to use our spiritual gifts to minister to one another, and thus build up and strengthen the body of Christ.

No one member of the body has every gift. But together, every gift needed to strengthen the church is in the body. The needs of members are met when we serve—or minister—to one another. God places the ministry gifts of the apostle, prophet, evangelist, pastor, and teacher to lead and provide guidance to His church (Ephesians 4:11). Furthermore, God gives believers the gifts of wisdom, knowledge, faith, healing, miracles, discerning of spirits, and divers tongues. Many gifts given by the One Spirit are used to build up the one body (1 Corinthians 12:8-10).

Perhaps you are gifted to speak; God will use you to encourage believers who may be down. Perhaps you are gifted to teach; God will use you to share the truth of His Word and strengthen believers in their walk. Perhaps you have the gift of assistance; God will use you to assist other believers. Whatever your gift, God requires you to be a good steward of what He has endowed within you so His church will be blessed and strengthened to be a light in a dark world.

Today, commit to serve using the gifts God has given you.

Dear Lord, thank You for the gifts with which You've blessed me. I will use them to glorify You and edify Your church. Amen.

FOLLOW THE WAY OF PEACE

Let us therefore follow after the things which make for peace, and things wherewith one may edify another.

ROMANS 14:19, KJV

Sometimes we can be impractical, and not very spiritual, in our Christian walk. We are swayed by our opinions and judgments more than the love of God, which serves to harmonize and unify us. We criticize others based on what we think or feel, instead of encouraging one another in the Word of God. Consequently, our encounters become about what divides us instead of what unites us. We easily place stumbling blocks in our brother's or sister's path, or set a trap wherein they might fall. We end up with fragmented and dysfunctional relationships. But, the apostle Paul says there is a better way!

We know that there is great diversity in the body of Christ. We share faith in Jesus Christ but don't all worship the same, or engage in the same spiritual practices. While many are taking a stand on being identified as Christians, others are stepping back from the association. Many move away from the church as an institution and devalue it in their lives.

Since we all come from various cultures and backgrounds, we are bound to have some differences. Yet the apostle Paul is saying, stop nitpicking about things that don't really matter in the Kingdom any way. Focus on what matters—righteousness, peace, and joy in the Holy Spirit. He reminds the church that we all have to stand before God and give account for our lives, and that we are all on equal ground with that reality! As such, none are in position to render personal judgments that make us better than others.

The apostle Paul says, how about focusing on the things that bring about peace and that build up one another? He's telling us to find what we do have in common and celebrate that. He encourages us to be kind and patient even as we follow our personal convictions.

❧

Lord, help me to be a peacemaker! I thank You that I think thoughts of peace and rest in the peace of God daily. Grant me peace in my soul, so that I can extend this peace to others and share in the peace of others. Help me to speak words that edify others and make for peace. Thank You, God. And so it is!

LOVE IS THE SOLUTION

*But if you bite and devour one another [in partisan strife], be careful that
you [and your whole fellowship] are not consumed by one another.*
GALATIANS 5:15, AMP

As we consider the events that occurred eleven years ago on
this eleventh day of September, we can't help but be reminded
of the underlying issues that led to such a catastrophic destruction
of life. Terrorists from another country purposed in their hearts
to destroy the United States, aiming at what they considered to be
the centers of American power. Those who plotted the destruction
were filled with so much anger and hatred that it penetrated their
hearts right to the core and drove them to an act that ultimately
led to their own destruction. Of course there is nothing that can
change for those terrorists, but what about us? How can we make
sure that we are not consuming or being consumed by one another?

In today's passage, Paul reflected on the attacks launched
against him—spiritual attacks, verbal attacks against his character
and apostolic authority. He was concerned not just for his own
reputation but for the overall health of the church. He was
adamant that backbiting, strife, and anger destroy a fellowship.
They consume or eat away at the very core of a congregation. Using
today's analogy, those who act out of bitterness and anger terrorize
the church and ultimately end up consuming themselves.

Ironically, before Paul was converted to Christ, he attacked the
church. Just as Paul could consider his own attacks on the church
in addressing the Galatians, we must consider our own ways as it
relates to the church. Are we allowing things such as backbiting,
envy, jealousy, strife, and works of the flesh to terrorize us and
affect others?

We must slow down and operate out of the abundance of love
for one another. The terrorists' anger at a nation led them not to
only destroy those whom they hated but also themselves. Let us let
go of anger and allow the love of God to overtake us so that we may
handle one another as it would truly please God.

*Father, help me to let go of the anger that can lead me away from how You
truly want me to deal with others. Strengthen me to focus on pleasing You
by loving others. In Jesus' Name. Amen!*

It Looks Good on You

In the same way, you who are younger, submit yourselves to your elders. All of you, clothe yourselves with humility toward one another, because, "God opposes the proud but shows favor to the humble."

1 Peter 5:5, NIV

Going natural is all the rage now. Styles of the 70s call us back to a time before perms and pinstripes were the thing and a kinky curl with a little height was more than just a style. It was a statement and the envy of every up-and-coming young mobile, hoisting a sign of strength. Sometimes mistaken for arrogance, the young were misunderstood by their observing elders who couldn't get with the new way they were expressing themselves. The young and eager looked good, but needed to learn from those whose experiences had been tested by trusting God. There were lessons of humility and serving being taught and learned.

Peter learned firsthand what clothing oneself in humility looked like. He witnessed a real life picture of it as he watched Jesus clothe Himself in humility when He washed His disciples' feet (John 13). He saw Jesus put on the apron as an outer garment but could see He was wearing something more significant on the inside. Peter may have realized that, as Jesus attached the apron to His side, He had attached His disciples to His heart. He saw Jesus consider others before Himself. Jesus illustrated the Old Testament Proverb that today's passage echoes by showing us a picture of the grace that can be upon us when we serve one another.

We, too, are to serve one another. Christ's example shows we can silence selfishness and let humility speak by placing ourselves under the authority of someone with greater wisdom and maturity, and by walking respectfully with those who are more knowledgeable about the things of God.

The once rebellious, opinionated Peter, now matured, speaks words of wisdom to us. No outer garment takes the place of inner submission and humility. Resist prideful urges of thinking too much of yourself and serve others in a gracious, God-honoring way. It will look good on you!

Father, help me resist the urge to be arrogant or prideful. Remind me I have a lot to learn, and I thank You for putting people in my life to teach me. In Jesus' Name. Amen.

In-House Love

As we have therefore opportunity, let us do good unto all men, especially unto them who are of the household of faith.

GALATIANS 6:10, KJV

In the sixth chapter, the apostle Paul addresses the issue of how we should treat one another within the household of faith (or within our sacred community). His preference is that we show compassionate love toward one another.

In the first verse, we are told to restore our brother or sister who has been overtaken in a fault. Translated, that means that within the sacred community (which is the church), we should do what we can to support our brother or sister struggling with an issue. Our support should be given in the spirit of meekness, as if we, ourselves, were struggling with the same issue.

Paul goes on, in verses 7 through 9, to discuss the nature of sowing and reaping. If we sow to the flesh—or spend time catering to our fleshly desires—we shall, of the flesh, reap corruption or death. But, in contrast, if we sow to the spirit—or spend time catering to the fruit of the spirit—we shall, of the spirit, reap everlasting life. It becomes clear, then, that occupying our time with things of the spirit has far greater benefits than occupying our time with things of the flesh.

It's important, however, that we do not overlook the next point the apostle makes: in sowing and reaping, as with everything else in life, timing is everything! We cannot expect to reap before what we have sown has had proper time to fully develop. In verse 9, Paul says, "in due season we shall reap, if we faint not." In other words, when it's our season—and not a minute before—we will reap the benefits of what we have sown. The key is to not give up before harvest time! So—and this is the point—do good at every opportunity, especially for your brothers and sisters within our sacred community. Then, when harvest time comes, you'll not only reap abundantly, you will have also helped your brothers and sisters along the way. There should be compassionate love within our sacred community, what I like to call "In-House Love."

※

Lord, let Your compassionate love reign within our sacred community as we sow seeds in Your vineyard. Amen.

WATCH YOUR STEP

Let us not become conceited, provoking one another, envying one another.
GALATIANS 5:26, NKJV

Before a concert, the sound crew sets up the equipment. They lay cables along the floor to speakers positioned around the auditorium. Then they lay rubber shields over the cables to keep the audience from tripping over them. The shields are often painted bright yellow, so the audience will notice them.

In Galatians, Paul talks about heinous sins—adultery, fornication, idolatry, sorcery, envy, murders—and then he adds this comment: "Don't be conceited." Almost as an afterthought, Paul lays down a bright yellow rubber shield for us, warning: "Watch out! Don't trip over yourselves."

It's easy for us to become conceited, thinking more of ourselves than we ought. It's easy to become our own top priority and evaluate others according to their usefulness to our purpose. Even in conversations, we want to be on top. Someone has a story to tell us, but we want to tell a more impressive story. We can even compete about suffering. Someone tells a story of his or her difficult childhood, but we need to respond with, "That's nothing! When I was a kid..." We provoke one another as we strive to be the best, but we are envious of those who are clearly more accomplished.

It's easy to trip and fall headfirst into this way of thinking. What would help us catch ourselves? When we are conscious of God's love and what He has done for us, despite our faults, we can see the silliness of our conceit. Right in the middle of the conversation or the situation, we can pause, step back, and view others with love. With a spirit of humility, we can listen to what others have to say. If it's a positive tale, we can rejoice with them. If it's a story of challenge, we can listen with empathy. We can seek to hear what God wants us to hear and respond with love for our brothers and sisters. Instead of provoking jabs and envious comments, we can offer words of encouragement and support.

🌾

Oh Lord, make me aware of my own conceits. When I am tempted to compete for status and attention, give me a humble heart and a consciousness of Your love. Help me see my brothers and sisters with love and empathy. Amen.

RECEPTION AREA

Therefore receive one another, just as Christ also received us, to the glory of God.

ROMANS 15:7, NKJV

In the 1990s, when people were lauding the Apostolic Church of God in Chicago as a "mega church" and praising its pastor, Bishop Arthur M. Brazier, as a visionary, a longtime member once asked Bishop Brazier what he thought of it all. He answered, "Never think it's you." In other words, in the midst of what others deem as success, be conscious that success is God working for God's purposes. There is a reason for the blessing.

It's easy to become self-centered, to attend only to what we, ourselves, need and only recognize those we consider "like us." But God looks across His children. He sees those with more and He sees those who have less. He loves all His children, and He asks those who have more to receive those with less. The "more" may be money or skills that could help those in need. The "more" may be an education that helps those struggling to write or comprehend. The "more" may be a circle of friends or family that could embrace the isolated or the lonely. In the case of Paul, writing to the Romans, the "more" was Jewish Christians feeling more entitled to the church than the Gentile Christians. Today, the "more" may be an established place within the church, from which we can reach out to the new and tentative.

God tells us to receive others into our blessings with a generous, loving heart—never out of pride, never with condescension. We are not to operate from a position of status and importance, deigning to give crumbs to the pitiful. All that we have, God gave us. He asks that we share His gifts with others, conscious that no matter how advantaged we are, we would be lost and miserable if Christ had not received us. We have been received. What a blessing to contemplate! Two thousand years before we were born, Christ received us and sacrificed for us. He is our Friend, willing to give all for us. Now He asks that we, in kind, receive those He sends to us.

✺

Oh Jesus, thank You for receiving me. You have blessed me. I see Your hand in my life and I ask that You show me how to use those blessings to receive others. Amen.

NEIGHBORS

So he answered and said, " 'You shall love the LORD your God with all your heart, with all your soul, with all your strength, and with all your mind,' and 'your neighbor as yourself'." And He said to him, "You have answered rightly; do this and you will live." But he, wanting to justify himself, said to Jesus, "And who is my neighbor?" Then Jesus answered and said: "A certain man went down from Jerusalem to Jericho, and fell among thieves, who stripped him of his clothing, wounded him, and departed, leaving him half dead."

LUKE 10:27-30, NKJV

"Who is my neighbor?" That's a profound question. Unfortunately, in this passage, the lawyer asking the question was not pondering the profound issue of his neighbor's identity. Rather, he asked to establish limits on his love, to see whom he might exclude. So, Jesus surprised him and included a man who was half-dead.

God challenges us. When we try to justify ourselves, when we try to set limits on what is expected, God surprises us. He broadens the task and raises the expectation, so we are left dismayed, wondering how we can possibly do what He asks. The greatest challenge He gives us—the most daunting task—is to love God with all our heart, soul, strength, and mind—with everything we've got. Then, when we have nothing left, He piles on the second greatest challenge: to love our neighbors as much as we love ourselves, even if the neighbor cannot give us anything in return.

Such a task can seem overwhelming, especially when we are faced with real circumstances of caring for others in dire need or being there when it's too painful to be there. At those times, we have no choice but to throw ourselves into God's arms and cry, "Help!" That's exactly what God wants us to do. When faced with an emotionally impossible task, Abraham said, "God will provide" (Genesis 22:8). We, too, are asked to do what is emotionally impossible, but we have the assurance that God will provide the strength, the resilience, the courage, the emotional stability, and the resources to do what He has asked.

❧

Jesus, You have challenged me beyond my capabilities. You ask for more than I know how to give. I trust that You will make it possible, that You will provide. Amen.

STAYING FAITHFUL

For God is not unjust to forget your work and labor of love which you have shown toward His name, in that you have ministered to the saints, and do minister.

HEBREWS 6:10, NKJV

When Walter Clemons founded the Apostolic Church of God, in Chicago in 1932, he began with his family and some neighbors. In 1952, they acquired a church building, and he had a vision that someday that building would be overflowing. But when he died in 1958, there were less than one hundred members and the church was in debt. That year, Arthur M. Brazier was pastor of an equally small church, whose building had been purchased by the city to make way for an expressway. In 1960, he became pastor of the Apostolic Church of God. God led him to take that small but faithful congregation and build a tremendous ministry. By 1998, the Apostolic Church of God had nearly 20,000 members.

There are times when our work seems stalled or even in vain. We try to minister as best we understand, but our efforts seem fruitless. We have worked hard, but the accomplishment seems small. Yet the Scripture promises that when we are serving God faithfully, He does not forget us. It may be that our accomplishments are on a personal level, touching individual lives, and not on the public level that looks like success to others. Or God's timing for the work is longer than our view. The fruit is down the road, to be accomplished by someone who will build on what we have done. The point is that we remain faithful and trust God that His plans will be accomplished. He will not forget our efforts. It is God who will bring fruitfulness to the work. Furthermore, He will not forget us. He will be there for us, honoring our faithfulness.

Jesus, I am working every day, and some days don't seem to add up to much. I need Your guidance to be sure that I am on the right track. I need Your encouragement to let me know that I must remain faithful even when the successes seem small. I know Your work is beyond me, and that it will extend beyond my life. Allow me to use my days to accomplish Your purpose, whatever that may be. Amen.

Mountain of Forgiveness

And whenever you stand praying, if you have anything against anyone, forgive him, that your Father in heaven may also forgive you your trespasses.
MARK 11:25, NKJV

There are things people do that are wrong, and probably petty. Sometimes, we take offense at certain actions more from pride than from actual hurt—"He stepped on my foot," "She cut me off in line." Forgiving such trivial acts mostly involves "getting over" ourselves. When we extend ourselves to forgive petty wrongs, we feel good about ourselves and feel more generous and stronger. When we forgive quickly, we show we are glad God forgives us.

Yet, there are grievous sins that hurt so deeply we can hardly talk or breathe. The pain goes on for years when the losses are severe. Our spirits cry for justice, and forgiveness just feels wrong—too easy, too cheap. We feel that if we forgive, the world will become unbalanced and more dangerous.

In Mark 11:23, Jesus told His disciples that their faith could move mountains. Then, in verse 24, He said that when His disciples pray, they should forgive. Mountains and forgiveness—right there together. What a mighty mountain it is: a mountain of hurt, pain, and trauma that follows grievous sin. That mountain sits before us, blocking our view of everything else. Every day, we climb over anger and sorrow, trying to function. We hike up bitter trails and get lost in a wilderness of hostility.

What can move such a mountain? According to Mark 11:25, faith can. God is just and concerned about justice; He is "a just God and a Savior" (Isaiah 45:21). He will take care of balancing justice, and He will extend mercy, grace, and forgiveness. Can we turn it over to Him to repay what must be repaid? Can we trust God to make such decisions? We want justice, yet the Scripture says to use our faith. Therein lies our need for faith. Jesus paid it all; whatever justice we are due has already been paid by His blood.

We stand at the core of Christianity, trusting God to provide for our healing, to remove the mountain of pain, to offer justice, and to extend grace according to His sovereign will.

❧

Oh my Jesus, You paid for what has hurt me. You have already moved the mountain. Give me a heart to trust You, my just God and my Savior, so I may forgive and be forgiven. Amen.

WHO WILL WE CARRY

Bearing with one another, and forgiving one another, if anyone has a complaint against another; even as Christ forgave you, so you also must do.

COLOSSIANS 3:13, NKJV

Years ago, our church had its annual retreats at a camp in Wisconsin. Services were held in a large, circular barn, some distance from the dining hall. The retreat committee had noticed that after lunch, people chatted and hung out. It was difficult to get everyone to come back on time for the afternoon sessions. So the retreat committee had an idea. After lunch, they had a Rapture Drill. They rang the big bell at the top of the barn, and the retreaters had to enter the barn before the doors closed. Those who made it received paper "crowns of glory." Of course, the committee then opened the doors to let in the latecomers for the session. The idea worked. People ran from the dining hall to the barn. The latecomers were few, and sessions started on time. We took pictures of the fun.

After the retreat, I saw a picture that brought tears to my eyes. When we planned the Rapture Drill, we forgot about Donovan, who had cerebral palsy. Donovan could walk, but his balance was poor, and he couldn't run from the dining hall to the barn. In the picture was a large man who was running to the barn with Donovan in his arms. He carried Donovan into the barn to make the Rapture so they would both get crowns of glory.

When we are the strong ones, can we carry another who cannot run? Can we bear others when they have challenges? Can we forgive those who have slipped? We must be connected enough to see that someone else is struggling. With a kindly eye, we must notice that someone is having trouble balancing. They may need more than an encouraging word and a pat on the back. They may need to be picked up and carried. Someone may take undue advantage of our efforts, but we have to trust God to give us wisdom and discernment. The Scripture admonishes us: bear one another.

※

Jesus, You carried me when I couldn't make it. Please give me the strength and the wisdom to bear others. Take away my complaints. Give me a forgiving heart. Let me see others through the light of Your love. Amen.

FACING SIN

If we confess our sins, He is faithful and just to forgive us our sins and to cleanse us from all unrighteousness.

1 JOHN 1:9, NKJV

At twenty-two months old, Lori was fascinated by her mother's favorite scarf. Mommy told her not to touch it, but it was soft and pretty. She saw it lying on the bed and she picked it up and danced around. She stomped her feet on it, leaving a few footprints, and then she waved it in the air. She heard Mommy coming. Quickly, she dropped it behind her back, hoping Mommy wouldn't see that she had it.

We learn about sin early. We also learn early that we would like to avoid the consequences. Even as adults, sin is hard to face. We can lie and claim that we did not sin: "I didn't do it." We can claim it was not our fault by blaming the situation: "I had to do it." We can blame others: "He made me do it." We can blame our frailties: "I was drunk." We can minimize: "My sin is not as bad as his sin." John admonishes us to confess our sins. Face them. Be honest. Admit to them. Tell God. He loves us, and He wants us to be back in harmony with Him. He will forgive us, cleanse us, and bring us back to righteousness.

Wait a minute, though. Scripture tells us that He is "just to forgive." How can this be? When we have sinned, we ask for mercy and forgiveness, not justice. The big problem with admitting to sin is that justice will fall on our heads, and we will not be able to bear it. So here is where God has a plan. Jesus died for our sins. In all justice, God forgives us, because the consequences are paid for. What a loving God we serve, that He sent His only begotten Son to pay for our sins, so that we may confess and then be cleansed and restored.

❧

Oh my Jesus, You paid the price. I am so sorry for the sins I have committed. I thank You for making a way for me to face those sins, and to be honest about what I have done. I thank You for cleansing me and bringing me back in relationship with You. Thank You for loving me. Amen.

ONE BODY

So we, being many, are one body in Christ, and individually members of one another.

ROMANS 12:5, NKJV

There is a nerve bundle, composed of about 30,000 neurons, which connects the inner ear to the brain. Each neuron has a "best frequency"—a tone that elicits its most vigorous response. However, when a complex sound, like a word or music, passes through the ear, every neuron responds. Neurons don't say, "No, no! That's not my best frequency so I will stay silent!" Instead, each neuron responds—some more, some less—creating a complex pattern that uniquely represents the sound to the brain. Better yet, neurons can synchronize their responses according to the timing pattern of the sound, and they can focus on the sound according to the brain's dictates. Thus, the neurons' complex response is organized and useful to the brain.

We all have talents. Some of us have remarkable talents. But when the task at hand does not utilize our particular "best talent," how do we respond? Do we say, "No, no, that's not my ministry" or do we pitch in, as we are able? Even more, do we synchronize with others, working together in harmony, so our combined efforts are effective and productive?

The "members" of the body are the legs and arms. We are one body, connected, coordinated, and working together, not because we like each other or always approve of each other. We are connected because of Christ. Like the cells of the body, we can contribute to each circumstance, whether or not it's what we do best. For example, "I'm a great singer, but I can help the committee by putting these badges in order." Or, "I'm a great cook, but I can watch the children while the leader gets organized." We can coordinate our efforts together instead of running around individually, doing what looks good. We can follow leadership, making adjustments so that, together, our efforts are effective and productive. The body sets a high standard for us. Are we willing to become one body for Christ?

Jesus, thank You for letting me be a part of Your body. Give me a heart to work for You and with other saints, no matter if my role is small or large. Amen.

GIVE AS GOOD AS YOU GET

Forgive us our debts, as we also have forgiven our debtors.

MATTHEW 6:12, NIV

Don't you just hate it when people who owe you act as if they don't? Doesn't it make you angry when they claim they will pay you back but never do? Doesn't that kind of behavior make you question why you bothered to help? *Doesn't that just...*

Wait a minute. Doesn't that describe what we do to God? We know we vowed to pray more, but we only offer weak excuses for neglecting to "hit our knees." We know we said reading the Bible was going to be a priority this year, but time just got away. We know that God gave us an opportunity we didn't expect, or a few dollars when we needed it most, but we just said, "Thanks, Lord," as we went about our business. We know that Jesus went to Calvary for us, but we find really creative ways to justify living "raggedy." On occasion we claim that "everybody else seems to be doing it, so..." Or we present our own logic on the matter: "Just because our hearts were repentant when we received the Holy Ghost doesn't mean we really have to change, does it?"

We put a lot of *negative* energy into getting angry with people we believe owe us. What would happen if we put some *positive* energy into reflecting the power of God in our lives? We expect God to forgive us (or "dismiss" from His memory) the fact that we failed to keep that prayer vow, or that we didn't honor that promise to read the Word, but we have trouble dismissing from our memories the bitterness we hold against the person who owes us. We expect God to love us enough to forget that we made excuses for not tithing the extra money He provided, but we can't love enough to forget our anger toward others. Jesus makes it pretty clear: Because we are not faultless, we ask God to forgive us every day. The least we can do is to love Him enough to forgive others. That's just giving as good as we get!

※

Lord, help me to recognize and release the bitterness that I hold against those who have wronged me. Help me to honor Your forgiveness by extending the love of forgiveness to others. Amen.

A NEW ATTITUDE

Bless them which persecute you: bless, and curse not.

ROMANS 12:14, KJV

Even before becoming Christians, the members of the church at Rome lived in an environment where the abuse of power dictated the social norm. The rich exacted their will on the poor, and women and children, treated like property, could be sold into slavery, abused, or left to die in the most cruel poverty. In such a climate, it was easy to believe that persecution, domination, and disregard of others was the norm.

It is to this group of persecuted faithful that Paul wrote the words of Romans 12:14. Much like Jesus, who had given hearers a new perspective, Paul imparts to the members of the Roman church a list of attitudes and actions that are to be the marks of their faithfulness to Christ Jesus. Paul explained in chapter 11 that the riches of Christ were so great that Jew and Gentile alike could be saved. Now co-existing in the unity of Christ, they were to demonstrate that their love for one another was based on the love Christ showed to them.

What a fitting lesson for us. As saints of God, we exist in a community of faith comprising people who came from diverse backgrounds where "get them before they get you" is an appropriate response to most things. But now that we are saved, we must have a different attitude about that boss who deliberately denied the request for a leave when others were given that consideration without reason. Now that the blood of Jesus redeems us, that neighbor who does things to make life difficult can no longer be viewed as a person worthy of disdain.

We, like Paul's first audience, must "bless and not curse." Our blessing them will draw them to Christ. Our blessing them shares with them the same mercy that Christ freely gave to us. Our blessing them brings them before the Father and asks His blessing upon them. Our blessing them helps us to see with our Father's eyes and heart, and that is a blessing to us.

❧

Father, thank You for showing me a new way to look at those who show disregard for me. Help me to regard Your will above my own so my attitude will bless them and honor You. Amen.

WHERE DOES FORGIVENESS START?

Take heed to yourselves: If thy brother trespass against thee, rebuke him; and if he repent, forgive him.

LUKE 17:3, KJV

Clark and Marcus grew up together. They were college roommates and best man in each other's wedding. When Marcus started a charter school, Clark was glad to join him. They shared the financial burdens and the sacrifice of a new venture. They often talked about a legacy that could keep their families secure and strengthen their community. Their school quickly became a model for turning a profit while educating children, strengthening families, and building positive relationships that were transforming the neighborhood. It was a shock when Clark learned that Marcus negotiated the sale of the school to a franchise that operated in several states. Marcus also negotiated a new place for himself in the larger company, but he was doing it all without Clark.

We've all experienced betrayal that left deep and lasting pain, as well as a severed relationship where forgiveness and reconciliation were deemed impossible. In Luke 17, Jesus warns that while it is bad to sin, it is worse to cause someone else to sin. In concluding that premise, Jesus tells His disciples to watch themselves. He cautions that their actions could lead to sin—in them and possibly someone else. Jesus' solution appears in verse 3.

As our scenario implies, the sin might be caused by bitterness that never abates, anger that is never addressed, or retaliation that benefits no one but hurts everyone. Jesus indicates that it is best to go to the person and discuss the situation, calling the behavior into question. Then, if the person repents, forgive.

We often think that we can brush our pain aside and if it's gone long enough, it is as good as forgiven. Jesus tells us that forgiveness begins with prayerful honesty and openness as we face the situation and the person. Only when Christian confrontation of the *problem* is successful can we forgive the person, release the hurt, and restore our relationship—hopefully with the person, but definitely with the Lord. Only then can we, and hopefully the other person, remain in right relationship with God.

Lord, help me to release that which has held me too long. Help me to seek restoration and to forgive as You would forgive. Amen.

HUMBLED

And forgive us our sins; for we also forgive every one that is indebted to us.
And lead us not into temptation; but deliver us from evil.

LUKE 11:4, KJV

Luke 11, like Matthew 6, records a prayer that is read at funerals and weddings alike. It has been memorized in word and in song. Jesus spoke what is known as the Lord's Prayer because the disciples asked Him how to pray. Jesus' prayer was no doubt completely different from the way the religious leaders prayed in His time. Unlike the hypocrites whose prayer rituals He condemned (Matthew 6:5), Jesus did not stand and make a show of praying. We do not know if He prayed aloud or silently, in the Temple or in a private place. We only know that Jesus took the opportunity to teach them (and us) how to stand before Almighty God in prayer.

This final line of the prayer focuses on two pairs of connected concepts. The first is the link between forgiveness and sin. Sin is a departure from right. It is, in most cases, knowing what is right and choosing to go in another direction. Verse 4 is clear: we have known right and chosen to go in another direction! Because we have chosen to disregard—and disrespect God—we need forgiveness.

Forgiveness is a legal term meaning "to put aside the offense." God knows we've sinned; we do, too. Yet in prayer, we ask Him to put aside our offense. Moreover, we acknowledge before Him that others have knowingly chosen to do wrong to us, and we know we must also forgive them.

The second idea links temptation and evil. Our failure to forgive lures us more deeply into the sin of unforgiveness. In short, it leads us to evil—a downward spiraling crisis from which we cannot free ourselves. We are dependent on God to *keep* us from falling into the evil of sin. We are indebted to Him for *deliverance* from the evil that so easily draws us. In teaching us to pray, Jesus taught us that humility comes only when we confess our need.

❧

Lord, I confess now that I have sinned and I need Your forgiveness. I have been drawn by temptation; I need Your deliverance. Help me, O Lord, my Redeemer. Amen.

BECAUSE WE ARE FORGIVEN

Judge not, and ye shall not be judged: condemn not, and ye shall not be condemned: forgive, and ye shall be forgiven.

LUKE 6:37, KJV

Just after Jesus says to love our enemies (Luke 6:35), He says to be merciful (Luke 6:36) and not to judge others. With these words, Jesus links loving our enemies with mercy. Furthermore, He explains that doing good to those who mean us harm without the expectation of their returning good to us is a demonstration of the mercy our Father has shown us.

Jesus said a lot of hard things and today it is still difficult to grasp them and even harder to embrace them—but we must. God is the ultimate judge. He has all power and, because of His righteousness, should have turned His back on us and left us to our own destruction—knowing that when we appeared before His Court, we were already condemned. Yet God in His mercy declared a way for our salvation. Jesus Christ came in the flesh to take away our sin and now we stand justified in Him.

How do we show our gratitude? How do we show our understanding of the tremendous sacrifice made for our sakes? We do not give back what we have received! We do not judge those who treat us poorly and attempt to harm us. We do not judge them, because God, through Jesus Christ, provided a way for us not to face His judgment. We do not condemn them, because Jesus Christ has made certain that we will not face condemnation (Romans 8:1). We forgive our enemies because God forgave us.

Because we are forgiven, we are called to forgive others. Because we are forgiven, we are called to withhold judgment. Because we are forgiven, we have no room to condemn!

Lord, thank You for Your mercy. Help me to be merciful: to love despite ill-treatment, to encourage rather than judge, to help rather than condemn, to forgive rather than tolerate. Help me to embrace others, even those who do not love me, as You have embraced me simply because I am forgiven. Amen.

PRAYER WILL FIX IT

Therefore confess your sins to each other and pray for each other so that you may be healed. The prayer of a righteous man is powerful and effective.

JAMES 5:16, NIV

Anyone who has ever had arthritis or the flu will tell you that you can't just "get over it." The pain and discomfort will compel you to seek better health perhaps through a trip to the pharmacy or a family remedy that was both dreaded and effective in your youth. If the situation persists, you might make your way to the doctor. And throughout the ordeal, you would not hesitate to call on God to heal you or lead you to the help your body needs. If you know anyone who has battled cancer or suffered a stroke, you know that the efforts toward restoring health were more serious and prayer more fervent.

But what about the sickness that is not physical. Harboring anger, hatred, jealousy are signs of illness since God has not called us to harbor bitterness of any kind. Jesus' sacrifice on Calvary was offered out of pure love. God's call to us in the midst of our sin was a demonstration of divine love. The indwelling of the Holy Ghost is the power to love despite how our love is received. Like the flu, jealousy and anger are both obvious to others and contagious in all of our relationships. The sign that we have given in to the pain of bad memories or the cancer of hatred is that we can no longer see God's love for someone else.

James 5:16 offers a simple solution: confess and pray. If someone has offended you or if the darkness and bitterness of our heart has caused you to offend another, confess it. Apologize! If the person is no longer available, confess your sin to God and seek forgiveness. And above all, pray because your actions hindered that person, and perhaps others, from seeing God in your life. Pray for the person you have offended with your mean-spirited comments or nasty attitude. Humble yourself and ask the person to forgive you and to pray for you as well. Prayer is the only effective remedy. Prayer will heal your relationship and your soul. Prayer will fix it.

Lord, help me to face what I hold in my heart that is not like You. Help me now, Lord, to be made whole. Amen.

A MATTER OF HONOR

Never pay back evil with more evil. Do things in such a way that everyone can see you are honorable.

ROMANS 12:17, NLT

Nelson Mandela was held in a South African jail from 1964 until 1990. When he was released, he could have shown anger toward his jailer and the system that imprisoned him and placed South Africa's Black population in virtual bondage. But that was not the case. Upon his release, Mandela continued to work to change his country for the better and for freedom of all citizens. He also stunned the world by befriending Christo Brand, his jailer. Despite the circumstances that brought them together, Mandela said that knowing Brand reinforced his hope in all people.

Had Nelson Mandela sought revenge or dealt evil for the evil perpetrated against him, South Africa would be a very different country. Instead, he chose to treat all people with honor and to show everyone the power of peace. As a result, Mandela's honor was noted not only by his jailer, but also by an entire nation and the world. What a difference we could make in this world if our actions bespoke honor instead of anger? What example might we set for our children if our love overrode our regret?

But before we get too full of ourselves, we must realize that the honor would not be ours. Such honorable behavior cannot turn into bragging or conceit. The honor would belong to and reflect Jesus Christ. When our behavior is honorable, our Lord and Savior is honored. When our attitudes rise above our circumstances and find the good in others, despite their attitudes—and often the facades they show—we honor Him. When we find it in our hearts to turn the other cheek and pray for those who despitefully use us, we reflect the attitude of Jesus on Calvary's cross.

Perhaps we should remember this today and every day we are faced with an insult or an affront designed to disdain, disrespect, disregard, or deny our presence or our contribution: not repaying evil for evil is a matter of honor.

❧

Lord, thank You for being the living example of love in the face of humiliation. Help me to see those who seek to humiliate me with Your eyes and Your heart so my actions and attitudes bring honor to You. In Jesus' Name. Amen.

WHEN MONEY TALKS

No one can serve two masters. Either he will hate the one and love the other, or you will be devoted to the one and despise the other. You cannot serve both God and money.

MATTHEW 6:24, NIV

We all know about love triangles, where two people are madly in love until another person enters the picture and the ill-fated affair ends tragically. This is more than the stuff that gives us romantic comedies or tragic romance novels. This failure of trying to love two people also applies in our relationship with God.

In Matthew 6, Jesus teaches about our perception of money in terms of a love triangle and concludes that we cannot love God and Mammon. Mammon is an Aramaic word that implies "wealth personified as an evil taskmaster" who dominates our earthly striving for acceptance and position. In this verse, Jesus says that our human tendency is to serve money, not use it. Either we will strive to be defined by our relationship with God or by our relationships through money.[23]

We live in a society that worships the dollar; we even call it "almighty." We hide it, hoard it, store it, and put our lives on the line for it. We think we have no legacy unless we leave money to our children. We think we have no prestige unless we use it to position ourselves socially. Even when we don't have much of it, we determine our value according to money.

God demands a primary position in our lives. Money, though inanimate, slyly makes its way into our consciousness and tricks us into placing all effort on its gain. Jesus' rationale for a new perspective is clear. We will hate one and love the other, or be devoted to one and despise the other. When money calls, we neglect our tithes as part of our worship. When money talks, we skip our devotions in favor of overtime, claiming that "God knows what we need."

Most of us don't have enough money to think this applies to us, but it does and we must make a choice: who will we serve when money talks?

✣

Lord, Help me to keep the right perspective. Regardless of my circumstances, whether I stand in need or in comfort, help me to focus on You and to wholly yield to Your voice. Amen.

Run Together, Children

Don't laugh when your enemy falls; don't crow over his collapse.
PROVERBS 24:17, *THE MESSAGE*

The Special Olympics Office in Washington recorded a 1979 race where one athlete stumbled, fell, and wept openly on the track.[24] Two of the contenders responded by turning back to help the racer. The three then locked arms and crossed the finish line together. With the competitive nature of sports today, most people would quip that the point of the race was to win. Others would add, "By any means necessary."

These Olympians, however, demonstrate Proverbs 24:17, "Don't laugh when your enemy falls; don't crow over his collapse." Most translations link this Scripture to the one that follows it, "God might see, and become very provoked, and then take pity on his plight." In other words, God will be displeased with your attitude and give favor to your enemy. This Old Testament idea places God in the role of the ultimate avenger, the One who will settle the score. Nevertheless, this Scripture delivers several good lessons for us today.

God is not pleased with our human tendency to gloat when He has shown us favor. We must not think that we can have callus attitudes or inhospitable actions and God does not take notice. Instead, this text teaches us that we must examine our attitudes, being mindful of how we treat others even when those people may not have treated us kindly. When our attitudes cause us to lose focus of God's divine care, our hearts displease God.

Jesus brought this point home in Matthew 5:43-45 when He said that loving, blessing, and doing good to our enemies is an indication that we are children of God. Paul picks this up in Romans 12:20 and says, "If thine enemy hunger, feed him; if he thirst, give him drink: for in so doing thou shalt heap coals of fire on his head." Doing good to those who have mistreated us allows us to help them see God in our lives and convicts them to seek God in their own lives.

We may not always be able to lock arms with those who hurt us, but we must always lock hearts with God on the matter.

❧

Thank You, Lord, for showing me how to love my enemies and making it possible for me to do so. Amen.

We are Secured by Love

...ye were sealed with that holy Spirit of promise...
Ephesians 1:13, KJV

Living for God is not always easy. Sometimes we trip up along the way trying to love as He loves in the face of humiliation and rejection, trying to resist temptation even when "no one" is looking, or trying to hold up our heads when we've gone against the tide of popularity to stand on Truth. We don't always get it right, but nothing we do can change God's mind about us. Jesus declared that nothing—no person, no situation—can remove us from God's hand, the place where our lives are secure. The apostle Paul wrote that nothing could separate us from God's love. God owns us, and we have been marked by the Holy Spirit, whom Jesus promised—a "down payment" on our full inheritance.

As you close out the year and look ahead, toward another year of growing deeper in your faith and reaching higher heights on your Spirit-led, Spirit-filled journey, do so with an assurance of the Holy Spirit's abiding and guiding presence (you are not alone), the assurance of eternal salvation (you are His forever), and the assurance of the final perseverance of the saints (God will complete the work He has begun in you).

WHAT MATTERS MOST

There is only one thing worth being concerned about. Mary has discovered it and it will not be taken away from her.

LUKE 10:42, NLT

Have you ever felt rushed to prepare or rearrange things due to an unexpected visit or turn of events? Many challenges may arise and, even though you may feel restless, you move about anyway to get the job done. Scurrying around, you find you need all the help you can get. Well, let's imagine how Martha felt the day Jesus decided to visit. She was trying to make everything nice for His visit. In her flurry, she felt that no one was there to help her, and others must have been oblivious to the fact that she was overwhelmed. She asked how her sister, Mary, could be so uninvolved?

We can become so derailed, sidetracked, or distracted by life's events that we miss out on what matters most. Mary refused to miss the opportunity to be in the presence of what truly mattered most: Jesus. She recognized that there was only one thing worthy of her undivided attention. When was the last time you were in His presence? Were you too busy to take notice, or did you pause in that moment to let Him know He had your complete attention?

When someone takes the time to be with you, it is a sign of his or her love and care for you. We must learn to enjoy the time we have with God, our loved ones, and even the moments when we are alone. Don't allow the struggles of life to carry you away from what truly matters. Learn to be still, attentive, and aware of the current moment, as Mary demonstrated in this Scripture. Let us decide today to make what really matters most our top priority.

※

Father, help me come to a full understanding that there is one thing worthy of concern and that is You! I pray that You will help me come to a place where I am content with being with You alone—and that is enough for me. In Jesus' Name. Amen.

PLACE OF ASSURANCE

I assure you, most solemnly I tell you, the person whose ears are open to My words [who listens to My message] and believes and trusts in and clings to and relies on Him Who sent Me has (possesses now) eternal life. And he does not come into judgment [does not incur sentence of judgment, will not come under condemnation], but he has already passed over out of death into life.

JOHN 5:24, AMP

There are times in life when we come to a point where we must solely rely on God's Word for our lives. When we recognize that Christ's love for us has secured us for eternity, we find ourselves in a place of assurance. Life will challenge us, but we can keep an ear open for God's Word and what He is telling us. We can do this by reading His Word constantly, praying consistently, and seeking Him wholeheartedly.

While riding the mountains of life, we may become flustered, anxious, and feel close to the edge. These feelings may cause us to overreact, and possibly find ourselves somewhere we didn't necessarily want to be. But when we breathe in and cling to the truth of God, which comforts us, we can rest in the fact that we are safe in His care. Neither death, sin, judgment, nor anything else can keep Him from us if we only listen, believe, trust, cling to, and rely on Him.

Often, we choose to rely on the words of friends, loved ones, or social network buddies who may eventually let us down. Then we find ourselves in a dilemma, because we chose to listen to someone else instead of the One who listens no matter what. We can turn to Him because we know He is the way, the truth, and the life. Today, we must decide not to straddle the fence of fear, but to stand firmly in the place Christ has secured for us, to give us eternal life. Now that's assurance!

🕊

Father, help me to learn to hear Your voice and heed Your Word. Help me to lean on You in the rough times and the good. Help me to stand firm in You and Your eternal grace. In Jesus' Name. Amen.

TIME TO PAUSE

Stop toiling and doing and producing for the food that perishes and decomposes [in the using], but strive and work and produce rather for the [lasting] food which endures [continually] unto life eternal; the Son of Man will give (furnish) you that, for God the Father has authorized and certified Him and put His seal of endorsement upon Him.

JOHN 6:27, AMP

Many of us face the hustle and bustle of daily life. We fill our days working hard to get another car, a larger home, a better job, or take the next vacation. Our days are so focused on how we're going to get what we want, that we often don't have time to pause and take a breath. But sometimes we have to stop and evaluate what we're really trying to do. Will what we are doing now endure or enhance what we truly seek?

As we look at John 6:27, he tells us to stop, to pause. Why? Because it's time to do something else! The things to which we've dedicated our energy and time have only helped us temporarily. We must pause and consider why we do what we do. Are we trying to please someone other than God? Some of us have gotten off course and bought into what society dictates, but we must recognize that the desires of this world will soon perish, decompose, and waste away.

Where do we go from here? When we pick up from our pause, it will be time to work for, and produce, the things that matter for eternity. It's not enough to just work hard for things, it's important to let Jesus work in and through us. As we yield our everyday lives to Him, we will find ourselves full, experiencing the lush fruits of His Spirit where they are most needed. With the Lord helping us, the things we do will bring Him glory and honor.

🕊

Father, help me to pause in life and refrain from those things that are only temporary. Help me work to produce things that will endure! Father, I love You and am grateful You are always thinking of me. Amen.

COMMITTED TO THE CAUSE

Meanwhile his disciples urged him, "Rabbi, eat something." But he said to them, "I have food to eat that you know nothing about." Then his disciples said to each other, "Could someone have brought him food?" "My food," said Jesus, "is to do the will of him who sent me and to finish his work."

JOHN 4:31-34, NIV

Jesus often presented His actions as His Father's will and purpose. How many of us can say that most of what we do is because of the will and purpose of our heavenly Father? How many of us have chosen to abandon our own desires for the One who will raise us up on the last day?

When we begin to walk out the will of God for our lives, we discover how different our lives can be. It is then time to consider the changes needed in our lives to follow the lessons of Jesus. Once we make those changes, we can begin to do the will and purpose of God. Forsaking our own desires, we begin to realize that it is time to live out loud for God, refraining from being "Closet Christians" and moving toward being Christians "Sold-Out" for God.

As God's children, we live purposing that our actions reflect our heavenly Father. As we focus on His business and strive to do His work on the earth, we know He will work in and through us. We then live to spread the Good News that Jesus saves and begin to urge others to give their lives to Christ.

Even when Jesus faced death, He remained committed to the will of God. What are you facing right now? No matter where you find yourself, you will remain committed to the cause! Don't let life's challenges cause you to doubt. Remember the Word and look for Him in your situations. Decide today to commit yourself to His will and purpose, no matter what life throws in your path.

Lord, today I commit myself to Your will and purpose for my life. I pray that I will boldly spread Your Good News. Amen!

A PLACE TO BELONG

So Jesus said to those Jews who had believed in Him, if you abide in my word [hold fast to my teachings and live in accordance with them], you are truly my disciples.

JOHN 8:31, AMP

How many times have we sat down with a grandparent, aunt, or uncle who told us what they knew about our family history and the events that occurred? The stories they tell are so thrilling that we are drawn in, hanging on every word and waiting for what would come next. We begin to trust the storyteller, so we believe what he or she told us to be undoubtedly true. We believe we have learned more about who we are and our connections.

Jesus is sharing a story with His believers: if believers hold fast to His teachings, and live in accordance to them, then they are truly His disciples. Many of us are excited to say we are Christ followers, but we are slow to abide in His Word and follow His ways. As Christians, we must not only confess with our mouths that we are His disciples, but we must also clearly act as His disciples and do as He has taught us. Jesus connected to those who believed in Him and refused to be deterred by those who refused to believe. *What is deterring you from fully following His teachings?*

We must learn to abide in His Word! There will be times when we may have to withstand temptation and refuse to be swept away. We must decide to remain in His Word. Often, when we are not holding fast to His Word, we begin to revel in our own thoughts and drift away from what we know to be true. We begin to associate with people and things that do not reflect the teachings we have come to know.

Once we come to believe and abide in His Word, we will arrive at a place of belonging. We, in fact, will recognize that we are His disciples!

Lord, help me to believe and duly follow Your ways so I may truly be Your disciple. Help me to know that I always have a place to belong. In Jesus' Name. Amen.

THE KEY TO FREEDOM

And you will know the Truth, and the Truth will set you free.

JOHN 8:32, AMP

Have you ever stayed up late because you couldn't sleep, and you found yourself watching the infomercials on late-night television? Sometimes the more we watch, the more we are drawn in to believe the infomercials' convincing stories. We hope that the product will do what the advertiser promises, without truly knowing if the advertiser has told the truth.

Well, Jesus has made us a promise concerning truth. One way to know the truth is to know God's Word. That truth, in turn, becomes the key to freedom. Something happens when we realize the truth. Truth reinforces the information we hold and how we apply it. When we understand the character of Christ, we learn to trust Him more. We trust Him because He is the truth, and we know He cannot lie.

Lies hold us captive, and not knowing the truth can make us vulnerable to the enemy's attacks. Reading God's Word daily strengthens us so we can be free to fight the good fight of faith. In Matthew 4:1-11, Satan tempted Jesus when He was in the wilderness. The enemy thought he had found Jesus vulnerable and thought he had the upper hand on Him. Jesus didn't fight with idle chatter but with the Word of God. Not only *was* Jesus the Word, but He knew what was written about Him. Just like Jesus gave Satan the Word, we can remind Satan of the truth that sets us free. That truth *is* Jesus, and He makes us free! What is your strategy to remain free?

When confronted with the devil's schemes, Christ had a plan of action. We must have one, too, and then choose to follow through. Knowing that Christ has come to set us free, we only have to recognize the truth versus the lie. As we determine to know the Word, and put it into action, we will discover that our lives are strengthened and we have the real key to freedom!

※

Father, help me to know Your Word that I may not fall prey to the weapons of the enemy. I pray that I will remain free in You. In Jesus' Name. Amen.

.

A SECURED GIFT

And I give them eternal life, and they shall never lose it or perish throughout the ages. [To all eternity they shall never by any means be destroyed.] And no one is able to snatch them out of My hand.

JOHN 10:28, AMP

What a blessed assurance that we can rest in the wonderful gift presented to us in John 10:28! Jesus voluntarily gave us a very valuable and costly gift in eternal life. We can be confident in His declaration of the gift, which He gave us! What a joy and freedom to know we can rest and stand on His Word.

At times, the idea that this gift has been given to us—and we can't lose it—is hard to imagine! Have you ever received something so precious that you had to be ever-so-careful with it? You may have searched for a safe place to keep the gift, so you would not lose it or no harm would come to it. Well, we don't have to worry about losing this gift because it is secured. We are in His hand, under His full protection. What an honor to be in our Savior's hand! We can be grateful that we don't have to do anything to earn or keep this gift, because it can't be lost or taken away. It can't perish and it can never be destroyed! We can take this word to the bank; we don't have to worry any longer about our salvation and what we must do to protect it. Christ has secured us and taken on that responsibility because He loves us!

The next time we are concerned about life, and start to sink in the river of doubt about our salvation, let's meditate on Christ's words: "I give them eternal life, and they will never perish. No one can snatch them away from me" (John 10:28, NLT).

Lord, help me to be confident that Your Word is true, that I am are safe in Your hands, and that my salvation is secure! I love You for the wonderful gift You have freely given to me. Thank You so much. Amen!

A Perfect Opportunity

You don't have to wait for the End. I am, right now, Resurrection and Life. The one who believes in me, even though he or she dies, will live. And everyone who lives believing in me does not ultimately die at all. Do you believe this?

John 11:25-26, *The Message*

During a crisis, have you ever received a response that irritated you because it was not the solution you'd anticipated? To make matters worse, you may have felt that the one person you thought you could depend on let you down by slowly responding to your needs, even though the person knew you were in dire straits.

So it is in the story of Mary and Martha concerning the death of their brother, Lazarus. Jesus was aware of how sick Lazarus was, but He chose to wait until Lazarus had been dead four days before arriving. Can you imagine how Mary and Martha must have felt as others supported them during Lazarus' last days—and even afterward—but Jesus, whom they thought would be there during the most critical time of their lives, was nowhere to be found. Even after He showed up, the sisters anguished because they felt that if Jesus had been there, Lazarus wouldn't have died. Jesus said, "Your brother will be raised up" (John 11:23).

How reassuring would these words have been if Mary and Martha had taken comfort in them, and Jesus' presence, instead of reacting to their own desires and frustrations in that moment of crisis? How delightful would it have been to know that, in the end, they would see their brother again?

In John 11:25-26, Jesus gave the sisters the great hope He gives us: you do not have to wait until the end! He is, at this present moment, the resurrection and life. All we have to do is believe. What is God telling us to believe? Do we need to be reminded that God hasn't deserted us, no matter what we are facing? Let's trust that Jesus is waiting for the right moment, the perfect opportunity to demonstrate something awesome and miraculous in our lives!

❦

Dear Lord, help me to patiently wait on You and know that You are in control of all things. Sickness, finances, family members, and nations all respond at Your command. You are Lord of all. Thank You, Lord, for hearing me and loving me, Amen!

WELCOME ABOARD!

When he arrived and saw what grace (favor) God was bestowing upon them, he was full of joy; and he continuously exhorted (warned, urged, and encouraged) them all to cleave unto and remain faithful to and devoted to the Lord with [resolute and steady] purpose of heart.

ACTS 11:23, AMP

In today's society, there are many things that occupy our time—building a career, political involvement, assisting with neighborhood watches, providing child safety—the list could go on and on. But, as children of God, we must prioritize so we can remain faithful to our purpose of extending the kingdom of Christ. We must be devoted and committed to the Lord with the determination to do His will.

This passage from Acts 11, finds Barnabas arriving in Antioch, where the Gentile Christians were dedicated to the work, even in the face of resistance. Members of the early church found themselves at risk of losing their lives, or being thrown in jail, yet they still found a way to spread the gospel of Christ.

It seems that in today's society, everyone is taking a stand on some issue and calling it "right." But when we reflect on the church in Acts, we must ask ourselves, "Are we taking a stand for the truth of the gospel today?" If not, what is hindering us.

As Christians, we must take a stand for Jesus. We must learn to live the song we sing, making its words ring true in our collective and individual lives. We must decide to live for the cause of Christ and accomplish an awesome work for the Kingdom. As sons and daughters of our heavenly Father, we must not let the concerns of life deter us from working on our Father's behalf. We must focus on the arenas and actions that help us draw men and women to Christ.

Today, let's decide today to be totally "sold out" for God. Do you have a "made-up mind?" If so, welcome aboard! Fasten your seat belt and enjoy the entire ride.

❧

Father, thanks for allowing me to further Your Kingdom by spreading the Good News! Help me to study Your Word, pray, and walk a walk that pleases You and is an effective witness for the Kingdom. In Jesus' Name. Amen!

THEY'RE CHEERING US ON

Wherefore seeing we also are compassed about with so great a cloud of witnesses, let us lay aside every weight, and the sin which doth so easily beset us, and let us run with patience the race that is set before us, looking unto Jesus the author and finisher of our faith; who for the joy that was set before him endured the cross, despising the shame, and is set down at the right hand of the throne of God.

HEBREWS 12:1-2, KJV

Picture, in your mind's eye, the Christian journey set up as a race in an arena. We are the runners, and the stands are filled with the saints of old, cheering us on. Their life experiences bear witness to what we encounter during our race. When we feel isolated and lonely, Abraham speaks and says, "I've been there/done that; keep moving." God is directing our path even in the lonely, uncertain places. When we want to give up on our dreams, Joseph's voice is heard saying, "Keep hope alive; your dreams will come to pass." When we've been thrown in the lion's den of life, Daniel rises up and shouts, "He'll shut the lion's mouth and make his mane a cushion for peaceful dreams." When we are put on the hot seat or ostracized for boldly proclaiming our faith, Shadrach, Meshach, and Abednego sing out in chorus, "We've been there/done that; you won't even feel the flames."

Still there are times when we are publicly mocked and humiliated for living a godly life. That's when Jesus himself reminds us "for the joy that was set before Me, I endured the cross, despising the shame, and I now sit at the right hand of the throne of God," the place of power and authority, having finished His race.

While these personifications are just analogies, they beautifully illustrate the point the author was making in this Scripture, that we can take comfort in the fact that others have run this race before us and finished it with great joy. We should rehearse their stories and gain strength for our journey. If you listen closely, they are indeed cheering us on!

Lord, thank You for providing witnesses of Your keeping power. Help me to stay focused on the joy at the end of my journey. Amen.

Purposely Prepared

*Do you not know that in a race all the runners run, but only one gets the
prize? Run in such a way as to get the prize. Everyone who competes in the
games goes into strict training. They do it to get a crown that will not last;
but we do it to get a crown that will last forever. Therefore I do not run like
a man running aimlessly; I do not fight like a man beating the air. No, I
strike a blow to my body and make it my slave so that after I have preached
to others, I myself will not be disqualified for the prize.*

1 Corinthians 9:24-27, NIV

Our mission, as born-again Christians, is twofold: to purposely
live for Christ and to win souls for His Kingdom in the
process. In today's Scripture, the apostle Paul seeks to aid us in
our mission by comparing the Christian walk with the strategies
of two professional athletes: a runner and a boxer.

In the case of the runner, there are many competing for one
prize, yet each runner prepares, through disciplined practice, to
win the race. Runners often follow a strict regimen every day, that
includes exercise and proper diet, to maintain optimum speed
and endurance during the race. The runner's primary focus is to
know his or her body's strengths and limitations, and find a way to
maximize its potential during the race.

In the case of the boxer, there is only one opponent. Like the
runner, the boxer also prepares through disciplined exercise and
diet; but, since there's only one opponent, the boxer also studies
his opponent to learn his strengths and weaknesses. If the boxer is
to win the match, he must make every move count and not waste
energy swinging into thin air.

As Christians, we must, like the runner, maximize our spiritual
potential by studying and applying God's Word to our lives. And,
like the boxer, we should know the strategy of our enemy and use
the weaponry found in God's Word to defeat him.

❧

*Lord, thank You for Your Word, which is filled with everything I need
to finish my race and defeat the enemy of my soul. Help me to purposely
prepare for my journey. Enable me to discipline my body so that only Your
will is done through it. Amen.*

TIME TO REJOICE

Through Him also we have [our] access (entrance, introduction) by faith into this grace (state of God's favor) in which we [firmly and safely] stand. And let us rejoice and exult in our hope of experiencing and enjoying the glory of God.

ROMANS 5:2, AMP

Do you recall not having a way to enter someplace you needed or wanted to access? How disheartening and frustrating was it to know that there was nothing you could do but wait for someone to grant you access? At one point, we did not have entry into God's favor because we had not submitted our lives to Christ; we were children of wrath. But now, we have been granted access into God's grace by faith, in which we stand. We can now partake in the privilege of His favor. It is so wonderful to know that Christ has extended His grace to us, and we can stand firm!

Now that we are enjoying the riches of His grace, we can also rejoice in our hope of experiencing His glory. We can get excited about the fact that one day, because of His grace, we will see Him face-to-face. Oh, what a joy and assurance to know that we will not only hear of Him, but we will also be in His presence!

We can embrace this assurance the next time dark clouds hover over us, and we feel like there's nothing to look forward to. We have something far better than what this world has to offer. Remember: "whatsoever things are true, whatsoever things are honest, whatsoever things are just, whatsoever things are pure, whatsoever things are lovely, whatsoever things are of good report; if there be any virtue, and if there be any praise, think on these things" (Philippians 4:8, KJV). When we keep in mind what God has done for us, and remember that we will see Him and reign with Him, we will take time to *rejoice!*

Father, I take this time today to pause and acknowledge Your goodness and faithfulness to me. I am eternally grateful for the things You have done. I rest in the fact that You are God, and I look forward to the day when I will be in Your presence forever. Amen!

GIFT OF GRACE

For by grace are ye saved through faith; and that not of yourselves: it is the gift of God: Not of works, lest any man should boast.

EPHESIANS 2:8-9, NKJV

The late Bishop Arthur M. Brazier referred to this passage and the gift of grace often, and repeatedly read it in the hearing of his congregation. As a result, many in his congregation were fully persuaded that they were saved because of the grace of God. What a wonderful idea to consider: God was gracious enough to give us the most wonderful gift of salvation through faith.

It is great to know that salvation is not about our works, but rather His work—from start to finish. For many of us, it is hard to conceive that there is nothing we can do to earn salvation, but that is how God's love works! So often, at our jobs or in our communities, we have to do something to earn a place, to garner some respect, or to gain acceptance. Often, we have to perform all types of "tricks" before we earn the right to be part of a group or to be accepted in some manner.

Thank God, He doesn't operate like that! Make no mistake, there is nothing in us that God would view as useful or good. Nevertheless, God accepts us as we are, and He knows the plan He has for us. God knows what He can do with us once we are in His hands. When we receive His valuable gift, it enables us to partake in the great riches of His grace. As believers, we know what His gift offers us and how it enriches our lives. As we fully yield ourselves to Him and embrace the grace of our salvation, our lives both honor God and encourage others to partake in this wonderful salvation that is offered so freely.

Father, today I am humbled that You chose to bestow Your wonderful gift of salvation on me. Help me to value this gift always. In Jesus' Name. Amen!

A SEALED DEAL

And you also were included in Christ when you heard the message of truth, the gospel of your salvation. When you believed, you were marked in him with a seal, the promised Holy Spirit, who is a deposit guaranteeing our inheritance until the redemption of those who are God's possession—to the praise of his glory.

EPHESIANS 1:13-14, NIV

There are so many ways to hear the gospel today—television, radio, the Internet-not to mention the many churches around the country. By these various means, the message of Jesus Christ is reaching masses of people. We must never disregard the ways in which the message of the Gospel is spread because those are the tools that led many of us, and will continue to lead others, to Christ.

Still, there is a difference between *hearing* the gospel and *receiving* the Christ of the gospel. When we believe, we are marked with a seal of the promise, as the Holy Spirit becomes our secured inheritance. The seal indicates that we are fastened and preserved in Him! In Christ, we become heirs to *all* He is because we *are* His. We can be content because we have so much to look forward to in Christ. Since we are His, we can trust that we will receive all God has in store for us. We have no need to be impatient, to chase selfish desires, or become overwhelmed with the cares of this world. Rather, we can hold on to God with the assurance that we will one day receive everything He has promised us.

So let us praise God now. Let us decide to glorify His name. Let us lift up the name of Jesus because He has set us free. Let us proclaim this wonderful gospel and be strong in the faith. We were redeemed from sin and death, and that is reason enough to rejoice in Him. Christ has sealed the deal!

🦋

Today, Lord, I praise You and I hold on to the promises You have made to me. I resolve in my heart not to waiver or fret because I believe Your Word! Amen.

WORTH THE WAIT

Who are being guarded (garrisoned) by God's power through [your] faith
[till you fully inherit that final] salvation that is ready to be revealed [for
you] in the last time.

1 PETER 1:5, AMP

Many members of the military live in communities known as "bases." The base is a very tightly secured location that the troops stationed there call home. On the base, the troops are not only cared for, but they also reside in a safe haven. Although they are fully aware that their location is a temporary residence, the soldiers function on the base daily, until their service is over and they can go home.

Like the troops, believers are guarded by God's power. Under God's care, we have no need to worry or fear, for He is more than capable of handling any and every situation that may arise. As believers, we can rest in the hope that we have inherited our salvation, and it will be fully revealed when Jesus returns. When we are joined with Him, we will be whole, enjoying our completeness in Him. None of this is of our own doing. It is solely the power of God; that's why we must depend on Him! We are preserved by Him!

The act of preserving can involve many steps. We find an example in the way our grandmothers preserved fruit. It was a tedious task, with many procedures to follow to reach the desired outcome. The process involved using a paring knife to thinly peel away the skin, then removing the core, stem, and damaged parts of the fruit. The fruit had to be cooked, spices had to be added for flavor, and the filled jars had to be boiled then cooled. That would seem like a lot for one jar of preserves! But it was worth it. Likewise, at times it might appear that we are experiencing much in this journey, but we must trust that, in the end we are preserved and it will all be worth it.

❧

Father, today I trust that You know how to produce the best in me as I travel on this journey. Help me to be patient, to learn to enjoy this walk, and to always know that it is worth it. Amen.

CHRIST, OUR INTERCESSOR

Therefore he is able to save completely those who come to God through him,
because he always lives to intercede for them.

HEBREWS 7:25, NIV

The *Indiana Jones* films are classic adventure stories. Time and again, the hero is trapped in a dangerous situation and there seems to be no way out. Of course, at the last minute, a rescue comes from nowhere and the adventure continues. That cliffhanger life is great for the movies, but for most of us, looking back on our own hopeless situations is anything but a laughing matter.

Today, it is easy to see that what we needed long before we realized it was to be rescued from a life of sin, which led only to eternal death. Salvation doesn't keep us from facing some tough times, but we now have a hope and refuge because we can draw near to God. Without God, our troubles can be devastating; but with God, we have hope even in difficult times.

Unfortunately, in this life we may face many choices. When we try to figure out what we need to do, we sometimes revert to old habits and go to everyone except God. As a result, some of our choices can go against what God has instructed us to do, resulting in us pulling away from Him. Then, at the very last minute, we ashamedly realize the importance of going to the Mediator, who can resolve our issues and help us again feel the forgiveness of God.

Christ makes intercession for us. He goes before the Father for us. He is constantly and consistently working on our behalf. In Him, our salvation is secure. We no longer have to depend on ourselves to escape life's twists and turns; we can rely on the One who rescued us. Because of His intercession, we no longer face life without hope. Instead, we can face today and each day after with assurance, by drawing near to Him, knowing that He is close to us.

❧

Dear Lord, continue to draw me even closer to You. Being in Your care is the best place to be. Lord, thanks for salvation and for interceding for me. I am eternally grateful for what You've done. Amen.

AN INSEPARABLE LOVE

Nor height nor depth, nor anything else in all creation will be able to separate us from the love of God which is in Christ Jesus our Lord.

ROMANS 8:39, AMP

If you ever have one sheer moment of concern regarding God's love for you, look no further than Romans 8 for comfort. In this chapter, Paul reiterates God's love for us by identifying several powerful entities that are unable to separate us from His love. Neither nature nor gravity, depth of the sea nor height of the heavens can separate us from Him. No creature can keep us from Him; death can't hold us hostage. We can count on God to hold on to us and love us like we so need to be loved.

Paul explains that those who are in Christ are no longer condemned. We are sons and daughters who are now justified through Christ, despite our former guilt. Paul then asks two great questions. First, who can be against us if Christ is for us? Second, if God spared not His own Son, why would we doubt anything He would do for us? Imagine! God did all this while we were enemies, estranged from Him.

Whatever thoughts we might have had about Christ not loving us can be put away with Romans 8. Here, we can grasp the fact that there is nothing that can separate us from the love of God! He displayed His love for us long ago. God is devoted to us and has made it clear that He is not going anywhere. The love He has for us brings us even closer to Him; we are inseparable. It is wonderful to know that we can rest in His love right now. We can trust that He loves us in spite of our past; He loves us when we can't even love ourselves. He loves us despite what our accusers say and do. God loves us, period!

Father, help me to rest in the fact that You love me perfectly and nothing can—or will—persuade You otherwise. Thank You so much for giving Your Son, Jesus Christ, so that I could come to know Your love. Amen.

GOD IS ABLE

Now unto him that is able to keep you from falling, and to present you faultless before the presence of his glory with exceeding joy.

JUDE 1:24, KJV

Someone once said, "Never put a period where God places a comma." We could also say, never place a question mark where God puts an exclamation point! The life of faith seems to be filled with questions, but God, Who has all the answers, emphatically instructs us to trust Him and know that He is able to keep us.

The challenges we face in our Christian life are not totally different from those faced by believers of the first century. Jude wrote his short letter to warn and encourage believers in their walk. Jude warned about threats to the church—teachers who taught erroneously that grace is God's permission to sin (verse 4). He railed against leaders who were sexually immoral or bold in their selfish pursuits (verses 4, 7). He warned against those who disrespected, even rejected, authority. He gave grave warnings against those who were greedy, complainers, and grumblers (verses 11, 16).

In the midst of warnings that could have left believers questioning their faith, Jude closed his letter with a doxology—a blessing or ascription of praise to God. Instead of harping on the negative, Jude shifts to expound on the truth about God. Why close with a doxology? Because, in spite of any threat to the church or individual believers, Jude reminded them that God is able! Yes, even though Jude admonished them to do their part to stand and to build themselves up in their faith, he also admonished them to give glory to God.

The doxology is the final word on any matter pointing to the One who deserves all glory and honor, and in whom all majesty, dominion, and power reside. In the doxology, Jude assures us that God, through Jesus, has saved us and will enable us to stand before Him filled with joy and without blame at that last day.

Think about it. If God is able to keep us and sustain us to stand before His presence on *that* great day, how much more is He able to keep us and sustain us on *this* day?

※

Dear wise and gracious God, I praise You. You are indeed able to keep me and for this I give You glory!

THE TRUTH OF RECONCILIATION

And all things are of God, who hath reconciled us to himself by Jesus Christ, and hath given to us the ministry of reconciliation; To wit, that God was in Christ, reconciling the world unto himself, not imputing their trespasses unto them; and hath committed unto us the word of reconciliation.

2 CORINTHIANS 5:18-19, KJV

There can be no reconciliation without truth. Ask Archbishop Desmond Tutu, or other members of the Truth and Reconciliation Commission (TRC) of South Africa. The TRC was assembled after the end of apartheid, the legalized segregation system in which the minority Dutch held positions of power over the Black and Colored residents. During apartheid, many travesties were committed by the ruling class.

One of the features of the TRC was a committee set up to investigate human rights abuses that took place between 1960 and 1994. Anyone who had been a victim of violence could come forth and testify. Perpetrators could also come forth, acknowledge their actions, and request amnesty.[25] In an effort to unify the nation, the wise leaders of South Africa knew there could be no reconciliation without truth.

Some people think reconciliation between two estranged parties can occur by coming together, holding hands and singing "Kumbaya." Some desire reconciliation but want to sweep the truth of the conflict, alienation, or disconnection under the rug. Yet, in reality, there can be no reconciliation without truth telling. To reconcile means to be brought back together or to be brought back into favor. Fallen humanity was alienated from God because of sin. Yet God took the initiative to bring us back into favor with him through His Son, Jesus Christ. The truth of the matter is (and each of us at some point has to speak it), we were sinners and could not get to God on our own, and only God could bring us back to Him. Thank God He did just that and now has made us ministers of reconciliation. We are people who are called to share the Good News of Christ so that others may be reconciled back to God.

※

Dear Lord, thank You for Your Truth. I needed You when I could not get to You on my own. Thank You for sending Jesus so that I can live with You forever. Amen.

KEEPER OF THE FLOCK

The man runs away because he is a hired hand and cares nothing about the sheep.

JOHN 10:13, NIV

Teen girls used to advertise their babysitting skills to relatives and neighbors to earn extra money. Years ago, these young ladies would go door-to-door, describing their love for children, commitment to do an excellent job, and security in assuring the parents their child would be safe, cared for, and protected by them. Most often, they earned the job and prepared themselves for a quiet weekend evening of watching over a sleeping baby.

While on one babysitting job, a teen girl was confronted with a challenge. The baby she was "sitting" awakened, crying and in need. She nervously paced the floor holding the baby and desperately trying to sooth his discomfort. To no avail, her calls for help to friends rendered no counsel, and her parents were out for the evening. The baby's cries grew shrill, and this poor girl was at wit's end. So she laid the baby in his crib, wrapped him tightly in blankets, and bolted for the door, only to be startled by the unassuming parents coming in the front door. They had decided to end their evening out early.

The Word for today tells the story of the hired hand who left the sheep unattended the moment trouble arrived. He was unwilling to sacrifice his safety in protecting another person's property. To him, it was not worth the cost of injury or his life to guard the owner's sheep from imminent attack.

Praise God for our Lord and Savior, the one and only Good Shepherd. In this chapter, Christ, declares Himself the Good Shepherd, in one of His seven great I AM characterizations. Unlike the uncommitted employee, unwilling to endanger himself while watching over another person's flock, and the young, inexperienced teen sitter, who was ready to abandon an innocent, unprotected baby, Christ portrays Himself very differently.

Jesus Christ is the true Shepherd. He *watches over* and *protects* us, *calls* us by name, *provides* for us, and *leads* us. Ultimately, He *died* so we can have eternal life. Christ is the Good Shepherd, who became the Lamb of God.

❧

Father, I thank You for being the keeper of my soul. In Jesus' Name.

BODY OF THE SACRED ONE

What? Know ye not that your body is the temple of the Holy Ghost which is in you, which ye have of God, and ye are not your own? For ye are bought with a price: therefore glorify God in your body, and in your spirit, which are God's.

1 CORINTHIANS 6:19-20, KJV

When did we become conscious that our body is a holy place—the place of the Holy Spirit? When did we realize that we can't live however we please, wasting what God paid such a high price for? The spiritual part of us is not some kind of possession belonging to the physical part of us. God owns the whole work.

There will be times when the enemy will try to convince us that it's okay to abuse what Jesus so graciously paid His life for on Calvary. But, as God's children, we cannot yield to the trickery of the enemy, and we cannot take the temple of God and misuse it with worldly and carnal acts that are not pleasing to Him.

God did not design the human body to consume non-nutritious, health-hazardous foods. When we do so, we can become ill and, in the extreme, develop maladies difficult (sometimes impossible) to cure. Some of us force-feed what, under optimum conditions, the body would naturally reject. This same action happens in the spiritual realm; we cannot treat our spirits any kind of way and think that God is not going to reject it. Our total being belongs to Him, and He is a jealous God; so it is not whatever goes!

Hold on to the thoughts of how God paid such a high price for our lives, and in knowing that we should want to do right by Him in mind, body, and spirit. This body is not ours, and God has all the rights to it. So we should let people see God in and throughout our lives.

❧

God, Help me to glorify You in this body You have given to me. Amen.

GOD'S MAGNUM OPUS

For we are God's masterpiece. He has created us anew in Christ Jesus, so that we can do the good things He planned for us long ago.

EPHESIANS 2:10, NLT

In the classic movie *Mr. Holland's Opus*, a musician devoted his life to composing a world renowned *magnum opus* (masterwork/work of genius). He labored many years without completing the goal he set for himself. Finally, he resigned himself to a job more mundane (by his standard), of teaching music to high school students. His trials mounted year after year, but he persevered, without much grandeur, in his work of teaching.

Much to his surprise, at his retirement Mr. Holland realized he had accomplished far more than he perceived. For more than thirty years, he had touched the lives of hundreds of students, depositing lifelong values in them through music. His classroom provided a platform for him to inspire, encourage, redirect, and teach the importance of learning and achieving in any venue. Mr. Holland's *opus* had become his students and their success stories—not the great musical composition he longed for over the years.

Today's Scripture tells us that we are God's *magnum opus*—His masterpiece—and as such, God has great expectations for us. By His grace we are chosen to do special works specifically designed by Him that fit us perfectly. In the likeness of His Son, Jesus Christ, we navigate through life as *His special treasure,* serving to advance the Kingdom agenda and sowing seeds of righteousness. God uses every experience and every task, both good and bad, to grow us and strengthen us. As God's *masterpiece* we move forward in service to Him, serving others through our God-given, God-designed gifts and talents. We serve bringing glory to God, and never mistaking our personal accomplishments as earned credit in God's eyes. Instead, we serve based on the commitment in our hearts to serve Him in deed and in truth.

We are God's great work designed to do good works. Only what we do for Him will have an eternal impact.

❧

Father, thank You for creating me as a masterpiece. I am part of Your magnum opus. May my works for You flow out of the great work You are doing in me. Help me to be a more willing servant so my labor will reflect Your love for me. In Jesus' Name. Amen.

HEAVEN IN OUR VIEW

God Himself has prepared us for this, and as a guarantee He has given us His Holy Spirit.

2 CORINTHIANS 5:5, NLT

In our daily walk with the Lord, we are confronted on every side with issues. Conflicts in our families, problems on the job, failing health, discord in the community, and national dilemmas can appear overwhelming. We resign ourselves to press on and fight on. The miracle of it all is that we are not alone. Jesus Christ did not come to save us from our sins and then leave us to suffer through life, hoping and praying for that glorious day when we will see Him face-to-face. Christ loves us too much, and it cost too great a price for our earthly lives to be filled with misery and pain. Christ filled us with His Spirit, and took up residence in our hearts, as a constant reminder that He is with us to lead us and to guide us through life's long journey.

Today's Scripture shapes the focus of our earthly journey. The Lord knows our physical bodies will not withstand the maladies of life and, over time, will crumble and pass away. But we have a promise from God. Our daily challenges will be overcome, and our earthly bodies will one day be transformed into our heavenly bodies, with the promise of everlasting life. Our focus is heaven, and our goal is face-to-face fellowship with the Lord. As a down payment of that heavenly reward, God has given us the Holy Spirit to dwell within and strengthen us on our journey.

Our earthly bodies are destined to reach the finish line. We have heaven in our view because of the hope and the promise, or seal, of victory. As we cross that line, and lift our hands in victory, the brokenness, the weariness, the sorrow, and the pain in our physical bodies will be transformed into glorious bodies of righteousness and holiness. Glory to God!

Be encouraged. The Lord has equipped us to press toward the mark for the prize (Philippians 3:14). We will be draped in our heavenly garments, rejoicing eternally because heaven is our destination. Do you have heaven in your view?

🦋

Father, I bless Your Name for the promise of life eternal in Your heavenly kingdom. Amen.

TOUCHDOWN

For God loved the world so much that he gave his one and only Son, so that everyone who believes in him will not perish but have eternal life.

JOHN 3:16, NLT

During the fall season, all over the country, football games are being played. In the stands, from goal line to goal line, banners and posters are flying in support of the teams. One banner stands out over all the others with a scriptural reference to a very familiar passage, John 3:16. Why would someone wave a banner with this Scripture on it at a football game? What message is being sent to the Christian and non-Christian alike?

Since many of us are football fans, let us examine this special verse as if we are on that football field attempting to score an extraordinary goal. Getting started, we get the ball almost in the opponent's end zone. That's when things really get started as the Spirit convicts us and we finally catch the ball, miraculously realizing that *God so loved the world.* Suddenly we are at the 50 yard line because God, sovereign and matchless, loved us so completely and purely that we can now scramble down the field of life propelled by His Grace.

When we reach the 40, we truly understand that *God gave His only Son.* In His love for us, God willingly sacrificed what was most important to Him, so we can be victorious. We realize that without God's love and the sacrifice of His Son, we cannot navigate over the obstacles and challenges faced in life.

Moving forward on the field of life we have the goal line in sight. We're now at the 10 yard line and gaining speed as we believe ever more deeply in Jesus as Christ. Because God extended an unlimited, unrestricted invitation for all to trust Him, we have received salvation by faith and, as we continue to grow in faith, we even more fully embrace His love.

Then finally, we're in the end zone! Through Christ we have finally realized *eternal life*, everlasting fellowship with God. On the field of life, we cross the goal line and win! Praise God that the message of hope and life eternal are still available for all to receive. Now that is something to cheer about!

✹

Lord, thank You for eternal life I have in Your Son, Jesus Christ. Amen.

KNOW THAT YOU KNOW

These things have I written unto you that believe on the name of the Son of God; that ye may know that ye have eternal life, and that ye may believe on the name of the Son of God.

1 JOHN 5:13, KJV

The "old saints" used to admonish us to, "know that you know that you know." Their words were counter to those who gave an opinion about Jesus with, "I think…", or those who would speak about Jesus based on the testimony of Big Mama or someone else. These wise believers taught us that it wasn't enough to have a surface knowledge about Jesus, but we had to know that we knew Jesus for ourselves. Some of us are now the "older saints," and the message of long ago still holds: "we've got to know that we know!"

There are multiple levels of knowing. Let's take an excursion in the Greek language without it getting overwhelming or confusing. One word for "know" is *ginosko,* which means "to come to know." It can also mean "to know something through experience." There is another Greek word for know, *oida,* which means "to have knowledge." The difference between the two words is striking. Whereas *ginosko* is often used in the Bible to speak of a knowledge that grows progressively stronger with more experience, *oida* is used to speak of a "fullness of knowledge."

John was strategic in his use of Greek, in that he wanted his readers to understand that he had written from personal experience about the Jesus who lived, died, and rose again; so that we who came to believe and experience Jesus, could have *full knowledge* that we have the eternal life Jesus promised. John wrote to declare and disclose the full identity and mission of Jesus so that those who believed on Jesus would fully know, without doubt or speculation, that they indeed had eternal life.

So it is, like the old saints of the church, we join in and say, "we know that we know" that we have eternal life. We have full assurance that Jesus, Who is our life, who has transformed our lives, gives us eternal life.

Dear heavenly Father, thank You for eternal life and for the certainty of knowing that I have eternal life through Your Son, Jesus. I am forever grateful. Amen.

GOD'S PROMISE

He that overcometh, the same shall be clothed in white raiment; and I will not blot out his name out of the book of life, but I will confess his name before my Father, and before his angels.

REVELATION 3:5, KJV

God has made a promise to us in today's Scripture; it is simple and straightforward. The interpretation of His words is literal and prophetic—literal because Jesus is speaking directly to one of the seven churches referred to in Revelation 1:20; prophetic because today, even though we are not members of these seven churches, it is clear these churches are illustrative of congregations throughout the world, both in that generation and this generation.

This passage was written to the church in Sardis. God told them they were dead, meaning they were not living in the will of God. They were not as excited about Christ as they once were.

As we go through life's journey, we'll find ourselves, at some point, in a similar position as the church at Sardis. We're not always on the mountaintop; sometimes we're walking through the valley. Whether it's some tragedy that has come into our lives, or a situation of our own creation, we all have times in our lives when we feel like the church at Sardis.

God's warning here offers hope and a way to salvation, "Remember therefore how you have received and heard, hold fast and repent" (Revelation 3:3). These same words of admonishment are just as true for us today. We must hold fast to the Word of God we have heard and received! The Scriptures today bear witness to Christ's love for us; our salvation is secure and the Holy Ghost lives in us. We have the power within us to overcome. Whatever the problems in our lives, the Holy Ghost strengthens us and cleanses us from our sins. We will overcome and wear the white raiment of purity, not by our own power but by the power of the Holy Ghost that lives in us.

❧

Oh God, my heavenly Father, I love You and worship You today and I thank You for loving me enough to warn me. Thank You for my salvation. Father, forgive me for my transgressions. In Jesus' Name I pray. Amen.

THE GIFT OF ETERNAL LIFE

For the wages of sin is death; but the gift of God is eternal life through Jesus Christ our Lord.

ROMANS 6:23 KJV

How many of us have ever been shorted on our paychecks, or had some unauthorized withdrawals made against our checking account? What did we do? We marched right down to payroll, or to the bank, "Where is my money?" After all, we earned it. It is not unreasonable to expect our earnings to be there when they are due.

Suppose when we went down to payroll and the owner of the company met us there and said, "Here. We want you to have this new twelve-room mansion we just built, and your gold Rolls Royce is waiting outside." That's what God did. He gave us something worth more than the mansions, fancy cars, expensive clothes, or exotic vacations that our earnings can buy; God gave us eternal life through Jesus Christ.

Many of us who are parents chastise our children and warn them, "When you are disobedient you will be punished." We understand this; we are responsible for our actions and we accept the consequences for our actions. So when the apostle Paul writes, "The wages of sin is death," no one is surprised. We have seen the wrath of God toward the children of Israel for their disobedience. The apostle Paul wrote earlier, "for all have sinned and come short of the glory of God" (Romans 3:23).

When we are honest with ourselves and recognize the sin in our lives, when we realize that we are not perfect, when we understand that our goodness and humanitarianism still leave us short, that's when we can begin to comprehend the magnitude of the second part of today's Scripture: "but the gift of God is eternal life through Jesus Christ our Lord." We are saved by the grace of God, and our sins are cleansed by the blood of Jesus Christ.

Is it possible to thank God enough? Can we worship Him and praise Him enough? We can thank Him today from the bottom of our hearts.

Lord Jesus, thank You for eternal life. I love You today because You loved me. I will worship You in everything I do. I pray these things in Jesus' Name. Amen.

CHECK YOURSELF!

Who will render to every man according to his deeds: To them who by patient continuance in well doing seek for glory and honour and immortality, eternal life: But unto them that are contentious, and do not obey the truth, but obey unrighteousness, indignation and wrath.

ROMANS 2:6-8, KJV

Remember tattle-tales? They were the kids who were always ready to tell the teacher or a parent what another kid did wrong. Tattle-tales never told on themselves. They thought they were always so right that they could describe in detail where another kid went wrong! Actually, there is something in human nature that makes all of us think we are doing better than someone else. In his letter to the Romans, Paul points out this quality.

The Roman church was composed of both Jewish and Gentile believers who trusted Jesus Christ as their Savior. Paul's letter begins with genuine praise of the Roman Christians for their faithfulness. He then turns to discuss how Gentiles, who did not know God, engaged in crass, debased, and negative behaviors. Paul, however, does not give his Christian readers any excuse for thinking themselves to be better than the Gentiles around them. Yes, they were now filled with the Holy Spirit and believed Jesus Christ for salvation, but the root of sin was still sin. They condemned others and called for the wrath of God on Gentiles, but Paul reminded them that their own behavior displeased God.

In verse three, Paul says that God is not oblivious to sin in anyone—even in those who have declared a love for Him through Jesus Christ. In verse four, Paul reminds them that God was patient and gave them time and love, which led them to salvation. Finally, in verses six through eight, Paul says to be careful about judging others because God will reward everyone according to their deeds.

As adults we don't try to be tattle-tales, but we do often measure our "good" against someone else's "terrible," so that our "good" looks a little better and our bad doesn't seem as awful. Paul's words remind us that God is still watching and our true character is shining through.

❧

Dear God, I yield myself to You and confess my sin now. O Lord, strengthen me to follow You. Amen.

IT IS WRITTEN

But these are written, that ye might believe that Jesus is the Christ, the Son of God; and that believing ye might have life through his name.

JOHN 20:31, KJV

There are nearly six thousand colleges and universities in the United States today, and all offer courses in religious studies or history dealing with Christianity or Judaism, in some form or another, based on the Bible. There are more than two hundred Bible colleges and seminaries dedicated to studying and teaching the Bible. Not only is the Bible one of the world's bestselling books, but it is the bestselling book of all time. The Bible is also the most-read book of all time; more people have read the Bible than any book ever written.[26]

Why are people reading the Bible? As it turns out, there are a lot of reasons: the Bible is inspirational, with stories of faith and bravery; the Bible is a historical reference that aids archeologists and scholars to independently verify events and dates; the Bible gives us the most complete account of the life and ministry of Jesus Christ; we read the Bible to understand and know what "thus saith the Lord." All these are very good reasons to read the Bible.

In today's Scripture, the apostle John gives us another good reason to read the Bible—probably the most important reason— "that ye might believe that Jesus is the Christ, the Son of God; and that believing ye might have life through his name." People have studied God's Word, analyzed it, memorized passages, but gained very little from it. Why? Because they lacked the basic belief that Jesus Christ is the Son of God. This is where knowledge really begins.

Jesus said to Thomas, "because thou hast seen me, thou hast believed: blessed are they that have not seen, and yet have believed" (John 20:29).We are blessed today; we have not seen Jesus Christ but believe with all that is within us that He is the Son of God.

❧

Heavenly Father, I thank You today for Jesus Christ, and for Him dying for my sins. Thank You for Your Word. Through it I believed and now I am saved. Thank You for my salvation. In Jesus' Name I pray. Amen.

CHOOSE TO BELIEVE

He that believeth on him is not condemned: but he that believeth not is condemned already, because he hath not believed in the name of the only begotten Son of God.

JOHN 3:18, KJV

Quick! How many choices do you make in a day? What to wear? What to eat? Whether to exercise or what route to take to work? Now, how many of those choices are life-changing? How many have the potential to shape your character or determine your eternal destiny?

In this Gospel, John paints a portrait of how Jesus repeatedly challenged His disciples, the religious authorities, and the people of every village to rethink the choices God placed before them. When Nicodemus, a leader among the Pharisees, came to see Jesus secretly in the middle of the night, Jesus answered his queries with a simple statement: "You must be born again" (John 3:16). After this explanation of the depth of God's love, Jesus went on to say that God sent His Son not to condemn the world but to save it (verse 17), and that each person has a choice to either believe that Jesus is the Son of God or not (verse 18).

Believing Christ is to avoid condemnation and to have the assurance of eternal life. Condemnation comes from the rejection of Jesus as the Light of the World. Rejecting salvation through Jesus Christ is an indication of loving darkness—or evil—more than light.

When we accept Jesus as Lord and Savior, the Holy Spirit reveals to us where we come short in our relationship to God and to others. It is through the Holy Spirit that we are born again, not to mortal life and physical death, but to spiritual understanding and eternal life. The Holy Spirit is the assurance of God's love for us and our guide for daily living.

Today, we will make those ordinary decisions as we do every day. But we also are faced with life-changing choices. If we have the Holy Ghost, then today we can choose afresh to listen to the Spirit. If we are not saved, today is the day to believe Jesus and to choose eternal life.

✴

Lord, You know the choices I have failed to make and the times when I have heeded Your voice. Help me now to honor You in all I do. Amen.

BECAUSE OF LOVE

Why was this fragrant oil not sold for three hundred denarii and given to the poor?

JOHN 12:5, NKJV

Ever wonder why so much attention is given to a person's funeral? Much attention is given to the selection of the coffin, clothing, floral arrangements, and the program. In some instances, loved ones will go into debt to insure the deceased has a "proper burial." Why so much expense when that money could be put to good use for the living? One reason is because of love. We do these things sometimes at a great sacrifice to express our love and thankfulness for all that the person meant to us while alive. It gives us an opportunity to say, "We love you," one last time.

John writes the story of Jesus' friends Mary, Martha, and Lazarus. Jesus raised Lazarus from the dead and some time later joined the siblings for dinner. Mary loved Jesus and was so thankful to Him for what He did for her family, that she poured an expensive bottle of spikenard oil on His feet and dried them with her hair. An objection was raised as to why such a costly oil was used on Jesus' feet when it could have been used to help the poor. Jesus, knowing that He was going to soon die, responded by saying, "Leave Mary alone, she is preparing my body for my burial" (John 12:7).

Mary's example here is that she didn't wait for Jesus to die to show her gratitude, nor did she spare the cost. She anointed Jesus' feet with oil as a form of worship. The Holy Spirit prompts us to show God our gratitude with our gifts as well.

So it is we show our gratitude to our loved ones who have passed, as a testament to our faith in the eternal life promised the believer, and the security we have as we rest in knowing death really is not the end of the story—but our love (and God's love for us) lives on *eternally.*

Heavenly Father, thank You that You loved me, that Your Son, Jesus, paid the ultimate sacrifice with His life, that I might have the right to eternal life in heaven. Continue to bless me to use my gifts and talents to uplift the body of Christ. In Jesus' Name I pray. Amen.

A WIN-WIN SITUATION

For to me, to live is Christ and to die is gain.

PHILIPPIANS 1:21, NIV

May 10, 2007, two people died suddenly: a 75-year-old man of a heart attack and a 16-year-old boy of a gunshot wound. Family and friends were saddened by the man's death because it happened without warning. However, many of them agreed he lived a full, fruitful life. But the seemingly premature death of the honors student caused many to pause and question. Why is it that a young man with so much promise didn't live to graduate from high school, go to college, get married, have children, buy his first house, and so on? That's tragic, right?

Nothing is wrong with setting and pursuing such earthly goals or wanting those things for our children. Certainly, God takes joy in blessing our lives with such experiences. However, living the good life is not necessarily about the material goals we accomplish on earth.

The apostle Paul's chief goal was to serve Jesus Christ, to proclaim the Good News and draw others to the Lord. So whenever and however he would depart this life (for his life was often in danger), he would only gain more life: the fulfilled promise to every believer of eternity with Jesus Christ. For Paul there was no such thing as dying prematurely because he was living for Christ and looking toward the moment he would be absent from his body and present with the Lord (2 Corinthians 5:8).

We all want to live a long life, but if we strive to live a "purpose-driven" life in which our chief aim is to magnify the Lord in our day-to-day living—to proclaim His goodness, to love others, to do what He would do in any given situation—then the number of our days on earth don't matter, especially since the greater life comes after this one.

That 16-year-old young man died protecting a friend. He made himself a human shield and made the ultimate sacrifice—the very thing Jesus would do and did.[27]

Dear Father, thank You for creating me to live for You on earth and to live with You in heaven—forever. In Jesus' Name. Amen.

THE ULTIMATE GHOSTBUSTER

For in him all things were created: things in heaven and on earth, visible and invisible, whether thrones or powers or rulers or authorities; all things have been created through him and for him.

COLOSSIANS 1:16, NIV

Do you remember the 1984 hit movie *Ghostbusters*? In it, paranormal exterminators are hired by a woman whose apartment is haunted by a demonic spirit. Upon investigating the situation, the ghostbusters are outwitted by the spirit, who then possesses the woman. For the rest of the movie, they try to free her and destroy the demon once and for all. That's science fiction, but demons are real. They can take possession of a soul where the Holy Spirit does not reside, and they make it their business to try to oppress the born-again believer. Yet, we have the ultimate ghostbuster in Jesus Christ, who doesn't need a millisecond to exterminate any evil spirit.

When the apostle Paul writes that all things were created in Jesus Christ, he meant *everything,* including the demonic spirits that can come against us. He reigns over them, but, to be clear, He did not create them to be evil. They chose the way of rebellion. Demons are fallen angels, whose original purpose was the same as ours and any other created being: to glorify God. They know Christ is "the Holy One of God" (Mark 1:24), they must obey His commands (Matthew 8:16), and they know their fate (Matthew 8:29).[28] They know they are doomed and that we are set for life (one reason they come after us).

For sure, we cannot take lightly the influence Satan and his cohorts can have on our lives, particularly when we unwittingly lay out a welcome mat. However, let's remember that we serve the living God, who reigns supreme over them. Simply calling the name of Jesus will put them in check. Jesus is the source of life; therefore, everything is subject to His will and His authority, even the enemies of our faith. He has the final say, and here it is: Satan is already defeated and the church is already victorious.

❧

Dear Lord, thank You for reminding me that You are the Creator and You reign supreme. Not only are all things subject to You, but all things begin and end in You. Amen.

HE CALLS US BY NAME

My sheep hear my voice, and I know them, and they follow me: And I give unto them eternal life; and they shall never perish, neither shall any man pluck them out of my hand. My Father, which gave them me, is greater than all; and no man is able to pluck them out of my Father's hand.

JOHN 10:27-29, KJV

W hat's in a name? Our name is one of our most precious assets. It is our identifying marker to the world. Parents painstakingly consider names for their children and, for the most part, those names carry their children through life and define them. Names are important; they can carry power, promise, and potential. If there are ten people named Jack or Jill in a room, each will respond to the sound of his or her own name, yet we have a God who knows us all individually and calls us by our name in a manner only He can. He calls us by name and tells us His Name: Jesus. He, who calls us, holds us securely. His promise is that nothing or no one can pluck us out of His hands.

We may be tempted to think that our trials can come between God and us, but they can't. We might even think our past can come between God and us, but it can't. Even our feelings and emotions can't come between God and us because He, who calls us, knows us and loves us. Scripture reminds us that nothing can separate us from the love of God, which is in Christ Jesus (Romans 8:35). He is the Shepherd, who looks after us, leading us in and out in the pasture of our lives. When we hear His shepherd's call, we respond as obedient sheep. We are fed His Word and gratefully receive the gracious gift of eternal life.

We live loving, serving, and thanking the Lord for the gift that is reserved for us because we know our names are written in the Book of Life (Revelation 3:5). What joy to know the day is coming when we will hear Him call our names and acknowledge us as His before our heavenly Father!

Heavenly Father, we are the sheep of Your pasture—called, anointed, and appointed by You. Knowing my name is written in the Book of Life is an awesome privilege. Amen.

WHAT'S YOUR EXCUSE?

And they all with one consent began to make excuse.

LUKE 14:18A, KJV

We live in a world of excuses. At the drop of a hat, we have no qualms about making excuses for actions we know are inexcusable. Today's world is filled with growing moral decay, and even as Christians, we find ourselves tempted to commit—or actually engage in—behavior we know to be in direct opposition to God's Word. We sheepishly play the "blame game," not wanting to point the finger at ourselves, but rather to deflect the blame that falls squarely at our feet. Call it responsibility avoidance, call it "the devil made me do it," or call it what God calls it: sin! God has a remedy for those that name His Son as Savior and Lord. Let Him be Lord in your life and live according to His Word.

For many believers, the problem is a disconnect between our verbal confession and our actual profession. One of the great privileges of belonging to God is the eternal life that's promised to those who believe. Our response to what we believe is a dynamic way to reflect that truth now as we await the assurance to come. When our lives are laden with the guilt and shame that accompanies the sin-inflicted "blame game," we live far below our privilege as the heirs of Jesus Christ. We live *now* in light of the reality of what's *to come*. We practice now for our eternal lives of worship and adoration of our King. He has drawn us, and we have come to the Father.

Let's make it our business to allow what we know to be true to provoke us to live in the light of that truth. If God has saved us and promised eternal life, how do we live beneath that? We can't! Can we determine to hold to the promise of being secure with God forever? We can! So what's your excuse?

❧

Father, help what I say align with what I do. Help me not to make excuses when I elect something that betrays what I have received in You, but instead respond with a repentant heart that reflects the gratitude I have. I thank You for eternal life and I eagerly await the time when I will be with You forever. In Jesus' Name. Amen.

SEEING IS BELIEVING

And this is the will of him that sent me, that every one which seeth the Son, and believeth on him, may have everlasting life: and I will raise him up at the last day.

JOHN 6:40, KJV

"Will" is one of those words with multiple meanings. As a verb, it can mean "to wish or desire." As a noun, it can mean "a deliberative action or a legal document." God is very specific regarding His will. His will is that none should perish (Matthew 18:14). His will is that all would come into a saving knowledge of Him through His Son (1 Timothy 2:4). His will is that the eyes of our understanding be opened (Ephesians 1:18). His will is based on His love for us. We often want what we can see, but God invites us to want what we *cannot* see and thereby see Him. He wants us to want Him. When we see Jesus clearly, we can learn to want what He wants.

God's desire is for us to know in whom we have believed and to remain confident in our faith. In today's world, we are challenged with a frenzied media that promotes skepticism of the once-held understanding that "seeing is believing." Through technology and photographic manipulation, we know that what appears to be real is, in fact, fake. Being deceived by our eyes is not a new notion. Satan even tried to appear as an angel of light (2 Corinthians 11:14). If we can't believe what we see, what then can we believe? We are left questioning what or whom to believe.

We know and thank God that regardless of media manipulation or worldly skepticism, the truth of Jesus Christ stands. Jesus is the real deal. We have the remembrance of the writer of Acts with "To whom also he shewed himself alive after his passion by many infallible proof" (Acts 1:3). Those to whom He showed Himself became the church, and He is still revealing Himself today; Jesus is returning for His church. May His church stand firm, knowing that our lives lived in Him will result in a world that will see and believe.

🐦

Lord God, enable me to clearly see Jesus and live in such a manner that helps others believe that He is the Christ You have sent and believe in eternal life. Thank You! I'm one for whom He will return. Amen.

MAKING THE RIGHT CHOICE

He that believeth on the Son hath everlasting life: and he that believeth not the Son shall not see life; but the wrath of God abideth on him.

JOHN 3:36, KJV

Each day, we're faced with the task of making difficult decisions. Which bill do we pay to keep our families fed? Do we pay the mortgage or rent, or pay to keep the lights and gas on? How do we pay for medical treatment of a serious illness when there's no insurance? How do we accept God's favor when we feel so unworthy? Some of these decisions can be life or death choices. We find ourselves so caught up in the here and now that our focus on the now seems to neglect the truth of life *beyond* the now. We tend to concentrate on what's before us rather than the grander reality of the eternal life that is to come. We are urged to remember, "for the things which are seen are temporal; but the things which are not seen are eternal"(2 Corinthians 4:18).

God wants us to make the right choice in all things but particularly when it comes to making a decision about where we will spend eternity. The Word of God makes it indisputably clear that believing in God's Son, Jesus, leads to everlasting life. Not believing in the Son results in the wrath of God. Our growing tendency to get caught up in the cares of this world jeopardizes the comfort of resting in what is available to us as those who have believed in the Son. When we receive Christ by faith, we are received in the love of God. The simple solution of believing in the Son ushers us into the security of the Father's love. Don't become sidetracked and deceived by getting caught up in the affairs of this world; "Take therefore no thought for the morrow: for the morrow shall take thought for the things of itself. Sufficient unto the day is the evil thereof" (Matthew 6:34). Remember, we are making the right choice when we choose God's Son and live in His love.

❧

Father, I'm thankful that I've made the right choice in choosing to live for Jesus. Lord, grant me the wisdom to continually discern what is the correct choice when faced with life's decisions. Help me to not get sidetracked along the way. Amen.

THE POWER OF BELONGING

But as many as received him, to them gave he power to become the sons of God, even to them that believe on his name.

JOHN 1:12, KJV

There is a growing power shortage. Here on earth, we are depleting the finite fossil fuels used as sources for our energy needs. Oil and natural gas shortages are causing escalating prices and rationing. We're forced to turn to undesirable nuclear energy and underdeveloped sustainable, "green" technology to meet the world's increasing demand.

In the spiritual realm, we face powers of darkness that seek to destroy our Christian walk. But the writer of Ephesians reminds us, "we wrestle not against flesh and blood, but against principalities, against powers, against the rulers of the darkness of this world, against spiritual wickedness in high places" (Ephesians 6:12). The reality of a power struggle obliges us to look to the real power source instead of blindly searching for alternative power sources that are sure to fail. As the children of God, we can plug into an energy grid that never runs dry. Because Jesus has all power, when we plug into Him; we, too, have the power that comes with belonging to Him. Jesus, Himself, said, "All power is given unto me in heaven and in earth" (Matthew 28:18).

True power in this life, and the life to come, is not found in the ground or in the sky. It is not measured in barrels or cubic feet. It is found in faith in Jesus Christ. Faith in Christ taps the limitless resource that is God's power. Faith in Jesus Christ is the conduit that unleashes the power of believing. When we fail to receive the Father's power-filled invitation to become sons and daughters of God, we're doomed to a power failure in our lives. But when we respond to that invitation, we receive everything He has given through His Son, who gives us everything that is His. Whenever needed, God's power is available to us and there is no shortage or depletion. We can withstand anything that comes our way because all that belongs to Him is ours, including His power. !

❧

Heavenly Father, lead me to the power source that never runs dry. Through Your Holy Spirit grant me the power to withstand any blast the enemy may throw at me. In Jesus' Name. Amen.

THE VIEW INSIDE

But the fearful, and unbelieving, and the abominable, and murderers, and whoremongers, and sorcerers, and idolaters, and all liars, shall have their part in the lake which burneth with fire and brimstone: which is the second death.

REVELATION 21:8, KJV

Are you the type of person who fast-forwards the DVD player or turns to the end of the novel first without going through the entire story? The Bible provides a history of life on earth, from beginning to end. It opens with the awesomeness of God's creativity as He creates the heavens, earth, man, and woman. It ends with a picture of that same earth being destroyed while a new one—free from the domination of sin—takes its place. Fast-forwarding, or flipping to the end, our view is based on our position in Christ.

While the truthfulness and changelessness of the Bible is under attack, its power as the indisputable Word of God is the same. Attempts to categorize the Bible as nothing more than a book of poetry and parables is not only erroneous, it's a work of the evil one. If the Bible is just a book, then its words are *just* words. Nothing could be further from the truth! The Bible is our road map of history, life, and the future. In it are two foundational truths: 1) Man is sinful and the penalty of sin is death (Romans 6:23), and 2) Jesus is the only One who can pay that penalty because He is the perfect, sinless sacrifice. His death paid the debt for the whole world so we could live with Him and enjoy Him forever (1 John 2:2).

A day is coming when those who haven't placed their faith in Jesus will suffer the consequences of not turning to Him in faith. God is not mocked; those who fail to receive salvation in Jesus' Name will not be allowed to enter heaven, but will be watching from inside the lake of fire. For us, there will be a glorious view inside heaven's gate.

❧

Lord, You are the Alpha and the Omega, the Beginning and the End. I'm glad I know how the story ends! Help me remember that I have a place reserved for me inside heaven's gate. Amen.

WE SHALL OVERCOME

For whatsoever is born of God overcometh the world: and this is the victory that overcometh the world, even our faith.

1 JOHN 5:4, KJV

Do you know an "overcomer," someone who has been able to turn tragedy into victory? Someone who, when life throws them a curve ball, is still able to hit a home run? People like that have an uncanny knack for making something out of nothing. They're able to see the silver lining in every storm cloud. While many have overcome obstacles and hardships, there is the "ultimate overcomer." His name is Jesus.

During His earthly ministry, Jesus was able to overcome every stumbling block the devil placed in His path. These obstacles were in the form of attacks from Satan, Scribes, Pharisees, and even His own disciples. "These things I have spoken unto you, that in me ye might have peace. In the world ye shall have tribulation: but be of good cheer; I have overcome the world" (John 16:33). He overcame sin and death, and because of Him, we can overcome. Our faith in Christ opens the windows of heaven to His abounding grace.

His grace has made it possible for us to bear the difficulties that come our way. Today's life is filled with economic and moral challenges. As sojourners in this world, we are forced to navigate a landscape filled with both spiritual and natural obstacles. These impediments take many forms: attacks on our physical health, our prayer life, our familial and social relations, and our financial well-being. God is more than aware of the trials and tribulations we face. He even knows the number of hairs on our head! God reminds us that when we are born again, we are not reborn as powerless babes but as powerful saints of the living God. We receive power to overcome the difficulties we'll face in this mortal body. "But ye shall receive power, after that the Holy Ghost is come upon you" (Acts 1:8).

Jesus' life provides us with the ultimate model to overcome the obstacles we'll encounter as we live out this Christian walk. Overcoming obstacles requires great effort, but the rewards are even greater. Because of Jesus, we shall overcome!

❧

Father, I know that in You I have the power of the Holy Ghost to overcome all the obstacles I encounter as I walk this Christian journey. Thank You for giving me Your Son to demonstrate that I, too, can overcome. Amen.

DO NOT PRACTICE SIN

Those who have been born into God's family do not make a practice of sinning, because God's life is in them. So they can't keep on sinning, because they are children of God.

1 JOHN 3:9, NLT

"It is absolutely impossible to live a sin free life!" bellowed the passionate preacher. Tears ran down Mitzi's face. "Lord," she whispered, "I am so sorry I messed up. Forgive me, please." Mitzi was grateful for the pastor of her new Bible-teaching church. She was so thankful to know one indiscretion did not remove her from God's family. She was a child of God continually in need of God's grace.

Mitzi had been raised in a church tradition that taught "real" saints did not sin. In reality not only did members of that church sin, but they also hid their sin and put on their good church faces to hide their struggles. They talked against what they considered to be the "big sins" (such as fornication and adultery) while overlooking other sins (such as telling "little white lies"). In reality, all sin is missing God's mark and is an affront to a Holy God!

The apostle John, of the first century, grappled with the complexity of the sin issue also. God calls for us to be holy, yet we still live our Christian life in human flesh that is prone to error. John made it clear, "If we claim we have no sin, we are only fooling ourselves and not living in the truth" (1 John 1:8). Instead, John argued, anyone born of God does not practice sin. The believer may commit sin on occasion, but he or she will not be characterized by a life of habitual sin. The seed or life of God within will not allow the believer to consistently act contrary to his or her new nature.

Thank God for grace that frees us from leading a false life, and yet doesn't condemn us when we miss the mark. Like Mitzi, we come to realize that God's grace empowers us to grow spiritually, changing our nature.

❧

Lord, thank You for choosing me to be born into Your family. I thank You for the seed of righteousness within and for my new nature! Thank You for grace. Amen

No Turning Back

Now the just shall live by faith: but if any man draw back, my soul shall have no pleasure in him. But we are not of them who draw back unto perdition; but of them that believe to the saving of the soul.

HEBREWS 10:38-39, KJV

It's been said that you can't go home again, yet how many of us fondly reminisce about the "good old days." We "wax poetic" about how we didn't have much money, but a caring community more than made-up for it. We compare the freedom and safety of yesterday's idyllic upbringing with today's uncertain, manic environment. While there are some reasons to long for yesterday, there is more promise in making *today* the best ever. When we rewind our lives, we engage in a selective process. No matter how great the past, if it was lived in sin, it brings no pleasure to God.

The Jewish believers, who first received the letter to the Hebrews, were persecuted by the government and ridiculed by their own people. It would have been easy to return to Judaism and a life of comfort with no threat of death, but they had not turned back. The writer of Hebrews commends these Jewish Christians for standing strong through all manner of persecution. He then encourages them to stay strong, to not allow any pressure—even the pressure of a death sentence—to dissuade them from standing firm in their faith.

When we walk in the light of our new birth in Christ, there is no option to revisit our sinful past. Repentance means to turn away from sin, and to sin no more. Faith forges us to live holy in the present and future, despite the hard times that may come. This is the faith that brings pleasure to God when He looks at the life we lead. It is a faith that inspires us to look forward, with great expectation, to our eternal home. It is a faith that has no turning back.

❧

Lord, I look forward to that time when I will go home to spend eternity with You. Help me to use every waking moment to redeem the time, to bring honor and glory to Your holy name. Amen.

THE PERFECT MEDIATOR

And for this cause he is the mediator of the new testament, that by means of death, for the redemption of the transgressions that were under the first testament, they which are called might receive the promise of eternal inheritance.

HEBREWS 9:15, KJV

We live in a litigation-crazed world. If someone stubs a toe on the sidewalk, the person wants to sue because the curb is too high. If someone orders a beverage, he or she wants to sue because it is too hot or too cold. We are bombarded with advertisements from brash lawyers willing to take any claim—no matter how frivolous—to court. Greed and the chance of easy money have created a mantra of "sue first, forgive second."

Yet there is a higher court, a court that will determine where we will spend eternity. In that court, there are no frivolous claims. In that court, God is the judge. No matter how much we try to argue on behalf of our past, God's judgment is defined in the Old Testament and requires a death payment for sin. Under the Old Testament, no lawyer, no matter how persuasive, could argue on our behalf. We cannot stand before the Almighty Judge thinking that our wits, our charms, or our human efforts and accomplishments will help us. In God's court, we have only one Mediator: Christ Jesus. For there is one God, and one mediator between God and men, the man Christ Jesus (1 Timothy 2:5).

Over two thousand years ago, Jesus Christ entered this world as our perfect mediator. Because He is God, He is able to stand before us. Because He came to earth to live as a man, He stood in for us, taking our sin upon Him and paying our sentence of death. Jesus not only paid sin's debt, He is also our mediator—lawyer—before God's throne. When we live in Jesus, there is no fear of standing before God. With Jesus it's "Case Closed," and the sentence is eternal life. Jesus is our mediator, and He has never lost a case.

Lord, thank You for being my perfect mediator. Bless me to appreciate Your ultimate sacrifice by living a life that brings no shame or dishonor to You. Amen.

WE'RE IN THIS TOGETHER

If we suffer, we shall also reign with him: if we deny him, he also will deny us.
2 TIMOTHY 2:12, KJV

The suffering Savior is an iconic image but it's a visual that is in competition with other, more prosperous, images of Jesus Christ. Today's materialistic world tries to replace the Christ of the cross with the Christ of the cash register. A growing number of Christians are being drawn to the Gospel based on the promise of immediate prosperity rather than the promise of eternal life in the world to come. This is not to say that being born again doesn't have immediate benefits. The true blessings of being an heir of God are found not only in the spiritual prosperity of being a child of the King but also in partaking in the suffering and servanthood that Christ demonstrated during His earthly ministry.

It is God's will that none should perish (2 Peter 3:9), but the journey is not easy. "For unto you it is given in the behalf of Christ, not only to believe on Him, but also to suffer for his sake" (Philippians 1:29). We're in this race together, and Jesus Christ is our leader and our ultimate model. If He went through it, rest assured, we can, too. Despite the hardships, we cannot deny our relationship with Jesus or disavow His Lordship in our lives. It is God's desire to equip us with all the tools necessary to run this race called life. Being able to endure hardships provides a strong foundation for running this Christian race. When we exercise our capacity to suffer and serve in a Christ-like manner, we show a hungry world that our faith extends far beyond the superficial.

God likens our walk to refining gold, which produces a beautiful product at great cost: "That the trial of your faith, being much more precious than of gold that perisheth, though it be tried with fire, might be found unto praise and honour and glory at the appearing of Jesus Christ" (1 Peter 1:7).

※

Lord, bless me to never deny You in word or deed. Grant me the singular ability to endure suffering that will set the true image of what it means to be a Christian. Amen.

WORK AT IT

Wherefore, my beloved, as ye have always obeyed, not as in my presence only, but now much more in my absence, work out your own salvation with fear and trembling.

PHILIPPIANS 2:12, KJV

When a male child is born, he is fully equipped at birth to become a man, but he has to grow and mature into manhood. To do that, he needs a male role model. The influence of that example can be either direct or indirect. If direct, the boy can observe the man's example and decide to be the same type of person. Indirectly, the boy's observations can lead him to be the opposite of his male example. Both direct and indirect influences are instrumental in molding a boy into a man.

As in the birth of a male child, once we are born again spiritually, we, too, must grow and mature. When we are born again, we have everything we need, since we are filled with the power of the Holy Ghost and instantly saved from the guilt and penalty of sin. Paul explains that we are being delivered from the habit and dominion of sin. Our model is Jesus Christ, and His direct influence calls for us to be entirely conformed to His image.

Paul was an example to the saints at Philippi. In Philippians 2:12, Paul urges them to take responsibility for their own faith walk because the same God that was in him was in the Philippians. Even though Paul was absent from them, there was no reason for the Philippians to be afraid to move to the next level of spiritual maturity because God was with them. The Philippians did not need to be afraid to work at it, and neither should we.

Oh God, I want to grow in the knowledge of Your Word so I can live a life that's pleasing to You. Help me work out my salvation, growing and maturing in Your Word. Amen.

KEEPING CHRIST IN MIND

By which also ye are saved, if ye keep in memory what I preached unto you, unless ye have believed in vain.

1 CORINTHIANS 15:2, KJV

Our memories are the windows to our souls. They are valuable, therapeutic assets. Our memories allow us to revisit moments from our past that provide joy, encouragement, and healing when the cares of this world seem too depressing or overwhelming. Likewise, memory provides the ability to block painful past experiences, shut the door on areas of our lives that are best forgotten, and cope with present-day pressures. As Christians, our fondest memories revolve around receiving Jesus as our Savior and coming to know the power of Christ. The Lord wants us to always remember His Word and the journey we've traveled to walk upright before Him. These memories strengthen our faith and our ability to cope with future trials.

We are saved by faith (Ephesians 2:8), and our faith is strengthened when we remember the Word of God. In this text, Paul talks of remembering the preached Word. King David felt that committing God's Word to memory was so important that he referred to it as storing God's Word in his heart to ensure that he would not commit future sins against the Lord (Psalm 119:11).

When we commit God's Word to our hearts, we shut the door on memories of our sinful past, memories that the enemy could use to bring us down with feelings of guilt and shame. Memorizing God's Word, and its application to our struggles and triumphs in overcoming sin, strengthens us in our fight against Satan. With these memories stored in our souls, we realize our lives are not lived in vain. Memory strengthened with God's Word lets us know that what we do for Christ will last, and it assures us that the Lord will keep us in perfect peace because our minds are stayed on Him, in whom we trust (Isaiah 26:3).

Lord, bless me to commit Your Word to heart so when the storms of this world well up in my life, thoughts of Your saving hand will lead me safely to shore.

WORKING ON GRACE

And if by grace, then is it no more of works: otherwise grace is no more grace. But if it be of works, then it is no more grace: otherwise work is no more work.

ROMANS 11:6, KJV

Have you ever been the recipient of grace? Have you received unmerited favor or generosity for something you know you didn't deserve? Have you ever had a past indiscretion concealed? If you're a Christian, perhaps you can answer yes to many of those questions. It is because of God's grace that we are extended an invitation to salvation through Jesus Christ. And so it was important for the apostle Paul to make a keen distinction between grace and works.

Grace is a virtue that is hard to see or define, but you definitely know when you are its recipient. Even though works are important to the Christian faith, when it comes to salvation grace is superior. Works can show our love of the Lord, but if we're not careful, the spotlight can shift away from the Lord to focus on us. Grace is the reason Jesus went to the cross. If grace is so important to the Lord, it should be just as important to us. We need to contemplate grace.

In what areas of our lives can we extend grace to others? Is grace found in our relations with family members and coworkers? Can we see examples of grace in how we interact with someone who has committed a wrong against us? Can we find enough grace to forgive an act that seems unforgivable?

In many respects, these examples show how the grace of God has been extended to us. Shouldn't we do the same for others? Working on grace takes effort. If grace were an easy virtue, its value would be diminished. The Lord wants us to set a spiritual priority when it comes to grace and work: "Who hath saved us, and called us with a holy calling, not according to our works, but according to His own purpose and grace" (2 Timothy 1:9).

❦

God, grant me the ability to extend to others that wondrous grace You extend to me every waking day of my life. In Jesus' Name. Amen.

WALKING IN THE SPIRIT

But ye are not in the flesh, but in the Spirit, if so be that the Spirit of God dwell in you. Now if any man have not the Spirit of Christ, he is none of His.
ROMANS 8:9, KJV

To walk in the Spirit requires that we first have the Spirit of God—the "gift" of the Holy Ghost, whom the Lord gives to all who believe. On the Day of Pentecost (the day the church was born), Peter said, "Repent, and be baptized every one of you in the name of Jesus Christ for the remission of sins, and ye shall receive the gift of the Holy Ghost" (Acts 2:38). The Holy Ghost is our identifying marker, our seal in the Lord, "in whom ye also trusted, after that ye heard the word of truth, the gospel of your salvation: in whom also after that ye believed, ye were sealed with that Holy Spirit of promise" (Ephesians 1:13). Just before ascending to heaven, Jesus made this promise: "Ye shall receive power, after that the Holy Ghost is come upon you: and ye shall be witnesses unto me" (Acts 1:8). The Spirit grants us the power to resist the flesh and walk in the Spirit.

Where we walk and how we walk says a lot about us. As Christians, we are to walk in a manner worthy of our calling in God. We need to be careful when choosing which places to visit because, whether we like it or not, people are watching us. The Lord also watches us. "Dost thou not watch over my sin?" (Job 14:16b). Our walk is a reflection of our standing in Christ. Do we walk in the Spirit as God commands, or do we give in to sin and walk in the flesh? A pedometer measures the physical steps we take, but the Word of God serves as both a road map for the course we should take and a measure of how we walk. Similarly, the Holy Spirit is an active compass that lets us know immediately when we veer off course and walk in the flesh instead of the Spirit. Are you on course?

❧

Lord, order my steps. Grant me the power to walk where You want me to walk and to always acknowledge the Spirit wherever I go. Amen.

TO SEE HIM IS TO BELIEVE IN HIM

But shewed first unto them of Damascus, and at Jerusalem, and throughout all the coasts of Judaea, and then to the Gentiles, that they should repent and turn to God, and do works meet for repentance.

ACTS 26:20, KJV

Jesus is the most documented and most powerful man in history. His impact is so great that for centuries, history's time line was split into two: B.C. (Before Christ) and A.D. (Anno Domini, Year of our Lord). Yet in spite of all the irrefutable references to His deity and existence, we can still find a growing chorus of skeptics who are intent on questioning whether Jesus is real. During His earthly ministry even Jesus had to deal with naysayers who questioned if He was who He said He was. In fact, one of His disciples, Thomas, questioned if Jesus, with whom he walked, talked, ate, and slept had in fact risen from the grave (John 20:24-29).

Likewise, the Gospel and epistle writers wrote in response to the skepticism around this new faith in God. In this text, Paul gives his testimony to King Agrippa and explains how he spread the Gospel to combat disbelief and skepticism. Paul preached to Jews first, and then to Gentiles. His message was simple yet profound: repent, turn to God, and do works that meet for repentance.

Repeatedly, the Word points to paths where Jesus walked and to persons with whom Jesus talked, all in an effort to dispel any myths or stumbling blocks that would prevent people from believing that Jesus Christ is Lord. When Jesus appeared to Thomas, He said, "because thou hast seen me, thou hast believed: blessed are they that have not seen, and yet have believed" (John 20:29).

Today, we see Jesus not with our eyes, but with our hearts. Therefore, to see Him is to believe Him. To believe Him is to know we need Him. To receive Him is to take advantage of the greatest gift ever offered to humankind: salvation in Jesus' Name. If you have seen Him, believe Him, and live today to His glory and in His power.

※

Lord, thank You for opening my eyes to the Glory that can only be found in You. Help me to never take my eyes off You. Help me to see You more clearly and believe You more deeply each day. Amen.

ROOTS

But the ones on the rock are those who, when they hear, receive the Word with joy; and these have no root, who believe for a while and in time of temptation fall away.

LUKE 8:13, NKJV

Bishop Arthur M. Brazier once told this story: When he was young, he noticed a new saint who shouted, sang, and clapped in church with tremendous enthusiasm. Later, Bishop Brazier told his mother how he admired the man's great faith. She replied, "People can run real fast in the front door and then run right out the back." There's joy when we first understand the Gospel and when we first feel the welcoming grace of God, but we need more than initial enthusiasm. We need to put down some roots, grab hold, and stay.

The Christian walk is a journey, not a quick trip. Paul tells of our starting out as babes in Christ, needing milk (1 Corinthians 3:1-2), but eventually we must get to the meat. We need to face the deeper, harder issues of what God requires of us—facing the fact that the Christian walk can be difficult. There are perplexing places where we have to thoughtfully choose right from wrong. Certainly there are times of great blessing, but there are also times the blessing comes in the midst of struggle and sorrow. If we have no roots, the wind will blow us right off the path.

Let us sit and listen to the mothers and elders of the church. Make friends with a saint who has been saved for thirty, forty, or fifty years. There is a depth to their thinking that surpasses education. They know what is tried and true. Seek preachers and teachers of depth who provide insight to the Scriptures. Read the writings of people who have lived strong lives for Christ—Frederick Douglass, C.S. Lewis, Gardner C. Taylor, and others who have carefully thought about what it means to follow Christ. Let's take advantage of the opportunities God gives us to put down roots, and allow good teaching to sink into our hearts so we may grab strongly to God's truth.

Jesus, You saved me, not for the short term but for eternity. As I grow in Your grace, help me to be rooted and grounded in Your Word. Help me live so that I am more and more deeply anchored in You. Amen.

GOOD NEWS

And saying, "The time is fulfilled, and the kingdom of God is at hand. Repent, and believe in the gospel."

MARK 1:15, NKJV

Every day, we watch the news on television or on our computers, or read it in the newspapers. Typically, the news is not good. What would happen if we turned on the TV and heard the most incredibly good news imaginable? Would we embrace it?

At the beginning of His teaching ministry, Jesus announced a momentous time in the history of the world—a time when prophecies would be fulfilled, a time when God's will would be done on earth, as it is in Heaven. He announced a transformation in the relationship between God and humanity.

Can we grasp how incredibly significant that was? The ramifications of His ministry, His death, and His resurrection reach across 2,000 years to impact our lives in a most personal way. His Holy Spirit speaks in our lives, lifting us up from the fog of confusion that defined our lives before we repented. "Repent and believe," Jesus told the people. It is the same message we hear from the pulpit today: repent and turn away from sin. Believe the Gospel, the Good News, the remarkable news that God loves us so much that He sent His Son to die for our sins. For the people of His day, Jesus preached a startling new concept that many struggled to understand. In our day, we have heard this concept so often that we may miss its profound significance.

It sounds simple: repent and believe. Yet, He asks us to embrace a fundamental transformation in our hearts, our minds, and our souls. We step across a threshold into a light that we could not have previously imagined. We see things differently. We feel the Holy Spirit's guidance. We bask in grace, the unmerited favor of God. We call on God's protection. We seek His guidance. He is our Good Shepherd. *Surely goodness and mercy shall follow us* (Psalm 23:6). Let us begin this day rejoicing that the kingdom of God is at hand.

❧

Jesus, You brought us a message of hope and transformation. I thank You. Please give me a better understanding of how wonderful Your message is. Let Your message touch every moment of my day so Your will can be done in my life. Amen.

GOD'S LAW

And then I will declare to them, 'I never knew you; depart from Me, you who practice lawlessness!'

MATTHEW 7:23, NKJV

In a country that highly values freedom, we continuously struggle with the tension between freedom and law. Groups guard our rights to do as we please, while politicians promise to hire more police to enforce the law. We want to constrict others by law so we may feel safe, yet we do not want to be constrained. Jesus warns us against wanting unbridled freedom. Our God is a God of righteousness, justice, and order. Certainly there is joy and freedom in God's grace and mercy, but that does not give us permission to practice lawlessness.

Temptation may surround us, and whatever sin we are prone to may sneak up unexpectedly, even when we are committed to following God's laws. But if we demand, as a right, that we may violate those laws, then we can expect God's displeasure. It is a way of thinking like a spoiled child that demands whatever he or she wants. What a picture—that we would stand in God's face demanding to do whatever we wanted! Surely God would say, "Get away from me." If day-by-day we practice violating those laws, then of course God would say, "I never knew you, and you don't know Me."

When God knows us and we know God, we see that His laws are the best rules of life there can be. There are no improvements we can make. To decide for ourselves what is right, when clearly we are violating God's laws, is essentially saying, "I know better than God." Such a thought is the core of sin. It was Adam and Eve's mistake, and it is the mistake inherent in all sin. To live a lifestyle imagining one knows better than God is the epitome of pride. Such thinking does not lead to freedom, but instead slides toward destruction. We must trust that God's way is the best way.

❧

Oh God, my Father, You have laid out Your law for me. I want to obey You in all that I do. There are times when I follow my own thinking and I make a mistake, but Lord, I do respect Your laws. I want to know You, and I thank You for knowing me.

BUILD THE KINGDOM

Not everyone who says to Me, 'Lord, Lord,' shall enter the kingdom of heaven, but he who does the will of My Father in heaven.

MATTHEW 7:21, NKJV

There is a saying used at construction sites: "He can talk a good job," meaning one can talk about the job, but he or she doesn't accomplish very much. In construction, work is actually measured by how many bricks are laid and how much concrete is poured. Talking about work means little; it's the doing that matters. Jesus spent years working as a carpenter. Like today's construction workers, He appreciated the doing more than the talking. Do the will of my Father; don't just talk about it.

Sometimes people consider doing God's will a grand thing—building a huge ministry, being a great preacher, or receiving accolades from the far corners of the earth. But doing God's will is more often a day-to-day concept in the corner of the earth we live right now. It is kindness to those God sends your way. It is encouragement to those who are struggling right now. It is setting aside something we desire to help someone in need. There are those whom God anoints to do the grand things, but all of us can do the daily things.

We might be tempted to think of our daily actions as little things, but every brick counts. As we go through this day and strive to do God's will in every moment, we participate in the brick-by-brick building of God's Kingdom. We spread His Good News by our words, by our example, and by our choices. Whatever our occupation, whether it looks like ministry or not, if we stay in God's will, we will contribute to His Kingdom in ways we often do not appreciate. There will be a co-worker who knows he or she can depend on our honesty. There will be a customer who would prefer to work with us because he or she feels a sense of peace in our presence. We will understand that petty squabbles are not worth destroying relationships. We can remain calm when others are distressed or afraid. It's not because we talk about it; it's because of what we do each day.

❧

Jesus, this day is laid before me. Guide my thoughts, conversations, actions, and interactions. Let me do Your will each moment of this day. In Jesus' Name. Amen.

AN UNEARNED INHERITANCE

In whom also we have obtained an inheritance, being predestined according to the purpose of him who worketh all things after the counsel of his own will.
EPHESIANS 1:11, KJV

Ephesians is one of the most beautifully written books in the Bible. In it, we find superlatives used throughout—the apostle Paul's attempt to reveal the believer's security through the many blessings God has already provided. He begins the letter with an impressive list of blessings: we have been blessed with all spiritual blessings in heavenly places; we have been chosen in Him before the foundation of the world; He has predestinated us unto the adoption of children by Jesus Christ; we have been made accepted in the beloved; we have received redemption through the blood of Jesus; we have received the forgiveness of sins; grace has been abounded toward us in all wisdom and prudence; and we have been blessed to know the mystery of His Will. Wow! To think God has already made provision for all these blessings!

And if that wasn't enough, Paul then writes about the crowning jewel of blessings: we have obtained an inheritance. Notice the verbiage Paul uses here—almost clandestine in his approach. Paul speaks of us as having obtained an inheritance, which, if left unqualified, is not possible because to obtain would suggest that we somehow earned or deserved it. But Paul quickly qualifies his statement by saying that we are predestinated, according to the purpose of Him who worketh all things after the counsel of His own will. In other words, we have obtained this inheritance because God willed it so! And who can stand against the counsel of God's will? Surely He is the highest of all authorities, and His will settles our eligibility for the inheritance, whether we're deserving of it or not.

What a blessed people we are! What a great God we serve! To think God has made such wondrous provision for us. We should serve Him all the more with gladness and come before His presence with singing, for the Lord is good, His mercy is everlasting, and His truth endures to all generations.

🕊

Lord, thanks for so many blessings already given. Thank You for having the security of my salvation on Your mind before You formed the foundations of this world. Amen.

NOT MY WILL

Who has saved us and called us with a holy calling, not according to our works, but according to His own purpose and grace which was given to us in Christ Jesus before time began.

2 TIMOTHY 1:9, NKJV

There is a Christian woman in Egypt who works with children living in a Cairo garbage dump. They call her Mama Maggie. She founded Stephen's Children, an organization that provides clinics and schools for thousands of poor children. Mama Maggie was nominated for the 2011 Nobel Peace Prize, but when she speaks of her work, she begins with the words, "I am the least."[29] Her humility allows her to look into the eyes of the poorest children and see their pain and their needs. She is entirely attuned to an understanding that she is doing God's work.

Works alone do not save us; that is clear. What is less clear is that our calling is not our decision, either. We talk about "my ministry," claiming ownership of what we do for Christ. This sends us down the wrong road. If it is "my" ministry, then we get to decide its purpose and direction. Following leadership becomes secondary, which leads us to anger when the pastor wants to do it another way. We start to rail against obstacles in our path, although, if we really looked, we might see that God set up those obstacles in an attempt to send us in another direction. This can happen even after years in the ministry. The vision of fifteen years ago was fine, but now God wants some changes; yet we dig in our heels and bemoan how wonderful it used to be.

God wants it done "according to His purpose and grace." We have to resist that confident urge to have our *own* vision and decide how *we* are going to do it. Instead, we must seek God's purpose—beginning at the beginning and continuing down the path. Then we will see His Grace extended to the work. His unmerited favor will anoint the ministry, producing results far beyond what our vision and our efforts could possibly accomplish.

✷

Jesus, let me know what You want me to do today, according to Your purpose and grace. Let me trust You entirely, leaning on Your understanding, not my own. In Jesus' Name. Amen.

THE NAME ABOVE ALL OTHERS

There is salvation in no one else! God has given no other name under heaven by which we must be saved.

ACTS 4;12, NLT

Some people put great stock in names—such as the name on a handbag or a designer label. Some of those names have come to represent brands that stand for quality and elegance, and others for chic style. Besides impressing people with taste in clothes or accessories, what can those names really do for us? Today's Scripture tells of a name that exceeds all brands—and that is the name Jesus.

Jesus literally means "Jehovah our Savior." And though there have been others with the name Jesus, the authority for salvation rests in one: Jesus the Christ, the Son of God, the Savior of humankind, God incarnate. When the angel prophesied His birth, he told Joseph, "and he shall be called Jesus, for he shall save his people from their sin" (Matthew 1:21).

Earlier in Acts 3, Peter and John had healed a lame man by the authority of the name Jesus. When questioned about this miraculous deed, Peter proclaimed Jesus as Savior, and more than five thousand heard the word and believed. Yet Peter and John were thrown in jail and challenged by the religious elite, "by what power or authority have you done this?" (Acts 4:7). Peter proclaimed that what they did, they did by the authority of the name of Jesus of Nazareth, who was crucified, and who God had raised from the dead. In fact, they proceeded to proclaim that salvation could be found in no one else, for there is no other name to be found under heaven by whom we must be saved!

The name of Jesus is the name for salvation. Jesus supersedes the names of all other religious leaders. Jesus supersedes all religious formulas! The name Jesus is the name for healing, salvation and deliverance. In a day and age where so many people are trying to make names for themselves, isn't it good to know that we have been saved by the authority of the name that is backed up in heaven? There's no brand stronger than or as enduring as Jesus!

❧

Heavenly Father, I thank You for the power and authority that rests in the name Jesus! I am grateful that I have been saved through that mighty name! Amen.

LIVING A SHAMELESS LIFE

For I am not ashamed of the gospel of Christ: for it is the power of God unto salvation to every one that believeth; to the Jew first, and to the Greek.

ROMANS 1:16, KJV

Whether or not we admit it, we have all done something in our past or present that we are ashamed of. Some of us may be ashamed to admit how much we ate during Thanksgiving dinner. We may be ashamed of something we did to cause someone harm. A life that dwells on the past is not a productive life, however. It's like riding a bicycle forward while looking back over your shoulder.

Think how often God opened doors for us to witness, but we were reluctant to do so and felt so ashamed afterward. Given the opportunity, we want to share with others the power of the Gospel. What approach should we use?

Maybe we could start with something like, "Good evening, I am an ambassador of God, representing Jesus Christ and His Kingdom. Are you familiar with the power of God and how it can change your life through salvation?" That should grab someone's ear! Suppose we mention that Jesus said, "I am the way and the truth and the life. No one comes to the Father except through me" (John 14:6). How impressive! What would a stranger say if we shared that God provided salvation for us through grace, a grace that empowers men and women to receive forgiveness of their sins. Still, we could also share how one would be delivered from Satan's domination—Hallelujah! "No one on this earth can promise that power." Only God has all power; He allowed His Son Jesus Christ to die for our iniquities—past, present, and future.

How would we finalize our approach? What about informing others that the Gospel is contained in the greatest book ever written: the Bible. Oh! Do not forget to tell them about the grand prize to those willing to accept salvation: they will live a shameless life in eternity with our Father in heaven.

❧

My God, thank You for Your love and the ability to witness to lost souls each day. Please help me to be sincere and direct. In Jesus' Name I pray. Amen.

THE GAME CHANGER

He that believeth and is baptized shall be saved; but he that believeth not shall be damned.

MARK 16:16, KJV

Before meeting Jesus, the apostles had followed the Law of Moses and anticipated physical deliverance from Roman oppression. The three years they spent with Jesus had changed their perspective. They had witnessed first-hand the power of God. Yet, despite first-hand accounts of Jesus' Resurrection, the eleven apostles were struggling to believe that Jesus had risen from the dead, as He had said He would.

It is easy to sympathize with them. They were afraid of the Jewish officials who had wanted Jesus dead and the Roman government that carried out the execution. We can speculate that they were in shock, depressed, or just needed more time. But Mark 16:14 tells us that Jesus entered the room and rebuked them for their disbelief.

The event of Jesus' death, burial, and resurrection was the game-changer, and He had spent three years preparing them for it! Resurrection meant that all of the prophecy and the Law were fulfilled. Resurrection meant that deliverance was a matter of believing Jesus as the Son of God who gave His life that they (and we) could have eternal life. Jesus rebuked their disbelief because their faith would testify to the trustworthiness of His words, and His sacrifice, as they finally stepped into their true mission: to preach the gospel everywhere and to all people.

Our encounter with the game-changing gospel of Jesus Christ means that we, too, have to make a choice to believe or not believe that Jesus Christ rose from the dead for our sakes. Our baptism in Jesus' Name is our public confession of faith in Christ's power to take away our sins and to give us the gift of the Holy Ghost. Based on our belief in the Gospel message, we are saved from the judgment of God and born again into new life. Rejection of the Gospel is acceptance of condemnation at the judgment of God.

The Gospel message is still the game-changer. Despite our fears and worries, we can believe the report: Jesus Christ is alive!

🖎

Lord, help me to trust in Your word and to embrace baptism in Your Name as my public confession that I am Yours. Help me to spread the Good News of salvation to everyone I encounter. Amen.

JESUS CHRIST IS THE WAY

Knowing that a man is not justified by the works of the law, but by the faith of Jesus Christ, even we have believed in Jesus Christ, that we might be justified by the faith of Christ, and not by the works of the law: for by the works of the law shall no flesh be justified.

GALATIANS 2:16, KJV

For Roger, Gail was the woman he wanted for a wife; but, he felt that her family didn't think much of him, since he and his troubled family had always lived next door. Roger decided that winning the favor of his potential in-laws was the way to Gail's heart. His efforts included expensive gifts for their birthdays and cutting their grass when he mowed his mom's lawn.

As ridiculous as Roger's plan may seem, some of us try to earn God's favor the same way. We join every possible church auxiliary and eventually are so stretched that our reputation for faithfulness and quality of service is called into question. We make a big show of giving an offering or carry a huge Bible that we really don't open very often.

Likewise, Israel followed the Law of Moses as a way to gain God's favor. They knew that the prophets and the Law pointed to a Messiah who would lead all people to God, but they placed their trust in a cultural heritage that gave preference to the sacrifices they brought to the altar, the sacred feast days, and the foods that followed a strict standard.

In chapter two of Galatians, Paul recalls an incident where he reminded Peter that faith in the death, burial, and resurrection of Jesus Christ, not the works of the Law, is the only way to be right before God. Faith in Christ means trusting Him as Savior. It means being led by the Holy Spirit in all areas of our lives. Our actions should always honor God and give Him glory, but we can never work our way to heaven or earn a place in God's Kingdom. Regardless of our culture, race, or social status, Jesus Christ is the *only* way to be called righteous by God.

※

Thank You, Lord, for the security of salvation made possible through the sacrifice on Calvary's cross. Help me to trust and honor You in all I do. Amen.

OUR PERMANENT SOURCE OF CONFIDENCE

Therefore, he is able to save completely those who come to God through him,
because he always lives to intercede for them.

HEBREWS 7:25, NIV

For the really important things in life, permanent is better than temporary. Consider the uneasiness we feel when the bank we have trusted for years is taken over by another corporation. On a job, employees get nervous when "temporary management" is put in place. Children suffer during divorce because the security they need is frustrated. The uneasiness bred by temporary fixes makes us wonder what's next and whom we can trust.

Permanence breeds confidence. The writer of Hebrews puts forth a discussion of the Old Testament priesthood, the structure by which Israel sought God's forgiveness and guidance. Under the Law of Moses, the tribe of Levi was designated as the priests. The Levites took care of the Temple and made sure the Law was strictly followed. It was their job to offer the animal sacrifices, brought by the people to God, as a way of seeking God's forgiveness for sins. Generation after generation, the Levites served, leaving office only upon death.

But that was the rub. Each priest died! Regardless of their faithfulness to the job, they could not do it forever. Death made it necessary for a new priest to take their place. The Old Testament priesthood was temporary. The animal sacrifices were not the permanent fix for sin. The men who entered the Temple and prayed for the people were not there to do it forever. In fact, they had their own sins to confess.

But God had a permanent solution: Jesus Christ is our high priest forever. We can trust Him because He was with God from the beginning. In fact, He is God! (John 1:1-4). Jesus Christ came to earth as the sacrifice who takes away the penalty of sin and death forever. His resurrection gives us assurance of His priesthood and is the source of our confidence—that Jesus lives to intercede for us. Through the permanence of Jesus Christ we are saved forever and will one day live forever with Him.

※

My Lord and my Savior, thank You for the permanence of Your love and the
security of Your eternal grace. Amen.

ONWARD CHRISTIAN SOLDIERS

And now he has made all of this plain to us by the appearing of Christ Jesus,
our Savior. He broke the power of death and illuminated the way to life and
immortality through the Good News.

2 TIMOTHY 1:10, NLT

Reflecting on the old hymn "Onward Christian Soldiers" by
Sabine Baring-Gould provides a sense of intent and purpose
when singing the first verse: *"Onward Christian soldiers, marching*
as to war, With the cross of Jesus going on before. Christ, the royal
Master, leads against the foe; Forward into battle, see His banners go!"[30]

In our key Scripture today, the apostle Paul encourages his
young mentee, Timothy, to be strong and stand firm in the teachings
of his mother and grandmother, and to never be ashamed of sharing
the Good News. Paul's time is running out, but he wants to assure
Timothy that there is nothing more important than continuing to
spread the Gospel of Jesus Christ. He advises Timothy to stand
strong in the midst of opposition because the message of salvation
is greater than our challenges. The Good News brings hope and
anticipation of life eternal in God. God called us to this life by His
grace from eternity past, and our testimony is factual by Christ's
appearance.

It is important to boldly and confidently move forward in
our witnessing. Jesus told us to go and teach all nations of God's
saving grace. Persecution and suffering may come, but we are to
remain steadfast and unmovable in the work of the Lord. We can
ask ourselves how many times have we taken sides, supported, and
labored for an unsure, doubting, and weak individual. Probably
not as much as we should because the world's way is *only the strong*
survive. But our strength comes from the Lord and not ourselves.
He is on our side. Even though we may be ridiculed, shaken, and
turned back, Christ, the royal Master, leads against the foe.

So we have a charge this day to go out and tell others about the
love and mercy of Jesus Christ. He said He would never leave us
nor forsake us, so there is no need to be fearful. Onward Christian
soldiers!

❧

Father, in the Name of Jesus, how glad I am to have You by my side. I praise
You for giving me the victory through my Lord and Savior, Jesus Christ.
Amen.

BREAD FROM HEAVEN

Jesus replied, "I am the bread of life. Whoever comes to me will never be hungry again. Whoever believes in me will never be thirsty."

JOHN 6:35, NLT

Our personal walk with the Lord is defined by our individual life experiences. Jesus becomes real to us when we can perceive or identify His handiwork through the situations of our lives. When we get answers to a family problem, a surprising monetary blessing to pay a household debt, and even a physical miracle that heals a broken body, we know it is the Lord working in us and through us.

As a result of those personal experiences, when asked the question, "Who is Jesus Christ to you?" or "How do you know you are saved?", our responses will vary based on our individual relationship with the Lord. One may say, "Jesus is my light when I cannot see my way." Another, "Jesus is my everything, because I need Him in every area of my life." Still another might say, "Jesus is the Christ, the Son of the living God." All of those responses are true because when we received Christ into our hearts, He became our personal Savior; but there is another answer that should be given by all of us.

Today's text is one of the seven I AM statements of Jesus Christ. It was spoken sometime after the Sermon on the Mount, when, using the lunch of a young boy, Jesus fed more than five thousand with two fish and five loaves of bread. The crowd witnessed a true miracle of increase but still had doubts about Jesus' identity. They asked for another miracle because they were more interested in being physically fed than having their souls eternally saved.

Jesus wanted them to take the focus off what they could see and feel, and focus on His true identity: *I AM to your soul what these fish and loaves are to your body.* Jesus came to reveal the reason we can have faith in Him. He came down from heaven to seek those who would believe on His Name. In this miracle, Jesus revealed Himself to be the Bread of Life, the Bread from heaven—the One who saves us, keeps us, forgives our sin, and makes us whole.

Taste and see Him as He is!

Father, I thank You for meeting my needs according to Your riches in Glory. Amen.

FINAL DESTINATION

He said to me: "It is done. I am the Alpha and the Omega, the Beginning and the End. To the thirsty I will give water without cost from the spring of the water of life.

REVELATION 21:6, NIV

Some avid readers flip the pages of a book to read the final chapter before starting the first one. Without a story line, or any knowledge of the characters and subplots, they search to discover how the story ends before knowing how it starts. The book of Revelation is the final book of the Bible. It reveals, in detail, the final episode of all events and key individuals of the last days. The book of Revelation is the culminating account of King Jesus' triumphant battle against Satan.

This month, we celebrate and glorify the birth of Jesus Christ. Christmas Day is a day to share love with family and friends, following the example of God loving us and freely giving us His Son. Christ came to deliver us from the darkness of hell. He showed us a new life in salvation—eternal life in the presence of our Lord Jesus Christ. Today's highlighted verse begins with one of the statements made by Jesus as He hung on the cross: *It is done!* God's eternal plan of redemption is complete. The scarlet thread of redemption weaved itself in and around the lives of those who receive Christ as Lord and Savior, and will now live forever in the heavenly city called New Jerusalem. Christ identifies Himself as the Beginning and the End—all that was, all that is, and all that is to come, came by Him (Revelation 1:8). He was there in the beginning, and He will be there in the end. Jesus Christ *is* the Creator of the ends of the earth (Isaiah 40:28).

As God's chosen people, we have inherited eternal life and can freely drink from the life-giving waters that flow forever. Eternal life is ours, and we rejoice in knowing that the place that has been prepared for us is now ready for our occupancy (John 14:2-3). Rejoice and be glad! We know how the story ends! Jesus is ours forever!

✣

Father, I thank You for Your truth, which endures forever. I thank You for blessing me with life everlasting. Amen.

FOREVER SEALED

And this is what God has testified: He has given us eternal life, and this life is in his Son.

1 JOHN 5:11, NLT

This is the Christmas season. It is a beautiful time of year because it points to the birth of Jesus Christ. In this season, we often witness the love, peace, and compassion we extend to each other. The joy and anticipation of sharing gifts, fellowship, and love point to our desire to lay aside differences, demographics, and ideologies in the name of peace and harmony. Non-Christians would dispute this claim, but this holiday centers on the greatest gift bestowed unto this world—Jesus Christ. Jesus is the true and only reason for the season. No other gift imaginable measures up to salvation, grace, eternal life, and everlasting fellowship with Christ!

But Jesus is not just for *this* season. The first epistle of John, written by the apostle John, includes several statements that proclaim our secure position in Jesus Christ. Chapter five speaks of God's love, our victory over the world, the assurance we have in salvation, the promise of eternal life, our confidence in prayer, and the power of Christ dwelling in us and with us. Verse 11 emphatically states that God's abiding love seals, or guarantees, Christ's life in us and our life, by faith, in Him. In short, our life's power source comes from Christ, who dwells in us. Our thoughts, our emotions, and our spirits are joined with Christ, and He influences all we do. We love and live through Christ. We have eternal life because of the testimony of God and our power source, Jesus Christ. God testified that He loves us with an everlasting love and gave us eternal life—the most precious gift ever!

But there is more. Because of His victory over sin and death, Christ equipped us to overcome the influences of the enemy, and to have the victory over the world and sin. Our gift, wrapped in love and filled with faith, trust, and grace, is sealed with eternal life. By God's testimony and Christ's sacrificial gift, our place in heaven with God the Father is sealed forever.

❧

Father, in the Name of Jesus, I praise You and I celebrate the gifts You have given me in Jesus Christ. Amen.

ENDLESS LOVE

God showed how much he loved us by sending his one and only Son into the world so that we might have eternal life through him.

1 JOHN 4:9, NLT

We have all experienced love of some sort—parental love, spousal love, sibling love, puppy love, and even crazy love. As simple as it sounds, love is very complex, and its greatest point touches far beyond the depth of our hearts and minds. Here, we have some profound questions to consider: Can we experience or extend agape love—the God-kind of love—to one another? What is eternity? Will anyone ever reach it?

The Bible answers these questions. It says that God is from everlasting to everlasting. The Gospel of John opens with, "In the beginning was the Word, and the Word was with God, and the Word was God" (John 1:1, NIV). At the beginning of time, God was already there with love. The Bible tells us that God reveals Himself to be a loving, caring God. He watches over His people, protects them from their enemies, and disciplines them when they disobey. His love for His people reaches beyond the scope of our understanding. The Bible even uses the word "love" to describe God! God is the essence of all that is love. God's love supersedes any effort we might make to reach the height of His love. In its fullness, love is God and God is love.

The Scripture 1 John 4:9 extends the God-kind of love—the agape love—to us. God, through His immeasurable love for us, sacrificed—or gave up—His only Son, Jesus Christ, so we could live. God gave us His only Son to free us from a lifetime of bondage. That is unconditional love. We did not deserve it, we did not earn it, but the love of God manifested itself in the most precious gift ever: His Son, our Lord and Savior, Jesus Christ. In us, God's love becomes the hope and the expectation of living in the abundance of His eternal love.

🖋

Father, what manner of love is this that we are called Your children? Thank You, Father, for Your agape love. In Jesus' Name. Amen.

PAID IN FULL

So now there is no condemnation for those who belong to Christ Jesus.

ROMANS 8:1, NLT

We all know how it feels when we are unjustly accused of something. No matter how much we attempt to right the wrong, it does not sway the opinions of those who believe the charge. It remains implanted in their minds, and we feel wronged. How did Jesus feel when all of the wrongs of sinful people were placed on His shoulders? How was He able to overcome the overwhelming burden of the world's guilt and shame? He had been accused of things He never did but was willing to suffer and die for our transgressions. He took the blame and paid the price in full for the sins of this world. That unselfish act set us free!

An old hymn written as a poem speaks of the complete and final sacrifice Jesus made for our sins. Written by Elvina M. Hall (1865) and composed by John T. Grape, "Jesus Paid it All" speaks of the witness of Christ's complete redemption for man that left no hole or crevice that guilt or blame could seep through. Verse three says, *For nothing good have I Whereby Thy grace to claim—I will wash my garments white In the blood of Calvary's Lamb. Jesus paid it all, All to Him I owe; Sin had left a crimson stain—He washed it white as snow.*

Our Scripture today is a statement made by the apostle Paul as a result of previous statements made in chapter seven. In verse one, Paul says, there is, therefore, (for that reason, or consequently, for all that was said) now no condemnation, (blame, guilt, judgment) to us who are in Christ Jesus. Meaning, for all we did, for every sin committed, for every wicked deed done or spoken, we are forgiven and the sin is forgotten.

Jesus Christ became our replacement by standing before God on our behalf. He is our Advocate, our Judge, our Mediator. Accused of lying—declared not guilty. Accused of cheating—declared not guilty. Accused of stealing—declared not guilty. Jesus paid it all! We may stumble, trip, or even fall; Christ lovingly extends His grace and forgiveness.

Father, I thank You for being the Way, the Truth, and the Life. Help me to follow hard after You. Amen.

A WISE CHOICE

No, the wisdom we speak of is the mystery of God—his plan that was previously hidden, even though he made it for our ultimate glory before the world began. But the rulers of this world have not understood it; if they had, they would not have crucified our glorious Lord. That is what the Scriptures mean when they say, "No eye has seen, no ear has heard, and no mind has imagined what God has prepared for those who love him."

1 CORINTHIANS 2:7-9, NLT

Arthur W. Pink, a twentieth-century theologian, wrote in his book *The Attributes of God* that: "God is omniscient. He knows everything: everything possible, everything actual…. He is perfectly acquainted with every detail in the life of every being in heaven…. His knowledge is perfect. He never errs, never changes, never overlooks anything."[30]

In today's Scripture, the apostle Paul reminds the people of Corinth of God's attributes because their ungodly conduct and destructive behavior had weakened the church. He reminded them that the Holy Spirit had been given to them so they could spread the Good News of salvation and eternal life through Jesus Christ. This was God's plan from the beginning. Although the prophets told it, those with corrupt hearts could not understand or perceive it. They did not have the eyes, ears, or minds to comprehend what God had in store. Paul was urging the church at Corinth to allow the Holy Spirit to open its eyes, ears, and minds so it could operate as God intended.

Pink was right: our God knows everything and His knowledge is perfect. Yet, even when we realize this, we are incapable of understanding the depth of God's wisdom and the glory He has prepared for those who love Him. Like the Corinthians, we insist on thinking that we are in control of our lives; we are not! We must not attempt to follow our own judgment or to confuse God's wisdom with man's. God's wisdom is about the ultimate glory He perceived before the world began. The wise choice for us is to study God's Word to develop eyes, ears, and minds that help us follow God's wisdom. No turning back, no turning back.

Thank You, Father, for humbling my heart and keeping my eyes on You. In Jesus' Name. Amen.

DONE!

I have glorified thee on the earth: I have finished the work which thou gavest me to do.

JOHN 17:4, KJV

A rtists' portrayals of Jesus praying, with His eyes lifted toward heaven, are powerful. The Jews believed that praying with a bowed head and closed eyes was a "guilty" posture. Lifting the head, with eyes open toward heaven and hands lifted up, indicated that a person was guilt-free and quite confident in their right to approach the throne and be heard by God. While those artists' depictions are conjecture, there is no doubt that Jesus is the epitome of guiltlessness and confidence in calling out to the Father.

Throughout the Scriptures, we find God "calling those things which be not as though they were." Well, like Father, like Son! In today's Scripture, we find Jesus in prayer before the Father, saying, "What You've given me to do, I have done." Although He had yet to go to the cross, His commitment and assurance were finished works in the mind of Christ—what utter and complete dedication to His assigned task! And what confidence He has given to us.

Because of the commitment of Jesus to finish His course—to go to the cross for the salvation of humankind—we can stand with our heads raised and our eyes lifted toward our heavenly Father, knowing that when we pray, we are heard. The level of Jesus' commitment to bring us to God by His sacrificial death is overwhelmingly stunning! To die a horrible death for those who neither knew nor loved Him is the perfect picture of what sacrifice really is. We can, therefore, be confident in the knowledge that our place in Christ, and heaven, is secure. Since Christ so willingly sacrificed Himself for the joy of bringing us to Him, our minds should be squarely focused on our God-given assignments on the earth, without worrying whether what Christ did for us is good enough to get us into heaven! We can take confidence that God would never sacrifice His Son and then count that sacrifice as invalid. We, as believers, are secure. The work has been done!

❧

Father, thank You for the perfect sacrifice of Your Son. I gladly embrace and receive all that Christ's death affords me. In Jesus' Name. Amen.

SEEK TO LIVE

For thus saith the Lord unto the house of Israel, Seek ye me, and ye shall live.

AMOS 5:4, KJV

Our Scripture reference was written to Israel during a time when Israel was under the threat of being brought into judgment by God. God was reaching out to them, letting them know that they could live—the threat of judgment could be removed—if only they would seek Him for forgiveness and instruction on how to make things right again.

This is no different for us today. It is difficult to get a prayer through when there is something that stands between us and God, something we did and knew was wrong. It's called "sin." Unrepentant sin is a no-no for a smooth, uninterrupted relationship with our heavenly Father. We cannot reach out with the fervency required to approach God when we have "junk" standing between us. Confession and repentance are needed before we can pray with our whole hearts. He is encouraging us to seek Him and find the keys—the strategies—to live peaceably with Him and enjoy our relationship with Him.

The arms of God are wide open to receive those He loves! We have been granted access to the very throne room of God. We can take confidence in the fact that God wants us to be on good terms with Him. We can bring our sinful behavior to Him, knowing that He will forgive us, embrace us, restore us to right fellowship with Him, and reposition us on the right path.

We cannot allow anything to stand between God and us! The moment we commit sin is the moment we need to run—not walk—to Him, seeking forgiveness. God loves us so much that He would much rather we come to Him seeking His forgiveness, than be the recipients of His judgment. That process is made easier by the knowledge that we are secure enough in His love for us to seek Him with confidence.

Lord God, Your all-encompassing love has made me secure in my ability to seek Your face, regardless of the circumstances under which I do so. Your loving-kindness is great toward me, and for this, I shall ever be grateful! In Jesus' Name. Amen.

KEEP THE FAITH BABY!

I know that my Redeemer lives, and that in the end he will stand upon the earth.

JOB 19:25, NIV

Sylvia had been unemployed for three years. She had given up on getting a job in her field and went back to school to get training in another area; still no job. There were times that her refrigerator was empty and she had received the final turn-off notice for electricity. With tears streaming down her cheeks, she remained hopeful; she stayed in the Word every day and affirmed, "I have not given up on God. I know that God has plans for me."

The book of Job tells us of a similar story but worse by far. Job was a godly man who lost everything: his children, servants, wealth, and standing in the community. Even his body was covered with painful boils from head to toe. He endured unimaginable suffering day and night. Yet, in a heated discussion with two friends, and in spite of his pathetic situation, Job proclaimed his faith in God. He proclaimed he knew his God lived and that He would return to earth.

Job spoke these words of confidence in the life-giving power of his Redeemer. It's good to know that Job's Redeemer is also ours, and the hope we have in a resurrected Savior helps us hold on even during the most trying times. If God could raise Jesus from the dead, can He not raise us up out of our most dire situations? The Bible tells us God restored to Job over and above what he had lost before. After three long years, Sylvia was offered a job. Praise God!

These stories offer us hope and encouragement to face our struggles. Let us not give up on God, even when the situation seems hopeless. Let us remain steadfast in our faith. Our God is able to see us through every situation.

❧

Abba Father, I cannot thank You enough for the blessed life that You have bestowed upon me. I have had difficulties and low points in my life, but You have always brought me out and blessed me even more. I pray, Lord, that the unemployed, the sick and shut-in, the downtrodden will hold on to their faith and continue to wait on You for breakthroughs in their situations. In Jesus' Name I pray. Amen.

THE INDWELLING

And I will pray the Father, and he shall give you another Comforter, that he may abide with you for ever.

JOHN 14:16, KJV

During His time on earth, Christ continually and consistently showed the utmost care and concern for those who would become believers in the effectiveness of His cross work. He taught with loving concern, He healed with loving concern, and He died out of loving concern. He wanted to complete His Father's assignment, leaving no stone unturned. In His loving concern, He secured us by providing everything we would need relative to salvation.

In the Gospel of John, we have a stunningly beautiful picture of the Son, praying to the Father, asking that the Holy Spirit be sent to those who were predestined to become His. This is Christ making sure He provided for our need to have the strength, determination, fortitude, courage, and power to live a godly, overcoming life, one that brings glory and honor to God and puts on display the saving grace of God. Without this bequest, we simply would not be able to live for God.

The word "Comforter" is *parakletos* in the Greek and means "a person summoned to one's aid." This word is further rendered an advisor, a legal defender, a mediator, or an intercessor. The word "another" is *allos* in the Greek, and it means "another of the same kind." Just as Jesus shows the nature of the Father, so does the Holy Spirit show the nature of Jesus, because "He is another of the same kind."

Jesus goes further in saying, "that He may abide with you forever." In the Old Testament, the Spirit of God came upon people for specific tasks but only temporarily. Christ is now revealing to us that the Holy Ghost is going to take up His abode inside of us, to abide with us forever. What glorious news! How comforting it is to know we have the Holy Spirit—the Comforter—living in us, working through us, and interceding for us before God! We have become His dwelling, and He is ours.

✻

Mighty One, Your plan of salvation is perfect! You've thought of everything I need to make it in this life. You've given me the Holy Ghost, which is the indwelling power to live a godly life. Thank You for such an incredible gift! In Jesus' Name. Amen.

THE FIRM FOUNDATION

Nevertheless the foundation of God standeth sure, having this seal, The Lord knoweth them that are his. And, Let every one that nameth the name of Christ depart from iniquity.

2 TIMOTHY 2:19, KJV

The beloved Bishop Brazier used to cite a quote from Voltaire, who predicted that the Bible would be nonexistent in a hundred years. Voltaire, who died May 30, 1778, was a French Enlightenment writer. That's interesting because he made that comment more than three hundred years ago, yet the Bible is still being read globally every day! He—the "enlightened" one—is gone, but God's Word is still changing lives! The foundation of God indeed stands sure!

There always have been, and there will always be, enemies of the church. In fact, modern day churches are filled with those professing Christ but not living for Him. But those of us who are chosen in Christ, before the world was, are not the least bit concerned about the positions others may take regarding God's Word. We have this blessed assurance, even God's seal: God knows us! Everyone that He chose, He will bring to Himself in the last day. He is ever present to watch over His word to perform it—no matter the evils that bring a railing attack against it. We are kept by the power of God, standing sure on His word. God has so secured us in Himself, that we can accept that as fact! We can count on the unshakable kingdom of God standing until the end of time.

Difficulties may come in our walk with God as we seek to maintain our footing on the firm foundation, but we need only remember the seal—God knows His own. We can then renew our strength and regain our courage to forge ahead. Let evil and wicked behavior be far from us! God has granted us security; knowing that we are truly His fortifies us to put sin firmly in its place—outside our lives. With all that God has done out of His love for us, our lives should reflect our grateful appreciation for His kindness and generosity toward us!

Father, thank You so much for the foundation that stands sure. It gives me strength and courage to continue in Your ways and to be doubly committed to keep unrighteousness far from me. In Jesus' Name. Amen.

A LOVE THAT SACRIFICES

For it became him, for whom [are] all things, and by whom [are] all things, in bringing many sons unto glory, to make the captain of their salvation perfect through sufferings.

HEBREWS 2:10, KJV

One time, a mother was the recipient of a barrage of please and pretty-pleases by her daughter to buy her a very expensive item. The little girl kept after the mother for weeks. She would not give up! Though not a rich woman, she finally relented and bought the very expensive item for her beautiful little girl. Oh, the daughter was truly thrilled and heaped countless hugs and kisses on the mother! The extravagance of the gift was lost on the little girl until she was old enough to really understand sacrifices.

God chose to have His only begotten Son to suffer and die for us to bring us into right standing with Him, the maker and ruler of the universe. It was an extravagant way for God to show us His glory. Jesus' suffering and death was a splendid way to demonstrate true love and its sacrificial nature—our perfect example!

When the Scripture tells us "to make the captain of their salvation perfect through sufferings," it means that, through His sufferings, Jesus identified with us and showed us the perfect posture of love, giving, and sacrifice; God allowed the sacred suffering of His Son.

Christ is our pattern for true love. We see love that embraces sacrifice rather than eliminates it. True love is giving even when the cost is high. It gives even when it may be painfully sacrificial because that's what love does. That's what Christ did! We will emulate the Captain of our salvation and love others the way He has loved us!

✳

Holy Father, thank You for Your willingness to love me sacrificially. Teach me how to love myself and others with this same love. In Jesus' Name. Amen.

ME TOO!

Howbeit for this cause I obtained mercy, that in me first Jesus Christ might shew forth all longsuffering, for a pattern to them which should hereafter believe on him to life everlasting.

1 TIMOTHY 1:16, KJV

A very dear friend wanted, and very much needed, a new car, but she didn't qualify. Being out of work for seventeen months gave her some credit challenges. There are others with this same testimony. However, she prayed and went to the car dealership in spite of her creditworthiness, and God moved mightily on her behalf. She left the dealership—not with the used car she decided she would try for, but with a brand new car!

Our Scripture finds the apostle Paul saying to us that if he could gain mercy after all of the things he had done against Christ, then anybody could. Indeed, that is good news because if Paul could obtain mercy after living a hellacious life, then *me too!* The Bible said he was breathing out slaughter (Acts 9:1). He did everything he possibly could to stamp out Christianity in its infancy. Just as God's grace covered his sins, it will also cover ours. Paul's life speaks as a testimony to the power of God that brings others into the kingdom. It further speaks to the mercy that extends to us. We may not have the same sin résumé as Paul, but ours, too, puts us in the need of God's mercy.

If we remember who we were before we encountered the saving grace of the Lord Jesus Christ, we can testify like Paul that, irrespective of what we've done, God's grace is big enough to cover our sins.

People who knew us in our pre-saved lives can be the greatest recipients of the transforming power of God manifested in our born-again lives. Our new lives testify to the goodness, grace, love, and power of God. Old acquaintances and old friends are amazed at who we have become when they know who we were. They will want this mercy found in Jesus and testify, *"Me too!"*

Lord God, thank You for eradicating the sins of my past and causing my new life to draw others to You in spite of my past! I praise You because I am secure in Your never-ending love! In Jesus' Name. Amen.

GOD'S PRESERVING GRACE

Here is the perseverance of the saints who keep the commandments of God and their faith in Jesus.

REVELATION 14:12, NASB

John the apostle wrote the book of Revelation when the church of Jesus Christ was experiencing great persecution. Christ-followers were a threat to the imperial government because they would not worship the emperor as god but instead worshiped Jesus the Christ. As part of this wave of persecution, John was banished to the island of Patmos and there received revelation from the Lord to encourage the saints of that time and throughout all ages, with the following message: Jesus reigns supreme throughout all eternity and all those who trust in Jesus will ultimately be victorious.

Imagine the horrific conditions in which these first-century believers lived. They were threatened with death if they did not renounce Christ as their Lord. They were beaten, thrown to lions, ostracized, and shunned for their faith. Imagine the mental and emotional anguish they must have experienced. Yet they held to their faith, refused to deny their Lord, and often faced death. How did these believers persevere or endure such suffering? It was the grace of God.

Later theologians described this overcoming power in this way: "because of the temptations of the world and of Satan, those who are converted could not persevere in that grace if left to their own strength. But God is faithful, who, having conferred grace, mercifully confirms and powerfully preserves them therein, even to the end."[31] In other words, God's saving grace is also a preserving grace and ensures the believer that he or she is eternally secure, even through trials and tribulations.

Today, we may not face persecution by the government, but sometimes we experience situations and pressure that threaten our faith and tempt us to doubt God. Yet God's preserving grace ensures that we can endure heartache, financial downturns, or physical challenges. It assures believers that even the worst of trials will not separate us from God's love (Romans 8:38). Today, we can rejoice to know that if God brings us to it, grace will see us through it.

🖎

Dear Lord, thank You for the grace to persevere. I bless You for preserving me and keeping me by Your mighty power. Amen.

I Am a Christian, by the Grace of God

And I heard a voice from heaven saying unto me, Write, Blessed are the dead which die in the Lord from henceforth: Yea, saith the Spirit, that they may rest from their labours; and their works do follow them.

REVELATION 14:13, KJV

Stories abound of early Christians who were threatened with death if they did not recant their confession of faith in Jesus and turn to the worship of idols.

They were asked, "Are you a Christian?" To this query courageous Christians would reply, "I am a Christian, by the grace of God."[32] During particularly cruel times of persecution, especially during the times in which John wrote the Revelation, believers' unwillingness to renounce their faith in Jesus brought death. In each generation, no doubt, people have died proclaiming Jesus as Lord!

Yet in today's passage, God gives the apostle John the revelation that death is not the end of the story for believers. John wrote to Christians who were threatened with death in his time and to all ensuing generations. Those who die in the Lord are blessed. Christians may be tortured, beaten, whipped, or otherwise mistreated because they are in Christ and refuse to speak otherwise. Yet, what the Spirit affirmed is that all people who die in the Lord will enter into a place of rest where they will cease from their striving with ungodliness.

Though many Christians in the West are not threatened with death for holding firm to their confession of faith, we are threatened with unpopularity, fear, and being deemed as extreme if we take our Christian witness too far to the secular society in which we live. Some people in the world scoff that we believe in Jesus and go to church to worship. Being committed to our churches and doing good deeds may be met with ridicule.

But we can hold on to our faith in Jesus and be reminded of the works of Christians who went before us, unabashedly declaring, even in the threat of death, "I am a Christian, by the grace of God!" Just as their works of faith followed them, so will ours!

❧

Dear Lord, today, I boldly confess You as Lord in both word and deed, knowing that You will confess me before the Father in heaven. Glory to Your name!

WE'RE ALMOST THERE

And do this, knowing the time, that now it is high time to awake out of sleep; for now our salvation is nearer than when we first believed.

ROMANS 13:11, NKJV

Childhood road trips were always a mix of excitement and anxiety, so filled with anticipation that we couldn't stand the wait! It seemed that we would never reach our destination. Every so often, we would ask the grown-ups traveling with us, "Are we there yet?" In our childlike anticipation, not having a more developed sense of timing, we grew weary with waiting.

Eventually we would fall asleep, only to be awakened with, "Start getting yourselves together. We're *almost* there!" Knowing we were almost at the anticipated destination, the grown-ups did not want us to wait until the last minute to get ready. They wanted us to wake up, straighten our clothes, and wipe the sleep out of our eyes.

The life of the believer is much like a childhood road trip. When we trusted Jesus as Savior and were filled with the Holy Spirit, we began a journey that would take us from here to eternity. Like children, some of us have not developed a sense of timing for the eternal things of God, and we get impatient waiting for Him.

The apostle Paul helps us understand the significance of "getting ready." He says it is "high time" to wake up. In other words, it's the right hour or season for God to decisively bring His Kingdom to fruition. Paul calls the future realization of God's Kingdom "our salvation," not referring to the point in time when we first trusted in Jesus but to the point in time of Christ's return, when we will fully realize our eternal salvation. As you see, God's time is both present (this present age) and future (the age to come). Yet some of us grow weary waiting for the future age to come and are lulled to sleep by this present age.

So it is that Paul reminds us that we are closer now to our ultimate destiny than when we first believed. Today, we echo with Paul: "We're almost there." So wake up—our promised eternal reign is drawing near.

❧

Dear Lord, I know in my heart that we are almost there and I await Your return with great anticipation! Amen.

GOD IS FOR US!

What then shall we say to these things? If God is for us, who can be against us?
ROMANS 8:31, NKJV

In this present age, we face all kinds of challenges. It's part of living out the human condition in a fallen world. The child of God faces many pressures—physical illness, mental anguish, stress, potentially losing a home or livelihood to an uncertain economy, danger from violence within our neighborhoods. The list goes on. Throughout this eighth chapter, Paul acknowledges that the child of God will suffer (Romans 8:18) and will experience infirmities, or weaknesses (Romans 8:26). In today's passage, Paul raises a question to inspire us to think about the real meanings of the challenges we face.

In essence, Paul queries the believer: Are the challenges we face powerful enough to defeat us? He asks us to consider this: Though they are threats, are they powerful enough to destroy us? Paul knew that, if not put in proper perspective, "these things" could discourage believers in our walk with Christ. The enemy could use "these things" to cause believers to give up.

Interestingly enough, Paul answers his question with another: If God is for us, who can be against us? He used a provocative rhetorical technique to get the believer to think. In fact, his question could be turned into a statement: Since God is for us, no one or *no thing* is strong enough to succeed against us. At the heart of Paul's questioning is the assurance that God is for us!

Since God is for us, He gives us the Holy Spirit, who prays for us even when we don't know how to pray through the stresses of life (Romans 8:26). Since God is for us, He works all things together for our good (Romans 8:28). Since God is for us, He did not spare His own Son but gave Him up for us all (Romans 8:32). Since God is for us, He gives us overcoming power through Christ, who loved us (Romans 8:37).

Whatever we're facing, whatever has come against us, cannot destroy us nor overshadow the overwhelming fact that God is for us, has an eternal plan for us, and will keep us.

❧

Dear Lord, sometimes I feel overwhelmed. Today, I thank You for reminding me that You are indeed for me, watching over me so I may be an overcomer. Amen.

IT WILL BE WORTH IT ALL

For I reckon that the sufferings of this present time are not worthy to be compared with the glory which shall be revealed in us.

ROMANS 8:18, KJV

Too often in this old, fallen world, we experience physical, emotional, and mental pain, not unlike that experienced by the saints of old to whom the apostle Paul wrote. What are the sufferings of this present time? Heartache, body ache, loneliness, embarrassment, and the like all press on the child of God. Yet as devastating as these sufferings are, Paul reminded us that they do not compare with the glory that will be revealed in us. Because we are secured by God's love, we have a promised destiny that will outshine our present pain.

God, who is Spirit, is always with us, always present. Yet there are special manifestations of God's presence in which we experience His existence even more profoundly. Throughout Scripture, when God would arrive in special ways to reveal Himself to His people, that splendid presence was referred to as "God's glory." In the wilderness, God's glory was revealed to the children of Israel time and time again. On one occasion, Moses asked to see God's glory. Knowing Moses, in his earthly body, could not fully handle the weight of God, He placed Moses in the crevice of a rock and allowed him a glimpse of God's glory (Exodus 33:22).

So it is with us today; we glimpse God's glory when we meet Him in prayer. When we enter into worship, with hearts open and uncluttered, we get a glimpse of God's glory. Like Moses, our earthly bodies cannot fully handle the experience of God's glory. Yet, through our suffering, we yearn for more of His glory!

So we are assured that one day, when we are transformed to eternity, resting in His presence in heaven, God's full glory will be revealed, or manifested. The grandeur and splendor of God's glory will so greatly outshine the burdens of this earthly realm that then will we realize it was indeed worth it all!

✦

Dear Lord, thank You for glimpses of Your glory as I meet You in prayer and worship. I look forward to that day when Your glory will be fully revealed to me. Amen.

SHAPING UP TO BE SHIPPED OUT

Therefore let us not sleep, as do others; but let us watch and be sober.

1 THESSALONIANS 5:6, KJV

Monday morning, 6:35, the second snooze button has been depressed. The young man rolls over and asks, "Just ten more minutes, that's all." Time is passing by. He finally awakens thirty minutes later, and now he's rushing. He misses his connectors—a bus and a train. He sits, sighs, and waits.

Unlike the young man, we don't have to miss out on what's to come to us. Scripture tells us the second coming of our Lord will happen; it just doesn't tell us when it will happen. Therefore, in the meantime, we can prepare—but not lackadaisically—for when the second coming happens there is no waiting until we get our lives together. There is no, "*Lord just ten more minutes please. You know my heart.*"

We can't just slow down to prepare for our salvation in the Lord. Since we don't know the time, but know that it's near, our lives should be in order to fully connect with, or to, God. Our sleep could be tending to our personal business and not to the business of the Lord. Our sleep may be our day-to-day activities. Whichever it is, let's wake up and begin to prepare for the coming of our Lord. Being out of sin and into God is a start to getting one's life in order. Attending Bible class, reading the Bible, and praying to God are ways to getting one's life in order. Believing that Jesus died for our sins, having a confession of our heart, and being baptized in Jesus' Name is getting one's life in order.

We are in a time that the need for getting our life together (being right with Christ) is at hand. Again, no one knows the day, the place, or the time our Lord will return. We need to shape up so, when the time comes, we are ready to be shipped to heaven.

❧

God, thank You for Your love and kindness, I love You. Lord, I respect and cherish You with my life and my lips. My praises go up to You forever. In the Name of Jesus, I pray. Amen.

CONNECTED TO THE SOURCE

Abide in me, and I in you. As the branch cannot bear fruit of itself, except it
abide in the vine; no more can ye, except ye abide in me.

JOHN 15:4, KJV

In the film *It's a Wonderful Life*, Jimmy Stewart's youngest child, Suzu, develops a cold, when she walks home from school with her coat open, in an effort to protect a flower she had won as a prize. Not knowing that the cut flower would soon die, she seeks to revitalize it by asking her father to "give it a drink." As Stewart attempts to put the flower in a glass of water, the already withering petals fall apart in his hands. The scene does more than serve as a catalyst for Stewart's frustration. It also represents the pitiful condition of a life disconnected from its life-giving source.

In our Scripture, Jesus explains that as children of God, we must stay connected to our only life-giving force by abiding in Him. Like Suzu, we sometimes think we are abiding in Jesus when we "take a drink" of His Word while on the commuter train, or when we mumble a quick prayer just before a crisis hits. "Abiding" means to dwell, to remain, to endure.

Plant life faces fluctuating changes, from gentle rains to torrential storms, from mellow winds to raging hurricanes—yet they endure. While winter may bring blankets of snow, spring still yields sturdy trees and flowering plants. Our lives may face storms and billows but we must abide in Jesus if we expect to exhibit His beauty to the waiting world.

Jesus presents abiding as a two-way metaphor. We are to abide in Jesus, striving to be like Him in every way, while He abides in us. If we abide in Him, He provides for us. If we abide in Him, He develops us. If we abide in Him, He strengthens us.

When we attempt to do our own thing, to "bear fruit" on our own, to make a name for ourselves on our own merit, or to handle "our business" our way, we find our efforts to be fruitless. As our life-giving source, Jesus uses John 15:4 to give instructions for not only surviving, but for thriving.

❧

Thank You Lord, for the life-giving source of Your Holy Spirit, which helps
me to abide in You at all times. Amen.

COUNT YOUR BLESSINGS

And he said, Lord God of Israel, there is no God like thee, in heaven above, or on earth beneath, who keepest covenant and mercy with thy servants that walk before thee with all their heart.

1 KINGS 8:23, KJV

Have you ever heard the song "Count Your Blessings"? The chorus' lyrics are *"Count your blessings, name them one by one, And it will surprise you what the Lord hath done."*[29]

We often view life from the vantage point of our understandings, accomplishments, and problems (which, of course, can vacillate between "ego-tripping" and "singing the blues"). But what would happen if we took time to view life by remembering what God has done to us, for us, and through us? That's what King Solomon did.

Solomon succeeded his father, David, to the throne of Israel. That might not have been a big deal except that he was the youngest son, and before they died, some of his brothers had been pretty aggressive about becoming the next king. Solomon also accomplished something his father had not been able to do: he built the Temple, a permanent place of worship in Jerusalem.

In 1 Kings 8, the Temple is finished; God has given His approval by placing His glory upon it. Then Solomon, speaking to the congregation, tells of God's covenant with Israel and how God delivered the Israelites from Egypt. He remembers God's promises to his father and recalls all he was able to do because God allowed it. As he counts the blessings of God, Solomon declares with confidence and renewed encouragement that "there is no God like thee."

When counting God's blessings, the surprise is not that God has blessed but that the blessing leads us so powerfully into worship that we confidently renew our commitment to wholeheartedly follow Him. That's what happened to Solomon, and it will happen to us just as we sing in that little song: *When upon life's billows you are tempest tossed, When you are discouraged, thinking all is lost, Count your many blessings, name them one by one, And it will surprise you what the Lord hath done.*[33]

❧

Dear Lord, help me to see Your blessings, despite my distractions, so that I give You glory and never lose sight of Your love or my commitment to honor You. Amen.

HOPE IN LOW TIDE

The children of thy servants shall continue, and their seed shall be established before thee.

PSALM 102:28, KJV

People who fish tend to watch the tide. To the inexperienced person, high tide, which shifts many species of fish closer to the shore, seems the perfect time to fish. Yet it is low tide that produces real results. As one fisherman explains, "I can see the boulders...[and steer] away from harm."[34] Thus, low tide lets you see where you're really going.

Our lives are that way as well. When we're riding high, we can testify with confidence that God is on our side. But when we feel discouraged, when we can't understand why the plans we thought were God-directed suddenly seem God-forsaken, we must face our "low tide" and take a good look at our situation without allowing our hope to drift.

Psalm 102 was written by someone in such a "low tide" state that he felt it necessary to beg God to hear his prayer. His friends had forsaken him; he was frustrated and so distraught that he'd lost his appetite; his days seemed meaningless; and he'd fasted and prayed with no result. Yet, in the midst of his distress, the psalmist managed to write one truth that sustained him: God will endure forever. This acknowledgement sparked another truth: regardless of what we face, God's promise of mercy will be kept in every generation. The psalmist realized his hope in his "low tide."

There will be "low tides" in our lives. There will be times when we wonder who cares and whether our efforts make a difference. There will be times when loneliness and grief, sorrow and shame will rob us of joy and make us believe that the good times are impossible to recapture.

In those "low tide" moments, we must hold on to God's unchanging hand because in the "low tide," we find our faith. In the "low tide," we find strength in God's love. In the "low tide," we learn to appreciate even more the fact that, as God's children, our circumstances do not influence our position with Him.

❧

Lord, thank You for the strength, love, and deliverance You give me during my "low tides." Help me to always reach for Your hand and to remember that at all times, You always reach out to me. Amen.

TRAPPED? NEVER!

Whoever calls, "Help, God!" gets help. On Mount Zion and in Jerusalem there will be a great rescue—just as God said. Included in the survivors are those that God calls.

JOEL 2:32, THE MESSAGE

The James Bond film *Tomorrow Never Dies* has a great chase scene where Bond and his female companion ride a motorcycle through houses, over buildings, and through the streets of Saigon, while being chased by a series of cars and, finally, by a helicopter. As Bond steers onto a dead-end street, his companion looks at the wall ahead and the helicopter hovering just feet in front of them and declares, "Trapped!" Bond surveys the same situation and emphatically replies, "Never!" Perspective is everything.

The Old Testament book of Joel also opens with a chase scene: the vision of how God's judgment will come suddenly and devastatingly upon the earth. To his agricultural audience, the prophet describes the terror of an army that relentlessly devours every crop and destroys every animal, leaving the people without a place to hide—trapped.

Often we find ourselves living in the fear and anxiety of life's chase scenes when bills come due unexpectedly, illness attacks unannounced, accidents and crises arrive undeniably. In those times we may be aware of God's presence and even have what we think is strong faith. Yet we find ourselves staring into the face of the circumstances looming before us and the situations that have befallen us and think, "Trapped!"

Fortunately, the prophet Joel also gives us another perspective. *The Message* translates Joel 2:32 as, "Whoever calls, 'Help, God!' gets help." What a relief. We can stare in the face of our crises knowing that God will rescue. Whether the chase is "on" regarding money, family, job, or emotional pressure, we can have confidence that we are included in the survivors. Through the sacrifice of Jesus Christ we have been called out of darkness into God's marvelous light (1 Peter 2:9). By faith we will be delivered (Luke 4:18). By divine grace we will be helped (2 Corinthians 12:9). Through God's faithfulness we are never trapped! (Lamentations 3:23).

❦

Dear God, thank You that Your mercies are new daily, that Your faithfulness is great always, and that my deliverance is assured in You. Amen.

ANTICIPATION

When the seventh angel blows his trumpet, God's mysterious plan will be fulfilled. It will happen just as he announced it to his servants the prophets.

REVELATION 10:7, NLT

As a child, what created excitement for you just because you knew it was coming? Was it your birthday? A coming vacation? A special visitor? Or did the preparations for Christmas make waiting for the big day almost impossible?

Sometimes the anticipation of Jesus' return can be a point of anxiety as well. We have just passed two such anticipatory challenges in the past year. In 2011, October 21 was declared to be the end of the world. This year, December 20, 2012 was predicted to be "the end" based on the Mayan calendar. Such misinformation causes some Christians and non-Christians to lose faith that God will judge the world, that the "end time will come," and that the Bible and our Christian witness are true.

In the book of Revelation, John records many visions regarding these ending, or apocalyptic events. John is told not to record what was said in the final vision of Revelation 10:4. Instead, he is told that these things will come to pass and at the appointed time, "There will be no delay. When the seventh angel blows his trumpet, God's mysterious plan will be fulfilled. It will happen just as He announced it to His servants the prophets" (Revelation 10:6b-7).

When we read the Bible faithfully, we begin to comprehend—and to expect—the promises of God in our lives. Indeed, the promises are the foundation of our faith. We realize that the Holy Spirit is working in us and changing our attitudes and behaviors. We learn to be anxious for nothing, while being excited about Jesus. We recognize that we are sealed by the Holy Spirit until the Day of Redemption (Ephesians 4:30).

In Matthew 25:13, Jesus speaks a parable regarding His return and says, "Watch therefore, for ye know neither the day nor the hour wherein the Son of man cometh." While we won't know the exact day or the hour, we can be sure that "God's mysterious plan will be fulfilled ... just as He announced."

❧

Lord, help me to stand firm in faith that is based on the assurance of Your Word. Amen.

PRACTICE THE ART OF RE-GIFTING

And she shall bring forth a son, and thou shalt call his name JESUS: for he shall save his people from their sins.

MATTHEW 1:21, KJV

It's Christmas, probably the most misunderstood and misrepresented time of the calendar year. Modern American notions of Christmas range from Santa Claus and "visions of sugar plums," to three wise men, shepherds, and angels gathered in a nice, clean barn. Of course, there is the shopping, gifting, and re-gifting. Despite the festive atmosphere and general misunderstanding, there is only one true reason for this season, and His name is Jesus.

The detailed accounts of Jesus' birth open the Gospels of Matthew and Luke, but the prophecies of His birth are referenced throughout the Old Testament, while the New Testament is filled with the result. Our popular culture has been influenced by literature and art. As a result, we have some uniquely modern ideas about Christmas that don't fit the Bible. Nevertheless, the reason and intent of the season has never changed: Jesus came to save His people from their sins.

Of course, it is politically incorrect to talk about sin at Christmastime. This is not the time to acknowledge the evil in people's hearts, and it is not hospitable to acknowledge that some have turned away from God. Today, millions deny God's existence. Others claim to be Christians, but their actions and thoughts spew hatred and division.

So let's turn the tables on Christmas. This year, the gift you give to everyone on your list should be a simple statement of a fact that has never changed: Jesus came to save us from sin. What if, instead of just blessing the Christmas meal, you give an altar call? What if, instead of just helping your children wrap presents, you share the story of Jesus' birth, death, and resurrection? What if, instead of giving a gift card, you give a modern translation of the Bible? What if, this Christmas, you re-gift the greatest gift ever given—Jesus, who came to save His people from their sins.

Merciful Father, thank You for the gift of salvation, for the gift of Jesus, and for the gift of life in You. Amen.

SHOUT IT!

And they were shouting with a mighty shout, "Salvation comes from our God who sits on the throne and from the Lamb!"
                                        REVELATION 7:10, NLT

Here it is, the day after Christmas, and we know exactly who gave us each gift. Whether it's the fruitcake we knew was coming, the electronic gadget we hinted about all month, or the rather strange item we can't figure a use for, we know who gave each gift to us. In the next week, thank you cards and calls of appreciation will be issued, even if we haven't figured out that strange gift. But what about the best gift we've ever been given? What about the gift that will last two life times—this one and the one that is eternal? What about the gift of salvation that is ours though the sacrifice of Jesus Christ?

At Christmas, we tend to think only about the miraculous birth of Jesus. Our houses show depictions of Bethlehem, our hearts sing songs of the virgin birth and a Holy Night. But when do we say "thank you" for that gift, the gift of Salvation? In Revelation 6, John records his vision of a great earthquake that threatens all the people of the earth—rulers and peasants, rich and poor. Together, they ask for deliverance and wonder who can save them from the wrath of God. In Revelation 7, the destruction is ordered to a halt until the servants of God are sealed. Then suddenly, a crowd "too great to count, from every nation and tribe and people and language" stands before "the throne and before the Lamb" and shouts, "Salvation comes from our God who sits on the throne and from the Lamb!"

From the beginning, God planned our deliverance from our fallen state. Jesus Christ came from heaven to take away our sins and to restore us to a right relationship with our Father. What better gift could there ever be? We don't have to wait until Easter; we can show our appreciation today by shouting the Good News of why Jesus Christ, the Lamb of God, takes away the sins of the world.

※

Thank You, Lord, for taking away my sin and giving me new life in You. Thank You for salvation. Make me bold enough to declare Your Goodness through my words and my deeds. Amen.

WE, TOO, SING A NEW SONG

And they sang a new song: Worthy! Take the scroll, open its seals.
Slain! Paying in blood, you bought men and women, Bought them back
from all over the earth, Bought them back for God.

REVELATION 5:9, *THE MESSAGE*

Many names have been associated with the centuries' old struggle for civil rights in the U.S.: Nat Turner, Frederick Douglass, Sojourner Truth, Thurgood Marshall. For many people today, however, Martin Luther King's name has become synonymous with the freedoms and opportunities Americans from all backgrounds and ethnicities enjoy. However, as great an influence as he was, Dr. King's work was limited only to this world and this country. What might be said of a person who is able to free the people of all nations and backgrounds? What would we do in recognition of someone who could accomplish such a feat?

Revelation 5:9 records the vision John had while he was on the Isle of Patmos. In his vision, John saw God holding a scroll with seven seals. Simultaneously, John heard a question raised by an angel: "Who is worthy to open the scroll and break the seal?" When John realized that no one in heaven or on earth could do it, he wept. But as he did so, he was told not to cry. Raising his head, John saw the Lamb that had been slain. That Lamb was Jesus Christ, the only begotten Son of God, who was slain for the sins of humankind. At that moment, twenty-four elders and four living creatures responded in a spontaneous, new song of praise to the only One who could free people of all nations from sin. Only Jesus is worthy to open the book of God's Revelation so that the world may know God's judgment and be grateful for God's mercy.

Their song declared the worthiness of the Lamb that was slain. His name is Jesus, the One who came from heaven to be the Sacrifice on Calvary. His blood was shed to ransom us from the fate we deserved—eternal damnation. His blood rescued us and redeemed us from sin and its consequences. Now our lives sing praise to the One who bought us back for God!

❧

Thank You, Lord, that despite my flaws, failures, and struggles, Your sacrifice has made it possible that I, too, can now sing a new song in praise of You. Amen.

REVEALED

Now the Lord is that Spirit: and where the Spirit of the Lord is, there is liberty. But we all, with open face beholding as in a glass the glory of the Lord, are changed into the same image from glory to glory, even as by the Spirit of the Lord.

2 CORINTHIANS 3:17-18, KJV

In Exodus 34, Moses converses with God in Mt. Sinai where he receives the Law and the Ten Commandments. Moses' time in God's presence was so glorious that the residue of God's glory was still on Moses when he returned from the mountain to the waiting people below. Because the people did not have a relationship with God, they could not stand to view the glory of God as reflected on Moses' face. Moses wore a veil over his face to protect the people. Even though the veil was on Moses' face, it really veiled the people's hearts from the full knowledge of God's truth.

Paul's letter to the Corinthian church refers to this encounter between God with Moses. In 1 Corinthians 3:15, Paul says that even in his time, when the Law and the Ten Commandments (the Book of Moses) was read, the hearts of the Jewish people were still veiled so that they could not know the fullness of God. In verse 16, Paul explained that only when people understand that Jesus is the revelation of the fullness of God is the veil lifted from their hearts.

In I Corinthians 3, Paul writes of "the Spirit" four times. Finally, in verse 17, Paul explains that the Lord Himself is that Spirit. When believers are filled with the Spirit, the veil is lifted from our hearts and minds and we are given access to the power and glory of God. Our hearts are unveiled because, "where the Spirit of the Lord is, there is liberty." We, who have turned to Christ, now view the power and presence of God "with open face." No veil needed. We are blessed to see God's glory reflected in our own lives as we are "transformed into His likeness with ever-increasing glory" (1 Corinthians 3:17, TNIV).

Thank You, Lord, for the liberty You have given me so that I am free to love You and to live for You in every aspect of my life. Amen.

IN THE SHEPHERD'S CARE

And of Benjamin he said, The beloved of the Lord shall dwell in safety by him; and the Lord shall cover him all the day long, and he shall dwell between his shoulders.

DEUTERONOMY 33:12, KJV

How many metaphors can you think of for the care a parent gives a child? Is loving a child similar to caring for a precious flower? Is it at all like protecting an irreplaceable jewel? The metaphor we might not think of is shepherding, but the Bible uses just that to explain God's love for us.

The book of Deuteronomy explains the Law of God to a new generation who will soon pass into the Promised Land. In chapter 33, they are reminded of the blessings of Moses on each tribe. In verse twelve, the tribe of Benjamin, the son of Jacob by Rachel, is blessed. Benjamin's only brother, Joseph, was older than he and their mother breathed her last giving birth to this younger son.

In blessing Benjamin, Moses used the imagery of a shepherd who cares for His sheep. The lamb, though impervious to all danger, is in trouble despite its naïveté. It is the shepherd who keeps the lamb safe. This safety is not temporary; the lamb actually dwells in the sphere of the shepherd's safety with assurance of the shepherd's never-ending care, nurture, and guidance. The shepherd provides protection from harm—day and night. The shepherd does not sleep; he is on guard.

Sheep have a tendency to wander and get lost. As they graze, they concentrate so on the space they are covering, on dealing with their own appetites, that they become distracted and go astray. But the lost lamb is always found by the shepherd who carries the animal on his own shoulders back to the safety of the fold. If the lamb is cold, it is comforted by the heat of the shepherd's body. If the lamb is anxious, the closeness of the shepherd's neck is calming. All of this is because of the shepherd's love for his precious lamb. Like Benjamin, we are blessed because the Lord is our shepherd. We shall not want. Goodness and mercy will follow us and we will dwell in the house of the Lord—our Shepherd—forever (Psalm 23:1,6).

My Father and my Shepherd, thank You for Your endless blessings, protection, and love. Amen!

KEEP A TIGHT GRIP

He called you to this through our gospel, that you might share in the glory of our Lord Jesus Christ. So then, brothers and sisters, stand firm and hold fast to the teachings we passed on to you, whether by word of mouth or by letter.

2 THESSALONIANS 2:14-15, NIV

Riding a bus, subway train, or airport tram requires that we keep a tight grip, so when a turn or a sudden lunge happens, we won't stumble. Some people seem to balance effortlessly, but, should something unexpected happen, they are left scrambling for safety.

Our spiritual journey is not at all like riding a bus, except for one thing: we need to keep a tight grip! Life can lull us into believing that we can juggle job, family, and responsibilities without being shaken. But when life lunges in an unpredictable direction—job loss, family crisis, or a sudden inability to handle our responsibilities—our lives can be tossed and our faith tested in unexpected ways. In those times, we need to keep a tight grip on the Word of God.

In this chapter of the second letter to the Thessalonians, Paul warns that Satan will come to an end, but not before he attempts to destroy those who have chosen to follow Jesus Christ. Paul assures the Thessalonians that they must stand firm by holding "to the teachings we passed on to you."

Holding God's unchanging hand requires more than mental or emotional yearning. It is developed through our commitment to daily Bible reading and prayer. Our regimen must include the mid-week Bible class and Sunday school, where opportunities are given for small-group engagement with the Word.

Like the Thessalonians, God has called us through the message of the Gospel. We, too, will share in His glory, reign with Him, and live with Him eternally. But while salvation is ours from the moment we accept God's call, our journey is paved with struggles aimed at having us falter. So, while others make their New Year's resolutions, let us recommit to Bible study so we can "keep a tight grip" on what we were taught.

❦

Lord God, thank You for Your Word, which is able to keep me from falling. Help me to hide it in my heart so that I please You in all things. Amen.

WHAT'S THE BOTTOM LINE?

Verily, verily, I say unto you, He that believeth on me hath everlasting life.
JOHN 6:47, KJV

When Jesus told the people in His audience not to put their effort into temporary satisfaction, but to concentrate on that which would give them eternal life, they didn't get it. Instead, they asked, "What shall we do, that we might work the works of God?" (John 6:28). In other words, they asked, "What can we do to get it on our own?" For the next twenty-one verses, Jesus explained who He was and who sent Him. When they still didn't get it, Jesus cut to the bottom line: "He that believes on me has everlasting life" (John 6:4, KJV).

Before we call those people thick-headed, be warned that we do the same thing! We work all year for the temporary meat. We neglect to pray, forget to read the Bible, and take God's miracles for granted because we think we can work "this thing" on our own. But Jesus' bottom line is really quite clear: Believe in Jesus, place trust and confidence in Him, and realize that the priority is everlasting life.

Believing Jesus' bottom line means realizing that Jesus is God because only God can grant eternal life. It means recognizing that we no longer need to be anxious about our lives because God will take care of us each day, and He has already prepared our eternal home.

Tonight, African-American churches around the country will meet for a tradition known as Watch Night. This is more than waiting for midnight or finding a Christian way to celebrate New Year's Eve. We celebrate Watch Night believing that Jesus is God and that He will keep every promise He made. Watch Night means celebrating Jesus' bottom line—We have eternal life!

Lord, thank You for the realization that by placing my faith in Jesus Christ, I can face a new day and a new year knowing I have eternal life. Amen.

Notes

TRIBUTE
1. Interview with Bishop Arthur Brazier by Apostolic Church of God Vision Team, July 2, 2010

JANUARY
2. http://www.word-detective. com/081100.html#proofpudding (accessed July 12, 2011)
3. http://www.pbs.org/wgbh/aia/ part4/4p2967.html
4. Strong's Exhaustive Concordance of the Bible, entry 4632

FEBRUARY
5. "How Great Thou Art," by Carl Gustav Boberg (1885)
6. "Standing on the Promises," R. Kelso Carter (1886)
7. RayStedman.org
8. "When I Survey the Wondrous Cross," by Isaac Watts (1707)
9. "More Than Enough," lyrics by Robert Gay

MARCH
10. Spurgeon, Charles H. "February 18" in *Morning and Evening* (Peabody: Hendrickson Publishers, 1991) p. 79
11. Chambers, Oswald. "The Riches of the Destitute" in *His Utmost for My Highest*. (Grand Rapids: Discovery House Publishers, 1992).
12. McCabe, Robert V., The Meaning of "Born of Water and the Spirit" in John 3:5, http://www.

dbts.edu/journals/1999/McCabe. pdf, DBSJ 4 (Fall 1999) p. 107.
13. Walvoord, John F., Roy B. Zuck and Dallas Theological Seminary, *The Bible Knowledge Commentary: An Exposition of the Scriptures* (Wheaton: Victor Books, 1983-c1985). 2:281.
14. "My Soul's Been Satisfied," lyrics by George Jones

APRIL
15. Morgan, Robert, J. *Then Sings My Soul: 150 World's Greatest Hymn Stories* (Nashville: Thomas Nelson, 2003).

MAY
16. *Time Magazine*, Sept 1, 2002. http://www.time.com/time/ covers/1101020909/asurvivor.html http://www.moodyconferences. com/con_mainPage aspx?id=16216
17. "You Are My Sunshine," Jimmie Davis and Charles Mitchell (1940)

JUNE
18. 2nd Cor. 5:17, Barclay
19. "No One Ever Cared for Me Like Jesus," Charles F. Weigle (1932)

JULY
20. History.com Articles, Video, Pictures and Facts: http://www. history.com/topics/july-4th

21. "I Need You to Survive," David Frazier and Hezekiah Walker (2004)

AUGUST

22. http://www.biblestudytools. com/lexicons/greek/nas/psuche.html

SEPTEMBER

23. Duling, Dennis C. "Matthew" in *The Harper Collins Study Bible* (San Francisco: HarperSanFrancisco, 1989) p. 1679.
24. http://www.snopes.com/ glurge/special.asp

OCTOBER

25. South African History Online, http://www.sahistory.org/za/ contemporary-south-africa-truth-and-reconciliation-commission
26. http://home.comcast. net/~antaylor1/bestsellingbooks.html, http://www.christiananswers. net/q-eden/

NOVEMBER

27. http://mylifeofcrime. wordpress.com/2007/05/14/ blair-holt-murder-51007-chicago-il-the-boy-who-became-a-hero-with-his-murder/
28. Tenney, Merrill C., *Pictorial Bible Dictionary* (Grand Rapids: Zondervan, 1963, 1964, 1967), pp. 212-213.
29. The 2011 Global Leadership Summit, Willow Creek Community Church http:// www.willowcreek.com/events/ leadership/speaker_mama_ maggie_gobran.asp

DECEMBER

30. Pink, Arthur W., *The Essential Arthur W. Pink Collection: Volume 1, The Attributes of God* (Grand Rapids: Baker Book House, 1975), p. 17.
31. "Onward, Christian Soldiers," Sabine Baring-Gould (1865)
31. Council of Dort, 1618-1619
32. http://www.christian-history. org/justin-martyr-martyrdom.html
33. Reference: http://library. timelesstruths.org/music/Count_ Your_Blessings/
34. Reference: http://www.reel-time.com/forum/showthread. php?t=45240

Bible Abbreviations

AMP	Amplified Bible
ESV	English Standard Bible
KJV	King James Version
NASB	New American Standard Bible
NIV	New International Version
NKJV	New King James Version
NLT	New Living Translation
NRSV	New Revised Standard Version
TNIV	Today's New International Version

The Message

Contributors

Rev. Gwendalyn Francis Blair, a native of Gould, Arkansas (but reared in Chicago, Illinois), has committed her life to serving God and to helping His people achieve their fullest spiritual potential. She attended Loyola University and is currently in the process of returning to school to get her degree in Christian Ministry.

Rev. Cynthia Brawner is an ordained minister at the Apostolic Church of God, as well as a Sunday school instructor, a writer, a leader, and a National Board Certified Teacher. She is the daughter of Lloyd and Berdena Brawner, granddaughter of Mattie L. Hall, and niece of Wilbert Hall, Jr. and Patricia Clark.

Min. Anthony Briscoe is a son of God who has been entrusted with a poetic gift that ministers to many. Tony teaches, preaches, and writes the gospel of Jesus Christ with a transcendent style that captivates its hearers with passion and relevance for an emerging generation. He is a tech guy who uses it all for the glory of God. He is married to Larita and is the proud papa of Journey.

Pattie Caire has been a member of ACOG for more than thirty-two years and is currently the Special Events Manager for Saving Grace Ministries. Her first love is studying and teaching God's Word. Patti is also an editor who was honored to work on Bishop Arthur Brazier's *Saved by Grace and Grace Alone.*

Rev. Granada Cartwright serves on the ministry staff of the Apostolic Church of God. She delights to serve God and His people through teaching and equipping others. She enjoys good music, soulful conversations and quiet times of meditation. Her chief joys are to know and love Jesus; her husband, Erskine; and her children, Quinton Jeremiah and Jillian Alicia.

Rev. Donnie Collins is a an ordained full-time staff minister at the Apostolic Church of God and has served in numerous leadership roles on local, regional and national church levels, but he has found his greatest mission in teaching and training. He's a volunteer teacher in the Sunday school's elective department, ministers, counsels, teaches, leads and guides parishioners with a focus in moving people to higher levels of effectiveness through the knowledge and wisdom of the Word of God.

Beverly S. Curry, a longtime member of the Apostolic Church of God, is currently an instructor in the Elective Department of Sunday Morning Bible Study, works with communications for the Daytimers Bible study, and teaches adult Spanish classes. She has master's degrees in Secondary Spanish/Transitional and Political Science. She studied in Mexico for two years, taught secondary Spanish (bilingual) for twenty-four years, is a sports *aficionada,* and a devoted student of African-American history.

Darlene Dennard, creative writer and poet, has been a member of the Apostolic Church of God for twenty years, where she serves faithfully. Currently, she is a member of the ACOG praise team and associate editor of the *The Cross and Crown* newsletter. Previous ministry service includes Sanctuary Choir member and songwriter, and writing narration for the annual Easter and Christmas concerts for the Saving Grace Ministries.

Darryl W. Dennard is a nationally renowned, award-winning broadcast journalist who has hosted nationally syndicated programs like *The Black Enterprise Report*, *Minority Business Report* and the *Ebony-Jet Showcase*. A mentor, he is also a Sunday Morning Bible Study teacher and a leader in the youth and men's ministries at ACOG. He is married with two children and two grandchildren.

Rev. Shelli Dew is an ordained minister whose dedication in serving God's people is transparent in her areas of service, including Sunday school teacher, creative writer for marketing church events, and a former contributing writer for T*he Apostolic Light*, a Sunday school publication.

Renee Felker is the wife of Terrance Felker and mother of Christian and Cameron. Renee is a student in Christian ministry, and she loves to gather with family and friends. Her favorite Scripture is Philippians 4:13: "I can do all things through Christ who strengthens me."

Rev. Priscilla C. Green is an ordained minister at Apostolic Church of God, activist against all forms of abuse, a humanitarian, a community servant, a prolific motivational orator and writer, and an accomplished licensed hair designer. She attended Harrington College of Design.

Rev. Isaac Hayes is a Bible teacher and preacher at the Apostolic Church of God in Chicago. Isaac blogs at www.hotsministries.wordpress.com. His e-mail address is ichayes@hotsministries.com.

Wanda R. Jackson is a true intercessor and worshiper, and she's passionate about writing. She understands that writing is an extension of worship and a median through which God can minister to the heart of believers and non-believers. Sister Jackson received her academic training at the University of Arkansas at Fayetteville and Loyola University Chicago.

Dr. Willeta Johnson, a professional producer/arranger/composer, teaches physics and chemistry at Loyola University. A recipient of numerous awards and honors, she has congruently preached and written on biblical topics for more than twenty years. Contact: smuinc@gmail.com.

Dwayne Lee was born and raised in the Apostolic Church of God. A born-again Christian, he is the eighth child born to Julious and Barbara Lee, the husband of Carolyn Crossley-Lee, and the father of James D. Lee. Though an accomplished Gospel music artist, with lyrical credits to his name, this is Dwayne's first attempt at writing professionally.

Jennifer LuVert counts it an honor to write anything that inspires people to live for God. She is a graduate of Lawrence and DePaul universities who has edited publications for parents of pre-k students, the homeless, and disability professionals. A member of ACOG since 1991, she currently edits the *The Cross & Crown*.

Jacquelin McCord-Harris is a monthly columnist for *The Cross and Crown* and a contributing writer to a number of books, including *The Woman of Color Devotional Bible*. She is married with two daughters and two granddaughters, and she is the author and publisher of three children's books: *When We Get Straight*, *A Molehill is a Mountain*, and *Miss America and the Silver Medal*; and one for adults: *Fur Coats in My Closet*. More information on her books can be found at www.jsmccord.com.

Dr. Therese McGee is a clinical psychologist who works with traumatized children. She has been a member of the Apostolic Church of God since 1974, and was the editor of the church *NewsLetter* for twenty-four years. Currently, she teaches teenagers in Sunday Morning Bible Study and is married to minister and deacon Robert McGee Jr. They are the parents of three children and two grandchildren.

David Nuckolls was born February 21, 1952 to Gerald and Vera Nuckolls. He is one of fifteen grandchildren of District Elder Walter Clemons, the founding pastor of Apostolic Church of God. He received the Holy Ghost in August 1965, and he is currently working with the ACOG Youth Ministries.

Evangelist Nettie F. Ratcliffe is an ordained minister, staff member, and teacher at the Apostolic Church of God. She rejoices as she teaches about the mighty weapons that God has given to triumph over darkness, effecting change in the lives of hurting people, ministering encouragement and healing through the Word of God and prayer.

Rev. Kay Robinson is an ordained minister and a published author.

She is a prolific, well-sought after seminar and conference speaker. Anointed in the areas of teaching, the word of wisdom, the word of knowledge and the prophetic, she brings these gifts together in the area of deliverance for women. Her joy is to see God's people free to walk out their destiny in power and joy.

Dr. Jeanne Porter serves as an assistant pastor and the Ministerial Alliance Director at the Apostolic Church of God. She has written several books, including *Leading Ladies: Transformative Biblical Images for Women's Leadership* and *Leading Lessons: Insights on Leadership from Women of the Bible*. A leader, teacher, and preacher of the gospel, she believes in God's transformative power.

Rev. Samira E. Robinson is an ordained minister with the Apostolic Church of God and a featured columnist for the church's newsletter. She is the author of *This Side of Heaven—A Book of Poems, Prayers and Spiritual Writings* and facilitates poetry and self-development workshops in the community. Robinson holds a master's degree in Entertainment and Media management and has served as an adjunct professor for the City Colleges of Chicago.

Dr. Rosa Sailes is the Director of Editorial Curriculum for Urban Ministries, Inc., and she has several published books, papers, and articles. Dr. Sailes is celebrating thirty-five years of marriage and has been a member of the Apostolic Church of God for more than thirty years.

Rev. Delores Westbrook, is an associate minister of Apostolic Church of God and co-editor of the choir newsletter, *Choir Notes*. Her ministries consist of personal evangelism, administration, and teaching. She is proprietor of dsdivinedesserts.

Rev. Yolanda Williams is an associate minister, staff member, and volunteer administrator of the Apostolic Church of God. She's an encourager, wife (Kevin Williams), and mother (Jordan and Brittney). She believes that as you walk by faith and trust God, He will get you through the storm.

Acknowledgments

We thank God first and foremost for the creativity, energy, and passion in bringing this book to fruition. We thank our pastor, Dr. Byron T. Brazier, for being a man of vision; his heart for the growth of the people of God is without comparison. We thank the teams whose efforts went into making this 2012 devotional a reality.

Theological Framework Team:
Dr. Byron Brazier, Thomas Bolden, Dr. David Daniels, Jennifer LuVert, Dr. Jeanne Porter, and Dr. Rosa Sailes

Theological Reviewers:
Rev. Granada Cartwright, Dr. Jeanne Porter, and Dr. Rosa Sailes

Editors:
Caryn Bell, Freda Brown, Patti Caire, Patricia Gilmore, Pamela, Graves, Leah Hobson, Marla Martin, and Judith Stewart

Proofreaders:
Doris Franklin, Marsha McRoyal, April Morgan, Jacqueline Prince, and Evang. Nettie Ratcliffe

Graphics and Layout:
Apostolic Church of God Graphics Department

We thank Andrica Hamilton and the Saving Grace Book Center team for managing pre-orders and getting prepped to sell and distribute the 2012 Devotional. We thank Evang. Cynthia Brawner for taking on special assignments. We thank Earl Dortch for managing the development of our devotional book app.

This work has been a labor of love, and we are grateful!

ACOG Devotional Book Leadership Team
Patti Caire
Rev. Granada Cartwright
Jennifer LuVert
Dr. Jeanne Porter
Evang. Nettie Ratcliffe
Dr. Rosa Sailes